Covenant of Allah

Munawar Sabir

Order this book online at www.trafford.com
or email orders@trafford.com

Most Trafford titles are also available at major online book retailers.

Print information available on the last page.

ISBN: 978-1-6987-0884-3 (sc)
ISBN: 978-1-6987-0886-7 (hc)
ISBN: 978-1-6987-0885-0 (e)

Library of Congress Control Number: 2021914848

Trafford rev. 07/23/2021

Trafford PUBLISHING® www.trafford.com
North America & international
toll-free: 844-688-6899 (USA & Canada)
fax: 812 355 4082

To

my mother and father,
who set me onto the straight path of Allah.
To my wife, Eva,
whose curiosity and questioning
inspired me to the search for the truth.
And to my children—
Shamma, Sarah, Roxanna, and Laila—
who will one day light the path
of future generations
in the tradition of their forefathers.

He is Allah! There is no Deity but He, Knower of the hidden and the manifest.
He the Rahman (the Most Gracious), the Rahim, (Most Merciful.)

He is Allah; there is no Deity but He,

The Sovereign, The Pure, and The Hallowed,

Serene and Perfect,

The Custodian of Faith, the Protector, the Almighty,

The Irresistible, the Supreme,

Glory be to Allah. He is above all they associate with Him.

He is Allah, the Creator, the Sculptor, the Adorner of color and form.

To Him belong the Most Beautiful Names: whatever
so is in the heavens and on earth, Praise and Glorify
Him; and He is the Almighty and All Wise.

—Al-Hashr 59:18–24, Koran

Verily those who pledge their allegiance unto you, (O Muhammad)
pledge it unto none but Allah; the Hand of Allah is over their
hands. Thereafter whosoever breaks his Covenant does so to
the harm of his own soul, and whosoever fulfils his Covenant
with Allah, Allah will grant him an immense Reward.

—Al-Fath 48:10, Koran

Contents

Acknowledgments

Many years ago, I became conscious of recurring references in the Koran to a covenant between Allah and His believers. I wished to have an understanding of the terms of the covenant; my search and inquiries did not shed any more light on the subject. Little has been written on the subject of the covenant in Islam. I began my long journey in the quest of the covenant between Allah and the believers, and for over thirty years, I made mental and written observations on the subject, which had resulted in this book. Knowledge is a mountain of humankind's wisdom piled over thousands of years. Men and women receive knowledge and wisdom through the grace and mercy of Allah, adding up their insights and understanding to this mountain of wisdom. The mountain, thus, continues to rise and soar. I strode this mountain and drank from its mountain streams the wisdom of thousands of sages to quench my thirst for their knowledge.

Thirty-five years ago, I came across the book *The Covenant in the Qur'an* written by 'Abd al-Karim Biazer, which redirected my search to the source itself—the Koran. It was in the Koran that I found the answers to my search. And the search had resulted in this work. I discovered that the remedy to the ills of modern-day Islam lie in page after page of the holy book.

Over the years, I have found wisdom in thousands of sages, some of whom I have mentioned and the others not. They have all knowingly and unknowingly contributed to my miniscule understanding of the signs of Allah and of the divine wisdom. I wish to thank them all. May Allah bless all men and women of understanding who do beautiful works in the path of Allah and His creation.

I am touched and honored by the generous and encouraging message written by the great Muslim scholar and statesman of our time Dr.

Mahathir bin Mohamad. May Allah bless him for his incredible leadership of the *ummah.*

I used the English translations of the Holy Koran of Abdullah Yusuf Ali, Hashim Amir Ali, Marmaduke Pickthall, and N. J. Dawood. I found *A Concordance of the Qur'an* by Hanna E. Kassis most useful in deciphering the Arabic text of the Koran.

In my search of the covenant of Allah, I found the monumental work of Sachiko Murata and William Chittick, *Vision of Islam*, tremendously helpful; it should be an essential reading for everyone seeking the knowledge of the fundamentals of Islam.

I wish to acknowledge the love, understanding, and patience of my wife, Eva, and my daughters—Shamma, Sarah, Roxanna, and Laila—when for many hours, months, and years I was holed up in my study.

Finally, I wish to thank Hala Elgammal and Shamma Sabir for their helpful suggestions in the formatting and editing of this text.

Munawar Sabir

Message

I would like to commend this thesis of Dr. Munawar Sabir on the covenant of Islam (i.e., the agreement or undertaking by Muslims to fulfill their duties in return for the many blessings Allah promises the believers). Dr Munawar has chosen seventy-five verses of the Koran, thirty-seven of which begin with "O! Ye who believe" to illustrate the covenants that a Muslim enters into. I find Dr. Munawar's arguments very well grounded and persuasive. It is yet another attempt to clear the confusion in the minds of Muslims over the present state of Islam and the *ummah.*

We cannot say that the oppression and humiliation of the Muslims is preordained by Allah. We are taught and we know that all that is good that happens to us is from Allah and that all that is bad is from ourselves. If we are in the parlous state that we are now, it must be because of us because we are not following the teachings of Islam, or as Dr. Munawar puts it, we are not keeping to our covenants.

Historically, we know that when the ignorant Arab tribes embraced Islam, they were almost immediately successful, being able to set up a great civilization that lasted 1,300 years to give themselves as Muslims a place in the world arena, to gain respect from all quarters for themselves and for Islam. If today Muslims are looked down on and oppressed, it must be because of us, our failure to regard and practice Islam as a way of life, as *ad-deen*. We must therefore relook at the Koran and its teachings to see where we had gone wrong and afterward to make the necessary corrections in our understanding and practice of Islam.

I hope, in doing this, we will not end up in the creation of yet another Muslim sect that will only divide and weaken us. The one religion of Islam has become hundreds of different religions, each claiming to be the true Islam because of different interpretations of the teachings of the Koran and the Hadith. We do not need yet another interpretation and another sect. But we cannot deny that there is a need to return to the fundamental teachings of the Koran so that we can overcome the confusion that has resulted in the breakup of the Muslim *ummah* and in Muslims killing Muslims.

I pray and hope that this thesis by Dr. Munawar will not divide us again but will lead to a greater understanding of the teachings of Islam and a reunification of the Muslim *ummah.* Let us downplay our differences and seek common grounds so that we can at least say that all Muslims are brothers. Inshallah, with the restoration of our brotherhood, we can once again protect ourselves in this world and gain merit for the next world.

Dr. Mahathir bin Mohamad

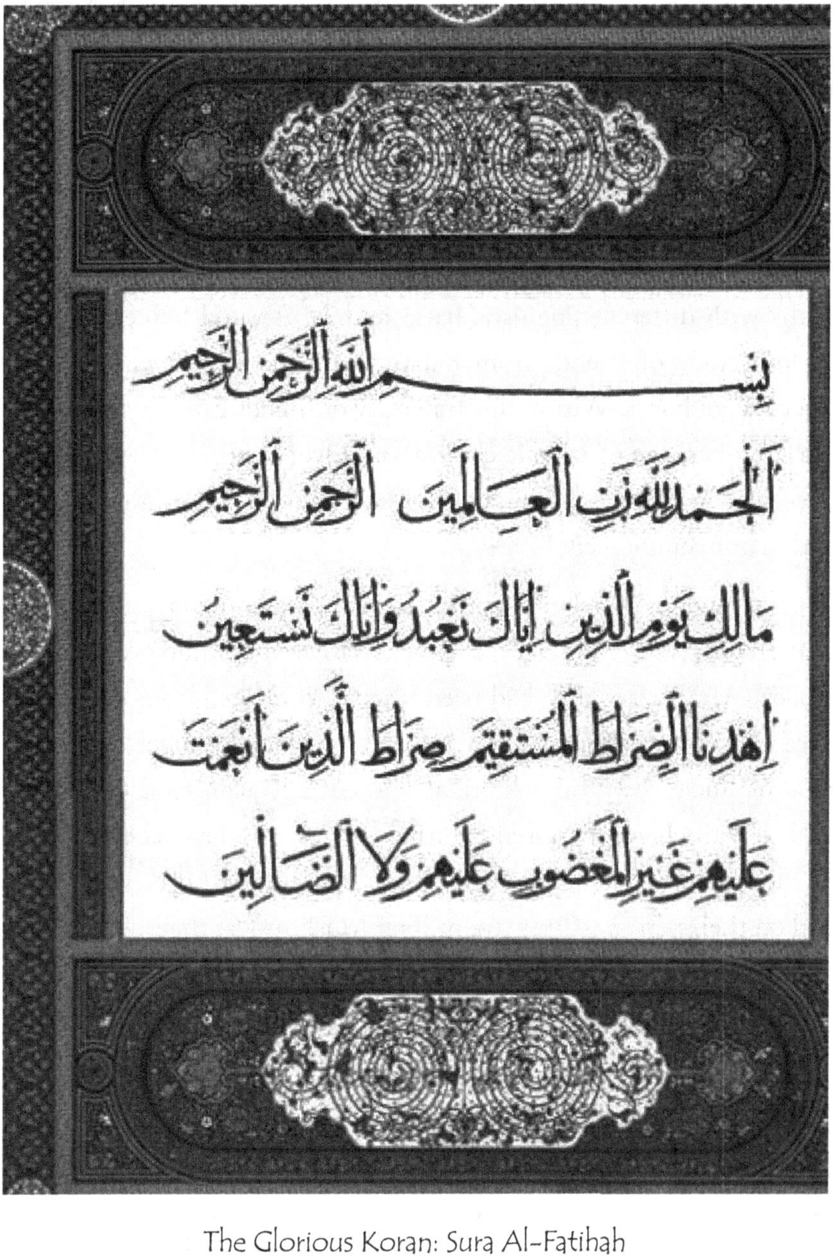
بسم الله الرحمن الرحيم
الحمد لله رب العالمين الرحمن الرحيم
مالك يوم الدين إياك نعبد وإياك نستعين
اهدنا الصراط المستقيم صراط الذين أنعمت
عليهم غير المغضوب عليهم ولا الضالين

The Glorious Koran: Sura Al-Fatihah

Introduction

My journey for the understanding of the covenant of the Koran and the search for the cause of repeated humiliation of Muslims began when I turned twelve. I had completed the recitation of the revelation (the Koran) under the guidance of a teacher known to his pupils as "Baba." The fog of time has obscured his real name from my memory, but the respect and love of him remains in my heart. Our community was multifaith and multiethnic, which gave us friends from many faiths with different linguistic backgrounds. Around home, we kept a close circle of friends from Baba's madrassa, which we attended after school hours. Within this fraternity of friends came awareness of our long heritage of Islamic civilization. Over this period, we all had developed a certain comfort and a sense of pride in our religious beliefs and in our common civilization.

My perception of Islam's unity, strength, and invulnerability was shattered that year. We had a flood of relatives move into our home in eastern Africa after they had been evicted from their homes in India because of their religion. They had lived in squalid refugee camps for months under dreadful conditions without adequate food or shelter, all the while being harassed by armed thugs who had relieved them of their homes, belongings, and in the end every item of value they had on their persons. Over five million Muslims lost their homes, and another quarter of a million were murdered or lost their lives through disease, starvation, and exposure to the elements.

Soon afterward came the broadcast declaring the partition of Palestine by the United Nations. This caused another diaspora; this time, Palestinians lost their homes to Jews, who had been earlier displaced by the Europeans through war, persecution, and perpetration of genocide by Germans with the acquiescence of the British, French, Italians, Poles, the Americans, and Catholic and Protestant churches.

The winds of change were blowing across the world. The Muslim peoples were beginning to win their battles for independence from colonial powers, weakened through the European wars for supremacy. The struggles raged on in Kashmir, Palestine, Indonesia, Malaya, Iran, Algeria, and Egypt in the 1950s, and similar battles for supremacy are still going on in subtler forms today. The West has given up the struggle for the crude form of colonial supremacy for the control of the Southeast, East Asia, and the Middle East. Now the battles for supremacy and control of wealth, minerals, trade, and natural resources of the world are now subtler. The control is now exercised through puppet regimes that rule and tyrannize their populations. The West quietly takes away wealth of these nations through unequal trade, privatized state utility companies, interest on loans, communication systems, and control over their agriculture, minerals, and oil industries.

Over the course of years of living and traveling in Africa, South Asia, Middle East, Western Europe, and North America, I realized that politics, international diplomacy, and trade are all controlled by the law of the jungle. Powerful nations have been able to inscribe these laws into legal jargon (with rules for negotiation, agreements, arbitration, etc.) to give an impression of fairness and civilized behavior. In reality, it is nothing of the sort. The laws that govern the United Nations, IMF, NATO, European Economic Union, GATT, G7, G12, and the World Trade Organization are all for the benefit of the most powerful, ensuring the survival of the fittest, perpetual capitulation, and subjugation of the weakest.

The covenant of Allah with the believers is a compact of divine guidance to faith, unity, and proper conduct for humans to live in mutual peace, respect, and harmony. It is the only comprehensive document governing human relationship, peaceful coexistence of humans, equality of man, justice, truth, and fair trade in existence for the survival of humankind.

- Allah! There is no god but He, the ever living, and the one who sustains and protects all that exists. (Al-Hashr 59:18–24, Koran)
- Stand firm for justice as witness to Allah, be it against yourself, your parents, or your family, whether it is against rich or poor, both are nearer to Allah than they are to you. Follow not your caprice lest you distort your testimony. If you prevaricate and evade justice Allah is well aware what you do. (An-Nisa 4:135, Koran)
- Be in taqwa of Allah, fear Allah as He should be feared, and die not except in a state of Islam.

  And hold fast, all together, by the Rope, which Allah stretches out for you, and be not divided among yourselves; and remember with gratitude Allah's favor on you; you were enemies, and He joined your hearts in love, so that by His Grace, you became brethren and a community. You were on the brink of the pit of fire, and He saved you from it. Thus, does Allah make His Signs clear to you that you may be guided. Let there arise out of you a band of people inviting to all that is good, enjoining what is right, and forbidding that is wrong. They are the ones to attain happiness.

  Be not like those who are divided amongst themselves and fall into disputations after receiving clear signs: for them is a dreadful penalty. (Ali 'Imran 3:102–5, Koran)
- To Allah belong all that is in heavens and on earth. He forgives whom He pleases and punishes whom He pleases. But Allah is Most Forgiving and Most Merciful. (Ali 'Imran 3:129, Koran)
- Fear the Fire, which is prepared for those who reject Faith.

  And obey Allah and the Rasool; that you may obtain mercy.

  Be quick in the race for forgiveness from your Lord, and for a Garden whose measurement is that of the heavens and of the earth, prepared for the righteous.

  Those who give freely whether in prosperity, or in adversity, those who restrain anger, and pardon all humans, for Allah loves those who do beautiful deeds. (Ali 'Imran 3:131–35, Koran)

- Fear treachery and oppression that afflicts not only those who perpetrate it but affects guilty and innocent alike. (Al-Anfal 8:24–25, Koran)
- Betray not trust of Allah, and His messenger, nor knowingly misappropriate things entrusted to you. (Al-Anfal 8:27, Koran)
- If you have taqwa of Allah, He will grant you a Criterion to judge between right and wrong and remove from you all misfortunes and evil and forgive your sins. (Al-Anfal 8:29, Koran)
- And fight the infidel until there is no more treachery and oppression and there prevails justice and Faith in Allah altogether and everywhere. (Al-Baqarah 2:-193, Koran)

  And there are those who bury gold and silver and spend it not in the way of Allah; announce unto them a most grievous penalty. (At-Tawbah 9:341, Koran)
- Be in Taqwa of Allah, fear Allah, and be with those who are true in word and deed. (At-Tawbah 9:11, Koran)
- Do not follow Satan's footsteps, if any will follow Satan's footsteps, he will command you to what is shameful, Fahasha, and wrong, Munkar. (An-Nur 24:21, Koran)
- You who believe! Be in taqwa of Allah Fear Allah and speak always the truth that He may direct you to the righteous deeds and forgive your sins. (Al-Ahzab 33:71, Koran)
- When you hold secret counsel, do it not for iniquity and hostility, and disobedience to the Messenger, but do it for righteousness and self-restraint...Secret counsels are only inspired by the Satan, in order that he may cause grief to the believers. Allah will exalt in rank those of you who believe and who have been granted knowledge. (Al-Mujadila 58:9–11, Koran)
- Bow down, prostrate and serve your Lord and do wholesome deeds that you may prosper. Perform jihad, strive to your utmost to Allah's cause as striving, (jihad) is his due. He has chosen you and Allah has not imposed any hardship in your endeavor to his cause. You are the inheritors of the faith of your father Abraham. It is He who named

you Muslims of the times before and now, so that Allah's Messenger may be an example to you and that you are an example to mankind.

Establish regular salaat, give regular charity and hold fast to Allah. He is your Mawla, Protector, the best of Protectors and the best Helper. (Al-Hajj 22:77–78)

Allah offered the believers His covenant, which the "Muslims" readily undertook. Some were remiss in their obligation to Allah of regular *salaat;* others forgot their obligation to provide for their kin and for those in need. Some of them let go of the rope that Allah stretched out to them and became divided and stranded, unable to find their way. This resulted in a situation whereby only a fraction of one and a half billion "Muslims" adhere to the covenant. Those who do not believe cannot be the righteous unless they submit out of their free will to the will and the law of Allah. The obedience to the covenant of Allah becomes obligatory to all those who pledge belief in Allah, His messengers, and His message in the scriptures. Allah proclaims His covenant to the believers by directly addressing the believers in seventy-five verses of the Koran. In these verses, there are thirty-seven commandments for the believers to follow in their daily lives. Those who believe, establish regular salat, and give regular charity are united and hold fast to Allah's rope; Allah is their *Mawla*, Protector and Helper. From the depths of darkness, He will lead them forth into light; those who reject Allah have no protector. For those who are divided among themselves fall into disputes and destroy the unity of Islam and have a dreadful penalty.

Muslims must understand that by letting go of their hold on Allah and by being disunited, they lose Allah's protection and earn His wrath and a dreadful penalty. The events of the last two hundred years in the Muslim world show that the "Muslims" have lost Allah's protection and have been devastated by pagan power and political and economic systems. Unless the "Muslims" adhere to Allah's covenant, their affairs will not change.

> If Allah is your Protector, none can overcome you, and if He forsakes you, then who can help you? Trust Allah and have faith in his sovereign power. (Ali 'Imran 3:160, Koran)

The human world, like the animal world, is a jungle. In small communities where everyone knows each other and relationships are governed by local mores and culture, there is peace. In the larger world, the law of the jungle applies, and the strongest and the fittest survive, leaving the weak at their mercy. The covenant of the Koran is the constitution of the world state that provides spirituality, nourishment, shelter, equality, human rights, peace, and protection under the laws of Allah as opposed to the laws of jungle. To achieve peace on the earth, there has to be total voluntary submission to Allah and His covenant. Allah's covenant is a guide to a straight path of peace and tranquility. In return for obeying the covenant, Allah promises His protection and guidance to the believers.

Since times historic, rulers have been autocratic—ruling at times with justice and at other times through tyranny. Behind the rulers are armies of sycophants who fill their own coffers. The actions of this group settle how much of Allah's bounty trickles down to the ordinary man. When Allah promised Adam that none of his progeny would go hungry or unclothed, He provided provisions for every living thing. Allah made man the conduit of His mercy to the ones in need and want. Man, in his greed and covetousness, misappropriated the provisions for the needy to himself. In doing so, he gained security, riches, and influence over others. Over thousands of years, theft and appropriation by force became the hallmark of the powerful. Nobility and aristocracy stole with style and genteelness, while common thieves and robbers did it with brutality and crudeness. Nevertheless, both classes contained criminals who got away with robbery because the robbers themselves enforced the laws.

The royals, merchants, and moneylenders financed the voyages of discovery in the fifteenth century. Usury was very much the kingpin of European commerce. European aristocracy, moneylenders, and merchants established the East India companies for trade. Such traffic was so lucrative and the profits so great that the European shipping and commerce degenerated into the wholesale piracy and plunder of the Orient. After pillaging the Asians and the American natives, European greed for gold and wealth had not been satiated. They embarked on illicit opium trade and trade in humans, all financed through usury. The wealth thus acquired provided the engine for the Industrial Revolution in Britain, Germany, and the Americas. It also fueled the search for more wealth and more colonies, this time in Africa.

Once the process of acquisition begins, there is no stopping. For wealthy nations and people alike, acquisition and spending are addictive. Like addiction to drugs and alcohol, addiction to acquisition leads to craving for more and more wealth. Wealth becomes an obsession to be had at whatever cost—pillage, plunder, murder, or war.

The descendants and the successors of the trading empires of the tall sailing ships acquired more wealth and became the owners of the largest banks, oil companies, armament complexes, food-processing industries, multimillion-acre genetic-engineering food farms, shipping companies, airlines, railways, mining conglomerates, power-generating complexes, construction companies, high-technology utility and telecommunication industries, liquor trade, gambling casinos, entertainment industry, illicit drug trade, and money laundering. To maintain their edge in international trading, they established think tanks, recruited the brightest university graduates, politicians, generals, economists, bankers, newspaper editors, and university professors to generate more wealth.

To continue to acquire more wealth, they established secret organizations. These secret societies select candidates for political posts, finance their campaigns, and have them elected. They plan the policies of the international organizations to dominate the world's commerce and trade. The better-known secret societies are the Council on Foreign Relations (CFR), Royal Institute of International Affairs, Trilateral Commission, and Bilderberg Group. The organizations meet in secret. The information given to the members is compartmentalized on a need-to-know basis. Faceless shadows in the inner circles of the secret societies decide the fate of nations and their economies in the back rooms. The presidents are their puppets, the intelligence services their instrument of operation, and the marines their storm troopers.

No world event ever occurs accidentally. The shadowy, faceless manipulators of these world events plan years in advance, instigating wars, inciting terrorism, and planning epidemics and food shortages. They own and manipulate the news media; people are fed selective, doctored information. The real events as they occur go unreported. The world is like a stage where the spectators see the drama on the screen while the real action is taking place behind the scenes. Likewise, war, torture, and sufferings in Palestine, Chechnya, Kosovo, and Iraq are mere diversions to keep the Muslims befuddled, while the real action is in Central Asian, Caspian, and the Middle Eastern deserts, where the wealth from oil, gas, aluminum, and gold is being removed every day to the West.

There is a satanic circle, the *circle of evil*, composing of shadowy, faceless people who all know one another and are in control of the world's wealth. This group comprising some of the world's richest men, Jewish moneylenders, Western royals, aristocrats, and business magnates manipulates and controls politicians, news media, universities, and the intelligence services of the Western democracies. These faceless conspirators are above the law, and their activities almost never hit the newsstands. Between them, they create circumstances in the Western and the Islamic worlds that allow them to place their puppets on the throne. These willing puppets—for instance, in Egypt, Jordan, Pakistan, Arabian Peninsula, and Central Asia—provide the faceless controllers reign over the Islamic lands. The circle of evil is composed of the Western world's richest men, both Jews and Christians; the Western world's corrupt political, military, and intelligence elite; and the Eastern world's corrupt Muslim rulers and greedy aristocracy.

The circle of evil deprives human kind of Allah's benevolence by diverting it to themselves. Of the total wealth and resources of the world, the circle of evil owns over 70 percent, while six billion people subsist on the remaining 30 percent. The prosperity of the un-Koranic Western world is an illusion, and this illusion has become the focus of inspiration for educated Muslim economists, planners, students, and businesspeople. Underneath the facade of prosperity and boundless riches of the West lies the bottomless pit of debt. The commerce, trade, industry, shipping, highways, spacious homes, office towers, boulevards, and automobiles are all run by the engine of massive debt. People's homes, household appliances, automobiles, holidays, and college education are all financed by money borrowed from the moneylenders of the circle of evil. The governments owe trillions of dollars to the circle as their budget deficits are financed by debt, whose interest amounts to a third of their national budgets. With the acquiescence of the people and their governments, the moneylenders create the illusion of immense wealth by printing money on fancy paper and then lending it to the governments and people. Further money is created by speculation on printed money and money trading. As if this was not enough, speculation on stocks generates further wealth through inside trading and fraudulent bookkeeping with the help of prestigious accounting firms.

How does the illusion of wealth affect the common man? The Western man and woman, during the last forty years, have been conditioned to pursue instant gratification of their needs and desires. The agenda of the circle is to make every human covetous and envious of others' possessions and to tempt every human to the immediate gratification of their desires. People can purchase a house, a car, household appliances, weekend cottage, and other luxury items on impulse, and loans at steep interest rates are readily available. The trading houses, industries, and municipal, provincial, and national governments do the same—borrow, borrow, borrow. The result is that the common consumer pays the ultimate price of paying the principal and interest, compounded on all this accumulated debt one way or the other. Without usury, a couple will pay annually at most ten thousand dollars for food, housing, transport, and utilities, while only one of them will go out to work. In the world of illusive prosperity and immediate gratification in a land of usury, the same couple at the time of their marriage will be in debt to the tune of $225,000 for their house, car, and appliances.

To survive, the couple, both husband and wife, will need to work full time for twenty-five years to repay their own debt and that of the three tiers of governments through taxation. The couple, when buying food, utilities, clothing, and manufactured goods, will pay extra in taxes—the debts of the producers and the debts of the governments—through payment of hidden taxes. The result is the illusion of prosperity through shiny granite office blocks, boulevards, busy airports, and bustling harbors, all driven on the wheels of usury. This couple, during their working life, will pay out directly and indirectly 60 percent of their earnings to the bankers of the circle of evil. All trade, businesses, industries, construction and housing markets, and governments are similarly indebted to the bankers of the circle of evil. Every person is in a rush to finish his forty- to sixty-hour workweek not realizing that through the payments of his debt, taxation, and purchases, 60 to 70 percent of his earnings will end up in the coffers of the circle of evil.

The circle of evil controls the policies of the world's governments through loans, bribery, and coercion. They control the political machinery through institutional manipulation and, in some countries, the judicial process. Secret organizations structured on the frame of freemasonry watch and manipulate politicians. The circle manipulates events around the world to perpetuate its control over the world's economy and its resources. Massacres, civil unrest, assassinations, and wars are perpetrated for the pursuit and benefit of profit.

The circle pays attention to the public mood and keeps the politicians and populations pacified. The media in the Western world is owned by a handful of people, members of the circle of evil. They control and manipulate the editorial content and news releases to the world. Media is used for mind control of the people. Newspapers and television are instruments for the shaping of public opinion on matters of importance. Polls are regularly held to gauge the success of their media campaigns.

During outcry and agitation against the Vietnam War, the street market was flooded with cheap marijuana and other drugs. The circle was making a killing in the sale of weapons and munitions and from the profits of war industry. It was not quite ready to end the war, even though thousands of American men had been killed. The drugs did have a calming impact worldwide. A new type of music introduced by artists such as the Beatles and the Rolling Stones was promoted on all broadcasting channels to pacify the youth.

The modus operandi of the circle is to keep every man and woman occupied in the quest of making a bare living. All thinking, cognitive, judgmental, and opinion-forming activities during the leisure times of people are discouraged by promoting amusements, games, sports, and movies shown on the television, which keep everyone busy and occupied in the life of trivia. Every person is busy making a living and having fun without ever thinking about the people who run the world.

Religion, especially Islam, poses a special threat to the circle of evil. There is a well-planned campaign to diminish the importance of religion in the life of people, especially the youth. In schools and universities, curricula are structured to denigrate the divine and the sublime; the common and the profane is pushed to the limit. The circle of evil is hostile toward the morality taught by the scriptures. Truth is the first casualty in the campaign to demolish the moral standards of the world.

When the president of the United States George W. Bush and the prime minister of Great Britain Tony Blair, as members of the United Nations Security Council and guardians of world peace, stood on the podium in front of world leaders and their own people, uttering falsehoods and lies to deceive the world to invade a sovereign country for the purpose of stealing its oil wealth, their moral standards and actions were akin to that of common thieves. Armed with these moral values, the leaders of the Western world and members of the United Nations Security Council set an ugly example to the youth of the world. Certainly, this is not a role model for democracy in the Islamic world.

The circle of evil has also initiated a sexual revolution in the Western world, which is fast spreading to the East. It started with the introduction of the contraceptive pill in the 1960s. Since then, the media controlled by the circle has extrapolated and encouraged lewd, open, and public display of sexual activity. What was shameful and profane has become an everyday norm. Prepubertal children are provided sex education in schools, teen pregnancies are common, 40 percent of births are out of wedlock, and divorce rate is now approaching 50 percent; this is not accidental. The media controlled by the circle first pushed for access to abortion for all, sex education for teens in schools, rights of people living out of wedlock, encouragement of homosexuality, and now acceptance of same-sex marriage.

The bankers and intelligence agencies of the circle of evil push drugs for profit among their own youth and adults. Their aim is satanic; to undermine the moral health of society to gain total control. The police arrest the small fry among the drug trade, but the big importers and the distributors are never caught. We are told that the spy agencies can spot a tennis ball lying on the ground from their satellites two hundred kilometers up in the sky. Why are these satellites blind to the large ships and airplanes carrying hundreds of tons of heroin and cocaine? People transferring a thousand dollars to an Islamic charity are incarcerated, whereas money launderers of millions of dollars of drug money are never questioned.

Adherence to the covenant of Allah reforms the individual. Through *iman* (belief), salat, fasting, and *taqwa* of Allah (awareness of Allah's presence), man becomes cognizant of the *furqan* (the criterion to distinguish between good and evil) and therefore follows the straight path of Allah. In doing so, the human performs good and beautiful deeds that please Allah. Helpful and charitable acts to the parents, the kin, the neighbors, the needy, and the sick and to the rest of mankind purify the believer. Frequent remembrance of Allah, beseeching His forgiveness, praising His magnificence, and showing gratitude for His grace and mercy is the obligation of every man. Forgiving others of their trespasses cleans anger, grudges, and rancor. Humility wipes out the ego. All actions with *taqwa* of Allah, with the knowledge that Allah is with you and sees you whether you see Him or not, help the believer to walk the earth in the glow of Allah's love. Walking on Allah's straight path, the believer recognizes the pitfalls where Satan has placed temptations of evil since Allah has bequeathed the believer the criterion to recognize the good from evil.

Every man aspiring to be a believer has to surrender totally to the will and the laws of Allah. Such a surrender involves accepting the covenant of Allah, which means a lifetime of adherence to it. Acting upon the covenant saves the believer from the temptations of Satan and his human manifestation—the circle of evil. The circle of evil is the enemy of Islam and of humanity. It corrupts the rulers of Islam, destroys the unity of the *ummah* and its prosperity, and attempts to deviate the Muslims from the message of the blessed *Nabi* Muhammad. Every believer should strive to expel Satan from his heart and also wage a jihad against his human manifestation the circle of evil. To do so, every believer has to recognize the circle of evil in his own community and country.

The circle of evil comprises the Western world's richest men, both Jews and Christians; the Western world's corrupt political, military, and intelligence elite; and the corrupt Muslim rulers and elite. Without the Muslim puppets of the satanic circle of evil, the *ummah* will be united; there will be a united Muslim country, the Dar es Salaam. And the believers will have no outside corrupting influences. To free the land of the believers from constant threats, subjugation, and exploitation, it is incumbent on every believer to wipe out the circle of evil from among their midst.

Islam is a religion of *faith, unity, truth, peace, justice, equality, and moderation*. The thirty-seven commandments of the covenant of Allah are applicable to every religion, nation, and race in the world.

According to the Koran, both Jews and Christians were given the covenant but failed to observe it. Allah's covenant is still accessible and open to all humans. Allah condemns extremism among the believers:

Commit no excess. Allah loves not people given
to excess. (Al-Ma'idah 5:87–88, Koran)

And there is no compulsion in religion, truth stands out
clear from error. (Al-Baqarah 2:254–57, Koran)

Extremism and compulsion in matters of faith are abhorrent to Allah. The acceptance of the trust of the covenant of Allah is voluntary on the part of man after he has, through knowledge and *iman* (faith), satisfied himself that Allah is the only reality and, on his own volition, surrendered to the will and the law of Allah. Man's submission to Allah opens him to the acceptance of His covenant. Allah is the Judge; He rewards and punishes. The religious police of the ulema, the Wahhabi, the Taliban, and the ayatollahs are guilty of *shirk* when they assume the role of Allah the Judge, the Awarder, and the Punisher. Every man is responsible to Allah for his or her own actions and is not accountable to the religious police, the ulema, the Wahhabi, the Taliban, and the ayatollahs, who on the Day of Judgment will stand all together in humility with the rest of humanity to give account of their own actions, both hidden and obvious.

"Muslims" around the world have been in spiritual, political, and economic decline for the last two hundred years. The obvious cause is the loss of faith in Allah, loss of unity among themselves, and deviation from the observation of the covenant of Allah. The result is predictable as Allah promises in the Koran:

If any among you turn back on his faith Allah will bring a people whom He loves and who love Him, and who are humble towards the Believers and stern towards the unbelievers, who perform jihad and strive in the cause of Allah and fear not reproaches of any blamer. Such is Grace of Allah which He bestows on whom He wills. Allah is All-Sufficient for His creatures and all-knowing. (Al-Ma'idah 5:54)

The answer is to go back to the basics of the blessed *nabi* Muhammad's message and the guidance from Allah to mankind, which are unreserved submission to Allah (*islam*) with full conviction that Allah is the only reality, absolute faith (*iman*) with the knowledge of the heart and the mind in that reality, and commitment to performing *ihsan*, doing good, wholesome, and beautiful deeds to benefit Allah's creation—man, animals, and the environment. *Islam*, *iman*, and *ihsan* together constitute the *din*, religion of the believers. Upon submission to the will of Allah, the believer makes a compact with Him and undertakes to abide by His covenant. Allah promises to be the Protector, Guide, and Helper of the believers. Allah blesses them and forgives their sins.

Mohamed Munawar Sabir
British Columbia, Canada
October 23, 2006, Ramadan 30, 1427

Andalusian manuscript from the sixth century AH. This copy of the Koran is on paper, 29 × 25 cm. It is written in a brown and red Andalusian script. Note the careful attention to recitation marks, voweling, verse divisions, and sura divisions. Located in the King Abdulaziz Public Library in Medina, Kingdom of Saudi Arabia.

Chapter One

In the Beginning

Several men climbed on the volcanic rocks at the edge of the oasis and gazed expectantly into the desert. At first, in the morning haze, they saw nothing; and then far in the horizon, they perceived a dust cloud that slowly approached closer and took the shape of riders on two camels. There was a spontaneous sigh of relief, followed by quiet whispering; this crowd had been awaiting this arrival for several days. All at once, men and women surged forward to meet the traveler and his companion.

The weary rider greeted the crowd, and several men and women begged him to alight and stay in their houses; the weary rider courteously declined, and his camel slowly moved on until it came to a date grove and knelt down to sit in front of a small dwelling. The camel's name was Qaswa. Unbeknownst to those present, that moment marked the beginning of a new era, a new century, a new millennium, and a new calendar. That precise moment was the beginning of a new civilization and of a new world empire, which arose out of oblivion.

The site where Qaswa sat down was to become the first seat of the government of that empire and the spot from which a new monotheistic faith would spread to every corner of the world. The weary traveler was Muhammad, the blessed *nabi* of God. He had fled from his enemies—his own tribe, the Quraish, who had vowed to kill him. He had come to Yathrib to seek protection and asylum. That moment of history was to change the world for all times to come; within ten years of that day, two of the mightiest empires the world had known, the Sassanian and the Byzantine, would kneel in front of Muhammad and his followers. Muhammad's companion was Abu Bakr, a true friend who had forsaken his wealth and comfort to support Muhammad at the time of his tribulation; he would succeed Muhammad as the leader of the Muslims.

Muhammad was born an orphan, his father having succumbed to an illness before his birth, and his mother died when he was five. Little is known of Muhammad's childhood, upbringing, and early life. From this inauspicious beginning arose a man whose influence on the civilization of man has not been surpassed by any other during the last two millennia. Muhammad taught that everything in the universe originates from the one and only reality of Allah and that man's ultimate salvation rests on the recognition of his absolute dependence and conscious submission to the will and the law of Allah. Muhammad, as the *nabi* and *rasul* of Allah, received the revelation of His word, law, and commandments, which he was commanded to spread to the whole mankind. Muhammad started receiving revelations from Allah at the age of forty, when Angel Gabriel first appeared to him and commanded:

> Proclaim! In the name of your Lord and Cherisher, Who created, Created man, out of a (mere) clot of congealed blood: Proclaim! And thy Lord is Most Bountiful, He who taught (the use of) the Pen. (Al-'Alaq 96:1–4, Koran)

Muhammad continued to receive revelations from Allah in fragments and at intervals for the next twenty-three years. He taught absolute belief in Allah, His revealed scriptures revealed through His angels and His *rasuls*, and the last day, the Day of Judgment. Recognition of Allah and total submission to Him is the supreme manifestation of faith of the Muslims.

Say: He is Allah, the One and Only; Allah, the Eternal, Absolute; He begets not, nor is He begotten; and there is none like unto Him. (Al-Ikhlas 112:1–4, Koran)

Allah's revelation to His blessed *nabi* is preserved in the Holy Koran. Allah has undertaken to preserve the truth and the veracity of His revelation in the Koran. The Koran sums up the faith of a Muslim as follows: belief in Allah, in the last day, in the angels, in the Koran, in the *rasuls* of Allah. Believers are told to spend (for the love of Allah) on one's kin, the needy, the orphans, the wayfarer, and the ones who ask; to be steadfast in prayer; to practice regular charity; to fulfill their covenant (with Allah); to be firm and patient in tribulation, adversity, and times of stress, pain, and panic; and to perform wholesome and beautiful deeds.

It is not righteousness that you turn your faces towards East or West; but it is righteousness to believe in Allah and the Last Day, and the Angels, and the Book, and the Nabiien; to spend of your substance, out of love for Him, for your kin, for orphans, for the needy, for the wayfarer, for those who ask, and for the ransom of slaves; to be steadfast in prayer, and practice regular charity, to fulfill the Covenant which you have made; and to be firm and patient, in pain (or suffering) and adversity, and throughout all periods of panic. Such are the people of truth, the God-fearing. (Al-Baqarah 2:177, Koran)

From the oasis of Medina, in the stark and sparsely populated deserts of Arabia, the message of Islam spread like wildfire around the world. Sixty years after the *nabi* of Allah was asked to proclaim His word, the message of Islam spread to Asia, Africa, and Europe and to the vast lands and populations of all the known continents. Vast landmass and populations were exposed to the message of Allah in all the three known continents within a short period. It was the faith in one merciful God and equality and brotherhood of all believers in the eyes of that God that brought vast numbers of people to the fold of Islam. The spread of Islam continued in the following centuries. Turks embraced Islam peacefully; so did a large number of people in the Indian subcontinent and the Malay-speaking world. Islam has continued to spread in Africa since its inception as well as in Europe and in the Americas.

Islam is a religion for all peoples that inhabit this earth regardless of their race, sex, or color. The Islamic civilization is based on unity and kinship (brother/sisterhood) of all believers who have submitted to the will of Allah. Therefore, today there are peoples of every race and color in the fold of Islam who stand in line, shoulder to shoulder, facing in one direction toward the Kaaba in unity, worshipping the one universal God, Allah. Every tribe, every nation, and every racial group that joined the fold brought their unique culture and civilization, which contributed to the building of the Islamic civilization. This global civilization created by Islam flowered for over twelve hundred years, pushing the boundaries of knowledge and learning in sciences, philosophy, literature, astronomy, mathematics, and music to such an extent that Arabic remained the major intellectual and scientific language of the world for over a thousand years.

This tradition of intellectual activity eclipsed at the beginning of modern times with the decay of united purpose, loss of unity, and infighting among the Muslim rulers. The rulers and the elite forgot the teachings of the Koran, ignored the welfare of their subjects, and began to indulge in a lifestyle of luxury and debauchery, alien to the teachings of Islam. The once mighty empire gradually broke down into about sixty principalities, each run by a ruler with a grandiose title of *shahinshah*, king, emir, imam, padishah, or caliph. Their populations were driven to poverty with the destruction of industry and trade, which in turn were taken over by European colonial interests. With virtually no zakat, no tax base, and little will or resource, each country fell victim to one or the other European power through force, treachery, bribery, or greed.

Ummah

The masses through this period of tribulation, adversity, and stress remained patient, steadfast, and united. Muslims from Nigeria to Indonesia remained united and close to their religion. They set up independence movements in their countries and assisted others in their war for freedom. They held on to the rope of Allah and had survived the turbulent nineteenth and twentieth centuries.

The *ummah*, the *nation of Islam*, the Dar es Salaam, the *abode of peace*, is still politically divided. Although the people, the Muslims as individuals, are united as they were at the time of the *nabi* of Allah, they live in countries divided by boundaries and frontiers, governed by visas and passports as they were before their subjugation by the colonials. Western economic interests control their economies and natural resources; their shores are patrolled by naval and air power and armies of these interests stationed in their harbors and on their land. Their rulers do not have a sanction from the subjects to rule over them, nor is there a process of consultation and consensus. Their rulers treat the wealth of the land as personal property and the countries as their personal fiefdom. They have secret pacts with non-Islamic countries to come to their aid in a struggle against their own people, the real owners of the land, Allah's vicegerents. The Western powers have a vested interest in preventing the unity of Islamic lands under one united flag, the unity that will terminate their one-hundred-year-old hegemony over the Muslim nation. The rulers of these impoverished Muslim nations are kept in power through force and subterfuge conducted by foreign intelligence agencies.

In the beginning, the Islamic civilization rose like the brilliant sun that illuminated the whole world; and then halfway along its course, there was a long eclipse that came with the Mongol invasion that devastated the eastern lands of Islam for more than a century and abolished the caliphate. With the rise of the Turks in the West, the Safavid in Persia, and the Mogul in India, there was another period of sunshine with a tremendous flowering of another civilization. Then came the darkness caused by thunderclouds, harbingering the invasions of the European powers and Russia. This was followed by complete darkness when most of the Islamic world came under European colonial rule. With the rise of Islam, there was a tremendous flowering of civilization lasting over eight hundred years. The flower garden was razed and plowed under by the Mongols for over a century. The Turks, the Safavid, and the Mogul patronized religion and learning. The knowledge of arts and sciences flourished once again until the colonial powers devastated the nurturing institutions in all the Muslim lands.

After the Second World War and with the dismemberment of the British, French, Dutch, and Spanish empires, the Islamic world once again gained its independence. Muslims around the world fought for their freedom and independence. Once again, the sun had risen, and the populace had altogether turned to Allah for His mercy.

Islam is a way of life, a *din*, in the straight path of Allah. There is an implicit assumption in the Koran that there exists an agreement between Allah and His creation, portrayed as a covenant—a mutual understanding in which Allah proposes a system of regulations for the guidance of humans. This guidance is presented in the form of commandments to be accepted and implemented by people. Allah then promised what He would do man willingly abides by these commands and regulates his life according to them. The concept of promise is clearly conditional on human obedience. The covenant of the Koran symbolizes the relationship between Allah and man; man becomes His steward, vicegerent, or custodian on the earth through submission and obedience to His will (*islam*) as expressed in His commands and is able to take advantage of Allah's promises and favors.

The concept of the covenant also symbolizes the relationship between humans among Allah's creatures and the rest of His creation. They all share in one God, one set of guidance and commandments, the same submission and obedience to Him, and the same set of expectations in accordance with His promises. They all can, therefore, trust one another since they all have similar obligations and expectations. In view of the Koran, humans, communities, nations, and civilizations will continue in harmony and peace so long as they continue to fulfill Allah's covenant.

Economics plays a significant role in the social structure of Islam, so significant that Allah did not leave the economic aspect of life to be solely determined by human intellect, experience, caprice, and lust. Allah made it subject to revelation. Thus, Muslims prosper when they follow Allah's laws and are subjected to scarcity when they turn to human systems.

The Koran promises peace and plenty for those who obey their covenant with Allah; for those who turn away from Allah's covenant, the Koran portends a life of scarcity and want.

> But whosoever turns away from My Message, verily
> for him is a life narrowed down, and we shall raise
> him up blind on the Day of Judgment.

> Thus do We recompense him who transgresses beyond bounds
> and believes not in the Signs of his Lord: and the Penalty of
> the Hereafter is far more grievous and more enduring.

> It is not a warning to such men (to call to mind) how many generations before them We destroyed, in whose haunts they (now) move? Verily, in this are Signs for men endued with understanding. (Taha 20:124, 127–28)

In the above *ayah* of the Koran, the word *ma'eeshat* comes from the word *ma'ashiyyat*, which is the recognized meaning of the word *economics*. The consequences of rejection of Allah's guidance are clearly portrayed: a life narrowed down or constricted is a miserable one—one of need, scarcity, unhappiness, poverty, hunger, disease, pestilence, and famine occurring at the same time or separately.

The Koranic covenant does not hold over the realization of the fruits of obeying or ignoring Allah's guidance until after death, nor does it hide it in spiritual abstractness. Observance of the covenant makes life on the earth economically, physically, and spiritually rich and happy. Nonobservance of the covenant makes life on the earth economically, physically, and spiritually miserable. In fact, the economic, physical, and spiritual condition of a people provides a pragmatic test of the soundness of the revealed guidance.

The Koran declares that people who transgress Allah's guidance are economically deprived in this world and will be worse off in the hereafter.

> Verily for him is a life narrowed down, and We shall raise him up blind on the Day of Judgment. (Taha 20:124, 127–28)

According to the Koran, economics and the observance of the moral code of Allah's covenant go hand in hand, and they cannot be separated from each other.

He has created the heavens and the earth for just ends; far
is He above having the partners they ascribe to Him!

He has created man from a sperm-drop; and behold
this same (man) becomes an open disputer!

And cattle He has created for you (men): from them you derive
warmth, and numerous benefits, and of their (meat) you eat.

And you have a sense of pride and beauty in them
as you drive them home in the evening, and as you
lead them forth to pasture in the morning.

And they carry your heavy loads to lands that you could
not (otherwise) reach except with souls distressed: for
your Lord is indeed Most Kind, Most Merciful.

And (He has created) horses, mules, and donkeys,
for you to ride and use for show; and He has created
(other) things of which you have no knowledge.

And unto Allah leads straight the Way, but there are ways that
turn aside: if Allah had willed, He could have guided all of you.

It is He Who sends down rain from the sky. From it you drink, and
out of it (grows) the vegetation on which you feed your cattle.

With it He produces for you corn, olives, date palms, grapes, and
every kind of fruit: verily in this is a Sign for those who give thought.

He has made subject to you the Night and the Day; the Sun and the Moon; and the Stars are in subjection by His Command: verily in this are Signs for men who are wise.

And the things on this earth which He has multiplied in varying colors (and qualities): verily in this a Sign for men who celebrate the praises of Allah (in gratitude).

It is He Who has made the sea subject, that you may eat thereof flesh that is fresh and tender, and that you may extract there from ornaments to wear, and You see the ships therein that plough the waves, that you may seek (thus) of the bounty of Allah and that you may be grateful.

And He has set up on the earth mountains standing firm, lest it should shake with you; and rivers and roads; that you may guide yourselves.

And marks and sign-posts; and by the stars (Men) guide themselves.

Is then He Who creates like one that creates not? Will you not receive admonition?

If you would count up the favors of Allah, never would you be able to number them; for Allah is Oft-Forgiving, Most Merciful. (An-Nahl 16:3–18, Koran)

Sama in the Koran signifies the universe and *ardh* man's domain on the earth pertaining to his social and economic world. Allah is the Lord of the heavens and the earth and all that is in between. The divine laws under which the universe functions so meticulously and smoothly should also apply to the economic life of man so that he might achieve a balanced, predictable, equitable, and just financial life. *Sama* is the source of Allah's benevolence to humanity and also of His universal laws that govern human subsistence and sustenance on the earth. *Ardh* controls man's economic life in this world. Allah's kingdom over the heavens and the earth sustains man's economic life and directly influences man's conduct and his obedience to Allah's covenant.

Ayahs in Sura An-Nahl are explicit: Allah created the heavens and the earth for just ends to bring peace, harmony, equilibrium, and justice to the universe. He is Allah the One, Lord of the creation. He sends water from the heavens for sustenance of life on the earth—the life of humans, plants, and animals. Allah sends sunshine to the earth to provide warmth and light to sustain human, plant, and animal life. Allah fashioned the moon and stars to create equilibrium in the universe, every object in its intended place, revolving in its fixed orbit in perfect harmony and balance. Allah knows the secrets and mysteries of the heavens and the earth, the so-called sciences, and the knowledge of particles, elements, cells, mitochondria, chromosomes, gravity, and black holes. He revealed only an infinitesimal portion to man, yet man is arrogant and boastful.

The commandments of Allah addressed to the believers are the fundamental principles of the covenant or the compact between Allah and man, which become obligatory when the fire of love for Allah is kindled in his heart and he submits to the will of Allah and becomes His servant and steward on the earth.

Say, "Come I will recite what your Lord has prohibited you from:

Join not anything in worship with Him:

Be good to your parents:

Kill not your children because of poverty, We
provide sustenance for you and for them.

Come not near to shameful deeds (lewd acts, fornication,
and adultery) whether open or secret.

Take not life, which Allah hath made sacred, except by the way of
justice or law: This He commands you, that you may learn wisdom.

And come not near the orphan's property, except to
improve it, until he attains the age of full strength,

And give full measure and full weight with justice.

No burden We place on any soul but that which it can bear.

Whenever you give your word speak justly
even if a near relative is concerned:

And fulfill the Covenant of Allah. Thus, He
commands you that you may remember.

Verily, this is My Way leading straight: follow it: follow not (other)
paths for they will separate you from His path. This He commands
you that you may remember." (Al-An'am 6:151–53, Koran)

This commandment, similar to the Ten Commandments of Moses, emphasizes tawhid and respect for parents; prohibits infanticide on the grounds of poverty, taking of life, lewd acts, adultery, fornication, and embezzlement of orphan's property; stresses honesty in trade; and emphasizes the individual's responsibility to be just. Allah commands humans to be righteous.

We need to pause and think about what brought the downfall and shame of the Muslims in the nineteenth and the twentieth centuries. The average Muslim forgot his covenant with Allah, and the words of the covenant lost their meaning. To blame was the life of ease and loss of faith among the ruling classes of the Muslim states. Such a state of ethics among the rulers and the elite could occur only when the Islamic community, the *ummah*, abdicated its authority and failed to execute its executive sovereignty over the conduct of its appointed imams.

The Islamic community has the moral responsibility that is implied in the primordial covenant referred to in the Koran as Allah's vicegerency on the earth. The Islamic society is made up of people with *taqwa* of Allah (God-fearing people), and it constitutes a "middle nation" or axial community (*ummah wast*) whose collective responsibility is to bear witness to the truth and act as an example for the rest of humanity. It is a nation of moderation that is averse to extremism. The community of believers enjoins what is right and forbids what is wrong.

This community also shuns life of ease, luxury, and quest for wealth for the sake of accumulation and the hoarding of such wealth. It abhors ostentation and the vulgar display of wealth. Wealth can only be used for necessities of daily living, kith and kin, the needy, the good of the community and the state, and the provision of food, shelter, education, and health care for every member of the community. Every member of the *ummah* is entrusted with the responsibility to ensure that his neighbors and clansmen do not suffer from hunger, illness, or any other deprivation. Every member also has the added responsibility, in consensus with the rest of the community, to select and appoint a devout, God-fearing, austere, competent, and humble person among themselves who will be granted with authority to manage the community's affairs (*ulil amri minkum*). Those with authority act in their capacity as the representative (*wakil*) of the people are bound by the Koranic mandate to consult the community in public affairs; consensus is the binding source of the law. The community, by consultation and in consensus, has the authority to depose any person charged with authority, including the head of state, in the event of disobedience of the covenant of Allah.

The rot in the Islamic world started with the establishment of the Umayyad caliphate in AD 661, when succession to the caliphate became hereditary, following the Persian and Byzantine tradition. The caliphs began to live in magnificent palaces surrounded by hundreds of courtiers, concubines, and eunuchs. When the Abbasid caliphs shifted their capital from Damascus to Baghdad, luxury, debauchery, and corruption continued to be the hallmark of the ruling elites. The tales of *The Arabian Nights* illustrate only a fraction of the debasement of the moral standards set by the Koran. This unabashed corruption of moral principles has continued among our ruling classes to this day. The Abbasid caliphate was finally abolished when Hulegu Khan's hordes plundered, razed, and looted much of the land and destroyed Baghdad, killing thousands of residents. It was written that waters of the Tigris turned red with the blood of thousands of victims for several weeks.

Allah has destroyed countless peoples for their lack of faith and unabashed corruption on the earth. Muslims also lost the mercy of Allah when they lost their faith and indulged in abominable behavior of extravagance and indulgence while their kin and clansmen went hungry. Allah's wrath was soon to follow.

> Allah sets forth a Parable: a city enjoying security and quiet, abundantly supplied with sustenance from every place: yet was it ungrateful for the favors of Allah: so, Allah made it taste of hunger and terror closing in on it, like a garment, from every side, because of the evil which its people wrought. (An-Nahl 16:112, Koran)

How many were the populations We destroyed because of their iniquities, setting up in their place's other peoples? (Al-Anbiya 21:11, Koran)

Allah calls to the home of peace, Dar es Salaam, those who believe in Allah, obey His covenant, and perform wholesome and beautiful deeds.

But Allah calls to the Home of Peace, Dar as Salaam, and guides whom He wills to the Straight path. To those who perform wholesome and beautiful deeds is beautiful reward. No darkness nor shall shame cover their faces! They are Companions of the Garden; they will abide therein forever. (Yunus 10:25–26, Koran)

The world of Islam is now waking up to the second dawn, having survived the darkness of adversity, servitude, and ignominy of the colonial occupation. It is once again heading toward the precipice of perpetual economic serfdom and servitude at an alarming rate. We are being led by self-appointed rulers whose agenda is to perpetuate their power and wealth at the cost of unity, well-being, honor, and freedom of the Islamic community.

The divine laws set by the Koran as the basis for an Islamic nation are these: The individual believer, both man and woman, is the vicegerent of Allah on the earth. The believer is entrusted with the responsibility for his own intentions, actions, and *iman.* Men and women are autonomous as individuals who unite to form the world community of Islam, the *ummah.* The believers, in this communion with Allah and with other believers, make decisions in consultation and consensus for the welfare and betterment of the whole community according to the laws laid down in the Koran. *The ummah as a whole, in consultation and in consensus, grants people from among themselves with authority to manage its affairs in accordance with the laws and commandments laid down by Allah in the covenant of the Koran.* Those given authority as the people's representative are bound by the Koranic covenant to consult the community in public affairs, and consensus is the binding source of the law. The *ummah* as a whole, in consensus, has the authority to depose the person in authority, including the head of state, for violation of the covenant of the Koran.

To those who perform wholesome and beautiful deeds, Allah promises Dar es Salaam, an abode of peace on the earth; abundance of rewards; and *Jannat* in the hereafter. For those who do beautiful deeds, neither darkness nor shame shall overcome them.

At the beginning of the twenty-first century, the community of Islam stands on the precipice behind our rulers, leading us to disunity, foreign domination, economic subjugation, humiliation, and serfdom for another two hundred years. The time has come for the *ummah* to exercise its divine right to unify and fulfill our obligations sanctioned by the covenant of the Koran. In doing so, we must first open our hearts to our faith and practice it according to Allah's commandments. Our actions should connote our true faith. Allah opens the heart of the believer who truly submits to His light (*nur*).

Farewell Address: During the last days of his prophethood and his worldly life on ninth day *Zul-hajj*, the blessed *rasul* of Allah summarized His message to mankind, the covenant of the Koran, the obligation of all believers to obey and follow. After midday prayers (Arafat), the blessed *nabi* delivered the historic hajj khutbah, which has come to be known as the farewell address. After giving praise to God and thanking Him for the bounties that he had conferred on the Muslims, the blessed *nabi* said:

- O People, listen carefully to my words for I may not be among you next year, nor ever address you again from this spot.

- People, just as you regard this month as sacred, so regard the life and property of every Muslim as sacred. Return the goods entrusted to you to their rightful owners. Hurt no one, so that no one may hurt you.
- Usury is forbidden.
- Satan has despaired in leading you astray in big things, so beware of his maneuvers in tempting you in small things.
- Women have rights over you as you have rights over them. Be good to them. You may soon have to appear before Allah and answer for your deeds. So, beware.
- Do not go astray after I am gone. O People, no Nabi will come after me, and no new faith will be born. Worship your Allah. Say your prayers. Keep fast during the month of Ramadan. Give of your wealth in charity.
- All Muslims, free or slaves have the same rights and the same responsibilities. None is higher than the other unless he is higher in virtue. Feed your slaves as you feed yourself. Do not oppress them. Do not usurp their rights. All distinctions between the Arabs the non-Arabs, the black, and the white are abolished. All Muslims are brothers.
- Do Good. Be faithful to your Covenant. Be kind to the orphans. Remember Allah Know that while man being mortal is bound to die, Allah being immortal will live forever[1].

Having spoken these words, the blessed *nabi* turned his face to Heaven and said, "Be my witness O Allah, that I have conveyed your message to your people."

Thereupon, the people corroborated, saying, "Yes, O Nabi of Allah, you have done so, and done it magnificently."

---

1 "Farewell address," abridged, in Muhammad Haykal, *The Life of Muhammad* (American Trust Publications), 486.

The Revelation: After the *zuhr* prayers on the ninth day of *Zul-hajj* on the tenth year of hijra, Allah announced to the blessed *nabi* in the presence of ten thousand people:

> This day have I perfected for you, your faith, and completed my blessings upon you, and have chosen for you Islam as religion. (Al-Ma'idah 5:4, Koran)

On that day, Allah in His mercy completed His message of the Koran and His covenant with mankind. The era of prophets and revelation had ended; there were to be no more prophets. Allah had shown His straight path to humans. The path to the *din* is in *islam* (submission), *iman* (faith), and *ihsan* (beautiful deeds). In the journey in this world, man is presented with Allah's covenant as his guide, *taqwa* of Allah as his shield against evil, and *furqan* (the criterion to distinguish between right and evil) as compass to the straight path of righteousness. If man accepts the path of Allah and follows Allah's covenant as his guide, *taqwa* of Allah as the shield against evil, and *furqan* as compass to the straight path, he becomes a *Momin*, a believer and one of the righteous. The way to righteousness is in the study of the Koran.

Every little bit of devotion makes the *nur* of Allah glow in the heart of the believer until he is connected to Allah and begins to follow His path. This communion between the believer and Allah becomes exclusive. Submission establishes the link between them. The believer asks, and Allah gives; the believer loves Allah, and Allah loves him in return. The believer asks for the straight path, and Allah shows him the way; the believer praises Allah, and Allah showers His mercy and grace upon him. The believer remembers Allah, and Allah responds to those who praise Him, thank Him, and ask Him. The believer, on his chosen journey on the path of Allah, is well equipped. He has Allah's protection, guidance, and direction.

Allah's *din* is divine. Allah is *Haqq,* and all truth emanates from him. The Koran is Allah's word on the earth and the expression of *haqq. Haqq* is the reality and the truth; *batil* refers to something that is imaginary or false. When humans add dogma and creed to Allah's *din,* it is not *haqq.* In matters of *din,* what is not absolute truth is not *haqq.* What is not *haqq* is *batil* (false or fabricated). What is not truthful cannot be a witness over Allah's word and *din.* All human additions to the *din* of Allah do not constitute the truth. Therefore, every human fabrication to the *din* after the completion of *wahiy* is *batil.*

***

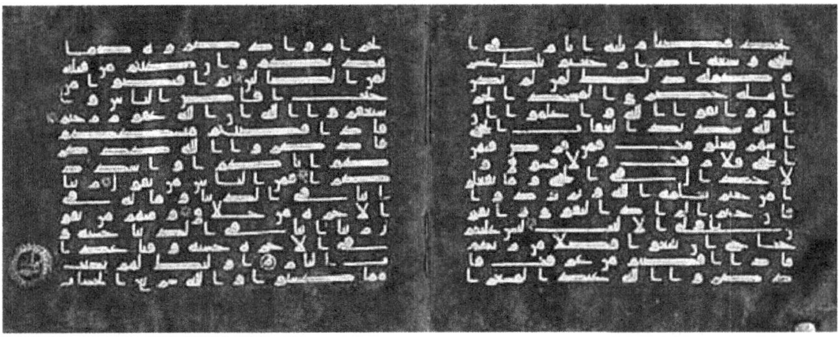

Two leaves of the famous Blue Koran depicting the Kufic script.

The famous Blue Koran. Vellums from (a) Rifaat Sheikh El-Ard Collection, Riyadh, Saudi Arabia, and (b) Beit al-Qur'an, Bahrain.

Date: Late ninth or early tenth century CE (c. AH 300).

Size: Each page is 37.5 × 28.6 inches.

Contents: The manuscript in (a) shows Sura Al-Baqarah verses 197–201.

Script and Ornamentation: Kufic. This page is from a nearly complete manuscript of the Koran that is a wonder of Islamic calligraphy. No more than three or four Koranic manuscripts on colored vellum are known, and of them, this splendid copy of the holy book is the most well known. It is a climax to the tradition of the vellum Koran in Kufic script. The script is gold, written on blue vellum. The end of verse 200 is marked with a golden circle bearing the Arabic letter *dal* and also with a silver medallion in the lower left-hand margin. Each verse is indicated by a small silver rosette, now tarnished and hardly distinguishable.

Location: Although most of the manuscript was originally in Kairouan, Tunisia, several folios are found in collections elsewhere.

Chapter Two

The Covenant of Allah: The Covenant of the Koran

Verily those who pledge their allegiance unto you, (O Muhammad) pledge it unto none but Allah; the Hand of Allah is over their hands. Thereafter whosoever breaks his Covenant does so to the harm of his own soul, and whosoever fulfils his Covenant with Allah, Allah will grant him an immense Reward.

—Al-Fath 48:10, Koran

There is an implicit assumption in the Koran that there exists an agreement between Allah and His creation, portrayed as a mutual understanding in which Allah proposes a system of regulations for the guidance of man. This guidance is presented in the form of commandments to be accepted and implemented by man. Allah then makes a promise of what He will do when man is willing to abide by these commands and regulates his life according to them. The concept of promise is clearly conditional on human obedience. The covenant of the Koran symbolizes the relationship between Allah and man; man becomes His steward, vicegerent, or custodian on the earth through submission and obedience to His will (*islam*) as expressed in His commands and is able to take the advantage of Allah's promises and favors.

Allah addresses those who believe in Him directly in seventy-five verses of the Koran, giving them guidance, advice, and a promise of rewards in this world and the hereafter. Those who do not believe in Him, the infidels (the *kafirun)* are promised a place in hell forever. A similar penalty is promised to those who submit to Allah according to their word but not their deeds; such people are the hypocrites or the *Munafiqeen*. The concept of the covenant also symbolizes the relationship between man and Allah's creatures and the rest of His creation. They all share one God, one set of guidance and commandments, the same submission and obedience to Him, and the same set of expectations in accordance to His promises. They all can, therefore, trust one another since they all have similar obligations and expectations. In view of the Koran, humans, communities, nations, and civilizations will continue in harmony and peace so long as they continue to fulfill Allah's covenant.

The Koran uses three terms for the word *covenant*:

- *'Ahd* is the more frequently used term than the other two. It means "commitment obligation, responsibility, pledge, promise, oath, contract, compact, covenant, pact, and treaty agreement." It also means "an era or epoch."
- *Mithaq* means "to put faith in"; it is a tie of relationship between two parties.
- *Isr* means "a firm covenant, compact, or contract that if not fulfilled constitutes punishment."

The covenant in the Koran contains several articles not unlike a modern legal agreement.

a) Names of the two parties of the covenant, the first one being Allah
b) Reminder of Allah's favors
c) List of commandments or conditions of the covenant
d) Promises and rewards
e) Warnings of disobedience
f) Affirmation and witness
g) Oaths by Allah's signs and favors
h) Signs of the covenant
i) Lessons from the past

In the covenant of Allah with the believers, for instance, in Sura Al-Ma'idah, the format of the pact is illustrated clearly:

a) In the name of Allah, Most gracious Most Merciful. O, who believe! Fulfill your obligations. (Al-Ma'idah 5:1, Koran)
b) And call in remembrance the favor of Allah unto you, and His Covenant, which He ratified with you. (Al-Ma'idah 5:7, Koran)
c) Forbidden to you are: carrion, blood, the flesh of swine, and that on which has been invoked the name of other than Allah: that which has been killed by strangling, or by a violent blow, or by a headlong fall, or by being gored to death: that which has partly eaten by a wild animal; unless you are able to slaughter it (in due form); that which is sacrificed on stone alters; forbidden is also the division of meat by raffling with arrows: that is impiety.
   This day those who reject faith have given up all hope of your religion: yet fear them not but fear Me.
   This day I have, perfected your religion for you, completed my favors upon you, and have chosen Islam as your religion. (Al-Ma'idah 5:3, Koran)
d) To those who believe and do beautiful deeds, for them there is forgiveness and a great reward. (Al-Ma'idah 5:8, Koran)
e) Those who reject faith and deny Our Signs will be companions of hellfire.
f) And remember Allah's favor to you and His covenant with which He bound you when you said, "we hear and obey", And fear Allah. Verily Allah is all knower of the secrets of your hearts. (Al-Ma'idah 5:7, Koran)
g) This day have I perfected your religion for you, completed my favors upon you, and have chosen Islam as your religion. (Al-Ma'idah 5:3, Koran)
h) Allah took a Covenant from the Children of Israel and We appointed twelve leaders from among them. And Allah said "I am with you if you establish salaat, practice regular charity,

believe in my Rasools honor and assist them, and loan to Allah a beautiful loan, Verily I will wipe out from you your evils, and admit you to Gardens with rivers flowing beneath; But if any of you after this disbelieved, he has truly wandered from the path of rectitude.

i) Therefore, because of breach of their Covenant, We cursed them and made their hearts grow hard. They perverted words from their meaning and abandoned a good part of the message that was sent them. Thou will not cease to discover treachery from them barring a few. But bear with them and pardon them. Verily Allah loves those who are wholesome.

Moreover, from those who call themselves Christians, We took their Covenant, but they have abandoned a good part of the Message that was sent to them. Therefore, We have stirred up enmity and hatred among them until the Day of Resurrection, when Allah will inform them of their handiwork.

O People of the Book! There has come to you Our Rasool, revealing to you much that you used to hide in the Scripture and passing over much. Indeed, there has come to you from Allah a light and a plain Book:

Wherewith Allah guides all who seek His good pleasure to ways of peace and safety, and leads them out of darkness, by His Will, unto the light, guides them to a Path that is Straight. (Al-Ma'idah 5:12-16, Koran)

The Commandments

The commandments of Allah addressed to the believers (men and women) are the fundamentals of the *din* of Islam. These commandments make up the covenant or the compact between Allah and His believers. The fulfillment of the covenant becomes obligatory to man when the fire of love for Allah is kindled in his heart, and he submits to His will, becoming His servant and steward on the earth.

Say, "Come I will recite what your Lord has prohibited
you from: Join not anything in worship with Him:

Be good to your parents: kill not your children because of
poverty, We provide sustenance for you and for them:

Come not near to shameful deeds (Fahasha) whether open or secret.

Take not life, which Allah hath made sacred, except by the way of
justice or law: This He commands you, that you may learn wisdom.

And come not near the orphan's property, except to
improve it, until he attains the age of full strength, and
give full measure and full weight with justice. No burden
We place on any soul but that which it can bear.

Whenever you give your word speak honestly even if a near
relative is concerned: And fulfill the Covenant of Allah.
Thus, He commands you that you may remember.

Verily, this is My Way leading straight: follow it: follow not (other)
paths for they will separate you from His path. This He commands
you that you may remember." (Al-An 'am 6:151–53, Koran)

These commandments are similar to the Ten Commandments of Moses. They emphasize tawhid and respect for parents; prohibits infanticide, taking of life, lewd acts, adultery, fornication, and embezzlement of orphans' property; stress honesty in trade; and underline a person's responsibility to be just. Allah commands humans to be righteous and to fulfill their covenant with Allah.

Commandments of the Covenant of Allah in
Sura Al-Baqarah (2 Medina 92)[2]

1.

O you who believe!

Seek help with patience, perseverance, and prayer.
Allah is with those who patiently persevere.

(2:153, Koran)

2

O you who believe!

Eat of good things provided to you by Allah and show your gratitude in worship of Him. Forbidden to you are the carrion, blood, and flesh of swine, and on any other food on which any name besides that of Allah has been invoked. If forced by necessity, without willful disobedience or transgressing due limits, one is guilt less. Allah is Most Forgiving and Most Merciful.

(2:172–73, Koran)

[2] The first number is the traditional sequence number of the sura, followed by the period during which the sura was revealed. The second number denotes the chronological sequence of the sura.

3

O you who believe!

The law of equality is prescribed to you in cases of murder. The free for the free, the slave for the slave, the woman for the woman. However, if any remission is made by the brethren of the slain, then grant any reasonable demand, and compensate him with handsome gratitude. This is a concession and a Mercy from your Lord. After this, whoever exceeds the limits shall be in grave penalty.

In the Law of Equality, there is a saving of life for you, O men of understanding; that you may restrain yourselves.

(2:178–79, Koran)

4

O you who believe!

Fasting is prescribed to you, for a fixed number of days in the month of Ramadan as it was prescribed to those before you, that you may practice self-restraint. If you are ill, or on a journey, the prescribed number of days of fasting should be made up afterwards. For those who cannot fast because of physical hardship, should feed the poor and needy but it is better to give more out of free will. However fasting is better. The Qur'an was revealed in the month of Ramadan, guidance to humankind for judgment between right and wrong. For every one except those ill or on a journey, this month should spend it in fasting. Allah intends to make it easy on you so that you may complete the prescribed period of fasting and to glorify Him to express your gratitude for His Guidance.

(2: 183–85, Koran)

5

O you who believe!

Enter into submission to the will of Allah, enter Islam whole-heartedly, and follow not the footsteps of Satan, for he is a sworn enemy to you!

(2:208, Koran)

6.

O you who believe!

Void not your charity by boast, conceit, and insult, by reminders of your generosity like those who want their generosity to be noted by all men but they believe neither in Allah nor in the Last Day. Theirs is a parable like a hard barren rock, on which is a little soil; on it falls heavy rain, which leaves it just a bare stone. And Allah guides not those who reject Faith.

And the likeness of those who give generously, seeking to please Allah and to strengthen their souls, is as a garden, high and fertile where heavy rain falls on it and makes it yield a double the amount of harvest, and if it receives not heavy rain, light moisture suffices it. Allah notices whatever you do.

(2:264–65, Koran)

The parable of those who spend their substance in the way of Allah is that of a grain of corn: it grows seven ears, and each ear has a hundred grains. Allah gives plentiful return to whom He pleases, Allah cares for all, and He knows all things.

Those who give generously in the cause of Allah, and follow not up their gifts with reminders of their generosity or with injury, for them their reward is with their Lord; on them shall be no fear, nor shall they grieve.

Kind words and the covering of faults are better than charity followed by injury. Allah is Free of all wants and He is Most Merciful.

(2:261–63, Koran)

7.

O you who believe!

Spend out of bounties of Allah in charity and wholesome deeds before the Day comes when there will be neither bargaining, friendship nor intercession. Those who reject faith are the wrongdoers.

Allah! There is no god but He, the Ever Living, the One Who sustains and protects all that exists. No slumber can seize Him or sleep. His are all things in the heavens and on earth. Who is there can intercede in His presence except as He permits? He knows what happens to His creatures in this world and in the Hereafter. Nor shall they know the scope of His knowledge except as He wills. His Throne doth extend over the heavens and the earth, and He feels no fatigue in guarding and preserving them for He is the Most High, Most Great.

Let there be no compulsion in religion: Truth stands out clear from Error: whoever rejects Evil and believes in Allah hath grasped the most trustworthy handhold that never breaks. And Allah hears and knows all things.

Allah is the Wali, protector of those who have faith. From the depths of darkness, He will lead them forth into light. Of those who reject faith their Wali (protectors) are the false deities: from light, they will lead them forth into the depths of darkness. They will be Companions of the Fire, to dwell therein (forever).

(2:254–57, Koran)

Those who spend of their goods in charity by night and by day, in secret and in public, have their reward with their Lord: on them shall be no fear, nor shall they grieve.

Those who devour usury will not stand except stands the one whom the Satan by his touch has driven to madness. That is because they say: "Trade is like usury", but Allah hath permitted trade and forbidden usury. Those who after receiving direction from their Lord, desist, shall be pardoned for the past; their case is for Allah to judge; but those who repeat (the offence) are Companions of the Fire; they will abide therein (forever).

Allah will deprive usury of all blessing but will give increase for deeds of charity, for He does not love ungrateful and wicked creatures.

(2:274–76, Koran)

8

Those who believe.

Those who do wholesome deeds, establish regular prayers and regular charity have rewards with their Lord. On them shall be no fear, nor shall they grieve.

(2:277, Koran)

9.

O you who believe!

Have taqwa of Allah, fear Allah, and give up what remains of your demand for usury, if you are indeed believers. If you do it not, take notice of war from Allah and His Rasool: but if you turn back, you will still have your capital sums.

Deal not unjustly, and you shall not be dealt with unjustly.

If the debtor is in a difficulty, grant him time until it is easy for him to repay. But if you remit it by way of charity, that is best for you.

(2:278–80, Koran)

10.

O you who believe!

When you make a transaction involving future obligations, write it down in presence of witnesses, or let a scribe write it down faithfully. Let the party incurring the liability dictate truthfully in the presence of two witnesses from among your own men and if two men are not available then a man and two women, so that if one of them errs then the other one, can remind him. If a party is mentally or physically or unable to dictate, let his guardian do so faithfully. The witnesses should not refuse when called upon to give evidence. Disregard not to put your contract in writing, whether it be small or large, it is more suitable in the eyes of Allah, more suitable as evidence, and more convenient to prevent doubts in the future amongst yourselves.

But if you carry out a transaction instantaneously on the spot among yourselves, there is no blame on you if you do not reduce it to writing. But neither takes witnesses whenever you make a commercial contract; and let neither scribe nor the witnesses suffer harm. If you do such harm, it would be wickedness in you. So, fear Allah; for it is Allah that teaches you. And Allah is well acquainted with all things.

If you are on a journey, and cannot find a scribe, a pledge with possession may serve the purpose. And if one of you deposits a thing on trust with another let the trustee faithfully discharge his trust, and let him fear his Lord. Conceal not evidence; for whoever conceals it, his heart is tainted with sin. And Allah knows all that you do.

(2:282–83, Koran)

Commandments of the Covenant of Allah in Sura Ali 'Imran (3 Medina 93)

11.

O you who believe!

If you listen to a faction among the People of the Book, (Jews and Christians) they would render you apostates after you have believed!

And how could you deny Faith when you learn the Signs of Allah, and amongst you lives the Rasool?

Whoever holds firmly to Allah will be shown a Way that is straight.

(3:100–101, Koran)

12.

O you who believe!

Be in taqwa of Allah, fear Allah as He should be feared, and die not except in a state of Islam.

And hold fast, all together, by the Rope, which Allah stretches out for you, and be not divided among yourselves; and remember with gratitude Allah's favor on you; You were enemies, and He joined your hearts in love, so that by His Grace, you became brethren and a community. You were on the brink of the pit of fire, and He saved you from it. Thus does Allah make His Signs clear to you that you may be guided.

Let there arise out of you a band of people inviting to all that is good, enjoining what is right, and forbidding what is wrong: they are the ones to attain happiness.

Be not like those who are divided amongst themselves and fall into disputations after receiving clear signs: for them is a dreadful penalty.

(3:102–5, Koran)

13.

O you who believe!

Devour not usury, doubled and multiplied; Be in taqwa of Allah (fear Allah) that you may prosper.

Fear the Fire, which is prepared for those who reject Faith.

And obey Allah and the Rasool; that you may obtain mercy.

Be quick in the race for forgiveness from your Lord, and for a Garden whose measurement is that of the heavens and of the earth, prepared for the righteous.

Those who give freely whether in prosperity, or in adversity, those who restrain anger, and pardon all humans, for Allah loves those who do beautiful deeds.

(3:130–34, Koran)

14.

O you who believe!

Take not into intimacy those outside your ranks: they will not fail to corrupt you. They only desire your ruin: rank hatred has already appeared from their mouths: what their hearts conceal is far worse.

We have made plain to you the Signs if you have wisdom.

Ah! You are those who love them, but they love you not, though you believe in the whole of the Book, when they meet you, they say, "We believe": but when they are alone, they bite off the very tips of their fingers at you in their rage. Say: "Perish in your rage; Allah knows well all the secrets of the heart."

If all that is good befalls you, it grieves them; but if some misfortune overtakes you, they rejoice at it.

But if you are constant and do right, not the least harm will their cunning do to you; for Allah compasses round about all that they do.

(3:118–20, Koran)

15.

O you who believe!

If you obey the Unbelievers, (kafaru) they will drive you back on your heels, and you will turn your back to your Faith to your own loss. Allah is your protector, and He is the best of helpers.

(3:149–50, Koran)

16.

O you who believe!

Be not like the Unbelievers, who say of their brethren, who were traveling through the earth or engaged in fighting: "If they had stayed with us, they would not have died, or been slain." So, that Allah may make it a cause of regret in their hearts. It is Allah that gives Life and Death, and Allah is seer of all that you do.

And if you are slain, or die, in the Way of Allah, forgiveness and mercy from Allah are far better than all they could amass.

And if you die, or are slain, it is unto Allah that you are brought together.

(3:156–58, Koran)

17.

O you who believe!

Persevere in patience and constancy; vie in such perseverance; strengthen each other; and be in taqwa of Allah, fear Allah that you may prosper.

(3:200, Koran)

Commandments of the Covenant of Allah
in Sura An-Nisa (4 Medina 94)

18.

O you who believe!

You are forbidden to take women against their will. Nor should you treat them with harshness, so that you may recant on part of the dower you have given them, and that is only where they have been guilty of open lewdness. On the contrary, live with them on a footing of kindness and equality. If you take a dislike to them, it may be that you dislike a thing, through which Allah brings about a great deal of good.

(4:19, Koran)

19.

O you who believe!

Squander not your wealth among yourselves in egotism and conceit: Let there be trade and traffic amongst you with mutual goodwill Nor kill or destroy yourselves: for verily Allah hath been Most Merciful to you. If any do that in rancor and injustice, soon shall We cast them into the fire: and easy it is for Allah. If you abstain from all the odious and the forbidden, Allah shall expel out of you all evil in you and admit you to a Gate of great honor.

And crave not those things of what Allah has bestowed His gifts more freely on some than others, men are assigned what they earn and women that they earn.

But ask Allah of His bounty. Surely, Allah is knower of everything.

(4:29-32, Koran)

???

20.

O you who believe!

Approach not prayers with a mind befogged until you understand all that you utter, nor come up to prayers in a state of un-cleanliness, till you have bathed. If you are ill, or on a journey, or when you come from the closet or you have had sexual intercourse, and find no water, take for yourself clean sand or earth and rub your hands and face. Allah shall blot out your sins and forgive again and again.

(4:43, Koran)

21.

O you who believe!

Obey Allah and obey the Rasool, and those charged amongst you with authority in the settlement of your affairs. If you differ in any thing among yourselves, refer it to Allah and His Rasool (The Qur'an and the Prophet's teachings). If you do believe in Allah, the last Day that is best, and the most beautiful conduct in the final determination.

(4:59, Koran)

22.

O you who believe!

Take your precautions, and either go forth
in parties or go forth all together.

There are certainly among you men who would tarry behind; if a misfortune befalls you, they say: "Allah did favor us in that we were not present among them."

But if good fortune comes to you from Allah, they would be sure to say – as if there had never been ties of affection between you and them – "Oh! I wish I had been with them; a fine thing should I then have made of it!"

Let those fight in the cause of Allah who sell the life of this world for the Hereafter, To him who fights in the cause of Allah – whether he is slain or gets victory – soon shall We give him a reward of great (value).

And why should you not fight in the cause of Allah and of those who, being weak, are ill-treated (and oppressed)? Men, women, and children, whose cry is: "Our Lord! Rescue us from this town, whose people are oppressors; and raise for us from thee one who will protect; and raise for us from thee one who will help!

(4: 71–75, Koran)

23.

O you who believe!

When you go forth in the cause of Allah be careful to discriminate and say not to the one who greets you with alaikum as salaam, "Though art not a believer".

Would you covet perishable goods of this life when there are immeasurable treasures with Allah. You were like the person who offered you salutation, before Allah conferred on you His favors. Therefore carefully investigate for Allah is well aware of all that you do.

(4:94, Koran)

24.

O you who believe!

Stand firm for justice as witness to Allah, be it against yourself, your parents, or your family. Whether it be against rich or poor, Both are nearer to Allah than they are to you. Follow not your caprice lest you distort your testimony. If you prevaricate and evade justice Allah is well aware what you do.

(4:135, Koran)

25.

O you who believe!

Believe in Allah, His Rasool, and the Book, which He has sent to His Rasool and the scriptures, which He sent to those before him. Any who deny Allah, His angels, His Books, His Rasools, and the Day of Judgment has gone astray.

(4:136, Koran)

26.

O you who believe!

Take not infidels (Kafirun) for awliya (friends and protectors) in place of believers. Would you offer Allah a clear warrant against yourselves?

(4:144, Koran)

Commandments of the Covenant of Allah
in Sura Al-Ma'idah (5 Medina 95)

27.

O you who believe!

Fulfill your Covenants.

(5:1, Koran)

28.

O you who believe!

Violate not the sanctity of the Symbols of Allah, or of the sacred month, or of the animals brought for sacrifice, nor the garlands that mark out such animals, nor the people coming to the Sacred House, seeking the bounty and good pleasure of their Lord. But when you are clear of the Sacred Precincts and of ihram, you may hunt, and let not the enmity of those who once debarred you from the sacred place make you guilty of bearing malice. Help one another in virtue and piety but help not one another in sin and acrimony. Be in taqwa of Allah, fear Allah, for Allah is swift in reckoning.

(5:2, Koran)

Forbidden to you for food is carrion, blood, flesh of swine and on which name other than of Allah has been invoked, also the strangled, the felled, the mangled or the gored and that has been sacrificed on alters; forbidden is also the division of meat by raffling with arrows: that is impiety.

This day have those who reject faith (kafaru) given up all hope of compromising your faith, fear them not, but only fear Me. This day have I perfected your religion for you, bestowed on you with My blessings, and decreed Islam as your religion.

(5:3, Koran)

29.

O you who believe!

When you arise for salaat, purify yourself by washing your faces, your hands to the elbows, wipe your heads, and wash your feet to the ankles. If you are unclean, purify yourself. If you are ill or on a journey or you come from call of nature, or you have been in contact with women and you find no water then take for yourself clean sand or earth and rub there with your faces and hands. Allah does not wish that you should be burdened, but to make you clean, and to bestow His blessings on you, that you might be grateful.

(5:6, Koran)

30.

O you who believe!

Stand firmly for Allah as a witness of fair dealing. Let not the malice of people lead you to iniquity. Be just, that is next to worship. Be with taqwa of Allah, fear Allah. Allah is well aware with what you do.

(5:8, Koran)

To those who believe and do deeds of righteousness,
Allah has promised forgiveness and a great reward.

(5:9, Koran)

31.

O you who believe!

Remember Allah's blessings on you. When a people planned stretching out their hands against you and Allah did hold back their hands from you to protect you from your enemies. Be in taqwa of Allah, fear Allah, and place your trust in Allah.

(5:11, Koran)

32.

O you who believe!

Be in taqwa of Allah, fear Allah. Perform Jihad and strive your utmost in Allah's Cause, and approach Him so that you may prosper.

(5:35, Koran)

33.

O you who believe!

Take not the Jews and the Christians as your friends and protectors (awliya). They are friends and protectors unto each other. He who amongst you turns to them is one of them. Allah does not guide those who are unjust and evil doers (zalimun).

(5:51, Koran)

34.

O you who believe!

If any among you turn back on his faith Allah will bring a people whom He loves and who love Him, and who are humble towards the believers, and stern towards unbelievers, who perform jihad and strive in the cause of Allah and fear not reproaches of any blamer. Such is the Grace of Allah, which He bestows on whom He wills. Allah is All Sufficient for His Creatures and all Knowing.

(5:54, Koran)

35.

O you who believe!

Take not for friends and protectors (awliya) those who take your religion for mockery, whether from amongst people of the book or from amongst the kafireen. Be in taqwa of Allah, fear Allah if you have faith indeed.

(5:57, Koran)

36.

O you who believe!

Make not unlawful the good things that
Allah hath made lawful to you.

Commit no excess; Allah loves not people given to excess. Eat of things, which Allah has provided for you, lawful and good. Be in taqwa of Allah, fear Allah in whom you believe.

(5: 87-88, Koran)

37.

O you who believe!

Forbidden to you are intoxicants and gambling, dedication of stones and divination by arrows. These are an abomination and Satan's handiwork; they hinder you from prayer and remembrance of Allah, and place enmity and hatred amongst you. Abstain from them so that you may prosper.

(5:90–91, Koran)

Commandments of the Covenant of Allah
in Sura Al-Anfal (8 Medina 113)

38.

O you who believe!

When you meet the infidel's rank upon rank, in conflict never turn your backs to them.

(8:15, Koran)

39.

Oh, you who believe!

Obey Allah and His Rasool and turn not to others when you should hear him speak. Nor be like those who say: "We hear" but listen not.

For the worst of creatures in the sight of Allah are those who neither listen, nor look or try to comprehend.

(8:20–22, Koran)

Obey Allah and His *rasul*; hear the *rasul*'s message. And grasp with your mind and heart the truth. The truth that Allah speaks of is tawhid, *nubuwwa*, and *Ma'ad*. Tawhid is accepting that there is no god but Allah and that He is the only one worthy of worship. As a principle of faith, tawhid explains the oneness of Allah and His creatures, including the angels connected to Him. Prophecy is the belief in the prophets of Allah and acceptance of their scriptures. *Ma'ad*, the return, is to Allah the Creator.

Do not be like those who say we hear but listen not. The worse of creatures in Allah's sight are those who neither listen nor look or try to comprehend and grasp the truth. Allah took the light from them, and they are left in the darkness.

40.

O you who believe!

Respond to Allah and His Rasool when He
calls you to that give you life.

And know that Allah intervenes in the tussle between man
and his heart, and it is to Allah that you shall return.

Fear treachery or oppression that afflicts not only
those who perpetrate it, but affects guilty and innocent
alike. Know that Allah is strict in punishment.

(8:24–25, Koran)

41.

O you who believe!

Betray not the trust of Allah and His Rasool. Nor knowingly misappropriate things entrusted to you.

(2:27, Koran)

42.

O you who believe!

If you have taqwa of Allah, He will grant you a Criterion to judge between right and wrong and remove from you all misfortunes and evil and forgive your sins. Allah is the bestower of grace in abundance.

(8:29, Koran)

Fight the infidel until there is no more treachery and oppression and there prevails Justice and Faith in Allah altogether and everywhere. If they cease, then Allah is seer of what they do.

If they refuse, be sure that Allah is your Protector, the Best to protect, and the Best to help.

(8:39–40, Koran)

43.

O you who believe!

When you meet the enemy force, stand steadfast against them, and remember the name of Allah much, so that you may be successful. And obey Allah and His Rasool, and do not dispute with one another lest you lose courage, and your strength departs and be patient. Allah is with those who patiently persevere.

(8:45–46, Koran)

Commandments of the Covenant of Allah
in Sura Al-Tawbah (9 Medina 114)

44.

O you who believe!

Take not for your protectors and friends (awliya) your kin who practice infidelity over faith.

Whosoever does that will be amongst the wrong doers.

(9:23, Koran)

45.

O you who believe!

The Mushrikun (unbelievers) are unclean, so let them not approach the Sacred Mosque. If you fear poverty, soon Allah will enrich you, if He wills out of His bounty, for Allah is All-Knowing, All Wise.

Fight those who believe not in Allah, the Last Day, nor forbid what has been forbidden by Allah and His Prophet, nor acknowledge the Religion of Truth from among the Jews and Christians until they pay jaziya in willing submission.

(9:28–29, Koran)

46.

O you who believe!

There are indeed many among the priests and clerics who in falsehood devour the substance of men and hinder them from the way of Allah. And there are those who bury gold and silver and spend it not in the way of Allah: announce unto them a most grievous penalty.

On the Day when heat will be produced out of that wealth in the fire of Hell, and with it will be branded their foreheads, their flanks, and their backs, "This is the treasure which you buried for yourselves: taste then, the treasures which you buried!"

(9:34–35, Koran)

47.

O you who believe!

What ails you? When you are asked to march forwards in the Cause of Allah you cling to the earth! Do you find the life of this earth more alluring than the hereafter? But little is the enjoyment of this life as compared with the hereafter! Unless you go forwards in Allah's cause, He will punish you and put other people in your place. But Him you will not harm in the least. Allah has power over all things. Whether you do or do not help Allah's Rasool, your leader, Allah strengthens him with His Peace and with forces that you do not see. The words of the infidels He humbled into the dirt but Allah's word is Exalted, High. Allah is Mighty, Wise. Go forth, advance! Whether equipped well or lightly, perform jihad strive your utmost and struggle with your wealth and your persons in the cause of Allah. That is best for you, if you knew.

(9:38–41, Koran)

48.

O you who believe!

Be in taqwa of Allah, fear Allah, and be with those who are true in word and deed.

(9:119, Koran)

49.

O you who believe!

Fight the unbelievers who surround you. Let them find you firm, and know Allah is always with those who have taqwa, who are Allah -wary.

(9:123, Koran)

Commandment of the Covenant of Allah in Sura Al-Hajj (22 Medina 112)

50.

O you who believe!

Bow down, prostrate yourself and serve your Lord, and do wholesome deeds that you may prosper. Perform Jihad; strive to your utmost in Allah's cause as striving (jihad) is His due. He has chosen you and Allah has imposed no hardship in your endeavor to His cause. You are the inheritors of the faith of your father Abraham. He has named you Muslims of the times before and now, so that Allah's Rasool may be an example to you and that you are an example to humankind.

Establish regular Salaat, give regular charity, and hold fast to Allah. He is your Mawla, protector, the best of Protectors and the best Helper.

(22:77-78, Koran)

Commandments of the Covenant of Allah in Sura An-Nur (24 Medina 110)

51.

Oh, you who believe!

Do not follow Satan's footsteps: if any will follow the footsteps of Satan, he will command to what is shameful (Fahasha) and wrong (Munkar): and were it not for the grace of Allah and His mercy on you, not one of you would have been unblemished: but Allah does purify whom He pleases: and Allah is all Hearer and all Knower.

Let not those among you who are blessed with grace and ample means hold back from helping their relatives, the poor, and those who have left their homes in Allah's cause. Let them forgive and overlook, do you not wish that Allah should forgive you? And Allah is Oft Forgiving, Most Merciful.

Those who slander decent women, thoughtless but believing, are cursed in this life and in the Hereafter: for them is a grievous Penalty.

(24:21-23, Koran)

52.

Oh, you who believe!

Enter not houses other than yours until you have asked permission and invoked peace upon those in them. If you find none in the house whom you seek, enter not unless permission is granted. If you asked to leave go back, it is best for you that makes for greater purity for you. Allah knows all that you do.

(24:27, Koran)

Commandments of the Covenant of Allah in Sura Al-Ahzab (33 Medina 111)

53.

O You who believe!

Remember the Grace of Allah, bestowed upon you, when there came down hordes to overpower you: We sent against them a hurricane and forces that that you did not see but Allah sees all that you do. Behold! They came on you from above you and from below you, your eyes became dim and the hearts gaped up to the throats, and you imagined various vain thoughts about Allah!

(33:9, Koran)

54.

O you who believe!

Celebrate the Praises of Allah often and Glorify Him in the morning and at night. It is Allah and His Angels Who send their blessings upon you, that He may lead you out of the depths of darkness into light. Allah is full of mercy to the believers! On the Day, they meet Him with the salutation: Salaam, He has prepared for them a generous Reward.

O Nabi, We have set thee as a witness, a bearer of glad tidings, as a Warner and as one who invites to Allah's Grace by His leave and as an inspiration and beam of light. Give glad tidings to the believers that they shall have from Allah bounty in abundance. And obey not the command of the Unbelievers (kafireen) and the hypocrites (munafiqeen), heed not their annoyances, and put your trust in Allah, for enough is Allah as Disposer of affairs.

(33:41–48, Koran)

55.

Allah and His angels bless the Prophet.

O you who believe!

You should also ask for Allah's blessings and peace on the Prophet.

(33:56, Koran)

56.

O you who believe!

Be you not like those who tormented and insulted Moses, but Allah cleared Moses of the slander they had uttered: and he was honorable in Allah's sight.

O you who believe! Fear Allah and speak always the truth that He may direct you to righteous deeds and forgive you your sins: he that obeys Allah and His Rasool have already attained the highest achievement.

We did indeed offer the Trust to the Heavens and the Earth and the Mountains; but they refused to undertake it, being afraid thereof: but man undertook it; he was indeed unjust and ignorant, so that Allah will punish the Hypocrites (munafiqeen), men and women, and the Unbelievers (Mushrikun), men and women, and Allah turns in Mercy to the Believers, men and women; for Allah is Oft-Forgiving, Most Merciful.

(33:69–73, Koran)

Commandments of the Covenant of Allah in
Sura Muhammad (47 Medina 107)

57.

O you who believe!

If you will aid (the cause of) Allah, He will aid you, and make your foothold firm. But those who reject Allah, for them is destruction, and Allah will render their deeds vain. That is because they hate the Revelation of Allah; so, He has made their deeds fruitless. Do they not travel through the earth, and see what was the end of those before them who did evil? Allah brought utter destruction on them, and similar fates await those who reject Allah.

That is because Allah is the Protector of those who believe, but those who reject Allah have no protector.

(47:7:11, Koran)

58.

O you who believe!

Obey Allah, obey the Rasool, and make not vain your deeds!

Those who reject Allah (kafiru), and hinder men from the Path of Allah, then die rejecting Allah; Allah will not forgive them.

Be not weak and ask for peace, while you are having an upper hand: for Allah is with you and will never decrease the reward of your good deeds.

The life of this world is but play and amusement: and if you believe, fear Allah, and guard against evil, He will grant you your recompense, and will not ask you (to give up) your possessions.

If He were to ask you for all of them, and press you, you would covetously withhold, and He would bring out your entire ill wills.

Behold, you are those invited to spend of your wealth in the Way of Allah: but among you are some that are parsimonious. But any who are miserly are so at the expense of their own souls. But Allah is free of all wants, and it is you that are needy. If you turn back (from the Path), He will substitute in your stead another people; then they would not be like you!

(47:33–38, Koran)

Commandment in the Covenant of Allah in Sura Al-Hujurat (49 Medina 109)

59.

O you who believe!

Be not presumptuous and impudent before Allah and His Rasool, but fear Allah: for Allah is He Who hears and knows all things.

60.

O you who believe!

Raise not your voices above the voice of the Prophet, nor speak aloud to him in talk, as you may speak aloud to one another, lest your deeds become vain and you perceive it not.

(49:2, Koran)

61.

O you who believe!

If an impostor (fasiq) comes to you with any news, ascertain the truth, lest you harm people unsuspectingly and afterwards become full of remorse for what you have done.

And know that among you is Allah's Rasool: were he, in many matters, to follow your desires, you would certainly fall into misfortune: but Allah has bestowed on you the love of iman (Faith), and has made it beautiful in your hearts, and He has made abhorrent to you disbelief, wickedness, and disobedience to Allah: such indeed are those who are the righteous (rashidun).

This is a grace from Allah, and a favor; and Allah is All Knowing and All Wise.

If two parties among the Believers fall into a quarrel, make peace between them: but if one of them transgresses beyond bounds against the other, then fight you all against the one who transgresses until he complies with the Command of Allah; but if he complies, then make peace between them with justice, and fairness: for Allah loves those who are fair and just.

The Believers are but a single Brotherhood: so, make peace and reconciliation between your two brothers; and fear Allah, that you may receive Mercy.

(49:6-10, Koran)

62.

O you who believe!

Let not some folk among you ridicule others: it may be that they are better than you are: nor let some women mock others: it may be that the others are better than them: nor defame or revile each other by offensive names: ill-seeming is wicked name calling for the one who has believed; and those who do not desist are indeed wrong doers (zalimun).

(49:11, Koran)

63.

O you who believe!

Avoid suspicion, for suspicion in some cases is sin; and spy not on each other, nor speak ill of each other behind their backs. Would any of you eat the flesh of his dead brother? No, you would abhor it.

Be in taqwa of Allah, fear Allah: for Allah is Forgiving, Most Merciful.

O humankind!

We created you from a single pair of a male and a female, and made you into nations and tribes, that you may know each other. Verily the most honored of you in the sight of Allah is the one with taqwa of Allah, the most righteous of you. And Allah is All Knowing, All Aware.

(49:12-13, Koran)

Commandment of the Covenant of Allah in
Sura Al-Hadid (57 Medina 97)

64.

O you who believe!

Be in taqwa of Allah, Fear Allah, and believe in His Rasool, and He will bestow on you the double portion of His Mercy: He will provide for you a Light by which you shall walk straight in your path, and He will forgive you; for Allah is Most Forgiving, Most Merciful:

That the People of the Book may know that they have no power whatever over the Grace of Allah that His Grace is entirely in His Hand, to bestow it on whomsoever He wills. For Allah is the Lord of Grace abounding.

(57:28–29, Koran)

Commandment of the Covenant of Allah in
Sura Al-Mujadila (58 Medina 98)

65.

O you who believe!

When you hold secret counsel, do it not for iniquity and hostility, and disobedience to the Rasool; but do it for righteousness and self-restraint; and be in taqwa of Allah, to Whom you shall be brought back.

Secret counsels are only inspired by the Satan, in order that he may cause grief to the Believers; but he cannot harm them in the least, except as Allah permits; and on Allah let, the Believers put their trust.

(58:9–10, Koran)

66.

O you who believe!

When you are told to make room in the assemblies, spread out and make room: ample room will Allah provide for you. And when you are told to rise up, for prayers, Jihad or other good deeds rise up: Allah will exalt in rank those of you who believe and who have been granted Knowledge. And Allah is well acquainted with all you do.

(58:11, Koran)

Commandment of the Covenant of Allah
in Sura Al-Hashr (59 Medina 99)

67.

O you who believe!

Be in taqwa of Allah and fear Allah and let every soul judge as to the provision he has sent forth for the morrow. Yes, be in taqwa of Allah and fear Allah: for Allah is well acquainted with all that you do.

And be not like those who forgot Allah, and He made them forget their own souls! Such are the rebellious transgressors (fasiqun)!

Not equal are the Companions of the Fire and the Companions of the Garden: it is the Companions of the Garden that will achieve felicity.

Had We sent down this Qur'an on a solid rock, verily, you would have seen it tremble and cleave asunder in deference to Allah. Such are the similitudes which We give out to men that they may reflect.

He is Allah, there is no Deity but He; Knower of the hidden and manifest. He is the Rahman (the Most Gracious), the Rahim, (Most Merciful.)

He is Allah, There is no Deity but He,

The Sovereign, The Pure and The Hallowed,

Serene and Perfect,

The Custodian of Faith, the Protector, the Almighty,

The Irresistible, the Supreme,

Glory be to Allah, He is above all they associate with Him

He is Allah, the Creator, the Sculptor, the Adorner of color and form. To Him belong the Most Beautiful Names: whatever so is in the heavens and on earth, Praise and Glory Him; and He is the Almighty and All Wise.

(59:18–24, Koran)

Commandments of the Covenant of Allah in
Sura Al-Mumtahanah (60 Medina 100)

68.

O you who believe!

Take not My enemies and yours as awliya (friends and protectors), offering them love and regard, even though they have rejected the Truth bestowed on you. And they have driven out the Rasool and yourselves from your homes, because you believe in Allah as your Rabb (Lord)! You have come out to strive in My Cause and to seek My favor, take them not as friends, holding in secret regard and friendship for them: for I know all that you conceal and all that you reveal. And any of you that do this has strayed from the Straight Path. If they were to gain an upper hand over you, they would treat you as enemies, and stretch forth their hands and their tongues against you with evil; and they desire that you should reject the Truth.

(60:1–2, Koran)

69.

O you who believe!

Befriend not people who have incurred Allah's wrath. They are already in despair of the Hereafter, just as the Unbelievers are in despair about those in graves.

(60:13, Koran)

Commandments of the Covenant of Allah
in Sura As-Saf (61 Medina 101)

70.

O you who believe!

Why do you promise what you do not carry out? Hateful is indeed to Allah that you say what you do not act upon. Allah loves those who fight in His cause in array of unison and solidarity.

(61:2–4, Koran)

71.

O you who believe!

Shall I guide you to a bargain that will save you from a painful torment? That you believe in Allah and His Rasool, and that you perform Jihad (strive to your utmost) in the way of Allah, with all that you own and in all earnestness: that will be best for you, if you but knew! He will forgive you your sins, and admit you to Gardens beneath which rivers flow, and to beautiful dwellings in Jannat of I (Gardens of Eternity): that is indeed the supreme blessing. And another favor will He bestow, which you will cherish; help from Allah and a speedy victory. So, give the glad tidings to the believers.

(61:10–13, Koran)

???

72.

O you who believe!

Be you helpers of Allah: as said Jesus, the son of Mary, to the Disciples, "Who will be my helpers in the work of Allah?" Said the Disciples, "We are Allah's helpers!" Then a portion of the Children of Israel believed, and a portion disbelieved: but We gave power to those who believed against their enemies, and they became the ones that prevailed.

(61:14, Koran)

Commandment of the Covenant of Allah in
Sura Al –Jumu'ah (62 Medina 102)

73.

O You who believe!

When the call is proclaimed to prayer on Friday, the day of assembly, hasten earnestly to the Remembrance of Allah, and leave off business and everything else: that is best for you if you but knew! And when the Prayer is finished, then may you disperse through the land, and seek of the Grace of Allah: remember and praise Allah a great deal: that you may prosper.

(62:9–10, Koran)

Commandment of the Covenant of Allah in
Sura Al-Munafiqun (63 Medina 103)

74.

O you who believe!

Let not your wealth or your children divert you from the remembrance of Allah. If any act thus, the loss is their own. And give freely, out of which We have bestowed on you, before death should come to each of you and he should say, "O my Lord! Why didst Thou not give me respite for a little while? I should then have given generously and be among the righteous. But to none does Allah give respite when his time has come; and Allah is well acquainted with all that you do.

(63:9–11, Koran)

Commandment of the Covenant of Allah in
Sura At-Taghabun (64 Medina 104)

75.

O you who believe!

Truly, among your wives and your children are some that are contenders of your obligations: so beware! But if you forgive them and overlook their faults, verily Allah is Most-Forgiving, Most Merciful. Your riches and your children may be but a temptation: Whereas Allah! With Him is an immense reward. So be in taqwa of Allah and fear Allah as much as you can; listen and obey; and spend in charity for the benefit of your own souls. And those saved from their own greed are the ones that prosper. If you loan to Allah a beautiful loan, He will double it for you, and He will forgive you: for Allah is both Appreciative (Shakoor) and Magnanimous (Haleem), Knower of what is hidden and what is manifest, Exalted in Might, Full of Wisdom. (64:14–18, Koran)

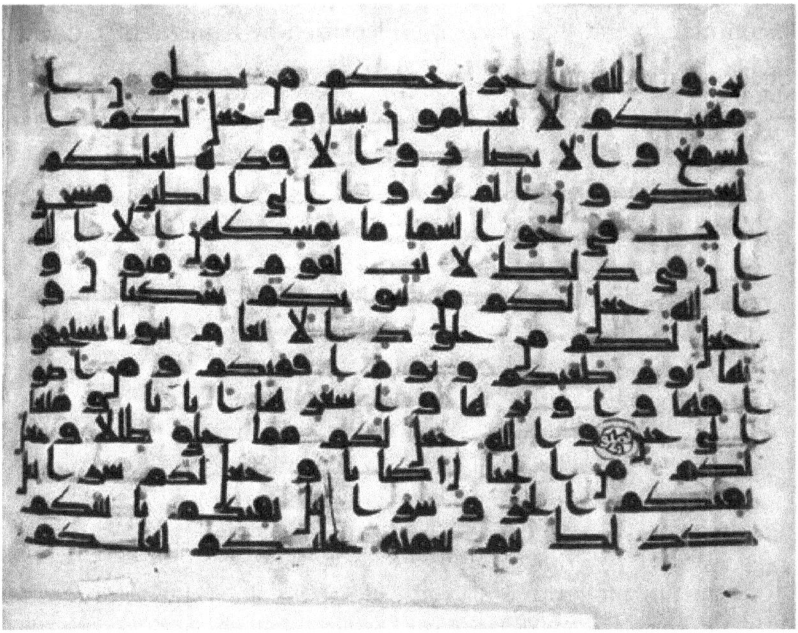

This copy of the Glorious Koran is in Kufic script with the signature of Hasan ibn Ali ibn Abi Talib. It consists of 122 pages of seven lines each. It is thought to have been reinscribed in the third century hijra or ninth century AD. Size: 17 × 11 cm. Endowed by Shah Abbas Safavid. Endowment deed written and prepared by Sheikh Muhammad Khadim Bahaii. Inscribed by Imam Hasan ibn Ali.

The Thirty-Seven Commandments

The essence of the Koran is in seventy-five verses in which Allah addresses the believers directly with the words *O you who believe!* In the following section, these seventy-five verses have been arranged in thirty-seven commandments of Allah according to the subject of the commandment. The suras are identified by name and traditional sequence numbers and the *ayah* marked with their number for easy recognition and verification of the source by the reader.

1. Belief in Allah

- He is Allah; there is no Deity but He, The Sovereign, The Pure, and The Hallowed, Serene and Perfect, He is Allah, the Creator, the Sculptor, the Adorner of color and form. To Him belong the Most Beautiful Names: whatever so is in the heavens and on earth, Praise and Glorify Him; and He is the Almighty and All Wise. (Al-Hashr 59:18–24, Koran)
- ALLAH! There is no god but He, the Ever Living, the One Who sustains and protects all that exists. No slumber can seize Him nor sleep. His are all things in the heavens and on earth. Who is there to intercede in His presence except as He permits? He knows what happens to His creatures in this world and in the hereafter. Nor do they know the scope of His knowledge except as He wills. His Throne extends over the heavens and the earth, and He feels no fatigue in guarding and protecting them. He is the Most High, Most Great. (Al-Baqarah 2:255, Koran)
- Join not anything in worship with Him. (Al-An 'am 6:151-153, Koran)
- Believe in Allah, His Rasool, and the Book that He has sent to His Rasool and the Scriptures that He sent to those before him. Any who deny Allah, His angels, His Books, His Rasools, and the Day of Judgment has gone astray. (An-Nisa 4:136, Koran)

- Verily, this is My Way leading straight: follow it: follow not (other) paths for they will separate you from His path. This He commands you that you may remember. (Al-An 'am 6: 151–53, Koran)
- Celebrate the Praises of Allah often and Glorify Him in the morning and at night. It is Allah and His Angels who send their blessings upon you, that He may lead you out of the depths of darkness into light. Allah is full of mercy to the believers! On the Day, they meet Him with the salutation: Salaam, He has prepared for them a generous Reward. (Al-Ahzab 33:41–48, Koran)
- Believe in Allah, His Rasool, and His Book which He has sent to His Rasool and the scriptures to those before him. Any who deny Allah, His Angels, His Books, His Rasools, and the Day of Judgment had gone far far astray. (An-Nisa 4:136, Koran)
- Be quick in race to forgiveness from your Lord for a garden whose measurement is that of the heavens and of the earth, prepared for the righteous.

  To those who give freely whether in prosperity or in adversity, those who restrain anger and pardon all humans, for Allah loves who do beautiful deeds. (Ali 'Imran 3:130–34, Koran)

2. The *nabi*, the *rasul*

- O Nabi, We have sent thee as a witness, a bearer of glad tidings, as a Warner and as one who invites to Allah's Grace by His leave and as an inspiration and beacon of light.

  Give glad tidings to the believers that they shall have from Allah bounty in abundance. And obey not the command of the unbelievers (kafireen) and the hypocrites (munafiqeen), heed not their annoyances, and put your trust in Allah, for enough is Allah as Disposer of affairs. (Al-Ahzab 33:41–48, Koran)
- Allah and His angels bless the Nabi you who believe! You should also ask for Allah's blessings and peace on the Prophet. (Al-Ahzab 33:56, Koran)

- Obey Allah and His Rasool and turn not to others when you should hear him speak. For the worst of creatures in the sight of Allah are those who neither listen, nor look or try to comprehend. (Al-Anfal 8:20, Koran)
- Be not presumptuous and impudent before Allah and His Rasool; be in taqwa of Allah, fear Allah: for Allah is He Who hears and knows all things. (Al-Hujurat 49:2, Koran)
- And how could you deny Faith when you learn the Signs of Allah, and amongst you lives the Rasool? Whoever holds firmly to Allah will be shown a Way that is straight. (Ali 'Imran 3:100–101, Koran)
- O you who believe! Fear Allah and speak always the truth that He may direct you to righteous deeds and forgive you your sins: he that obeys Allah and His Rasool have already attained the highest achievement. (Al-Ahzab 33:69–73, Koran)

3. And fulfill the covenant of Allah

- O you who believe fulfill your Covenants. (Al-Ma'idah 5:1, Koran)
- Verily those who pledge their allegiance unto you, (O Muhammad) pledge it unto none but Allah; the Hand of Allah is over their hands. Thereafter whosoever breaks his Covenant, does so to the harm of his own soul, and whosoever fulfils his Covenant with Allah, Allah will grant him an immense Reward. (Al-Fath 48:10, Koran)
- And fulfill the Covenant of Allah. Thus, He commands you that you may remember. (Al-An 'am 6:151–53, Koran)

4. Yes, be in taqwa of Allah and fear of Allah

(The word *taqwa* means "to be dutiful to Allah, to be wary of Allah, to be conscious of Allah, to be pious toward Allah, and to fear Allah." A person with *taqwa* always has Allah in mind with every action and word spoken "as if Allah sees you and you see Him.")

- Be in taqwa of Allah and fear Allah and let every soul judge as to the provision he has sent forth for the morrow. Yes, be in taqwa of Allah and fear Allah: for Allah is well acquainted with all that you do. (Al-Hashr 59:18–24, Koran)
- So be in taqwa of Allah and fear Allah as much as you can; listen and obey; and spend in charity for the benefit of your own souls. And those saved from their own greed are the ones that prosper. If you loan to Allah a beautiful loan, He will double it for you, and He will forgive you: for Allah is both Appreciative (Shakoor) and Magnanimous (Haleem), Knower of what is hidden and what is manifest, Exalted in Might, Full of Wisdom. (At-Taghabun 64:14–18, Koran)
- Humankind! We created you from a single pair of a male and a female, and made you into nations and tribes, that you may know each other. Verily the most honored of you in the sight of Allah is the one with taqwa of Allah, the most righteous of you. And Allah is All Knowing, All-Aware. (Al-Hadid 57:28–29, Koran)
- Be in taqwa of Allah, Fear Allah, and believe in His Rasool, and He will bestow on you the double portion of His Mercy: He will provide for you a Light by which you shall walk straight in your path, and He will forgive you; for Allah is Most Forgiving, Most Merciful. That the People of the Book may know that they have no power whatever over the Grace of Allah that His Grace is entirely in His Hand, to bestow on whomsoever He wills. For Allah is the Lord of Grace abounding. (Al-Hadid 57:28–29, Koran)
- Be in Taqwa of Allah and be with those who are true in word and deed. (At-Tawbah 9:11, Koran)
- Be not presumptuous and impudent before Allah and His Rasool; be in taqwa of Allah, fear Allah: for Allah is He Who hears and knows all things. (Al-Hujurat 49:2, Koran)

5. Worship Allah. Bow down, prostrate yourself, serve your Lord, and do wholesome deeds that you may prosper.

- Establish regular Salaat, give regular charity, and hold fast to Allah. He is your Mawla, Protector, the best of Protectors and the best Helper. (Al-Hajj 22:77-78, Koran)
- Those who do wholesome deeds, establish regular prayers and regular charity have rewards with their Lord. On them shall be no fear, nor shall they grieve. (Al-Baqarah 2:227-80, Koran)
- Seek help with patience, perseverance, and prayer. Allah is with those who patiently persevere. (Al-Baqarah 2:153, Koran)
- When you arise for salaat, purify yourself by washing your faces, your hands to the elbows, wipe your heads, and wash your feet to the ankles. If you are unclean, purify yourself. Allah does not wish that you should be burdened, but to make you clean, and to bestow His blessings on you, that you might be grateful. (Al-Ma'idah 5:6, Koran)
- Approach not prayers with a mind befogged until you understand all that you utter, nor come up to prayers in a state of un-cleanliness, till you have bathed. (An-Nisa 4:43, Koran)
- Bow down, prostrate yourself and serve your Lord, and do wholesome deeds that you may prosper. Perform Jihad; strive to your utmost in Allah's cause as striving (jihad) is His due. He has chosen you and Allah has imposed no hardship in your endeavor to His cause. You are the inheritors of the faith of your father Abraham. He has named you Muslims of the times before and now, so that Allah's Rasool may be an example to you and that you are an example to humankind. (Al-Hajj 22:77-78, Koran)
- When the call is proclaimed to prayer on Friday, the day of assembly, hasten earnestly to the Remembrance of Allah, and leave off business and everything else: that is best for you if you but knew! And when the Prayer is finished, then may you disperse through the land, and seek of the Grace of Allah: remember and praise Allah a great deal: that you may prosper. (Al-Jumu'ah 62:9-10, Koran)

6. Fasting during Ramadan

- Fasting is prescribed to you, in the month of Ramadan as it was prescribed to those before you, that you may practice self-restraint. The Qur'an was revealed in the month of Ramadan, guidance to humankind for judgment between right and wrong. For everyone except those ill or on a journey, this month should spend it in fasting. Allah intends to make it easy on you so that you may complete the prescribed period of fasting and to glorify Him to express your gratitude for His Guidance. (Al-Baqarah 2:178–79, Koran)

7. Zakat

- And the likeness of those who give generously, seeking to please Allah and to strengthen their souls, is as a garden, high and fertile where heavy rain falls on it and makes it yield a double the amount of harvest, and if it receives not heavy rain, light moisture suffices it.

  The parable of those who spend their substance in the way of Allah is that of a grain of corn: it grows seven ears, and each ear has a hundred grains. Allah gives plentiful return to whom He pleases, Allah cares for all, and He knows all things. Those who give generously in the cause of Allah, and follow not up their gifts with reminders of their generosity or with injury, for them their reward is with their Lord; on them shall be no fear, nor shall they grieve. Kind words and the covering of faults are better than charity followed by injury. Allah is Free of all wants and He is Most Merciful. (Al-Baqarah 2:261–63, Koran)

- Let not those among you who are blessed with grace and ample means hold back from helping their relatives, the poor, and those who have left their homes in Allah's cause. Let them forgive and overlook, do you not wish that Allah should forgive you? And Allah is Oft Forgiving, Most Merciful. (An-Nur 24:21–23, Koran)

- Spend out of bounties of Allah in charity and wholesome deeds before the Day comes when there will be neither bargaining, friendship nor intercession. Those who reject faith are the wrongdoers. (Al-Baqarah 2:254–57, Koran)

- Void not your charity by boast, conceit, and insult, by reminders of your generosity like those who want their generosity to be noted by all men, but they believe neither in Allah nor in the Last Day. Theirs is a parable of a hard barren rock, on which there is a little soil, washed by heavy rain, which leaves it just a bare stone. And Allah guides not those who reject Faith. And the likeness of those who give generously, seeking to please Allah and to strengthen their souls, is as a garden, high and fertile where heavy rain falls on it and makes it yield a double the amount of harvest, and if it receives not heavy rain, light moisture suffices it. Allah notices whatever you do. (Al Baqarah 2:264–65, Koran)

8. *Hajj*

- And proclaim the Pilgrimage to mankind; they will come to thee on foot and mounted on every kind of camel, lean on account of journeys through deep and distant mountain highways; that they may witness the benefits provided for them, and celebrate the name of Allah, through the Days Appointed, over the cattle which He has provided for them for sacrifice: then eat you thereof and feed the distressed ones in want. Then let them complete the rites prescribed for them, perform their vows, and again circumambulate the Ancient House. Such is the Pilgrimage: whoever honors the sacred rites of Allah, for him it is good in the sight of his Lord. Lawful to you for food in Pilgrimage are cattle, except those mentioned to you as exceptions: but shun the abomination of idols and shun the word that is false. (Al-Hajj 22:27–30, Koran)
- Violate not the sanctity of the Symbols of Allah, or of the sacred month, or of the animals brought for sacrifice, nor the garlands that mark out such animals, nor the people coming to the Sacred House, seeking the bounty and good pleasure of their Lord. Help one another in virtue and piety but help not one another in sin and acrimony. Be in taqwa of Allah, fear Allah, for Allah is swift in reckoning. (Al-Ma'idah 5:2, Koran).

9. Speak always the truth.

- You who believe! Have taqwa of Allah, fear Allah, and speak always the truth that He may direct you to righteous deeds and forgive you your sins: he that obeys Allah and His Rasool have already attained the highest achievement.
- We did indeed offer al-Amanah, (the Trust) to the Heavens and the Earth and the Mountains; but they shrank from bearing, being afraid of it, but man assumed it, and has proved to be a tyrant and a fool, (with the result) that Allah has to punish the munafiqeen, (truth concealers), men and women, and the mushrikeen, (unbelievers), men and women, and Allah turns in Mercy to the Believers, men and women; for Allah is Forgiving, Most Merciful. (Al-Ahzab 33:69–73, Koran)
- Let there be no compulsion in religion: Truth stands out clear from Error: whoever rejects Evil and believes in Allah hath grasped the most trustworthy handhold that never breaks. And Allah hears and knows all things.

  Allah is the Wali, protector of those who have faith. From the depths of darkness, He will lead them forth into light. Of those who reject faith their Wali (protectors) are the false deities: from light, they will lead them forth into the depths of darkness. They will be Companions of the Fire, to dwell therein (forever). (Al-Baqarah 2:254–57, Koran)

10. Follow not the footsteps of Satan. Reject all evil. Come not near shameful deeds (*Fahasha*), whether open or secret.

- Enter into submission to the will of Allah, enter Islam wholeheartedly, and follow not the footsteps of Satan, for he is a sworn enemy to you! (Al-Baqarah 2:208, Koran)
- Do not follow Satan's footsteps: if any will follow the footsteps of Satan, he will command to what is shameful (Fahasha) and wrong (Munkar): and were it not for the grace of Allah and His mercy on you, not one of you would have been unblemished: but Allah does

purify whom He pleases: and Allah is all Hearer and all Knower. (An-Nur 24:21–23, Koran)

- Come not near to shameful deeds (fornication, adultery, and shameful activities) whether open or secret. (Al-An'am 151–53, Koran)
- Whoever rejects evil and believes in Allah has grasped the most trustworthy handhold that never breaks. And Allah hears and knows all things. (Al-Baqarah 2:254–57, Koran)
- If you abstain from the all the odious and the forbidden, Allah shall expel out of you all evil in you and admit you to a gate of great honor. (An-Nisa 4:29–32, Koran)
- If you have taqwa of Allah, He will grant you a criterion to judge between right and wrong, and remove from you all misfortunes and evil and forgive your sins. Allah is the bestower of Grace in abundance. (Al-Anfal 8:29, Koran)

11. Unity of the *ummah*

- And hold fast, all together, by the Rope, which Allah stretches out for you, and be not divided among yourselves; and remember with gratitude Allah's favor upon you.

  Be in taqwa of Allah, fear Allah as He should be feared, and die not except in a state of Islam. And hold fast, all together, by the Rope, which Allah stretches out for you, and be not divided among yourselves; and remember with gratitude Allah's favor on you; you were enemies, and He joined your hearts in love, so that by His Grace, you became brethren and a community. You were on the brink of the pit of fire, and He saved you from it. Thus does Allah make His Signs clear to you that you may be guided?

  Let there arise out of you a band of people inviting to all that is good, enjoining what is right, and forbidding that is wrong. They are the ones to attain happiness.

  Be not like those who are divided amongst themselves and fall into disputations after receiving clear signs: for them is a dreadful penalty. (Ali 'Imran 3:103–5, Koran)

- Persevere in patience and constancy; vie in such perseverance; strengthen each other; and be in taqwa of Allah, fear Allah that you may prosper. (Ali 'Imran 3:200, Koran)
- This is a grace from Allah, and a favor; and Allah is All Knowing and All Wise. If two parties among the Believers fall into a quarrel, make peace between them: but if one of them transgresses beyond bounds against the other, then fight you all against the one who transgresses until he complies with the Command of Allah; but if he complies, then make peace between them with justice, and fairness: for Allah loves those who are fair and just. The Believers are but a single Brotherhood: so make peace and reconciliation between your two brothers; and fear Allah, that you may receive Mercy. (Al-Hujurat 49:6–10, Koran)

12. Obey Allah and His *rasul* and those charged with authority among you.

- Obey Allah and obey the Rasool, and those charged amongst you with authority in the settlement of your affairs. If you differ in anything among yourselves, refer it to Allah and His Rasool (The Qur'an and the Prophet's teachings). If you do believe in Allah and the last Day, that is best and the most beautiful conduct in the final determination. (An-Nisa 4:43, Koran)

13. Freedom of religion: Let there be no compulsion in religion.

- Let there be no compulsion in religion: Truth stands out clear from Error: whoever rejects Evil and believes in Allah hath grasped the most trustworthy handhold that never breaks. And Allah hears and knows all things. (Al-Baqarah 2:254–57, Koran)

14. *Awliya*: Allah is the *Waliy*, Protector of those who have faith. Take not infidels (*kafireen*) for *awliya* (friends and protectors) in place of believers.

- Allah is the Waliy, protector of those who have faith. From the depths of darkness, He will lead them forth into light. Of those who reject faith their waliy (protectors) are the false deities: from light, they will lead them forth into the depths of darkness. They will be Companions of the Fire, to dwell therein (forever). (Al-Baqarah 2:254–57, Koran)

- Take not into intimacy those outside your ranks: they will not fail to corrupt you. They only desire your ruin: rank hatred has already appeared from their mouths: what their hearts conceal is far worse. We have made plain to you the Signs, if you have wisdom. (Ali 'Imran 3:118–20, Koran)
- If you obey the Unbelievers, (kafaru) they will drive you back on your heels, and you will turn your back to your Faith to your own loss. Allah is your protector, and He is the best of helpers. (Ali 'Imran 3:149–50, Koran)
- Take not the Jews and the Christians as your friends and protectors (awliya). They are friends and protectors unto each other. He who amongst you turns to them is one of them. Allah does not guide those who are unjust and evil doers (zalimun). (Al-Ma'idah 5:51, Koran)
- Take not for friends and protectors (awliya) those who take your religion for mockery, whether from amongst people of the book or from amongst the kafireen. Be in taqwa of Allah, fear Allah if you have faith indeed. (Al-Ma'idah 5:57, Koran)
- Take not for your protectors and friends (awliya) your kin who practice infidelity over faith. Whosoever does that will be amongst the wrong doers. (At-Tawbah 9:23)
- Take not My enemies and yours as awliya (friends and protectors), offering them love and regard, even though they have rejected the Truth bestowed on you. And they have driven out the Rasool and yourselves from your homes because you believe in Allah as your Rabb (Lord)! You have come out to strive in My Cause and to seek My favor, take them not as friends, holding in secret regard and friendship for them: for I know all that you conceal and all that you reveal. And any of you that do this has strayed from the Straight Path.

  If they were to gain an upper hand over you, they would treat you as enemies, and stretch forth their hands and their tongues against you with evil; and they desire that you should reject the Truth. (Al-Mumtahanah 60:1–2, Koran)

- Befriend not people who have incurred Allah's wrath. They are already in despair of the Hereafter, just as the Unbelievers are in despair about those in graves. (Al-Mumtahanah 60:13, Koran)
- Allah is the Waliy protector of those who have faith. From the depths of darkness, He will lead them forth into light. (Al-Baqarah 2:254–57, Koran)
- Establish regular salaat; give regular charity, and holdfast to Allah. He is your Mawla, Protector, the best of Protectors and the best Helper. (Al-Hajj 2:277–78, Koran)

15. Jihad

- Make careful preparations and take precautions. Then go forth in groups or all together to the endeavor.

  There amongst you is he who will linger behind, if misfortune befalls you he will say, "Allah did favor him as he was not with you". When good fortune comes to you from Allah, he would wish that he had been with you.

  Those who swap the life of this world for the hereafter let them fight in the cause of Allah. Whosoever fights in the cause of Allah, whether he is slain or he is victorious, there is a great award for him from Allah.

  And why should you not fight in the cause of Allah, and for those men, women, and children, who are weak, abused and oppressed, those who beseech their Lord to deliver them from their oppressors, and those who ask Allah to send for them protectors and helpers. (An-Nisa 4:71–75, Koran)
- Remember Allah's blessings on you. When a people planned stretching out their hands against you and Allah did hold back their hands from you to protect you from your enemies. Be in taqwa of Allah, fear Allah, and place your trust in Allah. (Al-Ma'idah 5:11, Koran)

- Be in taqwa of Allah, fear Allah. Perform Jihad and strive your utmost in Allah's Cause, and approach Him so that you may prosper. (Al-Ma'idah 3:35, Koran)
- If any among you turn back on his faith Allah will bring a people whom He loves and who love Him, and who are humble towards the believers, and stern towards unbelievers, who perform jihad and strive in the cause of Allah and fear not reproaches of any blamer. Such is the Grace of Allah that He bestows on whom He wills. Allah is All Sufficient for His Creatures and all Knowing. (Al-Ma'idah 5:54, Koran)
- When you meet the infidels rank upon rank, in conflict never turn your backs to them. (Al-Anfal 8:15, Koran)
- Respond to Allah and His Rasool when He calls you to that gives you life. And know that Allah intervenes in the tussle between man and his heart, and it is to Allah that you shall return. Fear treachery or oppression that afflicts not only those who perpetrate it but affects guilty and innocent alike. Know that Allah is strict in punishment. (Al-Anfal 8:24-25, Koran)
- When you meet the enemy force, stand steadfast against them, and remember the name of Allah much, so that you may be successful. And obey Allah and His Rasool, and do not dispute with one another lest you lose courage, and your strength departs and be patient. Allah is with those who patiently persevere. (Al-Anfal 8:45-46, Koran)
- Whether you do or do not help Allah's Rasool, your leader, Allah strengthens him with His Peace and with forces that you do not see. The words of the infidels He humbled into the dirt, but Allah's word is Exalted, High. Allah is Mighty, Wise. Go forth, advance! Whether equipped well or lightly, perform jihad strive your utmost and struggle with your wealth and your persons in the cause of Allah. That is best for you, if you knew. (At-Tawbah 9:38-41, Koran)
- Fight the unbelievers who surround you. Let them find you firm, and know Allah is always with those who have taqwa, who are Allah-wary. (At-Tawbah 9:123, Koran)
- Remember the Grace of Allah, bestowed upon you, when there came down hordes to overpower you: We sent against them a hurricane

and forces that that you did not see but Allah sees all that you do. Behold! They came on you from above you and from below you, your eyes became dim, and the hearts gaped up to the throats, and you imagined various vain thoughts about Allah! (Al-Ahzab 33:9, Koran)

- If you will aid (the cause of) Allah, He will aid you, and make your foothold firm. But those who reject Allah, for them is destruction, and Allah will render their deeds vain. That is because they hate the Revelation of Allah; so, He has made their deeds fruitless. Do they not travel through the earth, and see what was the end of those before them who did evil? Allah brought utter destruction on them, and similar fates await those who reject Allah. That is because Allah is the Protector of those who believe, but those who reject Allah have no protector. (Muhammad 47:7–11, Koran)

- Be not weak and ask for peace, while you are having an upper hand: for Allah is with you and will never decrease the reward of your good deeds.

  The life of this world is but play and amusement: and if you believe, fear Allah, and guard against evil, He will grant you your recompense, and will not ask you (to give up) your possessions.

  Behold, you are those invited to spend of your wealth in the Way of Allah: but among you are some that are parsimonious. But any who are miserly are so at the expense of their own souls.

  But Allah is free of all wants, and it is you that are needy. If you turn back (from the Path), He will substitute in your stead another people; then they would not be like you! (Muhammad 47:33–38, Koran)

- When you are told to make room in the assemblies, spread out and make room: ample room will Allah provide for you. And when you are told to rise up, for prayers, Jihad or other good deeds rise up: Allah will exalt in rank those of you who believe and who have been granted Knowledge. And Allah is well acquainted with all you do. (Al-Mujadila 58:11, Koran)

- Why do you promise what you do not carry out? Hateful is indeed to Allah that you say what you do not act upon. Allah loves those who fight in His cause in array of unison and solidarity. (As-Saf 61:2–4, Koran)

- Shall I guide you to a bargain that will save you from a painful torment? That you believe in Allah and His Rasool, and that you perform Jihad (strive to your utmost) in the way of Allah, with all that you own and in all earnestness: that will be best for you, if you but knew! He will forgive you your sins, and admit you to Gardens beneath which rivers flow, and to beautiful dwellings in Jannat of adn (Gardens of Eternity): that is indeed the supreme blessing. And another favor will He bestow, which you will cherish; help from Allah and a speedy victory. So, give the glad tidings to the believers. (As-Saf 61:10–13, Koran)

Summary: Fight the infidel until there is no more treachery and oppression and there prevails justice and faith in Allah altogether and everywhere. If they cease, then Allah is the seer of what they do. If they refuse, be sure that Allah is your Protector, the best to protect and to help. And why should you not fight in the cause of Allah and for those men, women, and children who are weak, abused, and oppressed; those who beseech their Lord to deliver them from their oppressors; and those who ask Allah to send for them protectors and helpers?

16. Murder

- The law of equality is prescribed to you in cases of murder. The free for the free, the slave for the slave, the woman for the woman. But if any remission is made by the brother (family) of the slain, then grant any reasonable demand, and compensate him with handsome gratitude. This is a concession and a Mercy from your Lord. After this, whoever exceeds the limits shall be in grave penalty. In the Law of Equality, there is a saving of life for you, O men of understanding; that you may restrain yourselves. (Al-Baqarah 2:178–79, Koran)
- If anyone slew a person – unless it is for murder or for spreading mischief in the land – it would be as if he slew the whole people: and

if anyone saved a life, it would be as if he saved the life of the whole people. (Al-Ma'idah 5:32, Koran)

- Take not life, which Allah hath made sacred, except by the way of justice or law: This He commands you, that you may learn wisdom. (Al-An'am 6: 151–53, Koran)

17. Perseverance and patience

O you who believe! Persevere in patience and constancy; vie in such perseverance; strengthen each other; and fear Allah. that you may prosper.

***Şabr*, *şābir*, *şabbār*, and *şābara* denote the quality of patience and steadfastness, self-restraint, forbearance, endurance, and perseverance. One of Allah's ninety-nine names is *al-Şabur*, the Patient. It is one who does not precipitate an act before it's time but decides matters according to a specific plan and brings them to fruition in a predefined manner, neither procrastinating nor hastening matters before their time but disposing each matter in its appropriate time in the way of its needs and requirements and doing all that without being subjected to a force opposing Allah's will. *Şabr*, *şābir*, *şabbār*, and *şābara* are mentioned in the Koran sixty-nine times. Allah reassures the believers:**

- Believers, be patient, and vie you with patience. (Ali 'Imran 3:200, Koran)
- Pray for succor to Allah and be patient. (Al-A'raf 7:128, Koran)
- Be thou patient, Allah will not leave to waste the wage of good doers. (Hud 11:115, Koran)
- Be thou patient, Surely Allah's promise is true. (Ar-Rum 30:60, Koran)
- Bear patiently whatever may befall you. (Luqman 31:17, Koran)

- So, be thou patient with a sweet patience. (Al-Ma'arij 70:5, Koran)
- And be patient unto your Lord. (Al-Muddaththir 74:7, Koran)
- Believers, seek you help in patience and prayer. (Al-Anbya 21:153, Koran)
- But come sweet patience. (Yusuf 12:18, 83, Koran)
- Surely Allah is with the is with the patient. (Al-Baqarah 2:153, 249, Koran)
- Allah loves the patient. (Ali 'Imran 3:146, Koran)

18. Forgiveness

- Fear the Fire, which is prepared for those who reject Faith;

  And obey Allah and the Rasool; that you may obtain mercy.

  Be quick in the race for forgiveness from your Lord, and for a Garden whose measurement is that of the heavens and of the earth, prepared for the righteous.

  Those who give freely whether in prosperity, or in adversity, those who restrain anger, and pardon all humans, for Allah loves those who do beautiful deeds. (Ali 'Imran 3:130–34, Koran)

19. Theft, deception, fraud, dishonesty, and injustice

- Betray not the trust of Allah and His Rasool. Nor knowingly misappropriate things entrusted to you. (Al-Anfal 2:27, Koran)
- Conceal not evidence, for whoever conceals it, his heart is tainted with sin. And Allah knows all that you do. (Al-Baqarah 2:283, Koran)
- Be just, being just is next to worship. Be in taqwa of Allah; fear Allah. Allah is well aware of what you do. (Al-Ma'idah 5:8, Koran)
- Allah does not guide those who are unjust and evildoers. (Zalimun) (Al-Ma'idah 5:51, Koran)

Betray not the trust of Allah and His *rasul* nor knowingly misappropriate wealth entrusted to you, whether on behalf of an orphan or another party. Be honest in handling property, goods, credit, confidences, and secrets of your fellow men and display integrity and honesty in using your skills and talents. Whenever you give your word, speak truthfully and justly, even if a near relative is concerned. Similarly, the *amri minkum* (those entrusted with the administration of the affairs of the believers) should not betray the trust of Allah, the *rasul*, and the believers and knowingly misappropriate the wealth of the Muslims.

20. Usury and hoarding of wealth

Devour not usury, doubled and multiplied; be in *taqwa* of Allah (fear Allah) that you may prosper.

- Those that spend of their goods in charity by night and by day, in secret and in public, have their reward with their Lord: on them shall be no fear, nor shall they grieve.

  Those who devour usury will not stand except stands the one whom the Satan by his touch has driven to madness. That is because they say: "Trade is like usury", but Allah hath permitted trade and forbidden usury. Those who after receiving direction from their Lord, desist, shall be pardoned for the past; their case is for Allah to judge; but those who repeat (the offence) are Companions of the Fire; they will abide therein (forever). Allah will deprive usury of all blessing but will give increase for deeds of charity for He does not love ungrateful and wicked creatures. (Al-Baqarah 2:274-76, Koran)

- Those who believe and perform wholesome deeds, establish regular prayers and regular charity have rewards with their Lord. On them shall be no fear, nor shall they grieve.

- Fear Allah and give up what remains of your demand for usury, if you are indeed believers. If you do it not, take notice of war from Allah and His Rasool: but if you turn back, you will still have your capital sums.

Do not unjustly, and you shall not be dealt with unjustly.

If the debtor is in a difficulty, grant him time until it is easy for him to repay. But if you remit it by way of charity, that is best for you. (Al-Baqarah 2:277–80, Koran)

- Devour not usury, doubled and multiplied; be in taqwa of Allah (fear Allah) that you may prosper. Fear the Fire, which is prepared for those who reject Faith; and obey Allah and the Rasool; that you may obtain mercy.

  Be quick in the race for forgiveness from your Lord, and for a Garden whose measurement is that of the heavens and of the earth, prepared for the righteous.

  Those who give freely whether in prosperity, or in adversity; those who restrain anger, and pardon all humans; for Allah loves those who do beautiful deeds (Al-muhsinun). (Ali 'Imran 3:130–34, Koran)

- There are indeed many among the priests and rabbis who in falsehood devour the substance of men and hinder them from the way of Allah. And there are those who bury gold and silver and spend it not in the way of Allah: announce unto them a most grievous penalty.

  On the Day when heat will be produced out of that wealth in the fire of Hell, and with it will be branded their foreheads, their flanks, and their backs, "This is the treasure which you buried for yourselves: taste then, the treasures which you buried!" (At-Tawbah 9:34–35, Koran)

21. Be good to your parents. Allah forbids infanticide and abortion.

- Be good to your parents: kill not your children because of poverty, We provide sustenance for you and for them. (Al-An'am 6:151–53, Koran)

22. Women and equality

- You are forbidden to take women against their will. Nor should you treat them with harshness, so that you may renounce of the dower you have given them, and that is only permitted where they have been guilty of open lewdness. On the contrary, live with them on a footing of kindness and equality. If you take a dislike to them, it may be that you dislike a thing, through which Allah brings about a great deal of good. (An-Nisa 4:19, Koran)
- Truly, among your wives and your children are some that are contenders to your obligations so beware! If you forgive them and overlook their faults, verily Allah is most-Forgiving, Most Merciful. Your riches and your children may be but a temptation: Whereas Allah! With Him is an immense reward.(64:14-18, Koran)
- Those who slander decent women, thoughtless but believing, are cursed in this life and in the Hereafter: for them is a grievous Penalty. (An-Nur 24:21-23, Koran)
- And crave not those things of what Allah has bestowed His gifts more freely on some than others, men are assigned what they earn and women that they earn. (An-Nisa 4:29-32, Koran)

23. Wealth

- Squander not your wealth among yourselves in egotism and conceit: Let there be trade and traffic amongst you with mutual goodwill nor kill or destroy yourselves: for verily Allah hath been Most Merciful to you. If any do that in rancor and injustice, soon shall we cast them into the fire: and easy it is for Allah. If you abstain from all the odious and the forbidden, Allah shall expel out of you all evil in you and admit you to a Gate of great honor.

  And crave not those things of what Allah has bestowed His gifts more freely on some than others, men are assigned what they earn and women that they earn. But ask Allah of His bounty. Surely Allah is knower of everything. (An-Nisa 4:29-32, Koran)

- O you who believe! not your wealth or your children divert you from the remembrance of Allah. If any act thus, the loss is their own. And give freely, out of which We have bestowed on you, before death should come to each of you and he should say, "O my Lord! Why didst Thou not give me respite for a little while? I should then have given generously and be among the righteous. But to none does Allah give respite when his time has come; and Allah is well acquainted with all that you do. (Al-Munafiqun 63:9–11, Koran)
- O you who believe! among your wives and your children are some that are contenders of your obligations: so, beware! But if you forgive them and overlook their faults, verily Allah is Most-Forgiving, Most Merciful. Your riches and your children may be but a temptation: Whereas Allah! With Him is an immense reward. So be in taqwa of Allah and fear Allah as much as you can; listen and obey; and spend in charity for the benefit of your own souls. And those saved from their own greed are the ones that prosper. If you loan to Allah a beautiful loan, He will double it for you, and He will forgive you: for Allah is both Appreciative (Shakoor) and Magnanimous (Haleem), Knower of what is hidden and what is manifest, Exalted in Might, Full of Wisdom. (At-Taghabun 64:14–18, Koran)

24. Justice

- O you who believe! Fear Allah and speak always the truth that He may direct you to righteous deeds and forgive you your sins: he that obeys Allah and His Rasool have already attained the highest achievement. (Al-Ahzab 33:69–73, Koran)
- Stand firm for justice as witness to Allah, be it against yourself, your parents, or your family, whether it is against rich or poor, both are nearer to Allah than they are to you. Follow not your caprice lest you distort your testimony. If you prevaricate and evade justice Allah is well aware what you do. (An-Nisa 4:135, Koran)
- O you who believe! Stand firmly for Allah as a witness of fair dealing. Let not the malice of people lead you to iniquity. Be just, that is next

to worship. Be with taqwa of Allah, fear Allah. Allah is well aware with what you do. (Al-Ma'idah 5:8, Koran)

- Betray not the trust of Allah and His Rasool. Nor knowingly misappropriate things entrusted to you. (Al-Anfal 8:27, Koran)
- If you have taqwa of Allah, and fear Allah, He will grant you a Criterion to judge between right and wrong and remove from you all misfortunes and evil and forgive your sins. Allah is the bestower of grace in abundance. (Al-Anfal 8:29, Koran)
- Be in taqwa of Allah, fear Allah, and be with those who are true in word and deed. (At-Tawbah 9:119, Koran)
- Deal not unjustly, and you shall not be dealt with unjustly. (Al-Baqarah 2:277–80, Koran)
- Whenever you give your word speak honestly even if a near relative is concerned. (Al-An'am 6:151–52, Koran)
- And come not near the orphan's property, except to improve it, until he attains the age of full strength. (Al-An'am 6:151–52, Koran)
- And give full measure and full weight with justice. No burden We place on any soul but that which it can bear. (Al-An'am 6:151–52, Koran)
- If an impostor (fasiq) comes to you with any news, ascertain the truth, lest you harm people unsuspectingly and afterwards become full of remorse for what you have done. And know that amongst you is Allah's Rasool: were he in many matters to follow your desires, you would certainly fall into misfortune: but Allah has bestowed on you the love of iman (faith) and has made it beautiful in your hearts, and he has made abhorrent to you disbelief, wickedness, and disobedience to Allah: such indeed are those who are righteous (rashidun). (Al-Hujurat 49:6–10, Koran).

25. Knowledge

O you who believe! Allah will exalt in rank those of you who believe and who have been granted knowledge.

- When you are told to make room in the assemblies, spread out and make room: ample room will Allah provide for you. And when you are told to rise up, for prayers, Jihad or other good deeds rise up: Allah will exalt in rank those of you who believe and who have been granted Knowledge. And Allah is well acquainted with all you do. (Al-Mujadila 58:11, Koran)

26. Inviting to all that is good and right and forbidding what is wrong

- Let there arise out of you a band of people inviting to all that is good, enjoining what is right, and forbidding what is wrong: they are the ones to attain happiness. (Ali 'Imran 3:103–5, Koran)

27. Do not say to another Muslim, "You are not a believer."

- When you go forth in the cause of Allah be careful to discriminate and say not to the one who greets you with alaikum o salaam, "Though art not a believer". Would you covet perishable goods of this life when there are immeasurable treasures with Allah. You were like the person who offered you salutation before Allah conferred on you His favors. Therefore, carefully investigate for Allah is well aware of all that you do. (An-Nisa 4:94, Koran)

28: Suspicion and lack of trust

Avoid suspicion, for this, in some cases, is sin; spy not on each other, nor speak ill of each other behind your backs.

- Avoid suspicion, for suspicion in some cases is sin; and spy not on each other, nor speak ill of each other behind their backs. Would any of you eat the flesh of his dead brother? No, you would abhor it. Be in taqwa of Allah, fear Allah: for Allah is Forgiving, Most Merciful. (Al-Hujurat 49:12–13, Koran)

29. Do not ridicule other believers or revile each other with wicked names.

- Let not some folk among you ridicule others: it may be that they are better than you are: nor let some women mock others: it may be that the others are better than them: nor defame or revile each other by offensive names: ill-seeming is wicked name calling for the one who has believed; and those who do not desist are indeed wrong doers. (Al-Hujurat 49:11, Koran)

30. Secret counsels and pacts

Secret counsels are only inspired by the Satan so that he may cause grief to the believers.

- When you hold secret counsel, do it not for iniquity and hostility, and disobedience to the Rasool; but do it for righteousness and self-restraint; and fear Allah, to Whom you shall be brought back.
- Secret counsels are only inspired by the Satan, in order that he may cause grief to the Believers; but he cannot harm them in the least, except as Allah permits; and on Allah let the Believers put their trust. (Al-Mujadila 58:9–10, Koran)

31. Intoxicants and gambling

Forbidden to you are intoxicants and gambling:

- Forbidden to you are intoxicants and gambling, dedication of stones and divination by arrows. These are an abomination and Satan's handiwork; they hinder you from prayer and remembrance of Allah, and place enmity and hatred amongst you. Abstain from them so that you may prosper. (Qur'an 5:90-91 Al Ma'idah).

32. Forbidden to you are the carrion, blood, and flesh of swine and any other food on which any name besides that of Allah has been invoked.

- Eat of good things provided to you by Allah and show your gratitude in worship of Him. Forbidden to you are the carrion, blood, and flesh of swine, and on any other food on which any name besides that of Allah has been invoked. If forced by necessity, without willful disobedience or transgressing due limits, one is guilt less. Allah is Most Forgiving and Most Merciful. (Al-Baqarah 2:172–73, Koran)

33. Make not unlawful the good things that Allah hath made lawful to you.

- Make not unlawful the good things, which Allah hath made lawful to you. Commit no excess; Allah loves not people given to excess. Eat of things that Allah has provided for you, lawful and good. Be in taqwa of Allah, fear Allah in whom you believe. (Al-Ma'idah 5:87–88, Koran)

34. Contracts and agreements

When you make a transaction involving future obligations, write it down in presence of witnesses.

- When you make a transaction involving future obligations, write it down in presence of witnesses, or let a scribe write it down faithfully. Let the party incurring the liability dictate truthfully in the presence of two witnesses from among your own men and if two men are not available then a man and two women, so that if one of them errs then the other one, can remind him. Disregard not to put your contract in writing, whether it be small or large, it is more suitable in the eyes of Allah, more suitable as evidence, and more convenient to prevent doubts in the future amongst yourselves. (Al-Baqarah 2:282–83, Koran)

35. Respect other people's privacy

Enter not houses other than yours until you have asked permission and invoked peace on those in them.

- Enter not houses other than yours until you have asked permission and invoked peace upon those in them. If you find none in the house whom you seek, enter not unless permission is granted. If you asked to leave go back, it is best for you that makes for greater purity for you. Allah knows all that you do. (An-Nur 24:27, Koran)

36. This day I have perfected your religion for you.

We have made the Koran easy in your own tongue so that, with it, you may give glad tidings to the righteous and warnings to people given to contention. Therein is proclaimed every wise decree, by command, from our presence, for we are ever-sending revelations as a mercy from your Lord. We have explained in detail in this Koran, for the benefit of mankind, every kind of similitude.

- This day have those who reject faith (kafaru) given up all hope of compromising your faith, fear them not, but only fear Me. This day have I perfected your religion for you, bestowed on you with My blessings, and decreed Islam as your religion. (Al-Ma'idah 5:3, Koran)
- Ha Mim. By the Book, that makes matters lucid; We revealed it during the blessed night, verily We are always warning against Evil. Therein is proclaimed every wise decree, by command, from Our Presence, for We are ever sending revelations, as a Mercy from your Lord: for He is the hearer and knower. The Lord of the heavens and the earth and all that is in between them, if you have an assured faith. There is no god but He: it is He Who gives life and death, the Lord and Cherisher, your Lord and Lord of your forefathers. (Ad-Dukhan 44:1-8, Koran)
- So have We made the (Qur'an) easy in your own tongue, that with it you may give glad tidings to the righteous, and warnings to people given to contention. But how many (countless) generations before

them have We destroyed? Canst thou find a single one of them (now) or hear (so much as) a whisper of them? (Taha 19:97, Koran)

- We have explained in detail in this Qur'an, for the benefit of mankind, every kind of similitude: but man is, in most things, contentious. And what is there to keep back men from believing, now that guidance has come to them, nor from praying for forgiveness from their Lord, but that (they ask that) the ways of the ancients be repeated with them, or the Wrath be brought to them face to face? (Al-Kahf 18:54–55, Koran)

37. Wholesome and beautiful deeds

After his submission to the will and mercy of Allah, the believer is obliged to fulfill the covenant he has made with Allah. The compact of submission obliges the believer to perform wholesome and beautiful deeds.

Submission to Allah obliges the Believers to obey the Covenant and carry out their duty to their Creator and to their fellow man, and to Allah's Creation. And only those who 'have faith and do righteous acts' will have success in their earthly lives and in the hereafter. The phrase amilu al saalihaat, 'to do good, to perform wholesome deeds', refers to those who persist in striving to set things right, who restore harmony, peace and balance. The other acts of good works recognized in the Qur'an are to show compassion, to be merciful and forgive others, to be just, protect the weak, defend the oppressed, to be generous and charitable, to be truthful, and to seek knowledge and wisdom, to be kind, to be peaceful, to love others, and to perform beautiful deeds.

On those who believe and do good, will [Allah]
Most Gracious bestow love. 3

There are fifty such verses in the Koran that remind the believers of the rewards of righteous deeds. The following are some of the *ayahs* in the Koran that call the believers to perform wholesome and beautiful deeds:

Alladhina aaminu wa 'amilu al saalihaat.[3]

But those who believe and work righteousness. They are Companions of the Garden: therein shall they abide (forever). (Al-Baqarah 2:82, Koran)

Those who believe, do deeds of righteousness, and establish regular prayers and regular charity, will have their reward with their Lord: on them shall be no fear, nor shall they grieve. (Al-Baqarah 2:277, Koran)

As to those who believe and work righteousness, Allah will pay them in full their reward; but Allah loves not those who do wrong (zalimeen). (Ali 'Imran 3:57, Koran)

But those who believe and do deeds of righteousness, We shall soon admit to Gardens, with rivers flowing beneath, their eternal home, and therein shall they have companions pure and holy: We shall admit them to shades, cool and ever deepening. (An-Nisa 4:57, Koran)

But those who believe and do deeds of righteousness, We shall soon admit them to Gardens – with rivers flowing beneath – to dwell therein forever. Allah's promise is the truth, and whose word can be truer than Allah's? (An-Nisa 4:122, Koran)

---

3 Koran 2:25; 2:82, 277; 4:57, 122; 5:5; 7:42; 10:9; 11:23; 13:29; 14:23; 18:2, 88, 107; 19:60, 96; 20:75, 82, 112; 21:94; 22:14; 23:50, 56; 24:55; 25:70–71; 26:67; 28:80, 29:7, 9, 58; 30:15, 45; 31:8; 32:19; 34:4, 37; 38:24; 41:8; 42:22–23, 26; 45:21, 30; 47:2, 12; 48:29; 64:9; 65:11; 84:25; 85:11; 95:6; 98:7; 103:3.

If any do deeds of righteousness, - be they male or female – and have faith, they will enter Heaven, and not the least injustice will be done to them. (An-Nisa 4:124, Koran)

But to those who believe and do deeds of righteousness, He will give their due rewards, and more, out of His bounty: but those who are disdainful and arrogant, He will not punish with a grievous penalty; nor will they find, besides Allah, any to protect or help them. (An-Nisa 4:173, Koran)

To those who believe and do deeds of righteousness hath Allah promised forgiveness and a great reward. (Al-Ma'idah 5:9, Koran)

On those who believe and do deeds of righteousness there is no blame for what they ate (in the past), when they guard themselves from evil, and believe, and do deeds of righteousness – (or) again, guard themselves from evil and believe – (or) again, guard themselves from evil and do good. For Allah loves those who do good. (Al-Ma'idah 5:93, Koran)

But those who believe and work righteousness – no burden do We place on any soul, but that which it can bear – they will be Companions of the Garden, therein to dwell (for ever). (Al-A'raf 7:42, Koran)

To Him will be your return, of all of you. The promise of Allah is true and sure. It is He Who began the Creation, and its cycle, that He may reward with justice those who believe and work righteousness; but those who reject Him will have draughts of boiling fluids, and a Penalty grievous, because they did reject Him. (Yunus 10:4, Koran)

Those who believe, and work righteousness, their Lord will guide them because of their Faith: beneath them will flow rivers in Gardens of Bliss. (Yunus 10:9, Koran)

But those who believe and work righteousness, and humble themselves before their Lord, they will be Companions of the Garden, to dwell therein forever! (Hud 11:23, Koran)

For those who believe and work righteousness there is every blessedness, and a beautiful place of final return. (Ar-Ra'd 13:29, Koran)

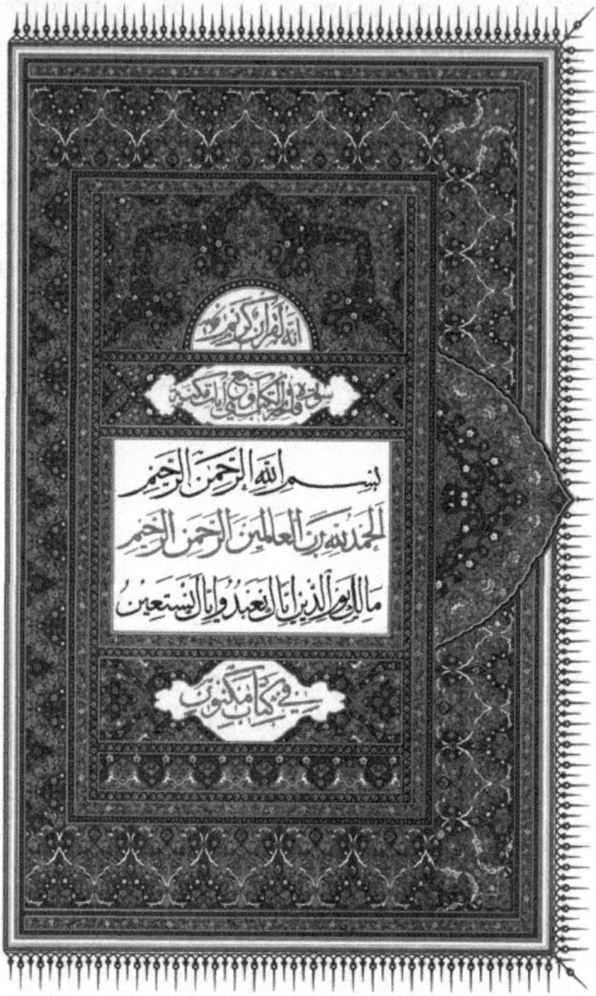

A complete copy of the Holy Koran in thuluth script. Date: about 10–11 century AH.

Six pages in the beginning and in the end have been reinscribed by Mirza Fazlallah, the famous bookbinder in the year AH 1315. It has 434 pages. Size: 50.5 × 35.0 cm. The two opening pages of this holy copy are illuminated, the beginning of Sura Al-Baqarah has been decorated with a gilt coupled top tablet dated the fourteenth century. Names or titles of the chapters: *riqa'* script with cinnabar on golden field. Binding: leather.

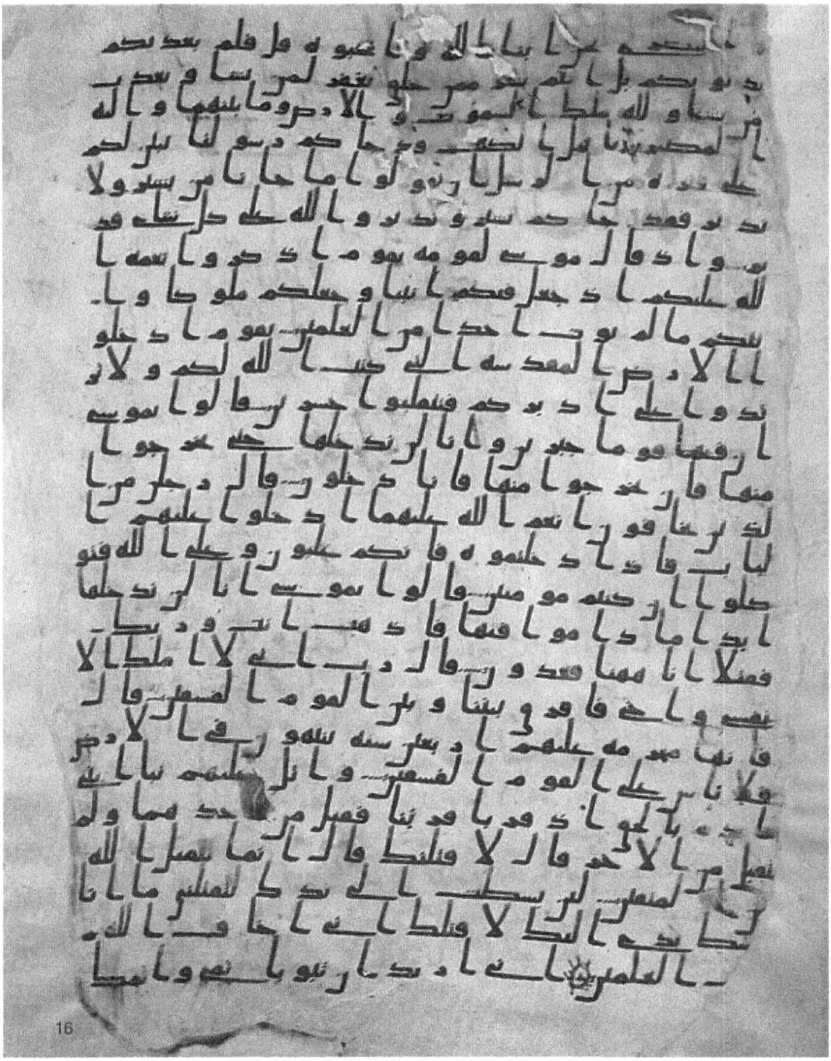

Ma'ili manuscript from first century AH. This is an example of what is thought to be one of the earliest styles of Koran copying. Dated to the first Islamic century. Located in the Tareq Rajab Museum in Kuwait.

Dhikr-e-Allah.

Chapter Three

The Covenant of Allah: The Thirty-Seven Commandments

The essence of the Koran is in the seventy-five verses in which Allah addresses the believers directly with the words "O you who believe!" The seventy–five verses or *ayahs* in this chapter contain the thirty-seven commandments of Allah[4]. They form the core of this belief of the believer and the nucleus of his *din.*

The synthesis of the three dimensions of *din* (religion)—*islam* (submission), *iman* (faith), and *ihsan* (performance of good deeds)—is what links the true believer to the divine through total submission and faith in the reality of the Creator, in addition to performance of virtuous and wholesome actions of devotion and worship of the Sublime and through beautiful deeds in the service of Allah and His creation. With this practice, the polarity between faith and actions is reversed; instead of faith being the prerequisite for practice, practice defines faith. This reverse polarity is a reminder that Islam is defined not only as a set of beliefs but also as a body of actions that reveal the inner convictions of the believer. This practice-oriented picture of Islam is dependent on the commandments of Allah in the verses of the Koran, and the traditions provide explanatory statements that act as a complement to the Koran. In this relationship, the Koran's word-centered approach to Islam in which the divine word arouses knowledge of Allah in the human consciousness, in contrast the Hadith (tradition) expresses a law-centered perspective on Islam,

---

[4] For references to the *ayahs* and the suras, please refer to "The Thirty-Seven Commandments" in chapter 2. In chapter 3, the *ayahs* from different suras have been combined according to subject matter.

in which the knowledge of spiritual realities is less important than performance of appropriate actions.

1. Belief in Allah

He is Allah, there is no Deity but He, Knower of
the hidden and the manifest. He is the Rahman the
Most Gracious, the Rahim, Most Merciful.

The Sovereign, The Pure and The Hallowed, Serene and Perfect,

The Custodian of Faith, the Protector, the
Almighty, the Irresistible, the Supreme,

He is Allah, the Creator, the Sculptor, the Adorner of color
and form. To Him belong the Most Beautiful Names,
whatever so is in the heavens and on earth, Praise and
Glorify Him; and He is the Almighty and All Wise.

There is no god but He, the Ever Living, the One
Who sustains and protects all that exists.

His are all things in the heavens and on earth. Who is there
to intercede in His presence except as He permits?

He knows what happens to His creatures in this world
and in the hereafter. Nor do His creatures know the
scope of His knowledge except as He wills.

His Throne extends over the heavens and the earth, and
He feels no fatigue in guarding and protecting them.

He is the Most High, Most Great.

Believe in Allah, His Messenger, and the Book that He has sent to His Messenger and the Scriptures that He sent to those before him. Any who deny Allah, His angels, His Books, His Messengers, and the Day of Judgment has gone astray. (An-Nisa 4:136, Koran)

Verily, this is My Way leading straight: follow it: follow not (other) paths for they will separate you from His path. This He commands you that you may remember. (Al-An 'am 6:151–53, Koran)

Islam: The Arabic word *islam* means "to resign oneself to or to submit oneself." In religious terminology, it means submission or surrender of oneself to Allah or to Allah's will. Allah is the only true reality, and everything else in the universe is dependent on Him for its reality and existence. Since Allah created the universe, all things in the universe are, as a result, totally dependent on Allah and thus are totally "submissive" to Him. Allah, being the Creator of all things, is the *Rabb*, the Sustainer of the whole creation. Thus God the Creator is the universal God.

The Koranic notion of religious belief (*iman*) as dependent on knowledge is actualized in practice in the term *islam*. This term signifies the idea of surrender or submission. The type of surrender Islam requires is a deliberate, conscious, and rational act made by a person who knows with both intellectual certainty and spiritual vision that Allah, who is the subject of Koranic discourse, is the reality.

A *Muslim* (fem. *Muslimah*) is "one who submits" to the divine truth and whose relationship with God is governed by *taqwa*, the consciousness of humankind's responsibility toward its Creator. However, consciousness of God alone is not sufficient to make a person a Muslim. Neither is it enough to be merely born a Muslim or to be raised in an Islamic cultural context. The concept of *taqwa* implies that the believer has the added responsibility of acting in a way that is in accordance with three types of knowledge: *ilm al-yaqin*, *ain al-yaqin*, and *haqq al-yaqin* (knowledge of certainty, eye of certainty, and the truth of certainty). The believer must endeavor at all times to maintain himself in a constant state of submission to Allah. Trusting in the divine mercy of his divine Master yet fearing Allah's wrath, the slave of Allah walks the road of life with careful steps, making his actions deliberate so that he will not stray from the straight path that Allah has laid out for him. It is an all-encompassing and highly personal type of commitment that has little in common with academic understanding of Islam as a civilization or a cultural system.[5]

The universality of religious experience is an important premise of the Koran's argument against a profane or secular life. This universalism has never been more important than it is in the present time when the majority of the believers do not speak Arabic. Such transcendence of culture is necessary for the Koran, as the vehicle of the word of God, to overcome linguistic and cultural differences and express itself in a metalanguage that can be understood even when its original Arabic is translated into a non-Semitic language such as English, Mandarin, or Hindi. Most people, whatever their experiences and cultural background, think in similar ways and have similar wants and needs. The Koran seeks to establish a common foundation for belief that is based on such shared perceptions and experiences. Over and over again, the Koran reminds the reader to think about the truths that lie behind the familiar or mundane things of the world, such as signs of God in nature, the practical value of virtue, and the cross-cultural validity of moral principles. The Koran, therefore, appeals to both reason and experience in determining the criterion for distinguishing between truth and falsehood.

---

[5] Vincent Cornell, "Fruit of Tree of Knowledge," in *Oxford History of Islam*, ed. John L. Esposito (Oxford University Press).

The most important theological point made by the Koran is that there is one God, Allah, universal and beyond comparison, the Creator, who creates and sustains both the material world and the world of human experience. All other forms of so-called truth are either false in their initial premises or contingently true only in limited situations. The recognition of this fact produces a profound effect on the human soul that it forever transforms the outlook of the believer.

Iman: Faith of Islam is based on certain knowledge that is both a liberation and a limitation. It is a liberation in the sense that certainty of divine reality allows the human spirit to expand inward, outward, and upward so that consciousness becomes three dimensional. Nevertheless, it is also a limitation because with the knowledge of Allah comes a concomitant awareness of the limits and responsibility imposed on a person as a created being. Unlike a secular humanist, a true Muslim believer who submits to Allah cannot delude himself by claiming that he is the sole author of his destiny as he knows that a person's fate is routinely controlled by factors beyond his control.

Ihsan: This means doing good, virtuous, and wholesome deeds. The third dimension of *din* is *ihsan*. The word *ihsan* is derived from the word *husn*, which designates the quality of being good, beautiful, virtuous, pleasing, harmonious, or wholesome. The Koran employs the word *hasana*, from the same root as *husn*, to mean a good or a beautiful deed. For example:

> Whatever beautiful touches you, it is from Allah, and whatever ugly touches you, it is from yourself. And We have sent thee as a Rasool to instruct humanity. And enough is Allah for a witness. (An-Nisa 4:79, Koran)

If any does beautiful deeds, the reward to him is better than his deed; but if anyone does evil, the doers of evil are only punished (to the extent) of their deeds. (Al-Qasas 28:84, Koran)

And for him who has faith and does wholesome works, his recompense shall be most beautiful. (Al-Kahf 18:88, Koran)

The word *ihsan* is a verb that means "to establish or to perform what is good and beautiful." The Koran employs the word *ihsan* and its active particle *muhsin* (the one who does what is beautiful and good) in seventy verses. The Koran often designates Allah as the One who does what is beautiful, and *al-Muhsin* is one of Allah's divine names. Allah's beautiful work is the creation of the universe of galaxies, stars, sun, and moon, all in their ordained orbits, destined in their paths by Allah's mysterious forces. All are shining and luminescent with Allah's blessed light (*nur*), providing life and vigor to billions of Allah's creatures so that they may acknowledge and praise their Creator, who made this beautiful and wholesome universe.

The Koran ascribes the love of Allah in about fifteen verses. One of the emotions most closely associated with *ihsan* is *hubb*. To have *ihsan* is to do what is beautiful. According to the Koran in five verses, Allah loves those who have *ihsan* because, by doing what is beautiful, they themselves have developed beautiful character traits and are worthy of Allah's love. In every Koranic verse where Allah is said to love something, the object is of this love are human beings, not the human species, whose traits and activities are beautiful.

The phrase *amilu al saalihaaat* (to do good, to perform wholesome deeds) refers to those who persist in striving to set things right, who restore harmony, peace, and balance. Other acts of good works recognized in the covenant of the Koran are to show humility, to be generous and charitable, to be truthful, to seek knowledge and wisdom, to be kind, to be peaceful, to love others, and to perform beautiful deeds.

Those who submit to Allah must believe in Allah, His blessed
Messenger, and the Book that Allah has sent to His Messenger, the
Qur'an, and the Scriptures that He sent to those Prophets before him.

Any one who denies Allah, His angels, His Books, His
Messengers, and the Day of Judgment has gone astray. Verily,
this is Allah's Way leading straight, follow it, and do not
follow other paths for they will separate you from Allah's
path. Do not join any other being in worship with Allah.

This He commands that you may remember.

Celebrate the Praises of Allah often, and Glorify
Him in the morning and in the night.

It is Allah and His Angels who send their blessings upon
you, that Allah may lead you out of the depths of darkness
into light. Allah is full of mercy to the believers!

On the Day they meet Him with the greeting
Salaam, He has for them a generous reward.

Be quick in race to forgiveness from your Lord for
He has prepared for the righteous a garden whose
measurement is that of the heavens and of the earth.

Allah loves those who do beautiful deeds, those who give freely in
charity whether in prosperity or in adversity, and those who restrain
anger and pardon all humans. Qur'an (various ayas composite)

2. The nabi, the rasul

- The Prophet and the Messenger of Allah. O Nabi, We have sent thee as a witness, a bearer of glad tidings, as a Warner and as one who invites to Allah's Grace by His leave and as an inspiration and beacon of light.
- Nabi, We have sent thee as a witness, a bearer of glad tidings, as a Warner and as one who invites to Allah's Grace by His leave and as an inspiration and beacon of light. Give glad tidings to the Believers that they shall have from Allah bounty in abundance. And obey not the command of the unbelievers (Kafirun) and the hypocrites (munafiqeen), heed not their annoyances, and put your trust in Allah, for enough is Allah as Disposer of affairs.
- Believe in Allah, His Messenger, and the Book that He has sent to His Messenger and the Scriptures that He sent to Prophets before him. Any who deny Allah, His angels, His Books, His Messengers, and the Day of Judgment has gone astray.
- Allah and His angels bless the Prophet You who believe! You should also ask for Allah's blessings and peace on the Prophet. Obey Allah and His Messenger and turn not to others when you should hear him speak. The worst of creatures in the Allah's sight are those who neither listen, nor see or try to comprehend. Be not presumptuous and impudent before Allah and His Messenger, be in taqwa of Allah, and fear Allah: for Allah is He Who hears and knows all things. And how could you deny Faith when you learn the Signs of Allah, and amongst you lives the Messenger? Whoever holds firmly to Allah will be shown a Way that is straight. O you who believe! Fear Allah and speak always the truth that He may direct you to righteous deeds and forgive you your sins: he that obeys Allah and His Messenger have already attained the highest achievement.

3. Covenant of Allah

- And fulfill your Covenant with Allah. Thus, He commands you that you may remember Verily those who pledge their allegiance unto you, (O Muhammad) pledge it unto none but Allah, the Hand of Allah is over their hands. Thereafter whosoever breaks his ***Covenant*** does so to the harm of his own soul, and whosoever fulfils his ***Covenant*** with Allah, Allah will grant him an immense Reward.

4. *Taqwa* of Allah

Be in taqwa of Allah and fear Allah and let every soul judge as to the provision he has sent forth for the morrow. Yes, be in taqwa of Allah and fear Allah, for Allah is well acquainted with all that you do.

(The word *taqwa* means "to be dutiful to Allah, to be wary of Allah, to be conscious of Allah, to be pious toward Allah, and to fear Allah." A person with *taqwa* always has Allah in mind with every action and word spoken "as if Allah sees you and you see Him.")

- So be in ***taqwa*** of Allah and be mindful of Allah as much as you can; listen and obey; and spend in charity for the benefit of your own souls. And those saved from their own greed are the ones that prosper. If you loan to Allah a beautiful loan, He will double it for you, and He will forgive you: for Allah is both Appreciative (***Shakoor***) and Magnanimous (***Haleem***), Knower of what is hidden and what is manifest, Exalted in Might, Full of Wisdom.
- Humankind! We created you from a single pair of a male and a female, and made you into nations and tribes, that you may know each other. Verily the most honored of you in Allah's sight is the one with ***taqwa*** of Allah, the most righteous of you. And Allah is All Knowing, All Aware.
- Be in ***taqwa*** of Allah, Fear Allah, and believe in His Messenger, and He will bestow on you the double portion of His Mercy: He will provide for you a Light by which you shall walk straight in your path, and He will forgive you; for Allah is Most Forgiving, Most Merciful. That the People of the Book may know that they have no power whatever over

the Grace of Allah, that His Grace is entirely in His Hand, to bestow on whomsoever He wills. For Allah is the Lord of Grace abounding.

- Be in *taqwa* of Allah and be with those who are true in word and deed. Be not presumptuous and impudent before Allah and His Messenger; be in *taqwa* of Allah, fear Allah: for Allah is He Who hears and knows all things.

5. Worship Allah

- Bow down, prostrate yourself and serve your Lord, and do beautiful deeds that you may prosper.
- Establish regular Salaat, give regular charity, and hold fast to Allah. He is your *Mawla*, Protector, the best of Protectors and the best Helper.
- Those who do wholesome deeds, establish regular prayers and regular charity have rewards with their Lord. On them shall be no fear, nor shall they grieve. Seek help with patience, perseverance, and prayer. Allah is with those who patiently persevere. When you arise for salaat, purify yourself by washing your faces, your hands to the elbows, wipe your heads, and wash your feet to the ankles. If you are unclean, purify yourself. Allah does not wish that you should be burdened, but to make you clean, and to bestow His blessings on you, that you might be grateful. Approach not prayers with a mind befogged until you understand all that you utter, nor come up to prayers in a state of un-cleanliness, till you have bathed. Bow down, prostrate yourself and serve your Lord, and do wholesome deeds that you may prosper. Perform Jihad; strive to your utmost in Allah's cause as striving (jihad) is His due. He has chosen you and Allah has imposed no hardship in your endeavor to His cause. You are the inheritors of the faith of your father Abraham. He has named you *Muslims* of the times before and now, so that Allah's Messenger may be an example to you and that you are an example to humankind.
- When the call is proclaimed to prayer on Friday, the day of assembly, hasten earnestly to the Remembrance of Allah, and leave off business and everything else: that is best for you if you but knew! And when the Prayer is finished, then may you disperse through the land, and

seek of the Grace of Allah: remember and praise Allah a great deal: that you may prosper.

6. Fasting during the month of Ramadan

Fasting is prescribed to you in the month of Ramadan.

- Fasting is prescribed to you, in the month of Ramadan as it was prescribed to those before you, that you may practice self-restraint. The Qur'an was revealed in the month of Ramadan, guidance to humankind for judgment between right and wrong. For everyone except those ill or on a journey, this month should spend it in fasting. Allah intends to make it easy on you so that you may complete the prescribed period of fasting and to glorify Him to express your gratitude for His Guidance.

7. Zakat

- And the likeness of those who give generously, seeking to please Allah and to strengthen their souls, is as a garden, high and fertile where heavy rain falls on it and makes it yield a double the amount of harvest, and if it receives not heavy rain, light moisture suffices it.
- The parable of those who spend their substance in the way of Allah is that of a grain of corn: it grows seven ears, and each ear has a hundred grains. Allah gives plentiful return to whom He pleases, Allah cares for all, and He knows all things. Those who give generously in the cause of Allah and follow not up their gifts with reminders of their generosity or with injury, for them their reward is with their Lord; on them shall be no fear, nor shall they grieve. Kind words and the covering of faults are better than charity followed by injury. Allah is Free of all wants and He is Most Merciful.
- Let not those among you who are blessed with grace and ample means hold back from helping their relatives, the poor, and those who have left their homes in Allah's cause.

- Spend out of bounties of Allah in charity and wholesome deeds before the Day comes when there will be neither bargaining, friendship nor intercession. Those who reject faith are the wrongdoers.

  Void not your charity by boast, conceit, and insult, by reminders of your generosity like those who want their generosity to be noted by all men, but they believe neither in Allah nor in the Last Day. Theirs is a parable of a hard barren rock, on which there is a little soil, washed by heavy rain, which leaves it just a bare stone. And Allah guides not those who reject Faith. And the likeness of those who give generously, seeking to please Allah and to strengthen their souls, is as a garden, high and fertile where heavy rain falls on it and makes it yield a double the amount of harvest, and if it receives not heavy rain, light moisture suffices it. Allah notices whatever you do.

8. Hajj

- And proclaim the Pilgrimage to mankind; they will come to thee on foot and mounted on every kind of camel, lean on account of journeys through deep and distant mountain highways; whoever honors the sacred rites of Allah, for him it is good in the sight of his Lord.
- And proclaim the Pilgrimage to mankind; they will come to thee on foot and mounted on every kind of camel, lean on account of journeys through deep and distant mountain highways; that they may witness the benefits provided for them, and celebrate the name of Allah, through the Days Appointed, over the cattle which He has provided for them for sacrifice: then eat you thereof and feed the distressed ones in want. Then let them complete the rites prescribed for them, perform their vows, and again circumambulate the Ancient House. Such is the Pilgrimage: whoever .honors the sacred rites of Allah, for him it is good in the sight of his Lord. Lawful to you for food in Pilgrimage are cattle, except those mentioned to you as exceptions: but shun the abomination of idols and shun the word that is false.

- Violate not the sanctity of the Symbols of Allah, or of the sacred month, or of the animals brought for sacrifice, nor the garlands that mark out such animals, nor the people coming to the Sacred House, seeking the bounty and good pleasure of their Lord. Help one another in virtue and piety but help not one another in sin and acrimony. Be in ***taqwa*** of Allah, fear Allah, for Allah is swift in reckoning.

9. Truth

Speak always the truth.

- You who believe! Have taqwa of Allah, fear Allah, and speak always the truth that He may direct you to righteous deeds and forgive you your sins: he that obeys Allah and His Messenger have already attained the highest achievement.
- You who believe! Have taqwa of Allah, fear Allah, and always speak the truth, that He may direct you to deeds of righteousness and forgive your sins: he that obeys Allah, and His Messenger has already attained the highest achievement.
- We did indeed offer al-Amanah, (the Trust) to the Heavens and the Earth and the Mountains; but they shrank from bearing, being afraid of it, but man assumed it, and has proved to be a tyrant and a fool, (with the result) that Allah has to punish the munafiqeen, (truth concealers), men and women, and the mushrikeen, (unbelievers), men and women, and Allah turns in Mercy to the Believers, men and women; for Allah is Forgiving, Most Merciful.

10. *Fahasha*

- Follow not the footsteps of Satan. Reject all evil. Come not near shameful deeds, ***Fahasha***, whether open or secret.
- Enter into submission to the will of Allah, enter ***Islam*** whole-heartedly, and follow not the footsteps of Satan, for he is a sworn enemy to you!

- Do not follow Satan's footsteps: if any will follow the footsteps of Satan, he will command to what is shameful (***Fahasha***) and wrong (***Munkar***): and were it not for the grace of Allah and His mercy on you, not one of you would have been unblemished: but Allah does purify whom He pleases: and Allah is all Hearer and all Knower.
- Come not near to shameful deeds (fornication, adultery, and shameful sexual activities) whether open or secret.
- Whoever rejects evil and believes in Allah has grasped the most trust worthy handhold that never breaks. And Allah hears and knows all things.
- If you abstain from the all the odious and the forbidden, Allah shall expel out of you all evil in you and admit you to a gate of great honor.
- If you have ***taqwa*** of Allah, He will grant you a criterion, ***furqan***, to judge between right and wrong, and remove from you all misfortunes and evil and forgive your sins. Allah is the bestower of Grace in abundance.

11. Unity of the *ummah*

- And hold fast, all together, by the Rope, which Allah stretches out for you, and be not divided among yourselves; and remember with gratitude Allah's favor on you.
- Be in taqwa of Allah, fear Allah as He should be feared, and die not except in a state of Islam. And hold fast, all together, by the Rope, which Allah stretches out for you, and be not divided among yourselves; and remember with gratitude Allah's favor on you; you were enemies, and He joined your hearts in love, so that by His Grace, you became brethren and a community. You were on the brink of the pit of fire, and He saved you from it. Thus, does Allah make His Signs clear to you that you may be guided?
- Let there arise out of you a band of people inviting to all that is good, enjoining what is right, and forbidding that is wrong. They are the ones to attain happiness.

- Be not like those who are divided amongst themselves and fall into disputations after receiving clear signs: for them is a dreadful penalty.
- Persevere in patience and constancy; vie in such perseverance; strengthen each other; and be in ***taqwa*** of Allah, fear Allah that you may prosper.
- If an impostor (***fasiq***) comes to you with any news, ascertain the truth, lest you harm people unsuspectingly and afterwards become full of remorse for what you have done. And know that amongst you is Allah's Messenger: were he in many matters to follow your desires, you would certainly fall into misfortune: but Allah has bestowed on you the love of ***iman*** (faith) and has made it beautiful in your hearts, and he has made abhorrent to you disbelief, wickedness, and disobedience to Allah: such indeed are those who are righteous ***(rashidun)***.
- This is a grace from Allah, and a favor; and Allah is All Knowing and All Wise. If two parties among the Believers fall into a quarrel, make peace between them: but if one of them transgresses beyond bounds against the other, then fight you all against the one who transgresses until he complies with the Command of Allah; but if he complies, then make peace between them with justice, and fairness: for Allah loves those who are fair and just.
- The Believers are but a single Brotherhood: so make peace and reconciliation between your two brothers; and fear Allah, that you may receive Mercy.

12. Obey Allah and His messenger and those charged with authority among you.

- Obey Allah and obey the Messenger, and those charged amongst you with authority in the settlement of your affairs. If you differ in anything among yourselves, refer it to Allah and His Messenger (The Qur'an and the Prophet's teachings). If you do believe in Allah and the last Day, that is best and the most beautiful conduct in the final determination.

13. Freedom of religion

- Let there be no compulsion in religion: Truth stands out clear from Error. Whoever rejects Evil and believes in Allah hath grasped the most trustworthy handhold that never breaks. And Allah hears and knows all things.

14. *Awliya*

- Allah is the ***Waliy***, protector of those who have faith. From the depths of darkness, He will lead them forth into light. Of those who reject faith their ***Waliy*** (protectors) are the false deities: from light, they will lead them forth into the depths of darkness. They will be Companions of the Fire, to dwell therein (forever)
- Take not into intimacy those outside your ranks: they will not fail to corrupt you. They only desire your ruin: rank hatred has already appeared from their mouths: what their hearts conceal is far worse. We have made plain to you the Signs, if you have wisdom.
- If you obey the Unbelievers, (***kafaru***) they will drive you back on your heels, and you will turn your back to your Faith to your own loss. Allah is your protector, and He is the best of helpers.
- Take not the Jews and the Christians as your friends and protectors (***awliya***). They are friends and protectors unto each other. He who amongst you turns to them is one of them. Allah does not guide those who are unjust and evil doers (***zalimun***).
- Take not for friends and protectors (***awliya***) those who take your religion for mockery, whether from amongst people of the book or from amongst the ***kafireen***. Be in ***taqwa*** of Allah, fear Allah if you have faith indeed.
- Take not for your protectors and friends (***awliya***) your kin who practice infidelity over faith. Whosoever does that will be amongst the wrong doers.
- Take not My enemies and yours as ***awliya*** (friends and protectors), offering them love and regard, even though they have rejected the

Truth bestowed on you. And they have driven out the Messenger and yourselves from your homes because you believe in Allah as your ***Rabb*** (Lord)! You have come out to strive in My Cause and to seek My favor, take them not as friends, holding in secret regard and friendship for them: for I know all that you conceal and all that you reveal. And any of you that do this has strayed from the Straight Path.

- If they were to gain an upper hand over you, they would treat you as enemies, and stretch forth their hands and their tongues against you with evil; and they desire that you should reject the Truth.
- Befriend not people who have incurred Allah's wrath. They are already in despair of the Hereafter, just as the Unbelievers are in despair about those in graves.

  Allah is the Waliy protector of those who have faith. From the depths of darkness, He will lead them forth into light.
- Establish regular salaat, give regular charity, and holdfast to Allah. He is your Mawla, Protector, the best of Protectors and the best Helper.

15. Jihad

- Fight the infidel (the one who do not believe in God) until there is no more treachery and oppression and there prevails Justice and Faith in Allah altogether and everywhere.
- There amongst you is he who will linger behind, if misfortune befalls you, he will say, "Allah did favor him as he was not with you." When good fortune comes to you from Allah, he would wish that he had been with you.
- Those who swap the life of this world for the hereafter let them fight in the cause of Allah. Whosoever fights in the cause of Allah, whether he is slain or he is victorious, there is a great award for him from Allah.

  And why should you not fight in the cause of Allah, and for those men, women and children, who are weak, abused and oppressed, those who beseech their Lord to deliver them from their oppressors, and those who ask Allah to send for them protectors and helpers.

Remember Allah's blessings on you. When a people planned stretching out their hands against you and Allah did hold back their hands from you to protect you from your enemies. Be in *taqwa* of Allah, fear Allah and place your trust in Allah.

Be in *taqwa* of Allah, fear Allah. Perform *Jihad* and strive your utmost in Allah's Cause, and approach Him so that you may prosper.

If any among you turn back on his faith Allah will bring a people whom He loves and who love Him, and who are humble towards the believers, and stern towards unbelievers, who perform jihad and strive in the cause of Allah and fear not reproaches of any blamer. Such is the Grace of Allah that He bestows on whom He wills. Allah is All-Sufficient for His Creatures and all Knowing.

- When you meet the infidels rank upon rank, in conflict never turn your backs to them.
- Respond to Allah and His Messenger when He calls you to that gives you life. And know that Allah intervenes in the tussle between man and his heart, and it is to Allah that you shall return. Fear treachery or oppression that afflicts not only those who perpetrate it but affects guilty and innocent alike. Know that Allah is strict in punishment.
- Fight the infidel until there is no more treachery and oppression and there prevails Justice and Faith in Allah altogether and everywhere. If they cease, then Allah is seer of what they do. If they refuse, be sure that Allah is your Protector, the Best to protect and the Best to help.
- When you meet the enemy force, stand steadfast against them and remember the name of Allah much, so that you may be successful. And obey Allah and His messenger, and do not dispute with one another lest you lose courage, and your strength departs and be patient. Allah is with those who patiently persevere.
- Whether you do or do not help Allah's Messenger, your leader, Allah strengthens him with His Peace and with forces that you do not see. The words of the infidels He humbled into the dirt, but Allah's word is Exalted, High. Allah is Mighty, Wise. Go forth, advance! Whether equipped well or lightly, perform *jihad* strive your utmost and struggle

with your wealth and your persons in the cause of Allah. That is best for you, if you knew.

- Fight the unbelievers who surround you. Let them find you firm, and know Allah is always with those who have ***taqwa***, who are Allah-wary.
- Remember the Grace of Allah, bestowed upon you, when there came down hordes to overpower you: We sent against them a hurricane and forces that that you did not see but Allah sees all that you do.
- Behold! They came on you from above you and from below you, your eyes became dim, and the hearts gaped up to the throats, and you imagined various vain thoughts about Allah!
- If you will aid (the cause of) Allah, He will aid you, and make your foothold firm. But those who reject Allah, for them is destruction, and Allah will render their deeds vain. That is because they hate the Revelation of Allah; so He has made their deeds fruitless. Do they not travel through the earth, and see what was the end of those before them who did evil? Allah brought utter destruction on them, and similar fates await those who reject Allah. That is because Allah is the Protector of those who believe, but those who reject Allah have no protector.
- Be not weak and ask for peace, while you are having an upper hand: for Allah is with you and will never decrease the reward of your good deeds.

  The life of this world is but play and amusement: and if you believe, fear Allah and guard against evil, He will grant you your recompense, and will not ask you (to give up) your possessions.
- Behold, you are those invited to spend of your wealth in the Way of Allah: but among you are some that are parsimonious. But any who are miserly are so at the expense of their own souls. But Allah is free of all wants, and it is you that are needy. If you turn back (from the Path), He will substitute in your stead another people; then they would not be like you!
- When you are told to make room in the assemblies, spread out and make room: ample room will Allah provide for you. And when you

are told to rise up, for prayers, ***Jihad*** or other good deeds rise up: Allah will exalt in rank those of you who believe and who have been granted Knowledge. And Allah is well acquainted with all you do.

Why do you promise what you do not carry out? Hateful is indeed to Allah that you say what you do not act upon. Allah loves those who fight in His cause in array of unison and solidarity.

- Shall I guide you to a bargain that will save you from a painful torment? That you believe in Allah and His Messenger, and that you perform ***Jihad*** (strive to your utmost) in the way of Allah, with all that you own and in all earnestness: that will be best for you, if you but knew! He will forgive you your sins, and admit you to Gardens beneath which rivers flow, and to beautiful dwellings in ***Jannat of adn*** (Gardens of Eternity): that is indeed the supreme blessing. And another favor will He bestow, which you will cherish; help from Allah and a speedy victory. So give the glad tidings to the believers.

16. Murder

- If anyone slew a person, unless it be for punishment for murder or for spreading mischief in the land, it would be as if he slew the whole people: and if any one saved a life, it would be as if he saved the life of the whole people.
- The law of equality is prescribed to you in cases of murder. The free for the free, the slave for the slave, the woman for the woman. But if any remission is made by the brother (family) of the slain, then grant any reasonable demand, and compensate him with handsome gratitude. This is a concession and a Mercy from your Lord. After this, whoever exceeds the limits shall be in grave penalty. In the Law of Equality there is a saving of life for you, O men of understanding; that you may restrain yourselves.

  If anyone slew a person, unless it is for murder or for spreading mischief in the land, it would be as if he slew the whole people: and if anyone saved a life, it would be as if he saved the life of the whole people.

- Take not life, which Allah hath made sacred, except by the way of justice or law: This He commands you, that you may learn wisdom.

17. Perseverance and patience

- You who believe! persevere in patience and constancy; vie in such perseverance; strengthen each other; and fear Allah; that you may prosper.

***Şabr*, *şābir*, *şabbār*, and *şābara* denote the quality of patience and steadfastness, self-restraint, forbearance, endurance, and perseverance. One of Allah's ninety-nine names is *al-Şabur*, the Patient. It is one who does not precipitate an act before its time but decides matters according to a specific plan and brings them to fruition in a predefined manner, neither procrastinating nor hastening matters before their time but disposing each matter in its appropriate time in the way of its needs and requirements and doing all that without being subjected to a force opposing Allah's will. *Şabr*, *şābir*, *şabbār*, and *şābara* are mentioned in the Koran sixty-nine times. Allah reassures the believers:**

- Believers! be patient and vie you with patience. (Ali 'Imran 3:200, Koran)
- Pray for succor to Allah and be patient. (Al-A'raf 7:128, Koran)
- Be thou patient, Allah will not leave to waste the wage of good doers. (Hud 11:115, Koran)
- Be thou patient, Surely Allah's promise is true. (Ar-Rum 30:60, Koran)
- Bear patiently whatever may befall you. (Luqman 31:17, Koran)
- So, be thou patient with a sweet patience. (Al-Ma'arij 70:5, Koran)
- And be patient unto your Lord. (Al-Muddaththir 74:7, Koran)

- Believers! seek you help in patience and prayer. (Al-Anbya 21:153, Koran)
- But come sweet patience. (Yusuf 12:18, 83, Koran)
- Surely Allah is with the is with the patient. (Al-Baqarah 2:153, 249, Koran)
- Allah loves the patient. (Ali 'Imran 3:146, Koran)

18. O you who believe! Be quick in the race for forgiveness from your Lord.

- Those who give freely whether in prosperity, or in adversity, those who restrain anger, and forgive all humans, for Allah loves those who do beautiful deeds.
- Fear the Fire, which is prepared for those who reject Faith.

  And obey Allah and the Messenger; that you may obtain mercy.

  Be quick in the race for forgiveness from your Lord, and for a Garden whose measurement is that of the heavens and of the earth, prepared for the righteous.

  Those who give freely whether in prosperity, or in adversity, those who restrain anger, and pardon all humans, for Allah loves those who do beautiful deeds. Qur'an 3:130-134. Ali Imran

19. Theft, deception, fraud, dishonesty, and injustice

- Betray not the trust of Allah and His Messenger. Nor knowingly misappropriate things entrusted to you. Conceal not evidence, for whoever conceals it, his heart is tainted with sin. And Allah knows all that you do. Be just, being just is next to worship. Be in taqwa of Allah; fear Allah. Allah is well aware of what you do. Allah does not guide those who are unjust and evil doers (*Zalimun*).
- Betray not the trust of Allah and His Messenger. Nor knowingly misappropriate wealth entrusted to you, whether on behalf of an orphan or another party. Be honest in handling property, goods,

credit, confidences, secrets of your fellow men and display integrity and honesty in using your skills and talent. Whenever you give your word, speak truthfully and justly even if a near relative is concerned. Similarly, the ***amri minkum***, those entrusted with the administration of the affairs of the Believers should not betray the trust of Allah, the Messenger, and the Believers, and knowingly misappropriate the wealth of the people.

20. Usury and hoarding of wealth

- Devour not usury, doubled, and multiplied; Be in taqwa of Allah (fear Allah) that you may prosper.
- Those that spend of their goods in charity by night and by day, in secret and in public, have their reward with their Lord: they shall have no fear, nor shall they grieve.

  Those who devour usury will not stand except stands the one whom the Satan by his touch has driven to madness. That is because they say: "Trade is like usury," but Allah hath permitted trade and forbidden usury. Those who after receiving direction from their Lord, desist, shall be pardoned for the past; their case is for Allah to judge; but those who repeat (the offence) are Companions of the Fire; they will abide therein (forever). Allah will deprive usury of all blessing but will give increase for deeds of charity; for He does not love ungrateful and wicked creatures.
- Those who believe and perform wholesome deeds, establish regular prayers, and give regular charity have rewards with their Lord. They shall have no fear, nor shall they grieve.
- Fear Allah and give up what remains of your demand for usury if you are indeed believers. If you do it not, take notice of war from Allah and His Messenger: but if you turn back, you will still have your capital sums.
- Deal not unjustly, and you shall not be dealt with unjustly.
- If the debtor is in a difficulty, grant him time until it is easy for him to repay. But if you remit it by way of charity, that is best for you.

Devour not usury, doubled, and multiplied; Be in *taqwa* of Allah (fear Allah) that you may prosper.

- Fear the Fire, which is prepared for those who reject Faith; and obey Allah and the Messenger; that you may obtain mercy.
- Be quick in the race for forgiveness from your Lord, and for a Garden whose measurement is that of the heavens and of the earth, prepared for the righteous.
- Those who give freely whether in prosperity, or in adversity; those who restrain anger, and pardon all humans; for Allah loves those who do beautiful deeds (*Al-muhsinun*).
- There are indeed many among the priests and clerics who in falsehood devour the substance of men and hinder them from the way of Allah. And there are those who bury gold and silver and spend it not in the way of Allah: announce unto them a most grievous penalty.
- On the Day when heat will be produced out of that wealth in the fire of Hell, and with it will be branded their foreheads, their flanks, and their backs, "This is the treasure which you buried for yourselves, taste then, the treasures which you buried!"

21. Be good to your parents. Allah forbids infanticide and abortion.

- Be good to your parents: kill not your children because of poverty, We provide sustenance for you and for them. (Al-An'am 6:151–53, Koran)

22. Women and equality

- You are forbidden to take women against their will. Nor should you treat them with harshness, so that you may renounce of the dower you have given them, and that is only permitted where they have been guilty of open lewdness. On the contrary live with them on a footing of kindness and equality. If you take a dislike to them it may be that you dislike a thing, through which Allah brings about a great deal of good.

- Truly, your wives and your children are contenders to your obligations so beware! If you forgive them and overlook their faults, verily Allah is Most-forgiving, Most Merciful. Your riches and your children may be but a temptation. Whereas Allah! With Him is an immense reward.
- So be in ***taqwa*** of Allah and fear Allah as much as you can; listen and obey; and spend in charity for the benefit of your own souls. And those saved from their own greed are the ones that prosper. If you loan to Allah a beautiful loan, He will double it for you, and He will forgive you: for Allah is both Appreciative (***Shakoor***) and Magnanimous (***Haleem***), Knower of what is hidden and what is manifest, Exalted in Might, Full of Wisdom.
- Those who slander decent women, thoughtless but believing, are cursed in this life and in the Hereafter: for them is a grievous Penalty.
- And crave not those things of what Allah has bestowed His gifts more freely on some than others, men are assigned what they earn and women that they earn. But ask Allah of His bounty. Surely Allah is knower of everything.

23. Wealth

- Squander not your wealth among yourselves in egotism and conceit: Let there be trade and traffic amongst you with mutual goodwill Nor kill or destroy yourselves: for verily Allah hath been Most Merciful to you. If any do that in rancor and injustice, soon shall We cast them into the fire: and easy it is for Allah. If you abstain from all the odious and the forbidden, Allah shall expel out of you all evil in you and admit you to a Gate of great honor.
- And crave not those things of what Allah has bestowed His gifts more freely on some than others, men are assigned what they earn and women that they earn. But ask Allah of His bounty. Surely Allah is knower of everything.

  O you who believe! Let not your riches or your children divert you from the remembrance of Allah. If any act thus, the loss is their own.

- And spend something (in charity) out of the substance which We have bestowed on you, before Death should come to any of you and he should say, "O my Lord! Why didst Thou not give me respite for a little while? I should then have given (largely) in charity, and I should have been one of the doers of good."

24. Justice and truth

- Stand firmly for Allah as a witness of fair dealing.
- Let not the malice of people lead you to iniquity. Be just, that is next to worship. Be with *taqwa* of Allah, fear Allah.
- O you who believe! Fear Allah and speak always the truth that He may direct you to righteous deeds and forgive you your sins: he that obeys Allah and His Messenger have already attained the highest achievement.
- Stand firm for justice as witness to Allah be it against yourself, your parents, or your family, whether it be against rich or poor, Both are nearer to Allah than they are to you. Follow not your caprice lest you distort your testimony. If you prevaricate and evade justice Allah is well aware what you do.
- O you who believe! Stand firmly for Allah as a witness of fair dealing. Let not the malice of people lead you to iniquity. Be just, that is next to worship. Be with *taqwa* of Allah, fear Allah. Allah is well aware with what you do.
- Betray not the trust of Allah and His Messenger. Nor knowingly misappropriate things entrusted to you.
- If you have *taqwa* of Allah, and fear Allah, He will grant you a Criterion to judge between right and wrong and remove from you all misfortunes and evil and forgive your sins. Allah is the bestower of grace in abundance.
- Be in *taqwa* of Allah, fear Allah and be with those who are true in word and deed. Deal not unjustly, and you shall not be dealt with unjustly.

- Whenever you give your word speak honestly even if a near relative is concerned. And come not near the orphan's property, except to improve it, until he attains the age of full strength.
- And give full measure and full weight with justice. No burden We place on any soul but that which it can bear.
- If an impostor (fasiq) comes to you with any news, ascertain the truth, lest you harm people unsuspectingly and afterwards become full of remorse for what you have done. And know that amongst you is Allah's Messenger: were he in many matters to follow your desires, you would certainly fall into misfortune: but Allah has bestowed on you the love of iman (faith) and has made it beautiful in your hearts, and he has made abhorrent to you disbelief, wickedness, and disobedience to Allah: such indeed are those who are righteous (rashidun).

25. Knowledge

- O you who believe! Allah will exalt in rank those of you who believe and who have been granted Knowledge.
- Proclaim! and thy Lord is Most Bountiful, He Who taught (the use of) the Pen, Taught man that which he knew not. O my Lord! Enrich me in knowledge.
- When you are told to make room in the assemblies, spread out and make room: ample room will Allah provide for you. And when you are told to rise up, for prayers, *Jihad* or other good deeds rise up: Allah will exalt in rank those of you who believe and who have been granted Knowledge. And Allah is well acquainted with all you do. (Al-Mujadila 58:11, Koran)

  Proclaim! In the name of thy Lord and Cherisher, Who created, Created man, out of a (mere) clot of congealed blood: Proclaim! and thy Lord is Most Bountiful, He Who taught by the Pen, Taught man that which he knew not. (Iqra 96:1-5, Koran)

  And he who brings the Truth and believes in Truth, such are the men who do right (Az-Zumar 39:33, Koran)

High above all is Allah, the King, the Truth! be not in haste with the Qur'an before its revelation to thee is completed, but say, "O my Lord! Enrich me in knowledge." (Taha 20:114, Koran)

Is one who worships devoutly during the hours of the night prostrating himself or standing (in adoration), who takes heed of the Hereafter, and who places his hope in the Mercy of his Lord, (like one who does not)? Say: "Are those equal, those who know and those who do not know? It is those who are endued with understanding that receive admonition. (Az-Zumar 39:9, Koran)

26. Inviting to all that is good and right and forbidding what is wrong

- Let there arise out of you a band of people inviting to all that is good, enjoining what is right, and forbidding what is wrong: they are the ones to attain happiness.

27. Do not say to another Muslim, "You are not a believer."

- When you go forth in the cause of Allah be careful to discriminate and say not to the one who greets you with alaikum o salaam, "Though art not a believer." Would you covet perishable goods of this life when there are immeasurable treasures with Allah. You were like the person who offered you salutation, before Allah conferred on you His favors. Therefore, carefully investigate for Allah is well aware of all that you do.

28. Suspicion and lack of trust

- Avoid suspicion, for suspicion in some cases is sin; and spy not on each other, nor speak ill of each other behind their backs. Would any of you eat the flesh of his dead brother? No, you would abhor it. Be in taqwa of Allah, fear Allah: for Allah is Forgiving, Most Merciful.

29. Do not ridicule other believers or revile each other with wicked names.

- Let not some folk among you ridicule others: it may be that they are better than you are: nor let some women mock others: it may be that the others are better than them: nor defame or revile each other by offensive names: ill-seeming is wicked name calling for the one who has believed; and those who do not desist are indeed wrong doers.

30. Secret counsels and pacts

- When you hold secret counsel, do it not for iniquity and hostility, and disobedience to the Messenger; but do it for righteousness and self-restraint; and fear Allah, to Whom you shall be brought back.
- Secret counsels are only inspired by the Satan, in order that he may cause grief to the Believers; but he cannot harm them in the least, except as Allah permits; and on Allah let the Believers put their trust.

31. Forbidden to you are intoxicants and gambling.

- Forbidden to you are intoxicants and gambling, dedication of stones and divination by arrows. These are an abomination and Satan's handiwork; they hinder you from prayer and remembrance of Allah, and place enmity and hatred amongst you. Abstain from them so that you may prosper.

32. Forbidden to you are the carrion, blood, and flesh of swine and on any other food on which any name besides that of Allah has been invoked.

- Eat of good things provided to you by Allah and show your gratitude in worship of Him. Forbidden to you are the carrion, blood and flesh of swine, and on any other food on which any name besides that of Allah has been invoked. If forced by necessity, without willful disobedience or transgressing due limits, one is guilt less. Allah is Most Forgiving and Most Merciful.

33. Make not unlawful the good things that Allah hath made lawful to you.

- Make not unlawful the good things, which Allah hath made lawful to you. Commit no excess; Allah loves not people given to excess. Eat of things that Allah has provided for you, lawful and good. Be in *taqwa* of Allah, fear Allah in whom you believe.

34. Contracts and agreements: When you make a transaction involving future obligations, write it down in presence of witnesses.

- When you make a transaction involving future obligations, write it down in presence of witnesses, or let a scribe write it down faithfully. Let the party incurring the liability dictate truthfully in the presence of two witnesses from among your own men and if two men are not available then a man and two women, so that if one of them errs then the other one, can remind him. Disregard not to put your contract in writing, whether it be small or large, it is more suitable in the eyes of Allah, more suitable as evidence, and more convenient to prevent doubts in the future amongst yourselves.

35. Respect other people's privacy.

- Enter not houses other than yours until you have asked permission and invoked peace upon those in them. If you find none in the house whom you seek enter not unless permission is granted. If you asked to leave go back, it is best for you that make for greater purity for you. Allah knows all that you do.

36. This day, I have perfected your religion for you.

- We have made the (Qur'an) easy in your own tongue, that with it you may give glad tidings to the righteous, and warnings to people given to contention. Therein is proclaimed every wise decree, by command, from Our Presence, for We are ever sending revelations, as a Mercy from your Lord. We have explained in detail in this Qur'an, for the benefit of mankind, every kind of similitude.

- The Qur'an is a complete and perfect guide of Allah's Divine Commandments for the Believers and a warning to the disbelievers. Therein is proclaimed every wise decree, by command, from Our Presence, We have explained in detail in this Qur'an, for the benefit of mankind, every kind of similitude.

  This day have those who reject faith (***kafaru***) given up all hope of compromising your faith, fear them not but only fear Me. This day have I perfected your religion for you, bestowed on you with My blessings, and decreed Islam as your religion.

- Ha Mim. By the Book that makes matters lucid; We revealed it during the blessed night, verily We are always warning against Evil. Therein is proclaimed every wise decree, by command, from Our Presence, for We are ever sending revelations, as a Mercy from your Lord: for He is the hearer and knower. The Lord of the heavens and the earth and all that is in between them, if you have an assured faith. There is no god but He: it is He Who gives life and death, the Lord and Cherisher, your Lord and Lord of your forefathers.

- So have We made the (Qur'an) easy in your own tongue, that with it you may give glad tidings to the righteous, and warnings to people given to contention. But how many (countless) generations before them have We destroyed? Canst thou find a single one of them (now) or hear (so much as) a whisper of them?

- We have explained in detail in this Qur'an, for the benefit of mankind, every kind of similitude: but man is, in most things, contentious. And what is there to keep back men from believing, now that guidance has come to them, nor from praying for forgiveness from their Lord, but that (they ask that) the ways of the ancients be repeated with them, or the Wrath be brought to them face to face?

37. After his submission to the will and mercy of Allah, the believer is obliged to fulfill the covenant he has made with Allah as part of the compact of submission and has to perform beautiful, wholesome, and good deeds.

Submission to Allah obliges the believers to obey the covenant and carry out their duty to their Creator, to their fellow man, and to Allah's creation. And only those who "have faith and do righteous acts" will have success in their earthly lives and in the hereafter. The phrase *amilu al saalihaat* (to do good, to perform wholesome deeds) refers to those who persist in striving to set things right, who restore harmony, peace, and balance. Other acts of good works recognized in the Koran are to show compassion, to be merciful and forgive others, to be just, to protect the weak, to defend the oppressed, to be generous and charitable, to be truthful, to seek knowledge and wisdom, to be kind, to be peaceful, to love others, and to perform beautiful deeds.

Fifty verses in the Koran remind the believers of the rewards of righteous deeds. They begin with the words *Alladhina aaminu wa 'amilu al saalihaat*.

Those who believe, do deeds of righteousness, and establish regular prayers and regular charity, will have their reward with their Lord: on them shall be no fear, nor shall they grieve. (Al-Baqarah 2:277, Koran)

As to those who believe and work righteousness, Allah will pay them in full their reward; but Allah loves not those who do wrong (zalimeen). (Ali 'Imran 3:57, Koran)

On those who believe and do good, will [Allah] Most Gracious bestow love.

But those who believe and do deeds of righteousness, We shall soon admit to Gardens, with rivers flowing beneath, their eternal home, and therein shall they have companions pure and holy: We shall admit them to shades, cool and ever deepening. (An-Nisa 4:57, Koran)

But those who believe and do deeds of righteousness, We shall soon admit them to Gardens – with rivers flowing beneath – to dwell therein forever. Allah's promise is the truth, and whose word can be truer than Allah's? (An-Nisa 4:122, Koran)

If any do deeds of righteousness, - be they male or female – and have faith, they will enter Heaven, and not the least injustice will be done to them. (An-Nisa 4:124, Koran)

But to those who believe and do deeds of righteousness, He will give their due rewards, and more, out of His bounty: but those who are disdainful and arrogant, He will not punish with a grievous penalty; nor will they find, besides Allah, any to protect or help them. (An-Nisa 4:173, Koran)

To those who believe and do deeds of righteousness hath Allah promised forgiveness and a great reward. (Al-Ma'idah 5:9, Koran)

Sura Al-Fatihah: A leaf of the Aqiq Koran: Ustad Bahram Saleki. In the first six centuries of Islam, various Kufic scripts added beauty and clarity to the manuscripts of the Glorious Koran. However, this beautiful script was gradually superseded by other scripts because the elongated characters of the Kufic script increased the number of pages, which slowed down the publication of the Koran. With the advent of new technologies, the Aqiq Institute has designed a new Kufic script based on the Piramxz Kufic. This new script is delicate and beautiful. Ustad Bahram Saleki has inscribed this beautiful Aqiq Koran in this new, beautiful, and delicate script.

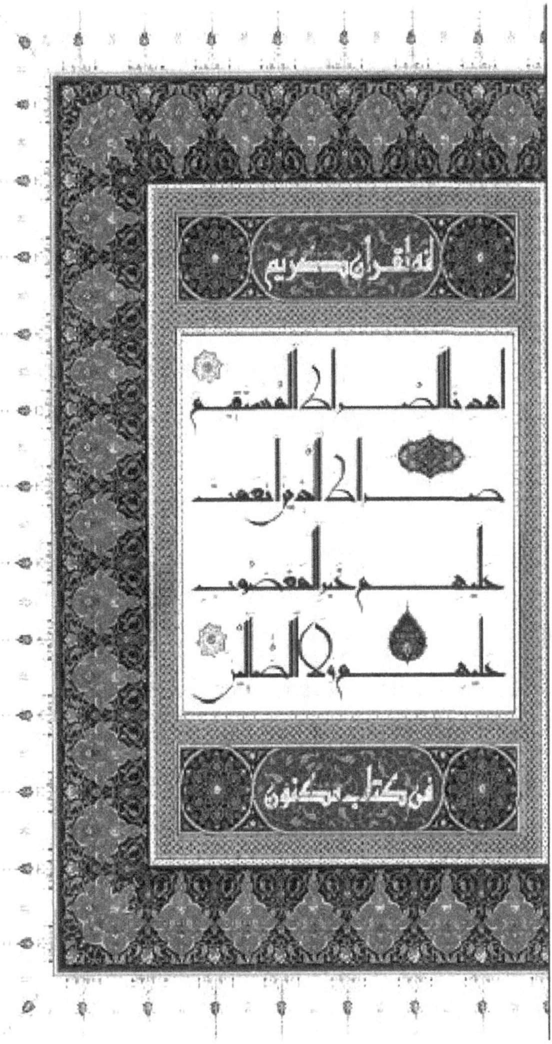

Sura Al-Fatihah: A leaf of the Aqiq Qur'an: Ustad Bahram Saleki.

Chapter Four

The Covenant: Islam and the Believer

Religion, or the *din* of Islam, has a multispatial influence on the individual believer in which he is aware of its three-dimensional impact on his intellectual, emotional, and physical being encompassing his total world of awareness and subconsciousness. The three dimensions are *islam* (total submission to the will of Allah), *iman* (faith), and *ihsan* (doing what is beautiful and wholesome). The synthesis of three dimensions of *din* (religion) is what links the true believer to the divine through total submission and faith in the reality of the Creator, in addition to performance of virtuous and wholesome actions of devotion and worship of the Sublime and through wholesome deeds in the service of the Creator and His creation. With this practice, the polarity between faith and action is reversed; instead of faith being the prerequisite for practice, practice defines faith. This reverse polarity is a reminder that Islam is defined not only as a set of beliefs but also as a body of actions that reveal the inner convictions of the believer. This practice-oriented picture of Islam is dependent on the traditions, which come as explanatory statements that act as a complement to one or more verses of the Koran. This relationship between the Hadith and the Koran is seen for example in the Hadith of Gabriel, which expresses a law-centered perspective on Islam, in which the knowledge of spiritual realities is less important than performance of appropriate actions in contrast to the Koran's word-centered approach to Islam, in which the divine word arouses knowledge of Allah in the human consciousness.

These dimensions are illustrated in Al-Baqarah in the description of a God-fearing person following his salutary obligations in the love of

Allah and the love of his fellow men in the form of *islam*, *iman*, and *ihsan*. All are acts interconnected yet separate.

It is not righteousness that you turn your faces towards East or West; but it is righteousness to believe in Allah and the Last Day, and the Angels, and the Book, and the Rasools; to spend of your substance, out of love for Him, for your kin, for orphans, for the needy, for the wayfarer, for those who ask, and for the ransom of slaves; to be steadfast in prayer, and practice regular charity, to fulfill the covenants which you have made; and to be firm and patient, in pain (or suffering) and adversity, and throughout all periods of panic. Such are the people of truth, the God-fearing. (Al-Baqarah 2:177, Koran)

In the Hadith of Gabriel, the blessed *nabi* takes a more earthly tack of the three dimensions of *din*, amalgamating *islam, iman*, and *ihsan* into practice that defines the path of the believer. 'Umar ibn al-Khattab said:

One day when we were with Allah's Rasool, a man with very white clothing and very black hair came up to us. No mark of travel was visible on him, and none of us recognized him. Sitting down before the Prophet, leaning his knees against his, and placing his hands on his thighs, he said "Tell me, Muhammad about submission."

The Blessed Nabi Muhammad replied, "Submission means that you bear witness that there is no god but Allah and Muhammad is Allah's Rasool, that you should perform salaat, the ritual prayer, pay the Zakat, fast during Ramadan, and make the pilgrimage to the House if you are able to go there."

The man said, "You have spoken the truth." We were surprised at his questioning him and then declaring that he had spoken the truth. He said, "Now tell me about faith (iman)."

He replied, "Faith (iman) means that you have faith in Allah, His angels, His Books, His Rasools, and in the Last Day and that you have faith in Allah's determination of affairs, whether good comes out of it or bad."

"You are correct," he said. "Now tell me about virtue (*ihsan*)." The Nabi said: "Virtue (doing good) is to worship Allah as if you see Him; for if you do not see Him surely, He sees you."

Then the man left. I remained for a while, and the Nabi said to me: "Oh Umar do you know who the questioner was?" "Allah and His Rasool know best," I replied. He said it was the angel Gabriel, who came to teach you your religion.

Islam: The Arabic word *islam* means "to resign oneself to, or to submit oneself," and in religious terminology, it means submission or surrender of oneself to Allah or to His will. Allah is the only true reality, and everything else in the universe is dependent on Allah for its reality and existence. Since Allah created the universe, all things in the universe are therefore totally dependent on Him and therefore are totally "submitted" to Allah. The Koran uses the term *islam* and its derivatives more than seventy times, in its broadest sense, that true religion is established by Allah alone and that everything in the universe praises and glorifies Him. All creatures, simply by existing, demonstrate the Creator's glory and perform acts that acknowledge Allah's mastery over them.

> Do they seek for other than the religion of Allah? While all creatures in the heavens and on earth have, willing or unwilling, bowed to His Will (accepted Islam), and to Him shall they all be brought back. (Ali 'Imran 3:83, Koran)

> Don't you see that to Allah bow down in worship all things that are in the heavens and on earth, the sun, the moon, the stars, the

> hills, the trees, the animals, and a great number among mankind? But a great number are (also) such as are fit for Punishment: and such as Allah shall disgrace, none can rise to honor: for Allah carries out all that He wills. (Al-Hajj 22:18, Koran)

All the prophets have submitted themselves to Allah's will and hence have been called Muslims in the Koran. In the same way, their followers who have submitted to Allah's will are believers (Muslims); however, the ones who have received earlier revelations but later changed them and confined themselves to partial truth, and in their pride, closed their minds to the whole truth are on their own. There are some people of the book who bow down in prayer, have faith in Allah, and in the last day perform virtuous deeds and who are among the righteous.

> Not all of them are alike: of the People of the Book are a portion that stand (for the right); they rehearse the Signs of Allah all night long, and they prostrate themselves in adoration.
>
> They believe in Allah and the Last Day; they enjoin what is right and forbid what is wrong; and they hasten (in emulation) in (all) good works: they are in the ranks of the righteous.
>
> Of the good that they do, nothing will be rejected of them; for Allah knows well those that do right. (Ali 'Imran 3:113–15, Koran)

> The religion before Allah is Islam (submission to His Will): nor did the people of the Book dissent there from except through envy of each other, after knowledge had come to them. But if any deny the Signs of Allah, Allah is swift in calling to account. (Ali 'Imran 3:19, Koran)

The true religion in the sight of Allah is only through submission to Allah and those who reject it will be in the ranks of the unguided.

If anyone desires a religion other than Islam (submission to Allah), never will it be accepted of him; and in the Hereafter he will be in the ranks of those who have lost (all spiritual good). (Ali 'Imran 3:85, Koran)

***Iman* (faith):** Faith in Islam, like in any religion, is never blind. Although belief in the unseen is important, there comes a point when a spiritual human being transcends the level of simple faith. At this point, the person's spiritual consciousness has penetrated the fog of the unseen, leading to knowledge of true nature of things. The Koran speaks of this progression from *faith* to *knowledge* as an inward metamorphosis in which belief (*iman)* is transformed into certainty (*yaqin).* This certainty is expressed in the Koran in terms of the three types of knowledge of Allah.[6]

The basic and fundamental knowledge is the knowledge of certainty (*ilm al-yaqin*, Koran 102:5). This type of certainty refers to knowledge that results from human capacity for logical reasoning and the appraisal of what the Koran calls "clear evidences" (*bayyinat)* of Allah's presence in the world. This knowledge also comes through the study of Koran, the earlier scriptures, the teachings of *Nabi* Muhammad, books of theology, and the study of Allah's signs. The knowledge of certainty is rational and discursive, a point that the Koran acknowledges when it admonishes human beings to

Say: "Travel through the earth and see how Allah did originate creation; so, will Allah produce a later creation: for Allah has power over all things." (Al-'Ankabut 29:20, Koran)

6 Cornell, "Fruit."

It is He Who gives life and death, and to Him (is due) the alternation of Night and Day: will you not then understand? (Al-Mu'minun 23:80, Koran)

Over time and under the influence of contemplation and spiritual practice, the knowledge of certainty may be transformed into a higher form of knowledge of Allah that the Koran calls the "eye of certainty" (*ayn al-yaqin*, Koran 102:7). This term refers to the knowledge that is acquired by spiritual intelligence, which believers in the East locate metaphorically in the heart. Before attaining this type of knowledge, the heart of the believer must first be "opened to Islam."

Is one whose heart Allah has opened to Islam, so that he has received enlightenment from Allah, (no better than one hard-hearted)? Woe to those whose hearts are hardened against celebrating the praises of Allah! They are manifestly wandering (in error)! (Az-Zumar 39:22, Koran)

Once opened, the heart receives knowledge as a type of divine light or illumination (*nur*) that leads the believer toward the remembrance of Allah. Just as with the knowledge of certainty, with the eye of certainty, the believer sees Allah's existence through Allah's presence in this world. With the eye of certainty, what lead the believer to the knowledge of Allah are not the arguments to be understood by rational intellect but the theophanic appearances (*bayyinat*) that strip away the veil of worldly phenomenon to reveal the divine reality underneath.

From the spiritual perspective, the one who perceives reality through the knowledge of Allah is a true "intellectual." Unlike the scholar, who develops his or her skills through years of formal study, the spiritual intellectual does not need book learning to apprehend the divine light. A spiritual intellectual can be anyone, scholarly or otherwise, whose knowledge extends outward to take in the physical world, upward to realize his ultimate transcendence of the world through his link with the Absolute, and then inward to reconcile all that with his intellectual and emotional self. Without such a vertical dimension of spirit, the scholar's knowledge, whatever its extent may be in academic terms, is of little worth.

The third and most advanced type of knowledge builds on the transcendent nature of knowledge itself. The highest level of consciousness is called the "truth of certainty" (*haqq al-yaqin*).

> But truly (Revelation) is a cause of sorrow for the Unbelievers. But verily it is Truth of assured certainty. So, glorify the name of thy Lord Most High. (Al-Haqqah 69:50–52, Koran)

It is also known as *ilm ladduni,* knowledge "by presence." This form of knowledge partakes directly of the divine reality and leaps off directly across the synapses of human mind to transcend both cognitive reasoning and intellectual vision at the same time. The truth of certainty refers to a state of consciousness in which a person knows the "real" through direct participation in it without resorting to logical proofs. This type of knowledge characterizes God's prophets and *rasuls*, whose consciousness of truth is both immediate and participatory, because what it is based on comes from direct inspiration.

Many Islamic scholars believe that divine inspiration could remain accessible to believers even after *Nabi* Muhammad's death. This possibility is symbolized in Islamic tradition by the figure of Khidr. Khidr first appeared in the Koran as an unnamed servant of Allah and as a companion of *Nabi* Musa (Moses). Khidr was endowed with knowledge of the unseen, which *Nabi* Musa lacked. The Koran describes this sage, who is not a *nabi* yet partakes of divine inspiration:

So, they found one of Our servants, on whom We had bestowed mercy from Ourselves and whom We had taught knowledge from Our own Presence. (Al-Kahf 18:65, Koran)

According to the Koran and the tradition, faith in Islam has as much to do with theoretical and empirical knowledge as it does with simple belief. This multidimensional concept of knowledge comprehends a reality that lies hidden within the unique world yet can be revealed to human mind and vision of spiritual intellect through the signs of Allah that are present in the world. In the Koran, Allah calls humanity:

So, I do call to witness what you see, and what you see not,

(This is) a Message sent down from the Lord of the Worlds.

But verily it is Truth of assured certainty. (Al-Haqqah 69:38–39, 43, 51, Koran)

The Koranic notion of religious belief (*iman*) as dependent on knowledge is actualized in practice in the term *islam*. The term *islam* signifies the idea of surrender or submission. Islam is a religion of self-surrender; Islam is the conscious and rational submission of the dependent and limited human will to the absolute and omnipotent will of Allah. The type of surrender Islam requires is a deliberate, conscious, and rational act made by a person who knows with both intellectual certainty and spiritual vision that Allah, who is the subject of Koranic discourse, is the reality itself.

The knower of God is a Muslim (fem. *Muslimah*), "one who submits" to the divine truth and whose relationship with God is governed by *taqwa*, the consciousness of humankind's responsibility toward its Creator. However, consciousness of God alone is not sufficient to make a person a Muslim. Neither is it enough to be merely born a Muslim or to be raised in an Islamic cultural context. The concept of *taqwa* implies that the believer has the added responsibility of acting in a way that is in accordance with three types of knowledge, *ilm al-yaqin*, *ain al-yaqin*, and *haqq al-yaqin* (knowledge of certainty, eye of certainty, and the truth of certainty). The believer must endeavor at all times to maintain himself or herself in a constant state of submission to Allah. By doing so, the believer attains the honored title of "slave of Allah" (*abd Allah*, fem. *amat Allah*), for he recognizes that all power and all agency belongs to God alone:

Allah has willed it. There is no power but Allah's. (Al Kahf 18:39, Koran)

Trusting in the divine mercy of his divine Master yet fearing God's wrath, the slave of God walks the road of life with careful steps, making his actions deliberate so that he will not stray from the path that God has laid out for him:

> Thee do we worship, and Thine aid we seek, Show us the straight Path, The Path of those on whom Thou hast bestowed Thy Grace, those whose (portion) is not wrath, and who go not astray. (Al-Fatihah 1:5–7, Koran)

It is an all-encompassing and highly personal type of commitment that has little in common with academic understanding of Islam as a civilization or cultural system.

The universality of religious experience is an important premise of the Koran's argument against profane or secular life. Taking a different tack from the Hadith (prophetic traditions that provide detailed instructions on how to act as a Muslim in specific ritual or moral context), the Koran is less concerned with defining creedal boundaries than with affirming the universal obligation to believe in one God. The Koran speaks of broad varieties of religious experience, to which every human being can relate. When dealing with religious practices, the Koran is less concerned with details of the ritual than with the meaning that lies behind the rituals it prescribes. The detail of the ritual practice, which serves to define Islam to most believers, is usually left for the tradition to define.

By speaking in a transcendental voice and presenting a discourse that is relevant to human experience in general, the Koran overcomes the cultural limitations of the western Arabian civilization, in which it was originally revealed, and makes it accessible to peoples of different cultural backgrounds throughout the world. This universalism has never been more important than it is in the present, when the majority of the *believers* do not speak Arabic. Such transcendence of culture is necessary for the Koran, as the vehicle of the word of God, to overcome linguistic and cultural differences and express itself in a metalanguage that can be understood even when its original Arabic is translated into a non-Semitic language such as English, Mandarin, Hindi, or Malay. An example of this metalanguage is found in the three types of knowledge already discussed. Most people, whatever their experiences and cultural background, think in similar ways and have similar wants and needs. The Koran seeks to establish a common foundation for belief that is based on such shared perceptions and experiences.

Over and over again, the Koran reminds the reader to think about the truths that lie behind the familiar or mundane things of the world, such as signs of God in nature, the practical value of virtue, and the cross-cultural validity of moral principles. What is good for Muslims is meant to be good for all human beings, regardless of gender, color, or origin. The Koran, therefore, appeals to both reason and experience in determining the criterion for distinguishing between truth and falsehood.

The most important theological point made by the Koran is that there is one God, Allah, universal and beyond comparison, the Creator, who sustains both the material world and the world of human experience.

> He has created the heavens and the earth for just ends far is He above having the partners they ascribe to Him! (An-Nahl 16:3, Koran)

All other forms of so-called truth are either false in their initial premises or contingently true only in limited situations. The recognition of this fact produces a profound effect on the human soul that has forever drawn humans in the search for the divine, which forever transforms the outlook of the believer.

The faith of Islam is based on certain knowledge that is both a liberation and a limitation. It is a liberation in the sense that certainty of divine reality allows the human spirit to expand outward and upward and then inward to transform the emotional and intellectual being so that consciousness becomes three dimensional. Nevertheless, it is also a limitation because with the knowledge of God comes a concomitant awareness of the limits and responsibility imposed on a person as a created being. Unlike a secular humanist, a true Muslim who submits to God cannot delude himself by claiming that he is the sole author of his destiny as he knows that a person's fate is routinely controlled by factors beyond his control.

***Ihsan* (doing, good, virtuous, and wholesome deeds):** The third dimension of *din* is *ihsan*. The word *ihsan* is derived from the word *husn*, which designates the quality of being good, beautiful, virtuous, pleasing, harmonious, or wholesome. The Koran employs the word *hasana*, from the same root as *husn*, to mean "a good or a beautiful deed." For example:

Whatever beautiful touches you, it is from Allah, and whatever ugly thing touches you, it is from yourself. And We have sent thee as a Rasool to (instruct) humanity. And enough is Allah for a witness. (An-Nisa 4:79, Koran)

If any does beautiful deeds, the reward to him is better than his deed; but if anyone does evil, the doers of evil are only punished (to the extent) of their deeds. (Al-Qasas 28:84, Koran)

The most significant Koranic usage of the word derived from *husn* is found in the adjective *husna*, most beautiful, which is applied to Allah's names. The Koran mentions Allah's most beautiful names in four verses. This means that Allah's attributes are more beautiful, more attractive, and more praiseworthy than attributes of anything else. Each divine name designates a superlative quality possessed by Allah alone. Allah is beautiful, and none is beautiful but Allah. Allah is majestic, and none is majestic but Allah. All of Allah's beautiful names can be placed in the formula of tawhid.

The Koran also uses the word *husna* as a noun, meaning "the best, the most beautiful," that which comprises all goodness, beauty, and desirability. *Husna* is the reward given to the devout and the faithful. By following the straight path of Allah and the teachings of the prophets and living up to the faith, human beings actualize God's most beautiful names in themselves and finally come to participate in everything that is most beautiful. The word *husna* is thus used to designate both the attributes of Allah and the ultimate goal of human beings, the reward that they experience in the next world.

And for him who has faith and does wholesome works, his recompense shall be most beautiful. (Al-Kahf 18:88, Koran)

For those who answer their Lord, are the most beautiful things
and those who answer Him not-theirs shall be an ugly reckoning,
and their refuge shall be in Gehenna. (Ar-Ra'd 13:18, Koran)

The word *ihsan* is a verb that means "to establish or to perform what is good and beautiful." The Koran employs the word *ihsan* and its active particle *muhsin* (the one who does what is beautiful and good) in seventy verses. The Koran often designates Allah as the One who does what is beautiful, and *al-Muhsin* is one of Allah's divine names. Allah created the universe of galaxies, stars, suns, and moons all in their ordained orbits, destined in their paths by Allah's mysterious forces, all shining and luminescent with Allah's blessed light (*nur*) that provides life and vigor to billions of His creatures.

He is the Knower of the unseen and the visible, and the Mighty,
the Compassionate, who made beautiful everything that He
created. And He created the human being from clay and made his
progeny an extraction of mean water. Then he proportioned him
and blew into him of His own spirit. (As-Sajdah 32:6–9, Koran)

It is Allah who has made the earth as the resting place for you, and
heaven a canopy, and He formed you, made your forms beautiful, and
provided you sustenance of things pure and good. Such is your Lord.
So glory to Allah, the Lord of the Worlds. (Ghafir 40:64, Koran)

He created heavens and the earth with His Reality (Haqq),
formed you and made your forms beautiful and to Him
is the homecoming. (At-Taghabun 64:3, Koran)

Love (*hubb*): The Koran ascribes the love of Allah in about fifteen verses. The emotion most closely associated with *ihsan* is *hubb*. To have *ihsan* is to do what is beautiful. Five verses of the Koran mention that

Allah loves those who have *ihsan* because by doing what is beautiful, they have developed beautiful traits that are worthy of Allah's love. In every verse of the Koran where Allah is said to love something, the object of this love is those human beings whose traits and activities are beautiful:

And spend of your substance in the cause of Allah and make not your own hands contribute to your destruction. Do what is beautiful. Surely Allah loves those who do what is beautiful. (Al-Baqarah 2:195, Koran)

Vie with one another, hastening to forgiveness from your Lord and to a Garden whose breadth is heavens and the earth, prepared for the god-wary, who give alms in both ease and in adversity and who restrain their anger and pardon people. Allah loves those who do what is beautiful. (Ali 'Imran 3:133–34, Koran)

Whosoever fulfils his Covenant and has Taqwa of Allah, surely Allah loves those with Taqwa. (Ali 'Imran 3:76, Koran)

There is no fault in those who have faith and do wholesome deeds in what they eat, if they are with Taqwa, have faith do wholesome deeds, and then have Taqwa, have faith and then are with Taqwa and do what is beautiful. Allah loves those who do what is beautiful. (Al-Ma'idah 5:93, Koran)

Truly Allah loves those who repent, and He loves those who cleanse themselves. (Al-Baqarah 2:222, Koran)

It is part of Allah's Mercy that that you deal gently with them. Had you been severe or harsh hearted, they would have broken away from you: so pass over their faults and ask for forgiveness for them; and consult them in the affairs. Then, when you have taken a decision, put your trust in Allah. Allah loves those who have trust. (Ali 'Imran 3:159, Koran)

Make things wholesome among them equitably and be just. Surely Allah loves the just. (Al-Hujurat 49:9, Koran)

Such verses reveal that Allah loves humans who do what is beautiful; who have *taqwa* and are God-wary; who repent, ask for forgiveness, and cleanse themselves; who have trust in Allah; and who are just and fair. Twenty-three verses in the Koran mention traits in humans that Allah does not love: the truth concealers (*kafirun*), the wrongdoers (*zalimun*), the workers of corruption (*mufsidun*), the transgressors (*ta'adda*), the immoderate, the proud, and the boastful.

In the Koran, Allah's love is always directed at humans, and such a love designates the special relationship between Allah and human beings, the special trust in the form of vicegerency given only to mankind. However, Allah does not love human beings whose love is not directed at Him. How can humans love Allah, about whom they know nothing? Once people come to know that Allah is lovable and the first spark for love of Allah lights up, according to the Koran, the person must follow the *nabi* by moving toward Allah through right practice, right faith, and doing what is beautiful. Through Allah's love, they will reach salvation. Allah commands the *nabi* to utter these words:

Say, if you love Allah, follow me and Allah will love you and forgive your sins. Allah is Forgiving, Compassionate. Say, "Obey Allah and the Rasool." But if they turn their backs, Allah loves not those who reject faith. (Ali 'Imran 3:31–32, Koran)

Allah wants people to love Him, and their love for Him follows His love for them. Human love precedes divine love. It is Allah who, in His mercy and bounty, kindles the spark of love for Him in the human heart. How is it possible for anyone to love Allah unless it is instigated by Him through His mercy, compassion, and guidance? How could a human exist without His mercy and love?

> O you who have faith, should any of you turn your back on your religion, Allah will bring a people whom He loves and who love Him, who are humble towards the faithful and disdainful towards the disbelievers, who struggle in the path of Allah and fear not the reproaches of any blamer. That is Allah's bounty, He bestows on whom so ever He will. Allah is all-embracing and all Knowing. (Al-Ma'idah 5:54, Koran)

Wholesomeness: *Islam* and Sharia (Islamic law) are concerned with everyday activities of the believer, differentiating right from wrong and guiding the person along the correct path. It defines *sin* as "breaking the commandments of Allah" and *good works* as "following Allah's instructions and the blessed *nabi's* conduct."

Iman adds a dimension to the understanding of human activity in that every human action in daily life reaches back into divine reality and that everything in the universe is governed by tawhid. Yet Allah has granted humans a freedom of choice that can upset the balance in the creation, of justice, of atmospheric elements, and of environmental pollution and cause the destruction of animal species, populations, cities, and agriculture through human actions. It tells people why they should be Allah's servants and explains which path they should follow to become His vicegerents. It makes clear that human activity is deeply rooted in the Real, and this has everlasting repercussions in this world and in the hereafter.

Ihsan adds to *islam* and *iman* a focus on people's intention to perform good and wholesome deeds on the basis of awareness of Allah's presence in all things. According to the Koran doing wholesome deeds, along with faith, will yield paradise.

> Whoso does wholesome deeds, be it male or female,
> and has faith, shall enter the garden, therein provided
> for without reckoning. (Ghafir 40:40, Koran)

> Those who have faith and do wholesome deeds, then we shall admit
> to gardens through which rivers flow. (An-Nisa 4:57, 122, Koran)

Another fifty verses in the Koran mention that people who perform wholesome deeds and have faith shall inherit the garden. The Koran uses the word *saalihaat* for wholesome deeds and the word *salihun* for wholesome people. The root word for both means "to be sound, wholesome, right, proper, good."

Another word used in the Koran, about thirty times, is *islah*, which means "establishing wholesomeness." In modern times, the word *islah* has been used to mean "reform." The word *sulh* is used in the Koran once to mean peace and harmony in family relationship. In modern times, the word *sulh* has come to mean "peace in the political sense."

While the Koran calls the wholesome people as *salihun*, it employs the opposite, *fasid,* for the corrupt, ruined, evil, and wrong. The wholesome are the ones who live in harmony with the Real (*Haqq*) and establish wholesomeness (*saalihaat*) through their words and deeds throughout the world. In contrast, the corrupt (*mufsidun*) destroy the proper balance and relationship with Allah and His creation. *Fasid* means "corrupt, evil, wrong."

Allah measures out the good and the evil, the wholesome and the corrupt. Humans have enough freedom to make their own choices;

if they make the choice to do beautiful and wholesome deeds motivated by faith and god-wariness (*taqwa*), they please Allah and bring harmony and wholesomeness to the world, resulting in peace, justice, mercy, compassion, honor, equity, well-being, freedom, and many other gifts through Allah's grace. Others choose to do evil and work corruption (*mufsidun*) to destroy the right relationship among the creation, causing hunger, disease, oppression, pollution, and other afflictions. In the universal order, corruption is the prerogative of humans, and vicegerency gives them the freedom to work against the Creator and His creation. Only misapplied trust can explain how moral evil can appear in the world. Modern technology; scientific advancement; nuclear, chemical, and biological weapons of mass destruction; genetic engineering of plants, animals, and humans; and exploitation of nonrenewable resources of the earth had made self-destruction of the human race and all life on the planet a distinct and imminent possibility.

> Corruption has appeared on the land and in the sea because what people's hands have earned, so that He may let them taste some of their deeds, in order that they may turn back from their evils. (Ar-Rum 30:41, Koran)

> When humans choose wrong and corrupt actions they displease Allah. Allah loves those who do what is beautiful, not those who do what is ugly.

> When he turns his back, he hurries about the earth to work corruption there and destroy the tillage and the stock. Allah loves not corruption. (Al-Baqarah 2:205, Koran)

Allah loves doing what is beautiful, and because of His love for those who do the beautiful, He brings them near to Himself, and His nearness is called Allah's mercy:

> Work not corruption in this world after it has made wholesome and call upon Allah in fear and hope. Surely the mercy of Allah is near to those who do what is beautiful. (Al-A'raf 7:56, Koran)

The covenant of Allah presents us with the scope of the freedom of choice that humans have in doing what is wholesome and beautiful or what is corrupt and ugly and in the human role among the creation that distinguishes right activity, right thought, and right intention from their opposites. It reminds us of how the scales of Allah's justice, the two hands of Allah—His mercy and His wrath—are reflected in the human domain, where people have been appointed Allah's vicegerents. Deeds of goodness and wholesomeness are associated with mercy, paradise, and the beautiful. Evil and corruption is rewarded with wrath, hell, and the ugly.

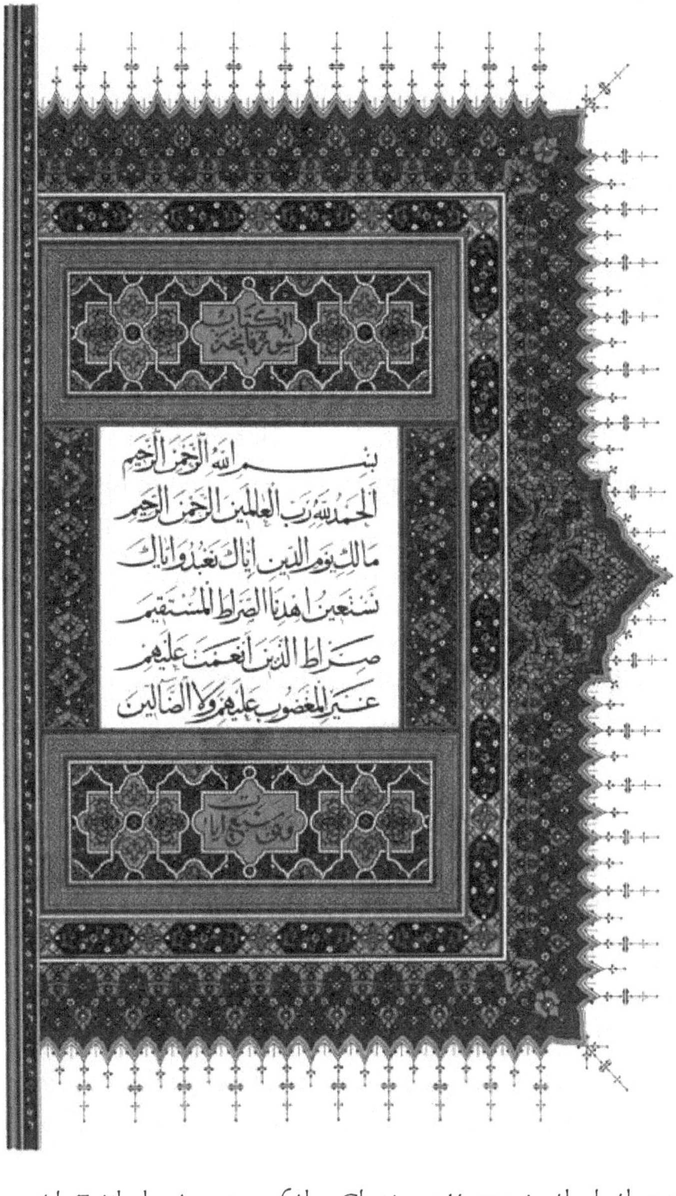

Sura Al-Fatihah: A copy of the Glorious Koran in thuluth script, inscribed by Haji Maqsud Sharif Tabrizi, dated AH 974, consisting of 465 pages of ten lines. Size: 36.7 × 24.5 cm. The two opening pages are illuminated, the headings of chapters in *riqa'* script with gold ink. Its annexed prayers are in *riqa'* script with gold ink. Paper: russet material, decorated with different designs. Binding: black goat leather.

Chapter Five

The Covenant of Allah: The Society and State

Allah is *al-Haqq*. Allah is the Real; there is nothing real but the Real. Everything other than Allah is unreal, ephemeral, illusory, transitory, vanishing, nothing. Everything derives its existence from Allah. Everything good, praiseworthy, permanent, and real belongs to Allah. Allah is independent. Everything in the heavens and the earth depends utterly on Allah for its existence and subsistence. Allah's reality is permanent and unchanging, everything else is relative, and everything else other than Allah has to be understood in relation to Him.

The sovereignty of the heavens and the earth belongs exclusively to Allah, whose will and command binds the Muslim community and state.

> To Allah belongs all that is in the heavens and on earth; and with Allah is the ultimate determination of all things. (Ali 'Imran 3:109, Koran)

> Behold, your Lord said to the angels: "I will create a vicegerent on earth." They said: "Would You place there one who will make mischief and shed blood? While we celebrate Your praises and glorify Your holy (name)?" He said: "I know what you know not." (Al-Baqarah 2:30, Koran)

The Koran declares that Allah has subjugated the earth and the entire created universe for the benefit of human beings.

> It is Allah who has subjected the sea to you, that ship may sail through it by His command, that you may seek of His bounty, and that you may be grateful. (Al-Jathiya 45:12, Koran)

The sovereignty of the Muslim state belongs to Allah. The *ummah*, through its covenant with Allah, is the repository of what is known as the "executive sovereignty" through the *ummah's* submission to the will of Allah. The *ummah* has the moral responsibility that is implied in the covenant, referred to in the Koran as the vicegerency (Koran 2:30-33). Those who uphold the requirements of the covenant are known as Allah's vicegerents (*khulafa*) on the earth. In the covenant of Allah, they are described as

> O you who believe! Fear Allah, and (always) say a word directed to the Right: That He may make your conduct whole and sound and forgive you your sins: he that obeys Allah and His Rasool, has already attained the highest Achievement. (Al-Ahzab 33:70–71, Koran)

The society that is made up of such God-fearing people (*muttaqeen*) constitutes a "middle nation" or axial community (*ummah wast*) whose collective responsibility is to bear witness to the truth and act as an example for the rest of the humanity—a nation of moderation that is averse to extremism:

> Thus, have We made of you an Ummah justly balanced, that you might be witnesses over the nations, and the Rasool a witness over yourselves; and we appointed the Qibla to which thou were used, only to test those who followed the Rasool from those who would turn on their heels (from the Faith). Indeed, it was (a change) momentous, except to those guided by Allah. And never would Allah make your faith of no effect. For Allah is to all people most surely full of Kindness, Most Merciful. (Al-Baqarah 2:143, Koran)

The *ummah* is a community of believers *(Jamma)* that enjoins good and forbids evil, a community that in its advocacy of truth is a witness over itself and over humankind. This community maintains itself in a permanent state of surrender to Allah (*ummah Muslimah*) as exemplified by the blessed *nabi* Muhammad and his followers in Medina.

> Whoever submits his whole self to Allah, and is a doer of good, has grasped indeed the most trustworthy handhold; and with Allah rests the End and Decision of (all) affairs. (Luqman 31:22, Koran)

> You are the best of Peoples, evolved for mankind, enjoining what is right, forbidding what is wrong, and believing in Allah. If only the People of the Book had Faith, it was best for them: among them are some who have Faith, but most of them are perverted transgressors. They will do you no harm, barring a trifling annoyance; if they come out to fight you, they will show you their backs, and no help shall they get. (Ali 'Imran 3:110–11, Koran)

The Koran is emphatic on the solidarity of the community of believers, a community that advocates unity and shuns separation, a community whose hearts Allah has joined in love so that, by Allah's grace, they become brethren unto one another. Allah repeatedly commands believers to call for all that is good, enjoining what is right and forbidding what is wrong. In the covenant of the Koran, Allah promises a dreadful penalty (*Azabu azeem*) to those creating a schism and division in the community of Muslims. The Muslim community of one and a half billion people around the world is a single unified *ummah* whose hearts have been joined in love by Allah and who are brethren unto one another, never to be divided into schisms, sects, principalities, states, or kingdoms. The individuals within the community of goodwill, both men and women, are equal in status and enjoy the same rights. Those ulema, preachers, imams, politicians, kings, and presidents who cause divisions and disputes among the *ummah* have been promised a dreadful penalty by Allah. They have been warned.

> And hold fast, all together, by the Rope which Allah (stretches out for you) and be not divided among yourselves; and remember with gratitude Allah's favor on you; for you were enemies and He joined your hearts in love, so that by His Grace, you became brethren; and you were on the brink of the Pit of Fire, and He saved you from it. Thus doth Allah make His Signs clear to you: that you may be guided. Let there arise out of you a band of people inviting to all that is good, enjoining what is right, and forbidding what is wrong: they are the ones to attain felicity. Be not like those who are divided amongst themselves and fall into disputations after receiving Clear Signs: for them is a dreadful Penalty. (Ali 'Imran 3:103–5, Koran)

> Verily, this Brotherhood of yours is a single Brotherhood, and I am your Lord and Cherisher: therefore, serve Me (and no other). (Al-Anbya 21:92, Koran)

The *ummah* is a community that is committed to truth and administers justice based on truth. The Muslim community is commanded by Allah to act justly to others and to one another and observe due balance in all their actions and follow a balanced path and not to transgress due bounds in anything. A human, man and woman, should be straight and honest in all his dealings.

> Of those We have created are people who direct (others) with truth and dispense justice therewith. (Al-A'raf 7:181, Koran)

> And the Firmament has He raised high, and He has set up the Balance (of Justice), In order that you may not transgress (due) balance. So, establish weight with justice and fall not short in the balance. (Ar-Rahman 55:7-9, Koran)

The Koran teaches that affairs of the believers should be conducted through mutual consultation (*ijma*) and decisions reached through consensus. Furthermore, the Koran proclaims consultation as a principle of government and a method that must be applied in the administration of public affairs. The sovereignty of Islamic state belongs exclusively to Allah, whose will and command binds the community and state. The dignified designation of the community in the Koran as vicegerent of Allah on the earth makes the *ummah* a repository of executive sovereignty in the Islamic state. The community as a whole, after consultation and consensus, grants people among themselves with authority to manage its affairs (*ulil amri minkum*). Those charged with authority act in their capacity as the representative (*wakil*) of the people and are bound by the Koranic mandate to consult the community in public affairs, and consensus is the binding source of the law. The community, by consultation and in consensus, has the authority to depose any person charged with authority, including the head of state, in the event of gross violation of the law.

> Those who hearken to their Lord and establish regular prayer; who (conduct) their affairs by mutual Consultation; who spend out of what We bestow on them for Sustenance; And those who, when an oppressive wrong is inflicted on them do not flinch and courageously defend themselves. (Ash-Shura 42:38-39, Koran)

Islam pursues its social objectives by reforming the individual. The ritual ablution before prayer, the five daily prayers, fasting during the month of Ramadan, and the obligatory giving of charity all encourage punctuality, self-discipline, and concern for the well-being of others. The individual is seen not just a member of the community and subservient to the community's will but also as a morally autonomous agent who plays a distinctive role in shaping the community's sense of direction and purpose. The Koran has attached to the individual's duty of obedience to the government a right of to simultaneously dispute with rulers over government affairs. The individual obeys the ruler on the condition that the ruler obeys the covenant of the Koran and Allah's commandments, which are obligatory to all Muslims regardless of their status in the social hierarchy. This is reflected in the declaration of the blessed *nabi*:

> There is no obedience in transgression;
> obedience is only in the righteousness.

The citizen is entitled to disobey an oppressive command that is contrary to the covenant of Allah.

> O you who believe! Obey Allah, and obey the Rasool, and those charged with authority among you. If you differ in anything among yourselves, refer it to Allah and His Rasool, if you do believe in Allah and the Last Day: that is best, and most suitable for final determination. (An-Nisa 4:59, Koran)

The dignity of the human being is a central concern of the Islamic law. Allah fashioned Adam in due proportion and breathed His Spirit into him, and Allah elevated Adam in rank above that of His angels. Allah bestowed dignity on the children of Adam, both men and women; gave them transport over land and oceans; gave them for the sustenance things, good and pure; and conferred on them special favors above a greater part of His creation. Allah elevated the children of Adam spiritually in rank above that of His angels and most of His creation. Allah also appointed the children of Adam as His vicegerents on the earth and promised them special favors.

The dignity of human beings is considered to have five special values—faith, life, intellect, property, and lineage—that must be protected by the law as a matter of priority. Although the basic interests of the community and those of the individual coincide within the structure of these values, the focus is nevertheless on the individual.

There is a clear message in Allah's proclamations in the Koran:

> We have honored the progeny of Adam; provided them with transport on land and sea; given them for sustenance things good and pure; and conferred on them special favors, above a great part of Our Creation. (Al-Isra 17:70, Koran).

> We have indeed created man in the best of moulds. (At-Tin 95:4, Koran)

The Koranic principle of enjoining good and forbidding what is evil is supportive of the moral autonomy of the individual. This principle authorizes the individual to act according to his or her best judgment in situations in which his or her intervention will advance a good purpose. The following saying of the blessed *nabi* also supports individual action by a believer:

> If any one of you sees an evil, let him change it by his hand, and if he is unable to do that, let him change by his words, and if he is still unable to do that let him denounce it in his heart, but this is the weakest form of belief.

This principle assigns to the individual an active role in the community in which he or she lives. The Koran annunciated the principle of free speech fourteen hundred years ago. Believing men and women are reminded that they are the best of people, witnesses over other nations. Such a responsibility carries with it a moral burden of an exemplary conduct of one who submits to the divine truth and whose relationship with Allah is governed is by *taqwa*, the consciousness of humankind's responsibility toward its Creator. The believer has the responsibility of acting in accordance with the three types of knowledge: the knowledge of certitude (*ilm al-yaqin*), the eye of certitude (*ain al-yaqin*), and the truth of certitude (*haqq al-yaqin*). With that knowledge and faith, the believer is well equipped to approach others to enjoin what is right and forbid what is wrong.

This moral autonomy of the individual, when bound together
with the will of the community formulates the doctrine
of infallibility of the collective will of the community,
Ummah, which is the doctrinal basis of consensus.

You are the best of Peoples, evolved for mankind, enjoining
what is right, forbidding that is wrong, and believing in Allah.
If only the People of the Book had Faith, it was best for them:
among them are some who have Faith, but most of them
are perverted transgressors. (Ali 'Imran 3:110, Koran)

The Koran addresses men and women who submit to Allah, who believe, who are devout, who speak the truth, who are righteous, who are humble, who are charitable, who fast and deny themselves, who guard their chastity, and who always remember Allah, promising them great recompense and forgiveness for their transgressions. In this address, Allah treats individual men and women evenly with a promise of a similar reward for their good acts. In Allah's eyes, all men and all women who do good deeds carry an equal favor with Him.

Allah admonishes both believing men and women to restrain from lustful stares, lower their gaze, and guard their chastity. He is well acquainted with men's intentions and actions. Allah also reminds women to dress modestly and that they should not display their adornments outside of their immediate family environment.

Allah then tells believers, men and women, to turn *all together* in prayer toward Him so that they may prosper. This can happen only when the believers, men and women, turn to Allah collectively as a community in a mosque as was customary during the lifetime of His *nabi*. According to the Koran, men and women are autonomous in their actions and deeds, are answerable to Allah for their own conduct and actions on the Day of Judgment, and will be rewarded and punished according to their deeds.

In a community, men as a group or as rulers of the state have no sanction from the covenant of Allah to enforce restrictions on the freedom of righteous and believing women. Men as a group do not have any authority over women as a group. To every man and to every woman, Allah has bestowed rights to *faith, life, freedom, intellect, and property, which include freedom of action and speech as well as education.* The authority of a ruler who denies these basic freedoms to men or to women is openly disputable. The individual obeys the ruler on the condition that ruler obeys the covenant of the Koran.

For Muslim men and women, for believing men and women, for devout men and women, for true men and women, for men and women who are patient and constant, for men and women who humble themselves, for men and women who give in charity, for men and women who fast (and deny themselves), for men and women who guard their chastity, and for men and women

> who engage much in Allah's praise, for them has Allah prepared forgiveness and great reward. (Al-Ahzab 33:35, Koran)

Absolute truth is only in Allah, universal and beyond comparison. All other so-called truths are either false in their initial premises or contingently true only in limited situations. The knower of Allah is a believer, a Muslim (one who submits to the divine truth and whose relationship with Allah is governed by *taqwa*). The seekers of truth are on a journey of discovery of knowledge, which extends outward to take in the physical world, upward through a link with the divine, and then inward to link with their emotions and the intellect, conscious and subconscious. The seekers are at various stages of their journey; their search takes them through differing intellectual pathways, through their diverse linguistic and cultural heritage, through their faith in God, and through their theoretical and empirical understanding of the faith. They comprehend the vision of divine reality through the signs of Allah that are present in the world itself. This multidimensional knowledge that comprehends the vision of the divine reality is unique to each human. This knowledge of the divine reality leaps directly across the synapses of human mind to transcend cognitive reasoning and occurs through direct participation and obedience of Allah and His covenant. This knowledge is not subject to creed or dogma. Therefore, the Koran admonishes:

> Let there be no compulsion in religion: Truth stands out clear from Error: whoever rejects Evil and believes in Allah hath grasped the most trustworthy handhold that never breaks. And Allah hears and knows all things. (Al-Baqarah 2:256, Koran)

Whosoever rejects evil and believes in Allah has His protection and guidance. The faith of the true believer as an individual is protected by

Allah's promise in the Koran. No hurt will come to those who follow the right guidance:

> O you who believe! Guard your own souls; if you follow right guidance, no hurt can come to you from those who stray. The goal of you all is to Allah: it is He that will show you the truth of all that you do. (Al-Ma'idah 5:105, Koran)

Absolute truth is only with Allah. The seeker of the road to divine mercy may take one of the many pathways leading to Allah's beneficence, and Allah does show the right path to whom He will:

> He doth guide whom He pleases to a Way that is straight. To those who do right is an abundant reward.

Therefore, it is not unto the ulema, the priests, the scholars, those in authority, and their religious police to criticize or restrain anyone from following a pathway different from theirs. The prerogative of judgment on anyone, a heretic or a believer, belongs only to Allah.

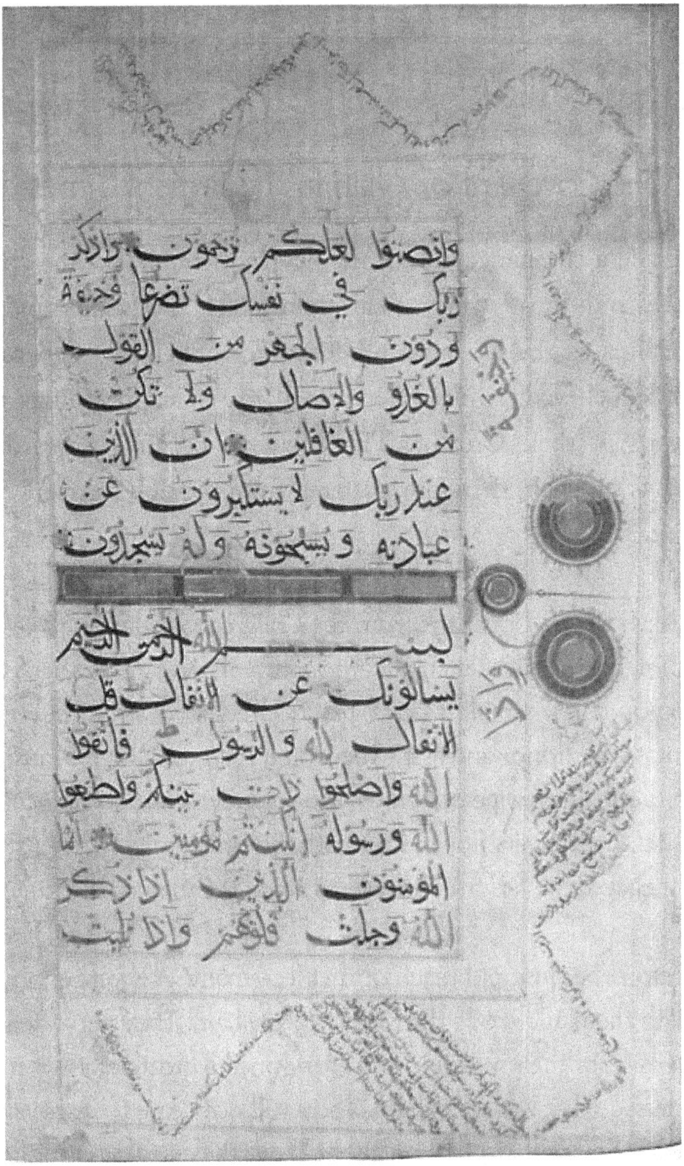

Bihari manuscript dated to the eighth century AD. This copy of the Koran consists of 246 pages, with 15 lines to each page. Most of the script is written in black except for the word *Allah*, which is in red ink. The Bihari script is said to resemble a sword or a ship. Located in the King Faisal Center for Research and Islamic Studies in Riyadh, Saudi Arabia.

Chapter Six

The Covenant of Allah in the Present Times

Allah made a covenant with all the people of the book, the children of Israel, and those who called themselves Christians and then the Muslims as the essential observation of their *din*. There were those who believed, while others opted to remain rebellious to the commands of their Creator. Those who chose to disregard their obligations to Allah, therefore, suffered from the dire consequences of rejection.

> Allah took a Covenant from the Children of Israel and We appointed twelve leaders from among them. And Allah said "I am with you if you establish salaat, practice regular charity, believe in my Rasools, honor and assist them, and loan to Allah a beautiful loan, Verily I will wipe out from you your evils, and admit you to Gardens with rivers flowing beneath. But if any of you after this disbelieved, he has truly wandered from the path of rectitude.
>
> Therefore, because of breach of their covenant, We were annoyed with them and made their hearts grow hard. They perverted words from their meaning and abandoned a greater part of the Message that was sent them. Thou will not cease to discover treachery from them barring a few. Nevertheless, bear with them and pardon them. Verily Allah loves those who are wholesome.
>
> Moreover, We took the Covenant from those who call themselves Christians, but they have abandoned a good part of the Message that was sent to them. Therefore, We have stirred up enmity and hatred amongst them until the Day of Resurrection, when Allah

will inform them of their handiwork. O People of the Book! There has come to you Our Rasool, revealing to you much that you used to hide in the Scripture and passing over much. Indeed, there has come to you from Allah a light and a plain Book, in which Allah guides all those who seek His good pleasure to the path of peace. He brings them out of darkness into light by His will and guides them to a straight path. (Al-Ma'idah 5:12–16, Koran)

The above sura and its verses show the importance of the Koran as

a light and plain Book from Allah where Allah guides all who seek His good pleasure to the path of peace. He brings them out of darkness into light by His will and guides them to a straight path.

The Koran is a guide and Allah's covenant, a code of conduct for all humans to trust and believe in the Creator, the one universal God, Allah. Allah leads all those people who believe in Him to His straight path and to the path of peace. The children of Israel disobeyed Allah, and they lost His favor. As for those who called themselves Christians, Allah took their covenant, but they abandoned a large part of the message Allah sent them, to trust and believe in the Creator, the one God of the universe. Thereafter, Allah stirred up hatred and enmity among them because of their transgressions. Having split into sects and nations, they have continuously battled among themselves for two thousand years over doctrine, gold, wealth, and possessions.

Allah has provided every human a guidance to His straight path through His covenant. Allah's covenant guides the believers to His way through its thirty-seven commandments. These commandments are the steps to peace and salvation for humankind.

The thirty-seven steps, pillars, or commandments comprise the essence of the believer's faith. Fulfillment of the commandments is not only a matter of faith of the believer; it is his *din*. Observation of the commandments of the covenant of Allah embraces the total belief system as ordained in the Koran. The fulfillment of the thirty-seven commandments of the covenant in awareness and *taqwa* of Allah unites the believer with Allah in a spiritual communion. This communion is not only with Allah but also, through Him, with other humans and with rest of Allah's creation. The phrase *amilu al saalihaat* (to do good, to perform wholesome deeds) refers to those who persist in striving to set things right, who restore harmony, peace, and balance. The other acts of good works recognized in the covenant of Allah are to show compassion, to be merciful and forgive others, to be just, to protect the weak, to defend the oppressed, to be generous and charitable, to be truthful, to seek knowledge and wisdom, to be kind, to be peaceful, to love others, and to perform beautiful deeds.

Therefore, a believer is one who has submitted of his own free will to the will and command of the one universal God (*islam*), maintains his faith (*iman*) in God in constant awareness of Allah's presence with him (*taqwa* of Allah), fulfills his covenant with Allah, and performs wholesome and beautiful deeds in the service of God and His creation (*ihsan*).

The Covenant of Allah

The First Commandment of Allah

Believe in Allah.

He is Allah, there is no Deity but He, Knower of the
hidden and the manifest. He is the Rahman the
Most Gracious, the Rahim, Most Merciful.
He is Allah; there is no Deity but Him,
The Sovereign, the Pure and the Hallowed,

Serene and Perfect,
The Custodian of Faith, the Protector, the Almighty,
The Irresistible, the Supreme,
Glory be to Allah; He is above all they associate with Him
He is Allah, the Creator, the Sculptor, the Adorner of color
and form. To Him belong the most beautiful names.
All that is in the heavens and on earth, praise and glorify Him; and
He is the Almighty and All-Wise. (Al-Hashr 59:18–24, Koran)

Allah is truly the only reality, and everything else in the universe is dependent on Him for its reality and existence. Since Allah created the universe, all things in the universe are therefore totally dependent on Allah and hence totally "submitted" to Him. The Koran uses the term *submission* (*islam*) and its derivatives more than seventy times in its broadest sense—that true religion is established by Allah alone and that everything in the universe praises and glorifies Him. All creatures, simply by existing, demonstrate the Creator's glory and perform acts that acknowledge Allah's mastery over them.

Verily I am Allah. There is no god but I, so worship Me, and
perform salaat in remembrance of Me. (Taha 20:14, Koran)

Long time ago, humankind was unaware of the Creator of the universe. The Creator God, Allah, sent His prophets to every community to enlighten humanity about the Creator and His creation. The prophets taught humans of the obligations of humankind to their Creator and to His creation.

Islam is the continuation of the message of Allah that *Nabi* Ibrahim (Abraham) began to spread around the Middle East in the fog of time. Ibrahim, who had lived in the mists of time in Urfa along the Euphrates River, believed in one God, who created the universe and everything in it. Ibrahim taught that God the Creator sustains every object, living and nonliving. Ibrahim placed his total trust in the universal God, Allah. He faithfully obeyed Allah's commandments and did Allah's bidding.

On one momentous occasion, Ibrahim was prepared to offer his most beloved son, Ishmael, in sacrifice at Allah's bidding. As it turned out, Allah was only testing Abraham's faith, and the child was miraculously saved by an angel. This test of faith became the foundation of belief and the *din* for mankind for all times to come.

There were those who unquestioningly followed Ibrahim, submitted their self to Allah, and put their trust in Him. In doing so, they became the believers, the *Muslims*. Muslims are those people who bow down and submit their total *self* to the Creator and do the His bidding. With time, *Nabi* Ibrahim's life story became an oral folklore; and by the time it came to be written in testaments, it had changed a great deal. Other prophets, thousands in number, followed Ibrahim, giving the same message as he did to all mankind: Submit yourselves to the Lord, your Maker. Believe in Him and place your trust in Him always. In return for this unconditional surrender to God, the believers are promised peace, security, and well-being in this world and the hereafter.

Submission to God sealed a covenant between God and His believers. Some communities forgot the message, and their prophet became their lord and master. In their minds, their lord became their tribal deity to be worshipped at an altar or in a shrine. Thus, their god became their tribal and personal savior. Priesthood took over the guardianship of their god and began to prescribe dogma and creed for the worshippers to obey. Both the gods and the devotees came to be the subject of creed and dogma crafted by rabbis, priests, and pundits of the temples, churches, and synagogues.

Communion with Allah: The twenty-first century is the time of awakening for Muslims. The last two hundred years of stupor and decadence in Islamic societies was also the time for assimilation and rejuvenation. Whereas in their decadence the Muslim rulers revealed their true colors to the believers, the believers grew in their knowledge of Allah and His commandments. In this period of adversity, believers also grew in numbers and strength not only within Islam but also within other religions. This century of enlightenment and awakening is also the century of decadence and evil. Increasing number of people, turned off by flagrant evil and falsehood of this period, turn to Allah, wishing to know Him and to receive His *nur* in their hearts. The more they seek Allah, the more things are revealed to them through the Koran and their faith.

At the time of the birth of *Nabi* Muhammad, people in general were ignorant and illiterate. Every living being connects to its source of sustenance, be it Mother Earth, the sun, and ultimately the Creator. The innate human yearning, the *fitra*, is for the thoughts of the Creator. Even though early thoughts link the child to the heavens, clouds, stars, and sun, eventually, the child turns to the thoughts of God. Despite the innate thoughts of God or *fitra*, early environment and culture decides the structure of the faith, but the innate spirituality in man persists. In the present day, the culture of hierarchy of priests and man-made dogma and creed has overpowered the instinctive spirituality of the modern humans.

Tawhid: The Koran laid the foundation of the idea of one universal God, and from this fount arose all that is known and all that will ever be known. This foundation had been laid in the first twelve years of Blessed *Nabi* Muhammad's prophecy, and it took another ten years to establish the precepts of truth, justice, covenant, equality, good, and evil. The Koran laid out these principles in clarity for all times to come.

In the sixth-century Arabia, at the time of the birth of the blessed *nabi*, the Arabian Peninsula was steeped in ignorance, superstition, spirit, and idol worship. There was no concept of one universal God. The people did not possess the know-how to grasp the concepts and precepts of knowledge of unity of Allah, the *taqwa* of Allah, and the criterion to distinguish between good and evil, *husna* and *Fahasha*. That distinction was fuzzy. In the Mediterranean world, the one God was a tribal deity of the Jews, and the God of Christians was accessible to man through the creed of Trinity, in which God had incarnated into the human Jesus, and Jesus into the divine God.

The blessed *nabi* Muhammad taught that everything in the universe originates from the one and the only reality of Allah and that man's ultimate salvation rests with the recognition of his total dependence on Him. This entails conscious submission to the will and the law of Allah. Muhammad, the *rasul* and the *nabi* of Allah, received the revelation of the word from Him. Allah commanded Muhammad to spread the word to the whole mankind. Today we believe that the universal God is the center of the belief of all the three monotheistic religions—Judaism, Christianity, and Islam. Nothing could be farther from the truth; for the Jews, God continues to be a tribal deity with His favorite children, and those who call themselves Christians, can only access God through His favorite son, Jesus. Yet God the Creator of the universe is the God of every particle and organism that was ever created. God, Allah, through the act and sustenance of His creation, is connected to each particle, every cell, and every soul. Thus, God is within reach of every bit of His creation. Islam, the surrender of one's whole self to God, is a way of life (*din*) to the straight path to Allah.

The Covenant of Allah: There is an implicit assumption in the Koran that there exists an agreement between Allah and His creation portrayed as a covenant, a mutual understanding in which Allah proposes a system of regulations for the guidance of humans. This guidance is presented in the form of commandments to be accepted and implemented by people. Allah then makes a promise of what He will do in the event that man willingly abides by these commands and regulates his life according to them. The concept of promise is clearly conditional on human obedience and submission (*islam*). The covenant of Allah symbolizes the relationship between Allah and the human; the human becomes His steward, vicegerent, or custodian on the earth through submission and obedience to His will as expressed in His commands and is able to take the advantage of Allah's promises and favors. The commandments of Allah addressed to the believers (men and women) are the fundamental principles of the covenant between Allah and man, which become obligatory to man when the fire of love for Allah is kindled in his heart and he submits to His will and becomes His servant and steward on the earth.

The covenant of Allah forms the basis of the practice of the *din*. The principles of the *din* written down, proclaimed, and stored on a shelf do not have any merit. It is only the practice of the principles that brings the *din* to life. It is the practice of the *din* that unites the believer to Allah and through Him to other believers. The believer understands his obligations to his *din*. To believe is to obey the covenant. Those who do not fulfill the covenant of Allah are not His believers. Islam, the *din*, is a divine call that stems from Allah's *wahiy* through the blessed *nabi* Muhammad. Allah's *wahiy* is the word from Him and constitutes the Koran. The blessed *nabi* Muhammad was the walking Koran when he carried Allah's word in his heart. The Koran, the word from Allah through *wahiy*, is the divine commandment. The word from Allah and the *wahiy* cannot be confused with human calls and systems. The prophets convey Allah's word. Prophets, as humans, also speak their own minds. Muhammad, the blessed *nabi* of Allah, was careful not to mix his own words with those of Allah. The blessed *nabi* said:

I am no more than a man; when I order you anything respecting religion, receive it, and when I tell you anything about the affairs of the world, and then I am nothing but a man.

No human has the prerogative to speak on behalf of Allah. Priests, imams, scholars, bishops, popes, and ayatollahs are all men like other men; some are more knowledgeable than the others. None, however, can represent Allah. They can represent their personal views on the meaning of scriptures; their opinions remain within the human domain.

A believer, a man or a woman, connects with Allah on submission, and then Allah is their hearts, and He is with them. Allah proposes a covenant, and the believer pledges on this with submission to Allah. Allah speaks to the believers in *seventy-five verses* of the Koran and, in a clear language, tells them all what is lawful and declared to be so and what is forbidden and unlawful. And Allah calls on His believers with the words *O you who Believe* and commands them to acts of faith and goodness in those seventy-five verses.

Obedience of every such command is jihad. A person is taught to obey the precepts of Allah's law in the Koran. Allah proclaims His law in the covenant to the believers in a simple, lucid language. Allah addresses the believers in the Koran and shows them the right way to follow Him. The observance of the covenant of Allah is the total belief system based on unity of one's personality in communion with Allah in total awareness and *taqwa* of Him and observance of the thirty-seven commandments of the covenant. This communion is not only with Allah but also through Him with other believers and with the rest of Allah's creation, both alive and inanimate. The phrase *amilu al saalihaat* (to do good, to perform wholesome deeds) refers to those who persist in striving to set things right, who restore harmony, peace, justice, and balance. The believer, man and woman, is then guided by

Allah and His *nabi* through the covenant to show compassion, to be merciful and forgive others, to be just, to protect the weak, to defend the oppressed, to be generous and charitable, to be truthful, to seek knowledge and wisdom, to be kind, to be peaceful, to love others, and to perform beautiful deeds.

This is Islam. In this communion between Allah and His believer, there are no priests, no imams, no scholars, nor any ulema. The believer does not need a book nor a university degree to know God. The believer does not need to know whether her folded hands should be above or below her navel or whether his pant legs should reach above or below his ankles. In the believers' communion with Allah, it does not matter if the prayers are led by a blind man or a lame woman so long as the person leading the prayer is with the *taqwa* of Allah. The believer, a man or a woman, reaches out to Allah in sincerity and bows down to Him in submission. Allah blesses him, and the believer praises Allah, who draws him closer. The believer asks for mercy, and Allah touches His devotee in love. The believer asks for forgiveness, and Allah pours His mercy on the believer. The believer loves Allah; in return, He promises the believer *Jannat.* When Allah bestows on the believer divine mercy, grace, and guidance, why will a believer burden himself with the baggage of human systems? Systems made up of laws, creed, and dogma fashioned by men?

Allah speaks to those men and women who believe in Him and guides them to the *din* of goodness, truth, unity, brotherhood, and justice. This guidance from Allah is summarized in seventy-five verses of the Koran, where Allah speaks to those who have submitted to Him and guides them to a way of life. Upon submission to the will of Allah, the believer affirms his covenant with Allah in which the believer pledges to live his life in accordance with His *din.*

Allah is the only reality, and it is through this reality that everything in the universe exists. Allah sustains and protects all that He has created. Everything that Allah has created is connected to Him through this act of creation. Allah sustains and protects His creation when those He created praise and thank Him for His beneficence. And Allah reassures His believers that He is aware of all that is hidden and all that is manifest. To Allah belongs all that is in the heavens and on the earth. Allah is the *Rahman* (the Most Gracious) and the *Rahim* (the Most Merciful). All of Allah's creatures in the heavens and the on earth praise and glorify Him with His most beautiful names. Allah is the Lord of everything that has ever existed or will ever exist. He alone is worthy of praise and worship. Joining anything in worship with Him is *shirk*, which upsets the human's relationship with Allah. Allah reminds His faithful,

> Believe in Allah, His Rasool, the Book that He has sent to His Rasool and the Scriptures that He sent to the Rasools before him. And those who deny Allah, His Angels, His Books, His Rasools, and the Day of Judgment have gone astray. Allah also says, "Verily, this is My Way leading straight, follow it, follow no other paths for they will separate you from My path".

> Verily those who pledge their allegiance unto you, (O Muhammad) pledge it unto none but Allah; the Hand of Allah is over their hands. Thereafter whosoever breaks his Covenant does so to the harm of his own soul, and whosoever fulfils his Covenant with Allah, Allah will grant him an immense Reward. (Al-Fath 48:10, Koran)

In the journey in this world, man is presented with Allah's covenant as his guide, *taqwa* of Allah as his shield against evil, and *furqan* (the criterion to distinguish between good and evil) as Allah's compass to the straight path of righteousness.

- If man accepts the path of Allah and follows Allah's covenant as his guide, *taqwa* of Allah as his shield against evil, and *furqan* as Allah's compass to the straight path, he becomes a believer and of the righteous.
- The way to righteousness is through Allah's guidance and in the covenant of Allah in the Koran. Every little bit of devotion makes the *nur* of Allah glow in the heart till the believer is connected with Allah and begins to follow His path.
- This communion between the believer and Allah becomes exclusive. Submission establishes the link between the believer and Allah. The believer asks, and Allah gives. The believer loves Allah, and Allah loves him in return. The believer asks for the straight path, and Allah shows him the way. The believer praises Allah, and Allah showers His mercy and grace upon him. The believer remembers Allah, and Allah responds to those who praise Him, thank Him, and ask Him.
- Allah's *din* is divine. Allah is *Haqq,* and all truth emanates from Him. The Koran is Allah's Word on the earth and the expression of *haqq. Haqq* is the reality and the truth; *batil* refers to something that is imaginary or false.
- When humans add dogma and creed to Allah's *din,* it is not *haqq*. In matters of *din,* what is not absolute truth is not *haqq*. What is not *haqq* is *batil* (false or fabricated). What is not truthful cannot be a witness over Allah's word and *din*.
- Therefore, all human additions to the *din* of Allah do not constitute the truth. Every human fabrication to the *din* after the completion of *wahiy* is *batil* or falsehood.

Allah is the Light of the heavens and the earth. The parable of His Light is as if there were a Niche and within it a Lamp: the Lamp enclosed in Glass; the glass as it were a brilliant star: lit from a blessed Tree, an Olive, neither of the East nor of the West, whose Oil is well-nigh luminous, though fire scarce touched it: Light upon Light! Allah doth guide whom He will to His Light: Allah doth set forth Parables for men: and Allah doth know all things. (Lit is such a light) in houses, which Allah hath permitted to be raised to honor; for the celebration,

> in them, of His name: in them is He glorified in the mornings and in the evenings, (again and again). (An-Nur 24:35–36, Koran)

Allah created His beings with love, and He nurtures His creation with love. His light illuminates the hearts of those who love Him, place their trust in Him, and submit to Him. Once their heart is open to Allah in submission, Allah's *nur* glows in the niche of the believer's heart, where the divine light, Spirit, and wisdom of Allah shines in man. The glow of the Spirit and wisdom shines with the brilliance of a star lit from divine wisdom, the tree of knowledge—the knowledge of Allah's signs. Allah is within those who believe. The believer's self, his *nafs*, is aglow with Allah's radiance—light upon light. The dwellings where Allah is praised and glorified in the mornings and in the evenings are aglow with Allah's *nur* and His knowledge.

When man is stripped of his raiment, veils of skin, flesh and bones, viscera, and circulating fluids, what is left over is nothing but his soul, his *self* (*nafs*). Removing the veils of self-admiration, self-image, and pride; wiping away covers of makeup and couture; removing masks and marks of social status; and stripping him of scars and years of greed and gluttony expose a tiny particle, the *nuqta,* that represents the self of man. This self is perhaps no greater than a little dot, the *nuqta.* The combined self of the entire human race, all the *nuqtas* combined, will perhaps not fill a small cup. Yet the ego of the human race through this minuteness of pride and arrogance has controlled the destiny of Allah's creation for thousands of years.

The *nafs,* unlike the Freudian ego, is capable of both good and evil. The *nuqta* of the *nafs* magnified a million times reveals a shiny disk, the mirror of the soul. The nature (*fitra*) of the *nafs* is to shine as a mirror with Allah's *nur.* When man walks the path of Allah in *taqwa of* Him with the knowledge that Allah is with him, watching him and guiding him, Allah's *nur* shines on the *nafs,* keeping it pure and safe.

Once the heart is open to Allah in submission, Allah's *nur* glows in the niche of the believer's heart, where the divine light, Spirit, and wisdom of Allah shine in the human. For those who believe, Allah is within. The believer's self is aglow with Allah's radiance, light upon light.

However, when the human's desires, cravings, and ego overpower his love and obedience for Allah, the shiny mirror of the *nafs* becomes obscured by the smoke of his desires, and he loses sight of the *nur* of Allah; and in this darkness, man trips into error and decadence. The effort required to keep focus on Allah's *nur* and the *taqwa* of Allah is jihad. And this jihad is the obedience of Allah's commandments when Allah calls on His believers with the words *O you who Believe* and commands them to do acts of faith and goodness in seventy-five verses of the Koran.

Obedience of every such command is jihad. The expression *in the path of Allah*, of course, is the path of right conduct that Allah has set down in the Koran. Jihad is simply the complement to *islam*, the surrender to the will of Allah. The surrender takes place in Allah's will, and it is Allah's will that people should struggle in His path. Hence, submission and surrender to Allah's will demands struggle in His path. Submission to Allah's command requires the believers to struggle against all negative tendencies in their self. Salat, zakat, fasting, and hajj are all struggles in the path of Allah. The greatest obstacles that people face in submitting themselves to Allah are their desires and cravings for the temptations of this world.

It is the *nafs* that directs intentions and actions of man to the good and the bad. *Nafs* is the seat of the qualities of self-admiration, arrogance, pride, hardheartedness, suppression of Allah's love, pointing to faults of others, lying, gossiping, cheating, backbiting, envy, jealousy, criticism of others, self-praise, bitterness, covetousness of the belongings of others even when one possesses what is better, lack of contentment, constant complaining, lack of gratitude, blindness to one's blessings, wishing for increase without effort, selfishness, greed and covetousness that knows no bounds, love of control, love of self and its desires, hatred for those who criticize even if it is for one's own good, love for those who praise even if it is in hypocrisy, rejection of advice and counsel, and the habit of talking about oneself. The same *nafs*, on the other hand, has a good side. When the human heart is open to Allah's *nur,* man becomes aware of Allah's presence with him, and all his actions become governed by the *taqwa* of Allah. The human becomes a believer, and all his intentions and actions are guided by Allah's presence in him.

Islam is a relationship between Allah and His believers. The *din* of Allah is an all-encompassing and highly personal type of relationship in which Allah's *nur* or light resides in the believer's heart. The believer is conscious of Allah's closeness and mercy. The believer obeys trusts and loves Allah, and Allah in return loves those who love Him and perform beautiful deeds.

Allah has granted knowledge and the wisdom of *furqan* and *taqwa* to the believers who have opened their hearts and minds to Him. Man has been granted the freedom of choice in doing what is wholesome and beautiful or what is corrupt or ugly. This knowledge reminds the human of the scales of Allah's justice; the two hands of Allah, His mercy and His wrath, are reflected in the human domain, where people have been appointed Allah's vicegerents. Deeds of goodness and wholesomeness are associated with Allah's mercy, paradise, and what is beautiful. Evil and corruption is rewarded with Allah's wrath, hell, and what is ugly. In the *nafs*, the *taqwa* of Allah drives away man's cravings for wealth, his inclination toward disobedience of Allah's commandments, and the unwholesome qualities of arrogance, pride, lying, gossiping, cheating, backbiting, envy, jealousy, self-praise, bitterness, covetousness of the belongings of others, ingratitude, blindness to one's blessings, selfishness, greed, covetousness, love of control, and love of self.

Obedience to the commandments of the covenant of Allah brings the believer closer to Him. By establishing regular salat, giving zakat, fasting, and traveling for the pilgrimage to the Kaaba, the believer holds on to Allah. Through this relationship with Allah, he becomes conscious of Allah's closeness and knows with certainty that Allah is aware of his intentions and actions. The believer is conscious that Allah is his *Mawla* or Protector. The believer is in *taqwa* of Allah.

- Verily, this is My Way leading straight: follow it: follow not (other) paths for they will separate you from His path. This He commands you that you may remember. (Al-An'am 6:151–53, Koran)
- Join not anything in worship with Him. (Al-An'am 6:151–53, Koran)
- Believe in Allah, His Rasool, and the Book that He has sent to His Rasool and the Scriptures that He sent to those before him. Any who deny Allah, His angels, His Books, His Rasools, and the Day of Judgment has gone astray. (An-Nisa 4:136, Koran)
- Celebrate the Praises of Allah often and Glorify Him in the morning and at night. It is Allah and His Angels Who send their blessings upon you, that He may lead you out of the depths of darkness into light. Allah is full of mercy to the believers! On the Day they meet Him with the salutation: Salaam, He has prepared for them a generous Reward. (Al-Ahzab 33:41–48, Koran)

The Second Commandment of Allah

Believe in Allah and in His *Rasool*

- Nabi, We have sent thee as a witness, a bearer of glad tidings, as a Warner and as one who invites to Allah's Grace by His leave and as an inspiration and beacon of light.
- Nabi, We have sent thee as a witness, a bearer of glad tidings, as a Warner and as one who invites to Allah's Grace by His leave and as an inspiration and beacon of light. Give glad tidings to the believers that they shall have from Allah bounty in abundance. Moreover, obey not the command of the unbelievers (kafireen) and the hypocrites (munafiqeen), heed not their annoyances, and put your trust in Allah, for enough is Allah as Disposer of affairs. (Al-Ahzab 33:41–48, Koran)
- Believe in Allah, His Rasool, and the Book that He has sent to His Rasool and the Scriptures that He sent to those before him. Any who deny Allah, His angels, His Books, His Rasools, and the Day of Judgment has gone astray. (An-Nisa 4:136, Koran)

Allah in His mercy, grace, and love for His creation has from the beginning of time communicated with humans and taught them all that they know about His workings, His universe, and His creation. Humans have always been resistant to accepting Allah's guidance regarding worship of Him and their relationship with other humans in matters of truth, justice, peace, equality, and sharing of their resources. Man's ego, selfishness, and greed always come in the way of his salvation. Allah inspired truthful men (prophets) with *taqwa* of Allah, humility, spiritual purity, and knowledge to convey His teaching and commandments to man so that he may continue to exist in the world during his short life in submission to Allah and in love, peace, and harmony with his fellow humans. To follow Allah's wisdom, man has to first submit himself unquestioningly to the mercy and will of Allah with the knowledge that, on an appointed day, he will meet his Maker to be questioned and judged on his conduct during his life on the earth.

> Those who have faith and do wholesome deeds, them we shall admit to gardens through which rivers flow. (An-Nisa 4:57, 122, Koran)

Allah will measure out the good and the evil, the wholesome and the corrupt deeds that humans carried out in their lifetime. Humans have enough freedom to make their own choices. If they make the choice to do beautiful and wholesome deeds (*saalihaat*) motivated by faith (*iman*) and God-wariness (*taqwa*), they please Allah and bring harmony and wholesomeness to the world, resulting in peace, justice, mercy, compassion, honor, equity, well-being, freedom, and many other gifts through Allah's grace. While others choose to do evil and corruption (*mufsidun*), destroying the right relationship among the creation, causing hunger, disease, oppression, pollution, and other afflictions. In the universal order, corruption is the prerogative of humans, and vicegerency gives them the freedom to work against the Creator and His creation. When humans choose wrong and corrupt actions, they displease Allah. Allah loves those who do what is beautiful, not those who do what is ugly:

> When he turns his back, he hurries about the earth to work corruption there and destroy the tillage and the stock. Allah loves not corruption. (Al-Baqarah 2:205, Koran)

> Obey Allah and His Rasool and turn not to others when you should hear him speak. For the worst of creatures in the sight of Allah are those who neither listen, nor look or try to comprehend. (Al-Anfal 8:20, Koran)

And how would ye deny Faith while unto you are rehearsed the Signs of Allah, and among you lives the Messenger? Whoever holds firmly to Allah will be shown a Way that is straight. (Ali 'Imran 3:101, Koran)

The Third Commandment of Allah

Fulfill the Covenant of Allah

- And fulfill the Covenant of Allah. Thus, He commands you that you may remember. (Al-An'am 6:151–53, Koran)
- Believers! Fulfill your Covenants. (Al-Ma'idah 5:1, Koran)
- Verily those who pledge their allegiance unto you (O Muhammad), pledge it unto none but Allah; the Hand of Allah is over their hands. Thereafter whosoever breaks his Covenant, does so to the harm of his own soul, and whosoever fulfils his Covenant with Allah, Allah will grant him an immense Reward. (Al-Fath 48:10, Koran)

  Those who break Allah's Covenant after it is ratified, and who sunder what Allah has ordered to be joined and do mischief on earth: these cause losses (only) to themselves. (Al-Baqarah 2:27, Koran)

  Those who fulfill the Covenant of Allah and fail not in their pledged word; Those who join together those things which Allah hath commanded to be joined, hold their Lord in awe, and fear the terrible reckoning. (Ar-Ra'd 13:20-21, Koran)

Islam is a way of life in the straight path to Allah. There is an implicit assumption in the Koran that there exists an agreement between Allah and His creation portrayed as a mutual understanding in which Allah proposes a system of regulations for the guidance of the humans. This guidance is presented in the form of commandments to be accepted and implemented by people. Allah then makes promise of what He will do in the event that man willingly abides by these commands and regulates his life in accordance with them. The concept of promise is clearly conditional on the human's obedience. The covenant of the Koran symbolizes the relationship between Allah and man; man becomes His steward, vicegerent, or custodian on the earth through submission and obedience to His will (*islam*) as expressed in His commands and is able to take the advantage of Allah's promises and favors.

The concept of covenant also symbolizes the relationship between humans and among Allah's creatures and the rest of His creation. They all share in one God, one set of guidance and commandments, the same submission and obedience to Him, and the same set of expectations in accordance with His promises. They all can, therefore, trust one another since they all have similar obligations and expectations. In view of the Koran, humans, communities, nations, and civilizations will continue to live in harmony and peace so long as they continue to fulfill Allah's covenant.

Economics plays a significant role in the social structure of Islam, so significant that Allah has not let the economic aspect of life to be solely determined by human intellect, experience, caprice, and lust. Allah has made it subject to revelation. Thus, Muslims prosper when they follow Allah's laws but subject themselves to scarcity when they turn to human systems. The Koran promises peace and plenty for those who obey their covenant with Him, and for those who turn away from Allah's covenant, the Koran portends a life of need, scarcity, and want.

> But whosoever turns away from My Message, verily
> for him is a life narrowed down, and We shall raise
> him up blind on the Day of Judgment.

> And thus, do We recompense him who transgresses beyond bounds and believes not in the Signs of his Lord: and the Penalty of the Hereafter is far more grievous and more enduring.
>
> It is not a warning to such men (to call to mind) how many generations before them We destroyed, in whose haunts they (now) move? Verily, in this are Signs for men endued with understanding. (Taha 20:124, 127–28, Koran)

In the above *ayah* of the Koran, the word *ma'eeshat* comes from the word *ma'ashiyyat,* which is the recognized meaning of the word "economics." The consequences of rejection of Allah's covenant and guidance are clearly portrayed. A life narrowed down or constricted is a miserable one, one of need, scarcity, unhappiness, poverty, hunger, disease, pestilence, and famine all at the same time or separately.

The Koran's covenant does not put off the realization of the fruits of obeying or ignoring Allah's guidance until after death, nor does it hide it in spiritual abstractness. Observance of the covenant makes life on the earth economically, physically, and spiritually rich and happy. Nonobservance of the covenant makes life on the earth economically miserable and physically and spiritually depressing. In fact, the economic, physical, and spiritual condition of a people provides a pragmatic test of the soundness of the revealed guidance.

Furthermore, the Koran declares that the people who transgress Allah's guidance and are economically deprived in this world will also be worse off in the hereafter.

> Verily for him is a life narrowed down, and We shall raise him up blind on the Day of Judgment.

According to the Koran, the economics and the observance of the moral code of Allah's covenant goes hand in hand, and they cannot be separated from each other.

He has created the heavens and the earth for just ends far
is He above having the partners they ascribe to Him!

He has created man from a sperm-drop; and behold
this same (man) becomes an open disputer!

And cattle He has created for you (men): from them you derive
warmth, and numerous benefits, and of their (meat) you eat.

And you have a sense of pride and beauty in them
as you drive them home in the evening, and as you
lead them forth to pasture in the morning.

And they carry your heavy loads to lands that you could
not (otherwise) reach except with souls distressed: for
your Lord is indeed Most Kind, Most Merciful.

And (He has created) horses, mules, and donkeys,
for you to ride and use for show; and He has created
(other) things of which you have no knowledge.

And unto Allah leads straight the Way, but there are ways that
turn aside: if Allah had willed, He could have guided all of you.

It is He Who sends down rain from the sky. From it you drink, and
out of it (grows) the vegetation on which you feed your cattle.

With it He produces for you corn, olives, date palms, grapes, and every kind of fruit: verily in this is a Sign for those who give thought.

He has made subject to you the Night and the Day; the Sun and the Moon; and the Stars are in subjection by His Command: verily in this are Signs for men who are wise.

And the things on this earth which He has multiplied in varying colors (and qualities): verily in this a Sign for men who celebrate the praises of Allah (in gratitude).

It is He Who has made the sea subject, that you may eat thereof flesh that is fresh and tender, and that you may extract there from ornaments to wear, and You see the ships therein that plough the waves, that you may seek (thus) of the bounty of Allah and that you may be grateful.

And He has set up on the earth mountains standing firm, lest it should shake with you; and rivers and roads; that you may guide yourselves.

And marks and signposts; and by the stars (Men) guide themselves.

Is then He Who creates like one that creates not? Will you not receive admonition?

If you would count up the favors of Allah, never would you be able to number them; for Allah is Oft-Forgiving, Most Merciful. (An-Nahl 16:3–18, Koran)

Sama in the Koran signifies the universe, and *ardh* is man's domain on the earth pertaining to his social and economic world. Allah is the Lord of the heavens and the earth and all that comes forth from them.

The divine laws under which the universe functions so meticulously and smoothly should also apply to the economic life of man so that he might achieve a balanced, predictable, equitable, and just financial life. *Sama* is the source of Allah's benevolence to mankind and of His universal laws that govern human subsistence and sustenance on the earth (*ardh*), controlling man's economic life in this world. Allah's kingdom over the heavens and the earth sustains man's economic life and directly affects man's conduct and his obedience to Allah's covenant.

The Fourth Commandment of Allah

Be in *Taqwa* of Allah

The word *taqwa* means "to be dutiful to Allah, to be wary of Allah, to be conscious of Allah, to be pious toward Allah, and to fear Allah." A person with *taqwa* always has Allah in mind with every action and word spoken, "as if Allah sees you and you see Him."

> Be in taqwa of Allah and fear Allah and let every soul judge as to the provision he has sent forth for the morrow. Yes, be in taqwa of Allah and fear Allah: for Allah is well acquainted with all that you do. (Al-Hashr 59:18–24, Koran)

> So be in taqwa of Allah and fear Allah as much as you can; listen and obey; and spend in charity for the benefit of your own souls. And those saved from their own greed are the ones that prosper. If you loan to Allah a beautiful loan, He will double it for you, and He will forgive you: for Allah is both Appreciative (Shakoor) and Magnanimous (Haleem), Knower of what is hidden and what is manifest, Exalted in Might, Full of Wisdom. (At-Taghabun 64:14–18, Koran)

Humankind! We created you from a single pair of a male and a female, and made you into nations and tribes, that you may know each other. Verily the most honored of you in the sight of Allah is the one with taqwa of Allah, the most righteous of you. And Allah is All Knowing, All-Aware. (Al-Hadid 57:28-29, Koran)

Be in taqwa of Allah, Fear Allah, and believe in His Rasool, and He will bestow on you the double portion of His Mercy: He will provide for you a Light by which you shall walk straight in your path, and He will forgive you; for Allah is Most Forgiving, Most Merciful. That the People of the Book may know that they have no power whatever over the Grace of Allah, that His Grace is entirely in His Hand, to bestow on whomsoever He wills. For Allah is the Lord of Grace abounding. (Al-Hadid 57:28–29, Koran)

Be in Taqwa of Allah and be with those who are true in word and deed. (At-Tawbah 9:11, Koran)

Be not presumptuous and impudent before Allah and His Rasool; Be in taqwa of Allah, fear Allah: for Allah is He Who hears and knows all things. (Al-Hujurat 49:2, Koran)

The believer protects himself by always keeping Allah in view with every action and thought, ensuring that his every action is in accord with Allah's way. Perform every act and utter every word as if you see Allah, and if you do not see Him, be aware that Allah not only sees your deeds but also knows your thoughts. To ensure that one is dutiful to Allah, conscious of His presence, and God fearing, the believer recites with every action:

In the name of Allah, Most Gracious, Most Merciful.

There is a distinction between two types of divine mercy. In the broader sense, mercy refers to Allah's gentleness and kindness to all His creation, for He brings into existence, nurtures, and protects it to its destination. In a narrower sense, Allah's mercy refers to closeness to Allah that is given to those with *taqwa* in contrast to the chastisement inflicted on those who have chosen to stay distant from Him. Their distance from Allah in itself is chastisement because to be distant from the wholeness and harmony of the Real (Truth) is to be overcome by the turmoil and chaos of the unreal (falsehood). Allah's mercy is achieved by *taqwa* of Allah, which itself demands both submission *(islam)* and faith *(iman)*.

> My Chastisement I mete out to whomsoever I will; but My Mercy extends to all things. That Mercy I shall ordain for those who are muttaqun, those who have taqwa and practice regular charity, and those who believe in Our Signs.
>
> Those who follow the Rasool, the Nabi of the unlettered, about whom they find mentioned in the Taurat (Torah) and the Injeel (Gospel). He bids them what is just and forbids them what is evil; he allows them as lawful what is good and pure and prohibits them from what is bad and impure; he relieves them of their heavy burdens and from the fetters that are on them. So, it is those who believe in him, honor him, help him, and follow the Light which is sent down with him, it is they who will prosper. (Al-A'raf 7:156–57, Koran)

The Fifth Commandment of Allah

Verily, I Am Allah. There Is No God but I, so Worship Me

Establish regular Salaat, give regular charity, and hold fast to Allah. He is your Mawla, Protector, the best of Protectors and the best Helper. (Al-Hajj 22:77–78, Koran)

Those who do wholesome deeds, establish regular prayers and regular charity have rewards with their Lord. On them shall be no fear, nor shall they grieve. (Al-Baqarah 2:280, Koran)

Seek help with patience, perseverance and prayer. Allah is with those who patiently persevere. (Al-Baqarah 2:153, Koran)

When you arise for salaat, purify yourself by washing your faces, your hands to the elbows, wipe your heads and wash your feet to the ankles. If you are unclean purify yourself. Allah does not wish that you should be burdened, but to make you clean, and to bestow His blessings on you, that you may be grateful. (Al-Ma'idah 5:6, Koran)

Approach not prayers with a mind befogged until you understand all that you utter, nor come up to prayers in a state of uncleanliness, till you have bathed. (An-Nisa 4:43, Koran)

Bow down, prostrate yourself and serve your Lord, and do wholesome deeds that you may prosper. Perform Jihad; strive to your utmost in Allah's cause as striving (jihad) is His due. He has chosen you and Allah has imposed no hardship in your endeavor to His cause. You are the inheritors of the faith of your father Abraham. He has named you Muslims of the times before and now, so that Allah's Rasool may be an example to you and that you are an example to humankind. (Al-Hajj 22:77–78, Koran)

When the call is proclaimed to prayer on Friday, the day of assembly, hasten earnestly to the Remembrance of Allah, and leave off business and everything else: that is best for you if you but knew! And when the Prayer is finished, then may you disperse through the land, and seek of the Grace of Allah: remember and praise Allah a great deal: that you may prosper. (Al-Jumu'ah 62:9–10, Koran)

The Koran, Allah's word, is the fundamental source of the believers' spiritual well-being. Recitation of the Koran imparts peace, tranquility, and closeness to Allah and also renews the believers' vows to obey Allah's covenant. All believers memorize some parts of the Koran, particularly Sura Al-Fatihah, and certain other verses to recite the salat. The salat is the daily renewal of the Koran in the believer, a daily rejuvenation of his or her covenant with Allah and communion with Him.

The *nabi* said, "Iman is knowledge in the heart, a voicing with the tongue, and activity with the limbs." The term *heart*, often used in the Koran, refers to a specific faculty or a spiritual organ that provides humans with intellect and rationality. Therefore, *iman* means confidence in the reality and truth of things and commitment to act on the basis of the truth that they know. Thus, *iman* involves knowledge and words and actions on the basis of that knowledge. The Koran is Allah's speech to the believers, and it is the foundation of everything Islamic. Thus, humans connect with Allah by speaking to Him. The believer speaks to Allah through daily salat and supplication (*du'a*). The words are accompanied by action of the body and limbs, symbolizing subservience, respect, and humility. The salat consists of cyclic movements of standing in humility in the presence of Allah, bowing down to Him, going down in prostration in the Lord's presence, sitting in humility, reciting verses from the Koran, and praising Allah. Recitation of the Koran serves to embody the Koran within the person reciting salat. Allah is the light, and His word, the Koran, is His luminosity. To embody the Koran through faith and practice is to become transformed by this divine light that permeates through the believer in his closeness to Allah. Such proximity to Allah's presence gives the worshipper a "luminous presence."

The Sixth Commandment of Allah

Fasting during Ramadan

Fasting is prescribed to you, in the month of Ramadan as it was prescribed to those before you, that you may practice self-restraint. The Qur'an was revealed in the month of Ramadan, guidance to humankind for judgment between right and wrong. For everyone except those ill or on a journey, this month should spend it in fasting. Allah intends to make it easy on you so that you may complete the prescribed period of fasting and to glorify Him to express your gratitude for His Guidance. (Al-Baqarah 2:178–79, Koran)

The month of fasting, Ramadan, is a month of self-reflection, self-discipline, prayer, and remembrance of Allah. This is a month of renewal of a believer's commitment to Allah's covenant and a vow to follow His guidance. During this month, there is heightened attention to the rules of right conduct, which helps the believer in his commitment to follow Allah's straight path during the following year. This month is a reminder to the believers of their obligation to Allah's creatures in need of sustenance, shelter, protection, peace, and other help.

The Seventh Commandment of Allah

Spend out of Bounties of Allah in Charity and Wholesome Deeds: Zakat

The parable of those who spend their substance in the way of Allah is that of a grain of corn: it grows seven ears, and each ear has a hundred grains. Allah gives plentiful return to whom He pleases, Allah cares for all, and He knows all things. Those who give generously in the cause of Allah and follow not up their gifts with reminders of their generosity or with injury, for them their reward is with their Lord; on them shall be no fear, nor shall they grieve. Kind words and the covering of faults are better than charity followed by injury. Allah is Free of all wants and He is Most Merciful. (Al-Baqarah 2:261–63, Koran)

Let not those among you who are blessed with grace and ample means hold back from helping their relatives, the poor, and those who have left their homes in Allah's cause. Let them forgive and overlook, do you not wish that Allah should forgive you? And Allah is Oft Forgiving, Most Merciful. (An-Nur 24:21–23, Koran)

Spend out of bounties of Allah in charity and wholesome deeds before the Day comes when there will be neither bargaining, friendship nor intercession. Those who reject faith are the wrongdoers. (Al-Baqarah 2:254–57, Koran).

Void not your charity by boast, conceit, and insult, by reminders of your generosity like those who want their generosity to be noted by all men, but they believe neither in Allah nor in the Last Day. Theirs is a parable of a hard barren rock, on which there is a little soil, washed by heavy rain, which leaves it just a bare stone.

And Allah guides not those who reject Faith. And the likeness of those who give generously, seeking to please Allah and to strengthen their souls, is as a garden, high and fertile where heavy rain falls on it and makes it yield a double the amount of harvest, and if it receives not heavy rain, light moisture suffices it. Allah notices whatever you do. (Al-Baqarah 2:264–65, Koran)

Alms are for the poor and the needy, and those employed to administer the funds; for those, whose hearts have been recently reconciled to the truth; for those in bondage and in debt; in the cause of Allah; and for the wayfarer: thus, is it ordained by Allah, and Allah is full of knowledge and wisdom. (At-Tawbah 9:60, Koran)

In the above verses, the clear indication is that a human is given bounty by Allah. In return, his obligation is to distribute the surplus after his needs have been met to the needy. The Koran specifies that the zakat be distributed to the *fuqara* (the poor who ask), to *al-masakin* (the poor and the needy who do not ask), to zakat administrators, to those who spread the light of Islam to those inclined, for freedom of those in bondage, to those in debt, for the cause of Allah, and for the wayfarer who treads the path for Allah's service.

In the covenant, the believer surrenders to Allah his life and belongings in return for His guidance, a place in paradise in the hereafter, and peace with prosperity in this world. Every believer according to his or her covenant with Allah has the obligation to extend the benefits that He has provided him or her to those who did not receive the same. Such acts of generosity will be rewarded by Allah with a place in *Jannat* (place of peace and plenty) in the afterlife. Life of *Jannat* is to be attained in this world also, provided the compact with Allah is adhered to. The believer is Allah's instrument in fulfilling His promise to Adam that, among his progeny, "*none will remain without food or clothes and none will suffer from heat or thirst*" (Taha 20:118, Koran).

In the verses below, Allah has promised those who believe and obey His covenant a reward for their acts of charity. He will double the harvest of their labors, forgive their sins, and provide them with His bounties, and they shall not grieve. Fear and grief arise from misfortunes, which cause anxiety, depression, and panic. Allah promises to safeguard the believers from misfortunes. And to those who devour usury, Allah will deprive all blessings. Obedience of Allah's covenant provides *Jannat* in the hereafter and a life of *Jannat*, peace, and plenty in this world. It also brings balance, harmony, and stability to the economic life of the world in that it meets the necessities of each person and eliminates unnecessary suffering.

O you who believe! Give of the good things that you have honorably earned, and of the fruits of the earth that We have produced for you, and do not even aim at giving anything which is bad, that you would not receive yourself except with closed eyes. And know that Allah is free of all wants, and worthy of all praise.

The Satan threatens you with poverty and bids you to unseemly actions. Allah promises you His forgiveness and bounties. And Allah cares for all and He knows all things.

He grants wisdom to whom He pleases; and those who are granted wisdom receive indeed a magnificent benefit, but none will grasp the Message but men of knowledge and understanding.

And whatever you spend in charity or devotion, be sure Allah knows it all. But the wrongdoers have no helpers. (Al-Baqarah 2:267–70, Koran)

The covenant of Allah has laid down principles and guidelines for the well-being of the economic life of the believers. Obedience of these principles will bring peace, harmony, spiritual enlightenment, and economic prosperity. Disobedience means misery, ruin, and Allah's wrath.

Land and sources of production do not become the personal property of individuals. *Ardh* is the source of life and means of sustenance and production of food and resources and therefore must remain available to the community, the *ummah.* Every Muslim, man and woman, who at the end of the year is in possession of about fifteen dollars or more in cash or articles of trade must give zakat at the minimum rate of 2.5 percent. Zakat is incumbent on all liquid, visible, movable, and immovable properties belonging to Muslims. Two and a half percent of all the liquid assets of a Muslim adult after deduction of reasonable amount of expenses for the maintenance of the person's family and other dependents is not an excessive amount of money. Allah constantly reminds the believers to practice regular charity. Giving to the needy with love and respect out of love of Allah is a profound act of spiritual cleaning. The more one gives in wealth and in kindness, the higher is his status with Allah.

In the united Muslim lands of the Dar es Salaam, if every adult man and woman gives minimum of *$15* in zakat, the total collected will amount to *$12 billion.* If every one of one thousand billionaires and one million millionaires in the Islamic world contributes a minimum of 2.5 percent of their liquid wealth in the way of Allah, the total collected will be in the tune of another *$50 billion.* If we approach another ten million prosperous businesspeople with liquid assets of five hundred thousand dollars to pay their minimum zakat, the sum collected from them will amount to another *$125 billion.* The total sum thus collected amounts *$187 billion.* Now we say to the same population that, in the twenty–first century, 2.5 percent is not really enough to feed and house a large population and ask for 5 percent of their liquid assets. The total collected will amount to *$379 billion*. Ten percent zakat on the same wealth will bring in *$758 billion annually*. Half this sum may then be used to feed, clothe, house, and educate the poor and needy population and the remaining half to create industries and jobs and job training for the people who have not been able to exit the cycle of poverty.

There is an estimated forty-five thousand tons of accumulated gold hoardings in the Islamic countries in the form of jewelry, gold bricks, gold bars, gold artifacts, and national treasures in museums with an estimated value of *$548 billion*. In addition, there is a hoard of precious stones worth another $100 billion. The zakat levy on the bullion and the precious stones will amount to another *$13 billion*. Even though the Islamic states have been milked dry by our elite and their colonial cohorts, the *ummah* acting in accordance with Allah's covenant shall be able to eradicate all poverty and destitution within the Dar es Salaam within *three years* with resources from within the community of believers amounting to *$3.95 trillion* without ever touching any of the government revenues.

Were the precepts of the covenant of Allah applied to the rest of humanity, all poverty, deprivation, and disease will disappear from the world in one year. Fewer than 10 percent of the world's people population own 80 percent of the world's wealth. This disparity has been caused by unbridled feudalism and capitalism in man's history. The total wealth of the world is estimated to be $300 trillion.

If every human gives away 2.5 to 5.0 percent of their surplus income in zakat to eradicate poverty, disease, and hunger in the global village, *$7.5 to $15.0 trillion* will become available, half of which might be used to eradicate hunger, illiteracy, unemployment, and disease annually and the remaining to build the world's infrastructure for environmentally sustainable agriculture and industrial production to sustain mankind. In no time, the world will be a stable place, with no wars, famines, epidemics, ignorance, and hunger.

The Eighth Commandment of Allah

Proclaim the Pilgrimage to Mankind: Hajj

And proclaim the Pilgrimage to mankind; they will come to thee on foot and mounted on every kind of camel, lean on account of journeys through deep and distant mountain highways; that they may witness the benefits provided for them, and celebrate the name of Allah, through the Days Appointed, over the cattle which He has provided for them for sacrifice: then eat you thereof and feed the distressed ones in want. Then let them complete the rites prescribed for them, perform their vows, and again circumambulate the Ancient House. Such is the Pilgrimage: whoever honors the sacred rites of Allah, for him it is good in the sight of his Lord. Lawful to you for food in Pilgrimage are cattle, except those mentioned to you as exceptions: but shun the abomination of idols and shun the word that is false. (Al-Hajj 22:27-30, Koran)

Violate not the sanctity of the Symbols of Allah, or of the sacred month, or of the animals brought for sacrifice, nor the garlands that mark out such animals, nor the people coming to the Sacred House, seeking the bounty and good pleasure of their Lord. Help one another in virtue and piety but help not one another in sin and acrimony. Be in taqwa of Allah, fear Allah, for Allah is swift in reckoning. (Al-Ma'idah 5:2, Koran)

For thirteen hundred years, Muslims have traveled to Mecca on foot, on horse, and on camelback, taking more than a year to complete the rituals of the hajj. This slow pace helps the believer in his spiritual and worldly quest to get acquainted with Muslims of other lands that have kept the *ummah* united. The hajj since then has been seen as a grand rite of passage from the life of this world to a communion with Allah in a grand festival of worship in devotion to Him. Hajjis have been treated as models of piety and blessedness.

In today's world, air travel has made hajj accessible to a large population, bringing the Muslim people closer into a well-knit community of one *ummah*. Increasing number of children and youth perform hajj rituals at the house of Allah and return to their communities inspired with a commitment of love and brotherhood for their fellow believers. The resurgence of such a sense of communion of the believers with Allah and with one another is the key to the unity and renewal of Islam.

The Ninth Commandment of Allah

Speak Always the Truth

O you who believe! Have taqwa of Allah, fear Allah, and always speak the truth, that He may direct you to deeds of righteousness and forgive your sins: he that obeys Allah and His Rasool, has already attained the highest achievement.

We did indeed offer al-Amanah, the Trust to the Heavens and the Earth and the Mountains; but they shrank from the burden, being afraid of it, but man assumed it, and has proved to be a tyrant and a fool, with the result that Allah has to punish the munafiqeen, truth concealers, men and women, and the mushrikeen, unbelievers, men and women, and Allah turns in Mercy to the Believers, men and women; for Allah is Forgiving, Most Merciful. (Al-Ahzab 33:69–73, Koran)

The very basis of Islam is truth or *haqq*. Every believer must always speak the truth. Allah guides the truthful to His path of righteousness. Without the truth, there is no *din* and no Islam. Allah's *din* is divine.

Allah is *Haqq*, and all truth emanates from Him. The Koran is Allah's word on the earth and the expression of *haqq*.

Haqq is the reality and the truth; *batil* refers to something that is imaginary and false. Those who believe in Allah only speak the truth. When humans add dogma and creed to Allah's *din*, it is not *haqq*. In matters of *din*, what is not absolute truth is not *haqq*. What is not *haqq* is *batil* (false or fabricated). What is not truthful cannot be a witness over Allah's word and *din*. Therefore, all human additions to the *din* of Allah do not constitute the truth, and every human fabrication to the *din* after the completion of *wahiy* is *batil* or falsehood. The truth in the believer connects to Allah through *haqq*, the essence of Allah.

In the same vein, it is falsehood that destroys the relationship between man and his Lord, and the same untruth destroys the relationship among humans. Without truth, there is no *din* and no Islam. And devoid of truth, the world of humans is barren, superficial, and false. Without truth, the Dar es Salaam cannot exist. All human transactions—whether personal, communal, national, or international—must always be based on the foundation of *haqq*.

The statecraft, diplomacy, and international relations of kings, sultans, and autocrats of the so-called democracies have, from the beginning of time, been based on deception and mendacity. It is through secrecy, falsehood, and systematic deceit and propaganda that the modern nation-states exist and control their populations. Modern democracy, in effect, grants custody of nation-states to politicians whose sophistication belies their art of deception. The economy of modern nation-states is founded on falsehood of usury and fake paper money.

Justice means fairness, fairness means truth or *haqq*, and *haqq* means the reality through Allah. Those who expect absolute truth from the adversarial system of the modern nation-state will not hear the truth. There will be peace, justice, and truth among the nations only when the people will make their rulers accountable to the truth in a public square and humiliate those who cheat and lie. In the Islamic state, truth will triumph over falsehood. The core of human values of the Dar es Salaam lies in truth and justice.

To live up to the trust of Allah, the vicegerency of man has to distinguish between good and evil, truth and falsehood, *'adl* and *zulm*. Falsehood is the abomination that corrupts the very basis of Allah's vicegerency and His covenant with man. The Koran discredits workers of corruption, the worst among them being the *Munafiqeen* (truth concealers), the hypocrites who claim to do good deeds but whose intentions are vile and harmful to others. Good deeds are based on truth and are therefore motivated by *iman* and *taqwa* of Allah. Corruption, dishonesty, and falsehood arise when humans—Allah's vicegerents on the earth—turn away from the covenant of Allah and forget the message of the prophets:

> But those who break the Covenant of Allah, after having pledged their word on it, and sever what which Allah has commanded to be joined together, and who work corruption on earth, on them shall be the curse and theirs is the ugly abode. (Ar-Ra'd 13:25, Koran)

The Tenth Commandment of Allah

Fahasha: Come Not near Shameful Deeds, Whether in Open or Secret

Allah calls the believers not to follow in the footsteps of Satan. Satan leads them to shame (*Fahasha*) and wrong (*Munkar*). Allah commands the believers not to approach shameful deeds in open or in secret. Whoever rejects evil and believes in Allah has His handhold that never breaks. Allah expels all evil from those who abstain from the odious and the forbidden, and He will admit them though the gate of great honor. Allah will grant those with *taqwa* of Allah the criterion and ability to judge between right and wrong, *furqan*. He will save them from them misfortunes and evil and forgive their sins.

Man has been granted the freedom to choose from the wholesome and beautiful or from what is corrupt and ugly. The core of the human—the *nafs*, the shiny mirror of the self—is tarnished by the dirt and the smoke of evil and the corrupt. The *taqwa* of Allah and the *nur* of Allah in man's heart blows away the dirt and smoke of evil and the ugly from the mirror of the human, *nafs*. Allah promises those who perform good, reject evil, and believe in Allah His handhold that will never loosen.

An *ummah* of one and a half billion believers in communion with Allah, surrounded with His *nur*, is the powerful force of good that will subdue all evil and the ugly from the face of the earth. A believer's life and soul is akin to a dew pond of crystal-clear spring from which a fountain gushes forth pure and refreshing. In the same manner, the cascades of beautiful deeds of the believer quench the thirst of the community of believers. Acts of indecency and shame, fornication, deceit, oppression, theft, and murder contaminate the dew pond with water so foul that the believer and his community fall prey to plague, pestilence, and diseases of the body and spirit. And they all lose the grace of Allah.

Rulers of Muslim states indulge in shameful deeds *Fahasha*, follow Satan's footsteps, and have lost the *taqwa* of Allah and the *furqan*, the criterion to distinguish right from wrong. Through the corrupt rulers, Satan spins his web, he schemes, and he triumphs. The Muslim nation-states are the dens of inequity, ignorance, illiteracy, oppression, falsehood, injustice, corruption, and they are deeply indebted to usurious, satanic economic systems. Believers in the Muslim countries are taken into custody, tortured, and imprisoned in their struggle for justice as commanded by the covenant of Allah. Some simply disappear, while others are killed in extrajudicial executions. Such brutality maintains the incumbent royals and dictators in power. Those whose actions betray the covenant of Allah displease Him, and they walk in arrogance in the path of the devil, who leads them to a cycle of shame and iniquity.

Enter into submission to the will of Allah, enter Islam wholeheartedly and follow not the footsteps of Satan, for he is a sworn enemy to you! (Al-Baqarah 2:208, Koran)

Do not follow Satan's footsteps: if any will follow the footsteps of Satan, he will command to what is shameful, Fahasha and wrong, Munkar: and were it not for the Grace of Allah and His mercy on you, not one of you would have been unblemished: but Allah does purify whom He pleases: and Allah is all Hearer and all Knower. (An-Nur 24:21–23, Koran)

Come not near to shameful deeds (fornication, adultery, and shameful activities) whether open or secret. Al-An'am 6: 151–53)

The Eleventh Commandment of Allah

And Be Not Divided among Yourselves

And hold fast, all together, by the Rope, which Allah stretches out for you, and be not divided among yourselves; and remember with gratitude Allah's favor on you; you were enemies, and He joined your hearts in love, so that by His Grace, you became brethren and a community. You were on the brink of the pit of fire, and He saved you from it. Thus, does Allah make His Signs clear to you that you may be guided.

Let there arise out of you a band of people inviting to all that is good, enjoining what is right, and forbidding that is wrong. They are the ones to attain happiness.

Be not like those who are divided amongst themselves and fall into disputations after receiving clear signs: for them is a dreadful penalty. (Ali 'Imran 3:103–5, Koran)

Persevere in patience and constancy; vie in such perseverance; strengthen each other; and be in taqwa of Allah, fear Allah that you may prosper. (Ali 'Imran 3:200, Koran)

This is a grace from Allah, and a favor; and Allah is All Knowing and All Wise. If two parties among the Believers fall into a quarrel, make peace between them: but if one of them transgresses beyond bounds against the other, then fight you all against the one who transgresses until he complies with the Command of Allah; but if he complies, then make peace between them with justice, and fairness: for Allah loves those who are fair and just. The Believers are but a single Brotherhood: so make peace and reconciliation between your two brothers; and fear Allah, that you may receive Mercy. (Al-Hujurat 49:6–10, Koran)

Just as the bond to Allah is indivisible, all the Believers shall stand behind the commitment of the least of them. All the Believers are bonded one to another to the exclusion of other men. (The Covenant of Muhammad)

The Communion of Believers: The believer's communion with Allah leads him to a communion with his fellow believers. In this relationship, the believers hold on to one another and to the rope that Allah has stretched to them. This rope is His covenant. The covenant of Allah thus becomes obligatory to each believer. After unity of Allah, tawhid—the unity of the *ummah* with Allah and the unity of the believers with one another—is the foremost commandment of Allah.

The Rope of Allah: Allah has ordained unity among the believers. He says to the believers, *"Hold fast, all together, the Rope, which Allah stretches out for you, and be not divided among yourselves"* (Ali 'Imran 3:103–5, Koran). When all the believers hold on to the rope that Allah casts to them, each believer connects to Allah; and through His mercy to each and every believer, the rope of Allah saves them from the turbulent waters of evil and falsehood. The rope of Allah is His covenant, and those who pledge their allegiance to Allah, His hand is over their hands. In this communion, every believer who clasps onto the rope of Allah, His covenant, connects with the believers through unity, goodness, and truth.

> Verily those who pledge their allegiance unto you (O Muhammad), pledge it unto none but Allah; the Hand of Allah is over their hands. Thereafter whosoever breaks his Covenant, does so to the harm of his own soul, and whosoever fulfils his Covenant with Allah, Allah will grant him an immense Reward. (Al-Fath 48:10, Koran)

Thus, in this communion of each believer with Allah, there is a communion among all the believers. Allah tells the believers,

> Let there arise out of you a band of people inviting to all that is good, enjoining what is right, and forbidding that is wrong. They are the ones to attain happiness. (Ali 'Imran 3:103–5)

Upon his submission to Allah, the believer has His mercy and protection, and Allah's hand is on the believer's hands. Upon rejecting evil, the believer grasps Allah's handhold that never breaks. Allah expels all evil out of those who abstain from all that is forbidden. Allah holds the believer's hand upon his submission to Him, and again, Allah holds the believer's hand when the he rejects all evil. In this condition of submission, faith, and performance of wholesome deeds, the believers form a community that has Allah's protection and guidance.

In His call to unity of believers, Allah says to them:

> Be not like those who are divided amongst themselves and fall into disputations after receiving clear signs: for them is a dreadful penalty. (Ali 'Imran 3:103–5)

> For those who lose their way and fight, Allah shows them a way to resolve their differences. "The Believers are but a single Brotherhood: so make peace and reconciliation between your two brothers; and fear Allah, that you may receive Mercy. Persevere in patience and constancy; vie in such perseverance; strengthen each other; and be in taqwa of Allah, fear Allah that you may prosper." (Al-Hujurat 49:6–10, Koran)

Believers in communion with other believers form a living *ummah*. This *ummah* is akin to a beehive, the community of honeybees. Millions of bees work together in harmony to maintain the integrity and concord of their community. Individual bees work in cooperation to build their hive of a preordained design of hexagonal units, to maintain required environment within bee nurseries, and to raise their young. In cohesion and unity, they gather and store honey and make wax for the mutual good of all. When threatened, the bees swarm altogether and prepare to fight unto death to protect their community from intruders. All their activity is intended for the mutual benefit, survival, and prosperity of their bee community. No single bee is seen to rebel for its own selfish reasons, for enrichment nor aggrandizement of self. Muslims are ordained to act with the same unity of purpose, in the way of Allah, for mutual benefit of the *ummah*. Allah bequeathed the honeybee, in His mercy, a genetic cipher that guides their conduct that nurtures their hive and pollinates Allah's garden.

Upon man, Allah has bestowed freedom of choice, whereby he may choose to do good or follow his cravings to do evil. He has the choice to do good for his kin, community, and humanity or to let the greed and craving of his *nafs* satisfy his desires. For those who submit to Allah and have faith in Allah, the Koran and the covenant of Allah are their guide. The Koran ordains unity and actions for the common good to the believers. For those who forsake the *ummah* to satisfy their lust and cravings—the kings and politicians of Islam—they have forsaken their Allah and their *din*. Allah will change the condition of the Muslims when they believe in Him and His messengers and perform right and beautiful deeds.

> Allah will not leave the Believers in the state in which you are now, until He separates what is evil from what is good. Nor will Allah disclose to you the secrets of the Unseen, but He chooses of His Messengers (for the purpose) whom He pleases. So, believe in Allah and His Messengers; and if you believe and do right, you have a reward without measure. (Ali 'Imran 3:179, Koran)

The communion of individual believers with Allah and with one another translates into an *ummah* in which the critical mass of goodness on the earth outweighs evil. In this union, the Real is supreme, and His writ is the ultimate. With Allah's *nur* in every heart, there is *haqq* (truth) on the earth, and peace will reign. People will share their substance; there will be no want and therefore no greed. Wars will be abolished. Ultimately, there will be no religion as there will be no priests. Man will be with his Allah and Allah with His creation.

The Twelfth Commandment of Allah

Be Thou Patient

O you who believe! persevere in patience and constancy; vie in such perseverance; strengthen each other; and fear Allah; that you may prosper.

Şabr, *şābir*, *şabbār*, and *şābara* denote the quality of patience, steadfastness, self-restraint, forbearance, endurance, and perseverance. One of Allah's ninety-nine names is *al-Şabur*, the Patient. It is one who does not precipitate an act before its time but decides matters according to a specific plan and brings them to fruition in a predefined manner, neither procrastinating nor hastening matters before their time but disposing each matter in its appropriate time in the way of its needs and requirements and doing all that without being subjected to a force opposing Allah's will. *Şabr*, *şābir*, *şabbār*, and *şābara* are mentioned in the Koran sixty-nine times. Allah reassures the believers:

- Believers! be patient and vie you with patience. (Ali 'Imran 3:200, Koran)

- Pray for succor to Allah and be patient. (Al-A'raf 7:128, Koran)

- Be thou patient, Allah will not leave to waste the wage of good doers. (Hud 11:115, Koran)

- Be thou patient, Surely Allah's promise is true. (Ar-Rum 30:60, Koran)
- Bear patiently whatever may befall you. (Luqman 31:17, Koran)
- So, be thou patient with a sweet patience. (Al-Ma'arij 70:5)
- And be patient unto your Lord. (Al-Muddaththir 74:7, Koran)
- Believers! seek you help in patience and prayer. (Al-Anbiya 21:153, Koran)
- But come sweet patience. (Yusuf 12:18, 83, Koran)
- Surely Allah is with the is with the patient. (Al-Baqarah 2:153, 249)
- Allah loves the patient. (Ali 'Imran 3:146, Koran)

For a man and a woman to be patient (*ṣabr*) requires endurance and discipline to affirm a rational resolve in opposing the impulses of passion or anger. It involves balancing two opposing desires. The believer has to overcome the impulse leading to rashness and haste and at the same time lean toward the inclination to delay the act. To be patient, one has to resolve the conflict between acts, anger and rashness on one hand and procrastination and delay on the other. Lack of *ṣabr*, self-restraint, patience, and self-discipline has overwhelmed the Muslim world at the beginning of the twenty-first century. The Muslim world has been rudderless and leaderless over one hundred years and poorly led during the previous one thousand years. The result is 1.5 billion individuals following their own instincts for the sake of mere survival.

Ṣabr teaches self-restraint in the matters of need and giving precedence to others over oneself in matters of need. Islam teaches that the elders, the sick, the needy, the women, and the children take precedence in matters of care, shelter, and food and that spirituality takes precedence over one's daily needs. Consideration and the well-being of the kin, the neighbor, and the fellow man requires a thought before fulfilling one's own requirements. The state of *ṣabr* in the Muslim world is obvious when one looks at the lineups at the bus and rail stations. People are being trampled at the holy sites. Old men, women, and the disabled were pushed and trampled during the holiest act of circumambulation of the Kaaba, at Safa and Marwah, and during the ritual stoning of the devil. The same is true in the shopping centers, down the streets, and inside the classrooms.

The extreme desire for immediate gratification of desires and cravings leads to small and major crimes. Lying, theft, and robbery are common acts involved in the impulse of possession of the unreachable. Military revolutions, palace coups, conspiracies, and conquests have brought power and wealth in the hands of people with vast but criminal ambitions. Such people lack perseverance, capacity for hard work, honesty, and *ṣabr.*

> Persevere in patience and constancy; vie in such perseverance; strengthen each other; and be in taqwa of Allah, fear Allah that you may prosper. (Ali 'Imran 3:200, Koran)

The Thirteenth Commandment of Allah

Theft, Deception, Fraud, Dishonesty, and Injustice

Betray not the trust of Allah and His *rasul.* Nor knowingly misappropriate wealth entrusted to you, whether on behalf of an orphan or another party. Be honest in handling property, goods, credit, confidences, and secrets of your fellow men and display integrity and honesty in using your skills and talents. Whenever you give your word, speak truthfully and justly, even if a near relative is concerned. Similarly, the *amri minkum*—those entrusted with the administration of the affairs of the believers—should not betray the trust of Allah, the *rasul*, and the believers and knowingly misappropriate the wealth of the Muslims. The populations of the Islamic lands are akin to the orphans whose land and heritage has been forcibly sequestered by conquest, soon to be redeemed and accounted for from the those who ceased it, who will on the appointed day be asked to account for every grain of sand and every grain of stolen gold. The Arabian Peninsula and other Muslim lands have been the plundering fields of the royal families and their kin for one hundred years in partnership with the circle of evil.

The rulers of the Arabian Peninsula and their royal relations regularly skim off the top third of the wealth of the *ummah* for their personal benefit. The dictators, the royals, and their circle of sycophants and cheerleaders in all Muslim nation-states have siphoned off the cream of their national wealth. Suharto, Benazir Bhutto, Nawaz Sharif, Pakistani generals, Reza Shah of Iran, Saddam Hussein, Anwar Sadat, Hosni Mubarak, kings of Arabian Peninsula, their families, and the inner circle of their regimes have plundered their nation's treasuries of billions of dollars over the years of their prolonged rein on power. However, the greatest pillage and plunder in history took place systematically when the descendants of ten barefoot, camel-herding Bedouins took control of the Arabian Peninsula with the help of British money and arms. In the latter half of the twentieth century, over a short period of forty-five years, they took a heist of $4.5 trillion. In the Arabian Peninsula, in the kingdoms of Oman, Kuwait, the United Arab Emirates, Qatar, Bahrain, and Saudi Arabia, there are now six kings and over two hundred billionaires and thousands of millionaires among this narrow circle of ten clans. Over this short period, these tent dwellers who had never been inside the confines of a dwelling now own hundreds of palaces in Arabia, Europe, and

America. Yet the plunder goes on. The total amount of petty cash taken out by the ever-increasing progeny of these Bedouin sheikhs in allowances, salaries, commissions, and expenses is to the tune of $125 billion annually, which is more than the total combined annual budget of nation-states of Pakistan, Afghanistan, Iran, Syria, and Jordan, with a population of 250 million people. The cost of security of these "royals" (90,000 troops), personal jets, helicopters, yachts, travel, and private royal air terminals in Jeddah, Riyadh, Dubai, and Doha is an additional $10 billion. At the same time, most of the Arabs and Muslims live in conditions of utter poverty and deprivation.

Two fundamental terms used in the Koran are *haqq* (right and honest means of income) and *batil* (wrongful and dishonest way of making money). The ways of making money approved by the Koran are halal, and those forbidden are haram.

Muslims the world over follow the verses of the Koran about fasting in Sura Al-Baqarah 2:183–87 but very conveniently ignore the following verse 188:

> O you who believe! Fasting is prescribed to you as it was prescribed to those before you, that you may (learn) self-restraint, (Fasting) for a fixed number of days; but if any of you is ill, or on a journey, the prescribed number (should be made up) from days later. For those who can do it (with hardship), is a ransom, the feeding of one that is indigent but he that will give more, of his own free will, it is better for him. And it is better for you that you fast if you only knew.

> Ramadan is the (month) in which was sent down the Qur'an, as a guide to mankind, also Clear (Signs) for guidance and judgment (between right and wrong). So every one of you who is present (at his home) during that month should spend it in fasting, but if anyone is ill, or on a journey, the prescribed period (should

be made up) by days later. Allah intends every facility for you; He does not want to put you to difficulties. (He wants you) to complete the prescribed period, and to glorify Him in that He has guided you; and perchance you shall be grateful.

When My servants ask thee concerning Me, I am indeed close (to them): I listen to the prayer of every suppliant when he calls on Me: let them also, with a will, listen to My call, and believe in Me: that they may walk in the right way.

Permitted to you, on the night of the fasts, is the approach to your wives. They are your garments, and you are their garments. Allah knows what you used to do secretly among yourselves; but He turned to you and forgave you; so now associate with them, and seek what Allah hath ordained for you, and eat and drink until the white thread of dawn appear to you distinct from its black thread; then complete your fast till the night appears; but do not associate with your wives while you are in retreat in the mosques. Those are limits (set by) Allah: approach not nigh thereto. Thus, doth Allah make clear His Signs to men: that they may learn self-restraint. (Al-Baqarah 2:183–87)

And do not devour each other's wealth dishonestly, nor use it as bait for the judges, with intent that you may devour dishonestly, and knowingly a little of (other) people's wealth. (Al-Baqarah 2:188, Koran)

There are several dishonest financial practices, cheating, bribery, stealing, embezzlement, hoarding, and swindling, but one mentioned specifically in the Koran is often overlooked. That is the one practiced by the aristocrats, clergy, clerics, and claimants of spiritual leadership all across the world:

O you who believe! There are indeed many among the priests and clerics, (leaders) who in falsehood devour the substance of men and hinder (them) from the Way of Allah. And there are those who bury gold and silver and spend it not in the Way of Allah: announce unto them a most grievous penalty. (At-Tawbah 9:34, Koran)

Like the politicians and dictators, these priests and spiritual leaders deceive the unlettered masses with false doctrines and fallacies to keep them entrapped in their web to safeguard their own power over people and wealth.

The Fourteenth Commandment of Allah

Obey Allah and Obey the *Rasul* and Those Charged among You with Authority

Obey Allah and obey the Rasool, and those charged amongst you with authority in the settlement of your affairs. If you differ in anything among yourselves, refer it to Allah and His Rasool (The Qur'an and the Prophet's teachings). If you do believe in Allah and the last Day that is best and the most beautiful conduct in the final determination. (An-Nisa 4:43, Koran)

The Koran teaches that all affairs of the individuals and of the Muslim community should be conducted through mutual consultation (*ijma*) and decisions arrived at through consensus. Furthermore, the Koran proclaims consultation as a principle of government and a method that must be applied in the administration of public affairs. The sovereignty of the Islamic state belongs exclusively to Allah, whose will and command binds the community and state. The dignified designation in the Koran of the community as vicegerent of Allah on the earth makes the Muslim community, the *ummah,* a repository of what is known as "executive sovereignty" of the Islamic state. The community as a whole, after consultation and consensus, grants people among themselves with authority to manage its affairs (*ulil amri minkum*). Those charged with authority act in their capacity as the representative (*wakil*) of the people and are bound by the Koranic mandate to consult the community in public affairs, and consensus is the binding source of the law. The community by consultation and in consensus has the authority to depose any person charged with authority, including the head of state, in the event of gross violation of Allah's law.

> Those who hearken to their Lord and establish regular prayer; who (conduct) their affairs by mutual Consultation; who spend out of what We bestow on them for Sustenance; And those who, when an oppressive wrong is inflicted on them do not flinch and courageously defend themselves. (Ash-Shura 42:38–39)

Islam pursues its social objectives by reforming the individual. The ritual ablution before prayer, the five daily prayers, fasting during the month of Ramadan, and the obligatory giving of charity all encourage punctuality, self-discipline, and concern for the well-being of others. The individual is seen not just as a member of the community and subservient to the community's will but also as a morally autonomous agent who plays a distinctive role in shaping the community's sense of direction and purpose. The Koran has attached to the individual's duty of obedience to the government a right to simultaneously dispute with rulers over government affairs. The individual obeys the ruler on the condition that the ruler obeys the covenant of the Koran and Allah's commandments, which are obligatory to all Muslims regardless of their status in the social hierarchy. This is reflected in the declaration of the blessed *nabi* that

There is no obedience in transgression;
obedience is only in the righteousness.

The citizen is entitled to disobey an oppressive command that is contrary to the covenant of the Koran. The blessed *nabi*, Allah's emissary, brought His word to the world and disseminated it to the populations of all the continents. Therefore, it is essential to obey and follow what Blessed *Nabi* Muhammad brought from Allah for mankind.

The Fifteenth Commandment of Allah

Let There Be No Compulsion in Religion

Let there be no compulsion in religion: Truth stands out clear from Error: whoever rejects Evil and believes in Allah hath grasped the most trustworthy handhold that never breaks. And Allah hears and knows all things. (Al-Baqarah 2:254–57, Koran)

The Koranic notion of religious belief (*iman*) is dependent on knowledge that is actualized in practice in the term *islam*. The term *islam* signifies the idea of surrender or submission. Islam is a religion of self-surrender; it is the conscious and rational submission of dependent and limited human will to the absolute and omnipotent will of Allah. The type of surrender Islam requires is a deliberate, conscious, and rational act made by a person who knows with both intellectual certainty and spiritual vision that Allah, who is the subject of Koranic discourse, is reality itself.

The knower of God is a Muslim (fem. *Muslimah*), "one who submits" to the divine truth and whose relationship with God is governed by *taqwa*, the consciousness of humankind's responsibility toward its

Creator. However, consciousness of God alone is not sufficient to make a person a Muslim. Neither is it enough to be merely born a Muslim or to be raised in an Islamic cultural context. The concept of *taqwa* implies that the believer has the added responsibility of acting in a way that is in accordance with three types of knowledge—*ilm al-yaqin, ain al-yaqin* and *haqq al-yaqin* (knowledge of certainty, eye of certainty, and the truth of certainty). The believer must endeavor at all times to maintain himself or herself in a constant state of submission to Allah. By doing so, the believer attains the honored title of "slave of Allah" (*abd Allah*, feminine: *amat Allah*), for he recognizes that all power and all agency belongs to God alone. Allah says to the believers,

> Let there be no compulsion in religion: Truth stands out clear from Error: whoever rejects Evil and believes in Allah hath grasped the most trustworthy handhold that never breaks. And Allah hears and knows all things. (Al-Baqarah 2:254–57, Koran)

Islam (submission) and *iman* (faith) arise out of the communion of a believer with his Maker. According to the Koran, *iman* is not just belief but also, in fact, knowledge. *Iman* is conviction that is based on reason and knowledge. The Koran does not recognize belief that involves blind acceptance. Islam does include acceptance of certain things that cannot be explained by perception through human senses. Our reason and thinking will compel us to recognize the existence of such things. *Iman*, according to the Koran, signifies conviction based on full mental acceptance and intellectual satisfaction. *Iman* gives us inner contentment, a feeling of *amn* (same common root). Thus, *iman* means to believe in something and to testify to its truthfulness, to have confidence in that belief, and to act in accordance with that belief.

There are five fundamental facts stated in the Koran that a believer must accept *iman* in:

1. *Allah:* Belief in Allah means that not only to profess obedience to Him and His covenant but also to show it in one's actions and to be in *taqwa* of Allah.
2. *The law of* mukafat *and the afterlife:* Belief in the law of *mukafat* means to have conviction that every action of man has an inescapable consequence of reward or retribution.
3. *Angels (*malaika*):* Angels are not the winged creatures depicted in children's literature. They are heavenly forces that carry out the laws of Allah governing the universe. They bow to Allah since they follow His orders. They also bow to humans because we are able to study, understand, and manipulate the laws of nature for the benefit of mankind.
4. *The revelations.*
5. *The rasuls:* Belief in revelations and *rasuls* implies that human intellect alone cannot safely reach the final destination without divine guidance in the form of *wahiy* (revelation) delivered by the *rasuls* to mankind. This guidance is to the whole humankind sent through many *rasuls*. The Muslim tradition began with Ibrahim, our father (Abraham of the Bible). The believers have a belief system and a course of action to be witness over the whole mankind and spread the message to them that began with *Nabi* Ibrahim and was completed with *Nabi* Muhammad.

Whereas the message of *wahiy* is divine and universal for all human races, man-made edicts, creed, and dogma directing the believers to beliefs and actions separate the believer in his communion with God. This is exclusive, and in this relationship, no man can intervene. Therefore, compulsion in matters of religion is only a human fantasy. In the same manner, the message of Hadith collections of the third century is human and therefore subject to error, and so it cannot be equated with the *haqq* of the Koran. Mullahs, scholars, Deobandi and

Brelvi priests, Wahhabi, Taliban, and ayatollahs who compel believers to conform to their own narrow beliefs assume the rights that are only Allah's prerogative.

The Sixteenth Commandment of Allah

Allah is the *Waliy*, Protector of Those Who Have Faith
Take Not Infidels for *Awliya* in Place of Believers

Take not infidels for Awliya (friends and protectors) in place of believers.

Oh, you who believe! Allah is the Waliy and the protector of the Believers. Allah commands Believers not to take people outside their ranks in closeness and confidence, who in their loathing for them wish them destruction.

The recurring theme in the Koran extols the believers to stand united. In this unity, all believers are bonded to one another to the exclusion of other men. Just as the bond to Allah is indivisible, all the believers shall stand behind the commitment of the least of them. In this scheme of things, there is no room for unbelievers and wrongdoers in the affairs of the believers.

Allah, in His covenant, reminds the believers repeatedly not to take the *kafirun* (infidels), Jews, and Christians as their *awliya* (friends and protectors) in place of believers. They are friends and protectors unto one another. He who among believers turns to them is one of them. Allah does not guide those who are unjust and evildoers (*zalimun)*. He who among the believers turns to them is among the *kafirun*, *mushrikun*, and the *zalimun*.

Allah is the Waliy, protector of those who have faith. From the depths of darkness, He will lead them forth into light. Of those who reject faith their Waliy (protectors) are the false deities: from light, they will lead them forth into the depths of darkness. They will be Companions of the Fire, to dwell therein (forever). (Al-Baqarah 2:254–57, Koran)

Take not into intimacy those outside your ranks: they will not fail to corrupt you. They only desire your ruin: rank hatred has already appeared from their mouths: what their hearts conceal is far worse. We have made plain to you the Signs if you have wisdom. (Ali 'Imran 3:118–20, Koran)

If you obey the Unbelievers, (kafaru) they will drive you back on your heels, and you will turn your back to your Faith to your own loss. Allah is your protector, and He is the best of helpers. (Ali 'Imran 3:149–50, Koran)

Take not the Jews and the Christians as your friends and protectors (awliya). They are friends and protectors unto each other. He who amongst you turns to them is one of them. Allah does not guide those who are unjust and evil doers (zalimun). (Al-Ma'idah 5:51, Koran)

Take not for friends and protectors (awliya) those who take your religion for mockery, whether from amongst people of the book or from amongst the kafireen. Be in taqwa of Allah, fear Allah if you have faith indeed. (Al-Ma'idah 5:57, Koran)

Take not for your protectors and friends (awliya) your kin who practice infidelity over faith. Whosoever does that will be amongst the wrong doers. (At-Tawbah 9:23, Koran)

Take not My enemies and yours as awliya (friends and protectors), offering them love and regard, even though they have rejected the Truth bestowed on you. And they have driven out the Rasool and yourselves from your homes because you believe in Allah as your Rabb (Lord)! You have come out to strive in My Cause and to seek My favor, take them not as friends, holding in secret regard and friendship for them: for I know all that you conceal and all that you reveal. And any of you that do this has strayed from the Straight Path.

If they were to gain an upper hand over you, they would treat you as enemies, and stretch forth their hands and their tongues against you with evil; and they desire that you should reject the Truth. (Al-Mumtahinah 60:1–2, Koran)

Befriend not people who have incurred Allah's wrath. They are already in despair of the Hereafter, just as the Unbelievers are in despair about those in graves. (Al-Mumtahinah 60:13, Koran)

Allah is the Wali protector of those who have faith. From the depths of darkness, He will lead them forth into light. (Al-Baqarah 2:254–57, Koran)

Establish regular salaat; give regular charity, and holdfast to Allah. He is your Mawla, Protector, the best of Protectors and the best Helper. (Al-Hajj 2:277-78, Koran)

These verses of the Koran often cause confusion among the believers, Christians, and Jews, yet the explanation is quite simple: the Koran recognizes only one true religion—the religion of those who have submitted themselves to the one universal God, have faith in that God, and perform wholesome and beautiful deeds. Allah sent thousands of His *rasuls* and *Nabiyyin* with a message to humankind. Some of the *rasuls* are named in the Koran, while others are not obvious to us. Millions of people who subscribe to the teaching of these *rasuls*—although they may on the surface be followers of Islam, Hinduism, Buddhism, teachings of Confucius, Christianity, and Judaism—have submitted themselves to one universal God, the Creator. They do His bidding as taught by the *rasuls*, and they perform beautiful and wholesome deeds in the service of Allah's creation. They seek peace and do not harm any humans. Such people are the believers of God, Allah, and they are *Muslims* according to the Koran.

There are millions of people who call themselves Muslims, Christians, Jews, and others who have not submitted themselves to the will of one God, their Creator; they do not have the same faith in the one universal God. Such people do not have the *nur* of Allah in their hearts; they create evil and mischief on the earth. Such people cause wars, murder whole populations, steal from nations, and profit from famines and destitution. Such are the people Allah warns us about. The believers should not take them as their *awliya*.

It is not only the Koran that makes the believers aware of the tricks of such people. Jesus spoke of them in these terms:

> Beware of false prophets, which come to you in sheep's clothing, but inwardly they are ravenous. You shall know them by their fruits. Do men gather grapes of thorns, or figs of thistles? Even so every good tree brings forth good fruit, but a corrupt tree brings forth evil fruit. "A good tree cannot bring forth evil fruit; neither can a corrupt tree bring forth good fruit." Every tree that brings forth bad fruit is hewn down and cast into the fire. Therefore, by their fruits shall you know them.

The Koran says:

> They have made their oaths a screen for their misdeeds, thus they obstruct men from the Path of Allah: truly evil are their deeds. That is because they believed, then they rejected Faith: so, a seal was set on their hearts: therefore, they understand not. When you look at them, their exteriors please thee; and when they speak, you listen to their words. They are as worthless as rotten pieces of timber propped up, unable to stand on their own. They think that every cry is against them. They are the enemies; so, beware of them. The curse of Allah be on them! How are they deluded away from the Truth! (Al-Munafiqun 63:4, Koran)

It should become abundantly clear to Muslims that the present world situation is the continuation of the Council of Clermont in 1095 CE when Pope Urban declared a crusade against Islam, a war till its destruction. There are powerful forces in the Euro-Christian world, which for the first time in history is not threatened by the barbarians or by any other force among themselves. The Christian West for the first time is united in NATO and the European Economic Community. The threats to Islam have been ongoing since the beginning of the Crusades and are now being renewed daily very subtly. In this battle, every component of the modern civilization has been harnessed against Islam—intelligence services, armed forces, diplomacy, economics and communications, and organizations such as the United Nations, the World Bank, the IMF, and the World Trade Organization.

The unwritten plan of the fundamentalist Christian, Jewish, and banking and oil interests that work in cohesion is to weaken and degrade the Islamic state and its military and economic infrastructure in such a way that Muslims will continue to be client states under American and

NATO hegemony. Muslim countries will continue to live in ongoing poverty and degradation under the despotic rule of incompetent, dishonest, and self-serving kings and dictators. Muslim and Arab states will be further divided into ministates so they can never be united to present a coherent, united front to the West. Iraq will break down into three fragments—Shiite, Sunni, and Kurdish. Saudi Arabia will be divided into the eastern Shia oil sheikhdom and the western Sunni religious kingdom centered on Mecca and Medina. Afghanistan will break down into Pashtun and Farsi components. Iran and Turkey will be forced to give up their Kurdish territories. Israel will absorb West Bank and Gaza and expel Palestinians to Jordan, which will come to be called a Palestinian state. Sunni Iraq will become the Hashemite kingdom. Sudan will become the Desert Arab republic in the north and oil-rich Christian in the south. Punjab and Sind in Pakistan will be absorbed into India. Baluchi and Pathan areas of Pakistan will join their brethren in Afghanistan. India will further break down into several countries. Indonesia will similarly disintegrate into several states. The wealth of all the new ministates will be administered by the United Nations to be controlled by America and Europe.

This is the plan of the *Yahudi-Salibi* think tanks funded by secret and faceless people and corporations. Several complete groups of *Yahudi* and *Salibi* planners have been embedded in the higher offices of the United States, Britain, Australia, and several European governments. They have been carefully and successfully planted into the NATO headquarters, the United Nations, the World Bank, and the IMF. The best-known example of the complete takeover of the planning for the Iraq War is in the Pentagon, the National Security Council, and the Office of the Vice President of the United States by the agents of the Israeli government and its security apparatus. After several years of covert operation in Washington, this group has sufficient backing that it is emboldened to come out in the open.

The covert and the obvious planning of the *Yahudi-Salibi* conspirators is thorough and detailed. Their agents speak Arabic, Farsi, Turkish, and Urdu fluently. They have been carefully planted in the diplomatic corps, intelligence services, armed forces, NGOs, various aid groups, commercial enterprises, airlines, and shipping and tourism services. Their function is to gather intelligence and to recruit corrupt and willing agents in the Muslim states to enhance the goals of the conspirators. A believer, aware of his history, has to pause and consider the effort and treasure that goes into such planning. This planning not only is worldwide but also dates back to the year 1095 CE, when Pope Urban called on his followers to destroy Islam. The expenditure on war against Islam since the 9/11 plot spent in the name of homeland security, covert and military action in Muslim countries, and war in Afghanistan and Iraq has totaled over a trillion dollars. Such worldwide planning, coordination, and financing could not possibly occur without an office, a full-fledged headquarters with staff and a head. Somewhere in this wide world, perhaps in Europe, in a stately home with boulevards and well-manicured gardens, there is a secret headquarters with a man overseeing the vast apparatus that controls the world's wealth and wants to control it in perpetuity. He has constant contact with his minions executing the policy set forth by an executive of stakeholders of wealth, Zionism, and Euro-Christianity who meet in secrecy.

Efforts by the believers to achieve unity and prosperity continue to be defeated. The average Muslim just cannot understand why the *ummah*'s efforts never come to fruition. As already mentioned, covert plans to defeat the believers' efforts toward unity are constantly formulated, discussed, and implemented.

There is a recurring cycle in Islamic history of destruction and humiliation of Islam by the manipulations of the circle of evil. The story starts sometimes with a scheming Jew who spins a web, meticulously planning to amass the world's wealth, and uses the power and the organization of the strongest Christian monarch by tempting him with acquisition of a world empire and its fabulous wealth. Then meticulous planning starts; the execution of such an expedition may take several years in which intelligence services, diplomats, and armed services play a role, while only the top select echelon is aware of all the moves on the chessboard. A willing victim, a weak Muslim—a *Munafiq*—with propensity toward greed and lust for power and usually endowed with overwhelming vanity and conceit is picked up, trained, and slowly eased into a position of power to be used at the opportune moment. A score of such people descended on Iraq and Afghanistan with the invasion of these countries. Ahmed Chalabi, Zalmay Khalilzad, Ibrahim al-Ja'fari, and Hamid Karzai were some of them, just to mention a few. Legions of the *Munafiqeen* are now standing in the wings, awaiting their rewards with the coming invasion of Iran.

An article on the subject written by Rowan Scarborough appeared in the *Washington Times* on February 20, 2006, that points to the intentions of the world's greatest military power. Though the article talks of a long war on terrorism, Osama bin Laden's religious ideology, and extremism, the underlying objective of the plan is to fight a long war against Islam. The covenant of Allah specifies each believer's obligation to the cause of Allah and to the unity of the believers. The Western Euro-Christian civilization, however, has yet to achieve the objectives of the one-thousand-year-old crusade called by Pope Urban in 1095 CE to destroy Islam.

The United States Joint Chiefs of Staff planners have produced a twenty-seven-page briefing on the war on terror that seeks to explain how to win the "long war" against the Muslims. The report states that, in this war, Islamic extremists may be supported by twelve million Muslims worldwide. Military planners worry that al-Qaeda could win if the "traditional allies prefer accommodation." The "traditional allies" refer to the traditional traitors of Islam in Egypt, Saudi Arabia, UAE, Kuwait, Jordan, Oman, Qatar, and Pakistan.

Al-Qaeda leader Osama bin Laden, the document states, "is absolutely committed to his cause. His religious ideology successfully attracts recruits. He has sufficient population base from which to protract the conflict. Even support of 1 percent of the Muslim population would equate to over 12 million 'enemies.'"

The unclassified production titled "Fighting the Long War—Military Strategy for the War on Terrorism" is a component of the Pentagon's ongoing campaign to explain that a lengthy struggle requires patience from the American people and Congress. The briefing was prepared for Rear Adm. William D. Sullivan, vice director for strategic plans and policy within the Joint Staff, which is under Marine Corps general Peter Pace, Joint Chiefs of Staff chairman. Admiral Sullivan used it to deliver a lecture in January to a national security study group at Mississippi State University. "It is an effort, when asked, to explain why we are doing what we are doing from a military perspective to fight the long war," said Air Force major Almarah Belk, spokeswoman for General Pace. The same core information is used in briefings by other speakers to explain this protracted planned war.

The Bush administration's effort to explain Iraq and the broader war includes more than briefings. In February 2006, Defense Secretary Donald H. Rumsfeld was in New York, talking to the Council on Foreign Relations, and General Pace addressed the National Press Club in the district. At the same time, President Bush was in Tampa, Florida. speaking on the war.

Bin Laden, the Joint Staff paper says, wants to "expand the Muslim empire to historical significance." And Iraq "has become the focus of the enemy's effort. If they win in Iraq, they have a base from which to expand their terror. Extremists now have an Emirate in Iraq that serves as a base of operations from which they can revive the Caliphate [Islamic rule]. . . . Baghdad becomes the capital of the Caliphate. The revived Caliphate now turns its attention to the destruction of Israel."

Admiral Sullivan's briefing contains a map that shows the bin Laden–style caliphate conquering North and East Africa, the entire Middle East, and Central and South Asia. This dire scenario can only happen if the United States is defeated in Iraq and Afghanistan. "The United States cannot be defeated militarily," the briefing claims, "the enemy knows this. But consider terror attacks weaken the world economy. Continued casualties weaken national resolve. Traditional allies prefer accommodation." The enemy has "inherent weaknesses," including "no military capacity to expand their fight beyond terrorist tactics."

"Americans will commit to a 'long war' if they are confident our leaders know what they are doing." This twenty-seven-page briefing clearly states, "Marginalizing an ideology requires patience and promoting reform from within. We cannot discredit all of Islam as we did with communism. It is a divine religion. We can only discredit the violent extremist[7]." Clearly, any believer reading this briefing will understand that any reference to bin Laden, extremists, and terrorism really points to mainstream Islam and the dangers posed to the *ummah.*

In this game, on one side of the chessboard are men with an attention span going back a thousand years to the Council of Clermont in 1095 CE, when Pope Urban declared a crusade against Islam. Their commitment and passion are fueled by a thousand years of pent-up hatred stored in Europe's political and ecumenical history. The ideologues are intellectuals with accumulated knowledge and information of Islamic history, the fault lines of the Muslim psyche.

---

7 Rowan Scarborough, "Military Plots a 'Long War' on Terror," *Washington Times*, February 20, 2006.

The players are in full control of the economics and the mercenary armed forces of the Muslim states. They are backed by wealth, intelligence services, and absolute military power of the West. At their beck and call are all the major players in the world of Islam. These "Muslim" *Munafiqeen* have been bribed, bought, or intimidated into subservience and service. Most of them are the descendants of the first-generation *Munafiqeen* who helped the West dismember the Ottoman Empire and establish Western control over the Middle East, Iran, Afghanistan, and Muslim India.

On the other side of the chessboard are the Muslim and Arab rulers whose attention span is constricted to one day at a time, devoted to staying in power and holding on to their ill-gotten wealth. In some, the attention span flickers from one alcoholic binge to the next, while others like King Fu'ad submerged in drinking and gambling. Kings, sheikhs, and presidents are virtually unaware of the demands of their *din* regarding their obligation to the *ummah.* Those in charge are oblivious to the dangers that lie ahead that will destroy their nations and their *din.* They are insensitive to the requirements of statecraft necessary to protect the world of Islam from the plots against it. In most cases, Muslim rulers themselves are a part of the conspiracy to destroy Islam. They form a part of the circle of evil—the circle of the *Yahudi*, *Salibi*, and *Munafiq* coalition out to destroy Islam.

The uninformed politico-military generals are confident that their parade ground skills are adequate to run the business of state and the *din* all across the Islamic world through Indonesia, Bangladesh, Pakistan, Afghanistan, Iraq, Syria, Turkey, Egypt, Libya, Algeria, and a host of West African countries; this curse of Islam has played havoc with the world of believers. The generals puff around in their fancy bemedaled uniforms like peacocks trying to dazzle their subjects with their shiny buttons. Islam has lost in this war time and again during the last two hundred years and will continue to do so unless the Muslims begin to take heed of their covenant with Allah and learn from their history. Allah addresses the believers repeatedly to emphasize the importance of unity among them. He repeatedly admonishes them not to take pagans, Christians, and Jews as their *awliya* in place of believers.

The Seventeenth Commandment of Allah

Fight the Infidel Until There Is No More *Fitnah*: Jihad

Fight the infidel until there is no more fitnah, treachery and oppression and there prevails Justice and Faith in Allah altogether and everywhere. If they cease, then Allah is seer of what they do. If they refuse, be sure that Allah is your Protector, the Best to protect and the Best to help. And why should you not fight in the cause of Allah, and for those men, women and children, who are weak, abused and oppressed, those who beseech their Lord to deliver protectors and helpers.

The Koranic use of the term *jihad* is "struggle." The Koran commonly uses the verb along with expression *in the path of Allah.* The path of Allah, of course, is the path of right conduct that Allah has set down in the Koran. Jihad is simply the complement to *islam*, the surrender to the will of Allah. The surrender takes place in Allah's will, and it is His will that people struggle in His path. Hence, submission and surrender to Allah's will demands struggle in His path. Submission to Allah's command requires the believers to struggle against all negative tendencies in themselves and in society that draw them away from Allah's path. Salat, zakat, fasting, and hajj are all struggles in the path of Allah.

The greatest obstacles that people face in submitting themselves to Allah are their laziness, lack of imagination, and currents of contemporary opinion. These weaknesses and events carry them along without resisting. It takes an enormous struggle to submit to an authority that breaks one's likes and dislikes of current trends and pressures of society to conform to the crowd.

The jihad, which is normally a daily inward struggle within oneself against temptations and evil, will sometimes take an outward form against the enemies of Islam. Such a war is permitted strictly in the path of Allah in today's contemporary world to fight *fitnah,* tyranny, and oppression and thus to enforce truth, justice, and freedom.

> And why should you not fight in the cause of Allah, and for those men, women, and children, who are weak, abused, and oppressed, those who beseech their Lord to deliver them from their oppressors, and those who ask Allah to send for them protectors and helpers. (An-Nisa 4:71–75, Koran)

The oft-repeated phrase in the Koran to proclaim jihad is to fight *fitnah*, tyranny, and oppression. Yet most of the wars in the Muslim world were civil wars, with Muslims killing other Muslims for the sake of territory, wealth, and power.

Life is a chain of emotions, intentions, and actions. Before each deed, man stops to intend an action. Each intention is the product of an emotion that acts on man's self, the *nafs*. The *nafs* may intend to act on its animal instincts of craving and lust, or in situations where the human *self* is sufficiently refined with the *taqwa* of Allah, man will follow the path of Allah as commanded by the covenant. The self is in continuous battle whether to follow its base cravings or to perform wholesome deeds. Such ongoing fluctuation of intent between the base and the honorable is stressful. Such stress leads to anxiety, anger, and depression, which in the end will cause an emotional turmoil and breakdown. When man intends to do his deeds with the knowledge that Allah is with him, that Allah is aware of his intent, and that Allah guides him to the right objective and action, there is peace and satisfaction.

When the believer is in *taqwa* of Allah, His *nur* cleans his *nafs* and aids him to obey the covenant of Allah. Jihad is this struggle that prepares the believer to follow and obey Allah's commandments without questioning. Jihad is the struggle of the individual on his way from the path of ignorance to the path of Allah. Man hears Allah's call though the noise and the commotion of the world and, through the eye of his soul, lets the *nur* of Allah into the niche of his heart. Allah's call is to obedience, goodness, and selflessness. Man bows down his head on the earth in submission and in humility to his Lord. The Lord guides, and the believer follows; the believer has faith in his Allah, and Allah holds his hand. Allah shows His believer the way to goodness, and the believer performs wholesome deeds. The *nur* of Allah glows in the believer's heart, and the believer accepts Allah in his heart.

This communion between the believer and Allah becomes exclusive. Submission establishes a link between the believer and Allah. Allah commands, and the believer follows. The believer asks, and Allah gives. The believer loves Allah, and Allah loves him in return. The believer asks for the straight path, and Allah shows him the way. The believer praises Allah, and Allah showers His mercy and grace upon him. The believer remembers Allah, and Allah responds to those who praise Him.

The *nafs*, unlike the Freudian ego, is capable of both good and bad. The *nuqta* of the *nafs*, when magnified a million times, becomes visible as a shiny disk, a mirror. The inherent nature (*fitra*) of the *nafs* is to shine like a mirror with Allah's *nur*. When man walks the path of Allah in *taqwa* of Him with the knowledge that Allah is with him, watching him and guiding him, Allah's *nur* shines on the *nafs*, keeping it pure and safe. However, when man's desires, cravings, and ego overpower his love and obedience for Allah, the shiny mirror of his *nafs* becomes obscured by the dirt and smoke of his desires, and he loses sight of the *nur* of Allah and trips into error and decadence.

The effort required to keep focus on Allah's *nur* and the *taqwa* of Him is the inner jihad. And this jihad is the obedience to Allah's commandments when He calls on His believers with the words *O you who Believe* and commands them to do acts of faith and goodness in *seventy-five* verses of the Koran. Obedience to every such command is jihad.

Jihad, foremost, is the struggle to fulfill the commandments of Allah in the covenant. The *taqwa* of Allah shines His light (*nur*) into core of man, in the self (*nafs*), that clears the smoke of evil and temptation from the *nafs*, allowing man to follow God. Once the believer has purified himself with Allah's *nur*, he has prepared himself for the external jihad. When the believer has purified his own *nafs* and soul with submission to Allah (*islam*) and faith (*iman*) in the only reality, the Lord, and by performance of wholesome deeds in the name of Allah, he is ready for the outer struggle for his *din* to fight the *fitnah* of tyranny and oppression.

The Blessed *nabi* of Allah wrote the following covenant in the first year of hijra in Medina. This is the essential constitution of the whole *ummah*. This is a covenant given by Muhammad to the believers.

1. They constitute one *Ummah* to the exclusion of all other men.
2. The believers shall leave none of their members in destitution without giving him in kindness that he needs by the way of his liberty.
3. No believer shall slay a believer in retaliation for an unbeliever, nor shall he assist an unbeliever against a believer.

4. All believers shall rise as one man against anyone who seeks to commit injustice, aggression, crime, or spread mutual enmity amongst the Muslims even if such a person is their kin.
5. Just as the bond to Allah is indivisible, all the believers shall stand behind the commitment of the least of them. All believers are bonded one to another to the exclusion of other men.
6. This Pax Islamica is one and indivisible. No believer shall enter a separate peace without all other believers whenever there is fighting in the cause of God but will do so only on the basis of equality and justice to all others. In every expedition for the cause of God we undertake, all parties to the covenant shall fight shoulder to shoulder as one man. All believers shall avenge the blood of one another when anyone falls fighting in the Way of Allah.
7. The pious believers follow the best and the most upright guidance. Whoever is convicted of killing a believer deliberatively but without righteous cause shall be liable to the relatives of the killed. Until the latter are satisfied, the killer shall be subject to retaliation by each and every believer.

Allah speaks to the believers about the struggle in His way:

Fight in the cause of Allah those who fight you, but do not transgress limits; for Allah loves not transgressors.

And slay them wherever you catch them and turn them out from where they have turned you out; for fitnah, tumult and oppression are worse than slaughter; but fight them not at the Sacred Mosque, unless they fight you there first; but if they fight you, slay them. Such is the reward of those who suppress faith.

But if they cease, Allah is Oft-Forgiving, Most Merciful.

And fight them on until there is no more fitnah, tumult,
or oppression, and there prevail justice and faith in Allah;
but if they cease, let there be no hostility except to those
who practice oppression. (Al-Baqarah 2:190–93)

And why should you not fight in the cause of Allah, and for those
men, women and children, who are weak, abused and oppressed,
those who beseech their Lord to deliver them from their oppressors,
and those who ask Allah to send for them protectors and helpers.

Those who believe, fight in the cause of Allah, and those who reject
Faith fight in the cause of Evil: so fight you against the friends of Satan:
feeble indeed is the cunning of Satan. (An-Nisa 4:75–76, Koran)

And slacken not in following up the enemy; if you are suffering
hardships, they are suffering similar hardships; but you have
hope from Allah, while they have none. And Allah is full
of Knowledge and Wisdom. (An-Nisa 4:104, Koran)

If Allah helps you none can overcome you: if He forsakes
you, who is there, after that, that can help you? In Allah, then,
let Believers put their trust. (Ali 'Imran 3:160, Koran)

We did indeed send, before you Rasools to their respective
peoples, with Clear Signs: To those who transgressed, We meted
out Retribution: and as a right those who earned from us,
We helped those who believed. (Ar-Rum 30:47, Koran)

Here is a declaration to the human, a guidance and advice
to those who live in awareness, Taqwa, of Allah!

So lose not hope nor shall you despair, for you shall achieve supremacy, if you are true in Faith.

If you have suffered a setback, verily a setback has been there for the other party too. We make such days of adversity go around amongst the humans so that Allah may distinguish those who believe and choose His witnesses from amongst them. And Allah loves not the evil doers.

Allah's objective is to distinguish the True Believers from those who reject Faith. (Ali 'Imran 3:138–41, Koran)

Wars and slaughter are abhorrent to Allah. Allah says:

If anyone slew a person, unless it is in retribution for murder or for spreading mischief, fasaad, in the land, it would be as if he slew the whole people. And if anyone saved a life, it would be as if he saved the life of the whole people. Take not life, which Allah has made sacred, except by the way of justice or law. This He commands you, that you may learn wisdom.

And then Allah declares to the believers that *fitnah*, treachery, and oppression are worse than slaughter and taking of life. *Fitnah*, treason, and oppression are so vile and repugnant to Allah that He commands the believers to fight those who assail them and inflict oppression:

"And slay them wherever you catch them and turn them out from where they have turned you out; for fitnah, tyranny and oppression are worse than slaughter; And fight them on until there is no more fitnah, tumult or oppression, and there prevail justice and faith in Allah; but if they cease, let there be no hostility except to those who practice oppression. (Al-Baqarah 2:190–93, Koran)

Allah's command to fight *fitnah*, however, is conditional:

> If the oppressors cease, let there be no further hostility except to those who practice oppression. Do not transgress limits. Allah does not love transgressors. (Al-Baqarah 2:190–93, Koran)

> When the Believers fight against fitnah and oppression, they fight in the cause of Allah. Those who reject faith in Allah, they fight in the cause of evil. (An-Nisa 4:75–76, Koran)

Fitnah: Allah has granted each believer a right to freedom; right to practice his and her *din* in accordance with his and her beliefs since, in Islam, there is no compulsion in matters of religion; right to life, which includes mental, physical, and emotional well-being; right safeguard to one's property; right to intellectual endeavors, acquisition of knowledge, and education; right to make a living; and right to free speech and action to enjoin good and forbid evil. In enjoying his freedoms, the individual ensures that his activities do not impinge on the similar rights of others. Oppression and tyranny—which deprives an individual believer, a community of believers, or their nation (the *ummah*) of their God-given right to such a freedom—is *fitnah* as described in the Koran. The perpetrators of such tyranny and oppression cannot belong to the fellowship of Allah, the fellowship of His covenant, nor the fellowship of the blessed *Nabiien* of Allah.

In the above *ayahs*, Allah commands the believers to fight such infidels until there is no more *fitnah*, treachery, and oppression and there prevails justice and faith in Allah everywhere. He orders them to slay them wherever they catch them and turn them out from where they have turned them out, for *fitnah*, tumult, and oppression are worse than slaughter. Allah has forbidden the taking of life. "Take not life, which Allah has made sacred, except by the way of justice or law."

Fitnah, tyranny, and oppression are so vile and repugnant that Allah commands the believers to fight those who assail them and inflict oppression. "Go forth, advance! Whether equipped well or lightly, perform *jihad* strive your utmost and struggle with your wealth and your persons in the cause of Allah." Allah loves those who fight in His cause in unison and solidarity. *Fitnah,* treachery, and oppression not only afflict those who perpetrate it but also affect everyone, guilty and innocent alike. Allah's command to fight *fitnah* is conditional, however: if the oppressors cease, let there be no further hostility except to those who practice *fitnah.* Do not transgress limits. Allah does not love transgressors.

In the twenty-first century, weakness, poverty, disunity, and fragmentation of the *ummah* arise from its lack of appreciation of the immense store of understanding and knowledge that is in the Koran. Muslims look at the word of Allah but do not see it. They listen to the word but do not hear it. Allah's *nur,* His light, is with them, but they do not let it enter their hearts. The mirror of their *nafs* is covered with the smoke of their greed and craving of worldly wealth. They cannot see Allah's *nur* through the smoky darkness in their heart. *Fitnah,* treachery, and oppression are by-products of darkened hearts, causing blindness to the *nur* of Allah. Without His *nur,* there cannot be *taqwa* of Allah; and in the absence of the consciousness of the reality of Allah, the darkened soul is open to the evil haunts of Satan.

Muslim societies have been plagued by *fitnah* and oppression since the death of the blessed *nabi.* In Muslim countries, *fitnah* is the result of the combination of internal and external forces. Although the perpetrators of *fitnah* often proclaim Allah as their Savior, their actions always belie their faith in Him.

Most believers, men and women, are not aware that Allah has granted each believer rights and freedom. Most do not know that when the blessed Muhammad died, every believer inherited the Koran, Allah's covenant, His *din*, and the Dar es Salaam. Every believer became the successor, inheritor, and the custodian of the blessed *nabi's* legacy till the end of time. Consequently, in the twenty-first century, majority of believers are unaware of their rights granted by Allah. They are unaware that Allah commands them to fight the *fitnah* of tyranny and oppression perpetrated by their self-appointed rulers, kings, military dictators, and infidel *awliya*, their Euro-Christian patrons.

Internal *Fitnah*: Hundreds of years of rule of sultans and later of the Western colonial masters produced three unique sources of internal *fitnah* that rule the roost in the Muslim societies of our day.

Priesthood. There is no priesthood in Islam; the believer has a highly personal and exclusive relationship with Allah. Such relationship does not permit the intervention of another human being between Allah and His believer. When the blessed Muhammad was taken up by Allah, every believer inherited the Koran, Allah's covenant, and His *din*. Every believer became the successor, inheritor, and custodian of the prophet's legacy till the end of time. The priests and clerics of Islam assumed the legacy of the pagan priesthood and began to speak on behalf of Allah. Through distortion and misrepresentation of the word of Allah and the pronouncements of His *nabi*, over the last fourteen hundred years, the priests and imams of Islam have created divisions and schisms to generate hundreds of self-righteous sects and subsects among the Muslims. Each sect is the enemy of the other. Every group has the dagger in the back of the other. This gradually smoldering *fitnah* of the priesthood is slowly consuming the body of the *ummah*.

Mercenary Armies of Islam: The blessed nabi said,

All believers shall rise as one man against anyone who seeks to commit injustice, aggression, crime, or spread mutual enmity amongst the Muslims. All believers are bonded one to another to the exclusion of other men. The believers shall leave none of their members in destitution without giving him in kindness that he needs by the way of his liberty.

However, this fight for unity, equality, and justice did not occur in the lands of Islam; the army of God and the army of Islam did not arise to fight in the cause of Allah to defend against *fitnah*, tyranny, and oppression and to seek retribution against injustice. The absolute loyalty of the army of Islam is to God, the Koran, and the *ummah*. The army of Islam defends the believers, their faith, their land, their wealth, and their honor and fights only against *fitnah* for truth and justice. In case of injury to the believers, their faith, their land, their wealth, and their honor, the believers are obliged to exact retribution.

No believer shall side with an unbeliever against a believer. Whosoever is convicted of killing a believer without a righteous cause shall be liable to the relatives of the killed. The killers shall be subject to retaliation by each believer until the relatives of the victim are satisfied with the retribution.

Had the Muslim communities stood united as one to avenge the blood of every fallen Muslim and rejected a separate peace with the pagans without all the Muslims participating in it, there would have been no *fitnah* and massacres in Algeria, Palestine, India, Afghanistan, Iraq, Bosnia, Chechnya, Kosovo, and Darfur. This unity demands revenge, retribution, and reprisal for every act of murder and injury in Dayr Yasin, Sabra, Shatila, Srebrenica, Jenin, Sarajevo, Falluja, Kosovo, Chechnya, Gujarat, Kashmir, Iraq, Guantanamo Bay, and Abu Ghraib. Had the Muslims stood up for one another and fought those who perpetrated *fitnah*, they would not have been groveling in the dustheap of humanity today.

Contrary to the stipulations of the covenant of Allah, the present six-million-man mercenary armies of Muslim states serve to bolster illegal regimes of *Munafiqeen*, the traitors to the cause of Islam. Instead of relieving the believers from *fitnah* and oppression, they cause them. They are the source of dichotomy and division in Islam; they are the defenders of the foreign hegemony over Islam. The armies of the sultans of the previous centuries and the rulers of modern times are the perpetrators of *fitnah*, and they are the enemies of Islam. They are the defenders of the borders created by the Western colonial powers that divide Islam today. They are the *fitnah*.

Rulers of Islam: Islam is a religion of voluntary submission of a human to the will of Allah after a considered conviction that He is the only reality and that everything else springs out of that reality. Allah has given every man the freedom of choice to submit or not to His will. There is no compulsion in matters of the *din*. Yet there are humans who by force of arms compel other humans to submit to their will. They demand obedience through imprisonment, torture, and murder. Every Muslim state in this day is a police state. Every Muslim ruler abuses his authority to plunder and debase the lands of Islam. Every Muslim state today is the source of *fitnah* that is eating into the heart and the soul of Islam.

1. The Fitnah of Priesthood: Islam is a relationship between Allah and His believers. The *din* of Allah is an all-encompassing and highly personal type of relationship in which Allah's *nur* resides in the believer's heart. The believer is conscious of Allah's closeness and mercy, obeys, trusts, and loves Allah, and Allah in return loves those who love Him and perform beautiful deeds.

Allah has granted knowledge and the wisdom of *furqan* and *taqwa* to the believers who have opened their hearts and minds to Him. Man has been granted the freedom of choice in doing what is wholesome and beautiful or what is corrupt and ugly. This knowledge reminds man of the scales of Allah's justice; the two hands of Allah, His mercy and His wrath, are reflected in the human domain, where people have been appointed Allah's vicegerents. Deeds of goodness and wholesomeness are associated with mercy, paradise, and what is beautiful. Evil and corruption is rewarded with wrath, hell, and what is ugly.

Everything in the universe is connected to Allah through its creation, birth, sustenance, existence, demise, and death. Every particle and atom spins at the command of Allah's majesty; it has done so for billions of years and will continue to do so at Allah's command. These particles and atoms continue to spin in the cells of the living when they are alive and when the cells are devoid of life at Allah's command. Nothing ever happens without Allah's will and knowledge. No human, howsoever proud or strong, is independent of Him. The newborn is thus physically connected to Allah through His mercy. The particles and atoms in his cells spin at Allah's mercy in life and in death. Through Allah's mercy, his cells grow and multiply with sustenance from Allah.

Every man and woman in this journey is born alone and innocent. The individual leads his short life in this world, and when he dies, he leaves this world alone. In death, his cells disintegrate, yet the particles and atoms continue to spin at Allah's command forever. His life was a miracle and a mirage. Now man was here, and in an instant, he was gone and all alone. The only reality is Allah. Every substance and relationship man accumulated is left behind—parents, friends, wealth, children, priests, kings, human laws, honors, comforts, and so on.

They all accompanied man to the edge of his life and then parted to wait for their own demise one day.

In this journey, man is presented with Allah's covenant as his guide, *taqwa* of Allah as his shield against evil, and *furqan* as Allah's compass to the straight path of righteousness. If man accepts the path of Allah and follows His covenant as his guide, *taqwa* of Allah as the shield against evil, and furqan as Allah's compass to the straight path, he becomes a believer and of the righteous. The way to righteousness is in Allah's guidance and covenant in the Koran. The way to righteousness lies in the inspiration from the Koran through the recitation of the Koran at leisure, at dawn, during the day, and under the glow of the lamp at night. Every little bit of devotion makes the *nur* of Allah glow in the heart till the believer is connected to Him and begins to follow His path. In this path, the believer does what is righteous and what is beautiful. Beautiful actions please Allah.

This communion between the believer and Allah is all exclusive. Submission establishes the link between the believer and Allah. The believer asks, and Allah gives. The believer loves Allah, and Allah loves him in return. The believer asks for the straight path, and Allah shows him the way. The believer praises Allah, and Allah showers His mercy and grace upon him. The believer remembers Allah, and Allah responds to those who praise Him, thank Him, and ask Him.

The believer on his chosen journey on the path of Allah is well equipped. He has Allah's protection, guidance, and direction. Does the believer need dogmas and laws based on human systems? Aren't Allah's word and the covenant sufficient as guidance? Allah is the absolute Truth (*Haqq*). All worldly, human, and priestly systems are not based on *haqq*. Allah is the only *Haqq*. What is not *haqq* is *batil*, the untruth. Those who let go of Allah's hand and clutch at the human priestly dogma and creed have fallen astray in Satan's footsteps.

The most important theological point made by the Koran is that there is one God, Allah, universal and beyond comparison, who creates and sustains both the material world and the world of human experience. Allah is *Haqq*, the absolute Truth. All other forms of so-called truth are either false in their initial premises or contingently true only in limited situations. The recognition of this fact is of paramount importance to all believers. That Allah is *Haqq* is undeniable. *Haqq*, the absolute truth, does not fall into the domain of human fancy nor human ideas, but it stands for beliefs that manifest in concrete form. These beliefs must be in harmony with the changing needs of time and with Allah's laws of the universe. No belief relating to this world can be called *haqq* unless its truth is established by the positive demonstration of Allah's reality. This truth is permanent and unchanging.

There is no priesthood in Islam. *Haqq* does not need priests. Yet there are people among the believers who talk like priests, dress like priests, and preach like priests. They are indeed the priests. They preach dogma and creed to the believers in the name of Allah and His blessed *nabi*. Yet what they preach distances the believers from Allah, the Koran, and the blessed prophet. The priests spread hatred among the believers and discord in the *ummah*. They concern themselves with obscure *Hadith* and man-made Sharia and *fiqh* that do not constitute the *din* of Allah. Their teachings and fatwas often contradict the Koran and the spirit of the blessed *nabi's* teaching.

If miraculously one day all the mullahs, self-proclaimed ulema, ayatollahs, imams, and Wahhabi preachers were to disappear from the face of this earth, from that day on, there will be no Shia, no Sunni, nor any other sect in the world. Every Muslim will be a believer of Allah. The mullahs, self-proclaimed ulema, ayatollahs, imams, and Wahhabi preachers sustain one another through their own inbred dogma and creed. In turn, the mullahs and priests sustain their sects through their man-made belief systems. It is a cycle in which the priests continue to perpetuate their creeds generation after generation with "quote and reference" to their earlier imams and priests, repeating distortions, misquotations, and misrepresentations. The believers cannot hear the gentle message of Allah over all the noise and commotion created by the mullahs and religious scholars in the world of Islam. In the same token, if there were no rabbis, Christian priests, ministers, clerics, preachers, pastors, bishops, popes, pundits, and mullahs, there will be no Judaism, Christianity, Hinduism, nor sectarian Islam. All those who believe in one God will then be servants of the same Allah, the religion of Abraham, Moses, Jesus, and Muhammad.

Yet priests have been with us since the times when man attained civilization. The priesthood of the Sumerian civilization left a powerful legacy on the generations to follow. Within a short time, the priestly culture spread to all human civilizations, to the Indus valley, Babylon, Egypt, Greece and Rome. Priesthood independently sprung up in the Americas.

Humans crave a belief in the supernatural. They seek comfort and security in the thought of supernatural protection from gods. Priesthood is ever present and ready to exploit this need. Sumerians and all other civilizations were served by many gods—gods of war, fertility goddesses, sun god, moon god, gods of rain, gods of death, and so on. Priests were at hand to provide the protection at a cost, an offering to gods. The cult of gods did not operate in isolation. Though communities had their own particular guardian gods, they did share other gods with other towns and villages. Devotees traveled to far, distant places to pay homage to their gods. There was considerable exchange and sharing of patronage, protection, and blessing of gods among varying communities. Priesthood became the original corporations and propaganda machine for their gods.

Such publicity also took advantage of the sense of weaknesses and vulnerabilities of the people. The greater the insecurity among the population, the more the devotees of particular gods were, the greater the wealth and influence of the priests. There were festivals of all sorts involving seasons, planting of seed, harvest, fertility, human sacrifice, fire, light, and many others. The priests began to control commerce, levy tithe, lend money on interest, organize professional armies, and provide temple prostitutes, alcohol, and protection against calamities. What mattered in the end was the power and wealth. Priesthood became a network of guilds connected through secret societies that began to control the affairs of the world for all times to come.

Thirty-eight hundred years ago, Blessed *Nabi* Ibrahim saw through the deceit and falsehood of the cult of false gods of Mesopotamia. He began to speak out. Being a danger to the cult of the priests, he was threatened to be silent or else. Thirty-two hundred years ago when Blessed *Nabi* Moses spoke against the same false gods, the priesthood persistently undermined and frustrated his efforts by worshipping the golden calf. Two thousand years ago, Jesus found the cult of the rabbis thoroughly objectionable. When he persisted in speaking against godlessness and corruption of the temple, the priests, and the moneylenders, he was nailed to the cross. Fourteen hundred years ago, Blessed *Nabi* Muhammad rebelled against the gods and priesthood of the Quraish; he was threatened with death and banished from his home. It was the same organism of priesthood developed by the Sumerians, whose descendants fought tooth and nail to protect their conspiratorial privileges, threatened by Ibrahim, Moses, Jesus, and Muhammad.

Priesthood created the cult of gods, spoke for their gods, and then assumed the power and wealth of the same gods. The corporation of gods run by priests in the days of *Nabi* Ibrahim is the longest-living organism, with its neurons and synapses running through the worshippers of the golden calf and then the Pharisees down to our times—the descendants of the priesthood of the Quraish, the enemies of the blessed *nabi* Muhammad. They appointed and directed kings. The ruling classes and the priest class successfully formed the system that controlled every Muslim's religion and exploited all Islamic societies.

The organism of priesthood had kept up with the times. It never let its tricks of trade get stale. The religions required periodic stimulation from wars, miracles, festivals, human sacrifice, and coronations. Whenever the true prophets won over adherents from the priesthood of gods, the counteroffensive was never far behind. Priesthood offered protection, vice, alcohol, gambling, and women to attract adherents to their gods. Priests directed trade and commerce and were the beneficiaries of usury. Priests foretold fortune and future, and for this supernatural prophecy, they gained influence and the gratitude of their followers.

Blessed *Nabi* Ibrahim (Abraham) reformed the Sumerian traditions in the name of the one true, merciful God. He left behind many followers with oral and perhaps written traditions that were passed on to the coming generations. The priesthood distorted his teachings. After eight lifetimes of seventy years, put end to end, *Nabi* Musa (Moses) taught his people the worship of one merciful God. Moses reformed the pagan Egyptian traditions of his people. He spoke with God on Mount Sinai through the smoke and haze of the burning bush and climbed down to the desert carrying the Ten Commandments of God inscribed on two stone slabs. After a lifetime of struggle with his people and their traditional priesthood, he left an oral and a written tradition. His people continued to revert to the pagan calf worship and pervert Allah's commandments.

When disputes arose questioning the divinity of *Nabi* Eisa (Jesus Christ), it was a difference of opinion among the priests of the fourth century. The priests assumed the prerogative of God and formulated a doctrine that defined the relationship between humanity and God. This relationship was to become so convoluted that no two Christians have the same understanding of their relationship to their Creator. The trinity of God has an incongruent understanding for each person and each sect. For the human of common understanding, Jesus is God. Jesus, in fact, became God on May 20, 325. On that day, Jesus became the Creator, the Word, the Judge, the Redeemer, and the only Way. In return, the priest class retained and augmented the special hierarchical status as it was among the Sumerians, Babylonians, Egyptians, Israelites, and Byzantines as the spokespersons of their God and gods. They retained the power to guide, legislate, teach, judge, excommunicate, and execute. The priests wore crowns, regalia, and jewels; they carried ornamental staffs to signify divine connection. Their processions into the places of worship in full regalia in pomp and circumstance resemble a spectacle and entertainment for the common folk than a true act of worship of the Creator. The priests speak in strange tongues and words incomprehensible to men and women.

Three hundred years after the blessed *nabi* Muhammad died, movements similar to ones that occurred after the times of the blessed prophets Ibrahim, Musa, and Jesus came to pass in Islam. Three months before the blessed *nabi* died, he performed the hajj. After midday prayers on the ninth day of *Zul-hajj* (March 632 CE) at Arafat, the blessed *nabi* delivered the historic hajj khutbah that has come to be known as the farewell address. When the blessed *nabi* delivered the hajj khutbah, he knew that he had completed his earthly mission and that his days in the world were numbered. The blessed Muhammad was aware that he was dying, yet he did not appoint a successor. He was a *nabi* and a *rasul.* Only Allah has the prerogative of appointing and sending His *rasuls* to this world.

When Blessed Muhammad died, he left in this world his mortal remains, the Koran, Allah's covenant, and the *din.* When the blessed Muhammad was taken up by Allah, every Believer inherited the Koran, Allah's covenant, and his *din.* Every believer became the successor, inheritor, and custodian of the prophet's legacy till the end of time. It was the negligence and the inability of the believer to assume his authority as the custodian of the prophet's legacy and Allah's covenant that degraded the *ummah* for over fourteen centuries.

After the *nabi* passed away, the succession to the blessed *nabi* Muhammad's presumed temporal authority became a problem from the very beginning. The period of the first four caliphs is regarded by the Muslims as the ideal period of Islamic history, when Islam was practiced perfectly. This is far from obvious when one looks at the contemporary records. For one thing, three of the four caliphs were assassinated.

What is the source of the continuing strife among the Muslims? Mecca in the pre-Islamic times was a pagan sanctuary with a cube-shaped shrine as the center of heathen worship. Kaaba housed over 360 gods, with the presiding god called Hubal. According to legend, in the fourth century of the Common Era, Amr ibn Luhayy, a descendant of Qahtan, a sheikh of Hejaz, placed an idol called Hubal inside the Kaaba after the Quraish group of tribes supplanted the Khuza'ah as the protectors of the holy ancient place. Luhayy had traveled to Hit in Mesopotamia and brought back with him the cult of the goddesses al-Uzza and Manat and combined it with the cult of Hubal, the god of the Khuza'ah. Hubal is considered to be of Aramaic origin, and its name is a variation of Baal, the Sumerian god (hu' Baal*)*. Hubal was one of the deities of Quraish before Islam.

Some of the deities of Kaaba had a universal following in the fourth century CE, when Christianity had not yet gained a popular following in the Middle East. Al-Uzza was Venus of the Greeks, Aphrodite of the Romans, and Isis of the Egyptians. Al-Lat was the Athena of the Greeks and Manat of the Arabs and represented the goddess of fate for the Persians and the Romans. Hubal was the Semitic Baal, Adonis of the Syrian and Greek Pantheon, and Tammuz, the consort of Ishtar, of the Babylonians. And a six-day "funeral" for this god was observed at the very door of the temple in Jerusalem, to the horror of the reformer Ezekiel. Temples for the worship of Baal, Adonis, Tammuz, Venus, Athena, Uzza, Aphrodite, and Isis were commonplace in the Byzantine and Roman Empires. These gods formed the collective pantheon of the known world before the advent of Islam.

Arab tribes from all over Arabia assembled once a year for mass worship of their gods. The occasion was also used by the visiting tribes for trade of goods and as a social gathering. The traders and their caravans plied between Arabia and destinations in the Byzantine and Persian Empires as well as Yemen. Over thousands of years, Arab traders had acquired the paramount position of intermediaries in the exchange of goods between the Indian and Mediterranean traders. The trade, maritime, and pilgrim connection provided Meccans and Arab tribes freedom, prosperity, affluence, and luxury that were not within the reach of people of other settled communities of the Middle East. The Meccans loved the luxury, wine, and revelry that wealth brought with it. To satisfy their passionate search for pleasure, they held their celebrations and drinking parties to find satisfaction in their slave girls in the center of the city right in front of the Kaaba. There in the proximity of more than 360 icons of gods belonging to over 300 Arabian tribes, the sacred elders, and the priests of the Quraish and their aristocracy held their salons and shared stories, wine, and pleasures of the flesh.

Pagan worship at the Kaaba gave rise to a number of offices assumed by the king or the head priest of Mecca. These offices were *hijabah, siqayah, rifadah, nadwah, liwa,* and *qiyadah. Hijabah* bequeathed maintenance of the house and guardianship over its keys. *Siqayah* was the provision of fresh water and wine to the pilgrims. *Rifadah* was the provision of food to the pilgrims. *Nadwah* was the chairmanship of all religious meetings and their arrangements. *Liwa* was one who carried the flag, and *qiyadah* was the commander and head of the army defending Mecca and its pilgrims. These offices claimed a tithe and levy on each pilgrim, trader, and inhabitant of Mecca, which made the Quraish priesthood very rich.

Qusayy ibn Kilab, a man who had been brought up in Syria in around 480 CE, dispossessed the reigning tribe of Mecca, the Khuza'ah, with the help of the Quraish and assumed all the offices associated with the Kaaba. Thereafter, his clan became the richest and the most influential family in Arabia. Wherever there is wealth, there is greed and craving. The descendants of Qusayy fell on one another to gain control over the guardianship, priesthood, and wealth earned by the gods of Kaaba. To avoid civil war and disintegration of the Quraish tribe, a peace treaty was worked out, and the offices of Kaaba were divided between the two contesting clans. The descendants of Abd Manaf (Hashim) were granted the *siqayah* and *rifadah*, and the descendants of Abd al-Dar (Abd Shams) kept the *hijabah*, the *liwa*, and the *nadwah*. This peace lasted till the advent of Islam. Hashim's descendants continued to provision water, wine, and food for the pilgrims. Abd Shams's descendants continued to administer the upkeep of the Kaaba and its defenses.

Most historians and Muslims do not recognize the relationship of pagan priesthood of the Quraish with Islam's later civil wars and its wars for acquisition of territory. After the blessed *nabi* died, there was an immediate though subdued struggle to revive the priestly power that had been destroyed by the fall of Mecca and the destruction of its gods. Though the powers that be could not revive the gods of the Kaaba, they could, however, take over Islam and bide their time till an opportune moment. With the rise of Islam and the conquest of Syria and Egypt, the choicest jobs of the new empire were given to the Quraish and to other Meccans. Whereas the descendants of Hashim—the providers of water, food, and wine to the pilgrims—stayed back in Mecca and Medina, the descendants of Abd Shams, the standard bearers of the army, were sent to the conquered territories. Among them was Mu'awiyah, the son of Abu Sufyan, the sworn enemy of Islam and the prophet. Both the son and the father were pagans till the last moment, till they could be pagans no more.

When Uthman ibn Affan was elected the third caliph, he filled the bureaucracy of the new empire with his kin, who were the descendants of Abd Shams. The corruption in the governance of Syria and the accumulation of wealth in the hands of Mu'awiyah and his kin incensed some soldiers to kill the caliph, Uthman. The grabbing power and wealth by one branch of the priestly family of the Quraish led to the murder of the caliph and a civil war between the next caliph, Ali ibn Abi Talib, and his stepmother-in-law, A'ishah, the blessed *nabi's* widow. Ali ibn Abi Talib, *Nabi* Muhammad's cousin and son-in-law (Hashmi), was elected caliph; but Mu'awiyah, son of Abu Sufyan of the clan of Abd Shams (Shamsi) who happened to be the governor of Syria at the time, refused to recognize him as the caliph. Five years of civil war resulted between Mu'awiyah, based in Damascus, and Ali ibn Abi Talib of Beni Hashim, based in Kufah.

This was a civil war among the descendants of Qusayy, who had earlier avoided a civil war and disintegration of the tribe of Quraish by dividing the spoils of their priestly inheritance. The gods of Mecca, who had provided power and wealth to the descendants of Qusayy, had been destroyed. This time, the war was fought for the control of wealth and power that the Islamic empire had garnered. Fighting among

Muslims, bloodshed, and killing of Muslims are strictly forbidden. This was a civil war among the Quraish and also among the prophet's immediate family. They had been used to bloodshed in their priestly days. Historians tell us about the battles, but we do not know of the conspiracies and family intrigues among the Quraish that undermined the new Islam's order. What actually followed was totally against the teachings of Allah, the Koran, and the blessed *nabi*. However, what did occur was a norm among the Quraish—a fight for the control and perpetuation of power of the priesthood.

In 661, Ali ibn Abi Talib was assassinated, and Mu'awiyah assumed the caliphate by force of arms and established the Umayyad dynasty, which ruled the Muslim world for ninety years, from 661 to 750. This was a victory of the dynasty of Abu Shams over the dynasty of Hashim. This war and struggle had nothing to do with the blessed *rasul* of Allah, the Koran, nor the *din* of Islam.

In 750 CE, there was another civil war among the Quraish; the descendants of Abbas, the blessed *nabi's* uncle, of the Hashim's clan rose in revolt and overthrew the Umayyad, the descendants of Abu Sufyan of the Abu Shams clan, with much bloodshed and killing of Muslims by Muslims. The Hashemite slaughtered every Umayyad they could find. Thereafter, the Abbasid dynasty ruled the Muslim empire until 861. Abandoning Damascus, the Umayyad capital, the Abbasids built Baghdad as their capital.

After the succession to the presumed *temporal* authority of the blessed *nabi* had been usurped by different priestly branches of the Quraish, a descendent of Abbas began to coerce clerics and judges to present him the authority to change the Koran. When Al-Ma'mun came to the throne, difficulties to his rule were increasing. To deal with these, Al-Ma'mun set up the so-called inquisition (*minhah*). The judges and people in authority had to state publicly that they believed that the Koran was created and rejected the view that it was an uncreated word of Allah. This was not a piece of theological hairsplitting but an important sociopolitical and legal question.

Soon after *Nabi* Muhammad's death, some people had the belief that the caliph was or should be a divinely inspired person whose decisions should be binding on Muslims. In other words, they wanted the caliph to carry a priestly authority both in temporal and spiritual matters, and this was also the viewpoint of the caliph Al-Ma'mun. If the Koran, though it was Allah's word, was created, then a leader inspired by Allah could presumably change it.

The opposite point of view was that of scholar-jurists, who had become an important class in Islamic lands. This, in effect, was a battle for the control of Islam between the descendants of the priesthood of Quraish, Qusayy's descendants, and the newly formed priest class from among the people. Quite a large population of the empire could not speak or read Arabic and required the services of ulema to understand the complex issues in the Koran. The scholars insisted that the Koran was the uncreated word of Allah and therefore unchangeable and that they alone were the authorized interpreters of the Koran, and only they could pronounce how it was to be applied to contemporary situations. That implied that it was they and not the caliph who had the final word. In fact, the descendants of the priesthood of Hashim and Shams or the newfangled ulema had neither the wisdom nor the authority to change or interpret the Koran. Allah addresses the Koran to the *nabi* and to those who believe. After the blessed *nabi* died, every believer inherited the Koran. When Allah speaks to those who believe, will He not inspire those whom He addresses with the understanding of His message?

The policy of inquisition was finally discontinued in around 850 CE because the people refused to accept the caliph's demands. It was a power struggle for the right to use the scriptures for the control of the religion as it had occurred among the pagans, the Israelites, the Jews, and the Christians.

Lady Fatimah and Ali ibn Abi Talib's descendants are held in high esteem by Muslims because of they descended from the blessed prophet. Ali ibn Abi Talib, his sons Hassan and Hussein, and their descendants also deserve veneration and honor by every believer because of their beautiful character and honorable conduct. Over the last fourteen hundred years, the lines of descent and pedigree have been dimmed by time, diluted with outside genes, polygamy, concubinage, and false claims of prophetic blood. The blessed *nabi* said in his farewell address, "None is higher than the other unless he is higher in virtue."

In matters of the *din*, every believer received the prophet's heritage, the Koran, and the *din*. Every believer receives Allah in his heart according to his virtue. The battles for the succession of the blessed *nabi* were the legacy of the pagan and priestly Quraish for the control of center of the new faith and the Kaaba. These past struggles of the Quraish are irrelevant in today's world. Total Koran is the total *din*. Men and priests do not intervene in the believer's relationship with Allah. The division of Islam into the Sunni and Shia sects was the result of infighting among the descendants of Qusayy for the control of Islam. This battle has continued to this day, with the priest class battling to control the pulpit and the throne of the Islamic state. Over the centuries, priests have raised the flag of *fitnah* with a claim to be God, a prophet, the Mahdi, an imam of the *din*, and a spokesperson of Allah. Their claims were for supremacy over the believers. True Muslims are believers of Allah. Believers of Allah and His *din* are not Shia, Sunni, nor any other sect, which are inventions and innovations of priests of the pagans, Sumerians, Israelites, and Christians.

If miraculously today, all the mullahs, self-proclaimed ulema, ayatollahs, imams, and Wahhabi preachers were to disappear from the face of the earth, from this day onward, there will be no Shia, no Sunni, nor any other sect in the world. Every Muslim will be a believer of Allah. The mullahs, self-proclaimed ulema, ayatollahs, imams, and Wahhabi preachers sustain one another through their own inbred dogma and creed. In turn, the mullahs and priests sustain their sects through their man-made belief systems. It is a self-perpetuating cycle in which the priests continue to recycle their creeds generation after generation with "quote and reference" to their earlier imams and priests, repeating distortions, misquotations, and misrepresentations. The believers cannot hear the gentle message of Allah over all the noise and din created by the mullahs and religious scholars in the world of Islam.

In the same token, if there were no rabbis, Christian priests, ministers, clerics, preachers, pastors, bishops, popes, pundits, and mullahs, there would be no Judaism, Christianity, Hinduism, nor sectarian Islam. All those who believe in one God would then be the servants of the same Allah, the religion of Abraham, Moses, Jesus, and Muhammad.

2. The *Fitnah* of the State and Mercenary Armies of Islam: The covenant of Muhammad and the covenant of Allah have established clear conditions when the believers will rise in arms and go to battle. The following conditions are summarized in the covenant of Muhammad written in the first year after hijra:

a) Defense of the unity of all believers: All believers shall rise as one against anyone who seeks to commit injustice, aggression, crime, or spread mutual enmity among the Muslims. All believers are bonded to one another to the exclusion of other men. The believers shall leave none of their members in destitution without giving him in kindness that he needs by way of his liberty.

b) Retribution against injustice: All believers shall avenge the blood of one another when anyone falls fighting in the way of Allah. Whoever is convicted of killing a believer deliberatively but without righteous cause shall be liable to the relatives of the killed. Until the latter are satisfied, the killer shall be subject to retaliation by each believer.

c) One and indivisible Pax Islamica: This Pax Islamica is one and indivisible. No believer shall enter a separate peace without all other believers whenever there is fighting in the cause of God except on the basis of equality and justice to all others.

However, this fight for unity, equality, and justice did not occur in the lands of Islam; the army of God and the army of Islam did not arise to fight in the cause of Allah to defend against *fitnah*, tyranny, and oppression and to seek retribution against injustice. The absolute loyalty of the army of Islam is to God, the Koran, and the *ummah*. The army of Islam defends the believers, their faith, their land, their wealth, and their honor and fights only against *fitnah* for truth and justice. In case of injury to the believers, their faith, their land, their wealth, and their honor, the believers are obliged to exact retribution. No believer shall side with an unbeliever against a believer. All believers shall avenge the blood of anyone who falls fighting in the cause of God. Whoever is convicted of killing a believer without a righteous cause shall be liable to the relatives of the killed. The killers shall be subject to retaliation by each believer until the relatives of the victim are satisfied with the retribution.

Had the Muslim communities stood united as one to avenge the blood of every fallen Muslim and rejected a separate peace with the pagans without all the Muslims participating in it, there would have been no *fitnah* and massacres in Algeria, Palestine, India, Afghanistan, Iraq, Bosnia, Chechnya, and Kosovo. This unity demands revenge, retribution, and reprisal for every act of murder and injury in Dayr Yasin, Sabra, Shatila, Srebrenica, Janin, Sarajevo, Fallujah, Kosovo, Chechnya, Gujarat, Kashmir, Iraq, Guantanamo Bay, and Abu Ghraib. Had the Muslims stood up for one another and fought those who perpetrated the *fitnah*, they would not have been groveling in the dustheap of humanity today.

The loyalty of the army of Islam is not to any individual, state, government, or party. The loyalty is to the precepts of the covenant of Allah and the covenant of the Koran. This army is an organism ordained by Allah with the stipulations for its conduct laid down by His covenant summarized below:

Wars and slaughter are abhorrent to Allah. Allah says:

> If anyone slew a person - unless it be for murder or for spreading mischief in the land - it would be as if he slew the whole people: and if anyone saved a life, it would be as if he saved the life of the whole people. (Al-Ma'idah 5:32, Koran)

> Take not life, which Allah hath made sacred, except by the way of justice or law: This He commands you, that you may learn wisdom. (Al-An'am 6: 151-53)

And then Allah declares to the Believers that *fitnah*, treachery, and oppression are worse than slaughter and the taking of life. *Fitnah*, treason, and oppression are so vile and repugnant to Allah that He commands the believers to fight those who assail them and inflict oppression:

> And slay them wherever you catch them and turn them out from where they have turned you out; for fitnah, tumult and oppression are worse than slaughter; And fight them on until there is no more fitnah, tumult or oppression, and there prevail justice and faith in Allah; but if they cease, let there be no hostility except to those who practice oppression. (Al-Baqarah 2:190–93, Koran)

Allah's command to fight *fitnah*, however, is conditional:

> If the oppressors cease, let there be no further hostility except to those who practice oppression. Do not transgress limits. Allah does not love transgressors. (Al-Baqarah 2:190–93, Koran)

> When the Believers fight against fitnah and oppression, they fight in the cause of Allah. Those who reject faith in Allah, they fight in the cause of evil. (An-Nisa 4:75–76, Koran)

Contrary to the stipulations of the covenant of Allah, the present six-million-man mercenary armies of the Muslim states serve to bolster illegal regimes of traitors to the cause of Islam. Instead of relieving the believers from *fitnah* and oppression, they cause them. They are the source of dichotomy and division in Islam; they are the defenders of the borders dividing the Islamic state. During the twentieth century, they had not successfully defended any Muslim people or a state. The Muslim armies and intelligence services in the twentieth century had detained, tortured, and killed more believers than their professed enemies did. State mercenary armies are a state within the Muslim state with loyalties to dubious and murky causes harmful to Islam.

What is the reason for the existence of Muslim mercenary armies? They bolster the corrupt and dishonest rulers and their governments against the wishes of their people. The Muslim rulers keep the Muslim world divided in the interests of the perpetrators of the external *fitnah*, the Euro-Christian powers. In return for their services to the interests of the United States and other Western governments, the Euro-Christian powers pay ten billion dollars annually to the mercenary armies of Egypt, Pakistan, Jordan, Oman, Morocco, Afghanistan, and Uzbekistan.

Their officer class receives additional benefits under the table to look after Western interests in their countries and in the Middle East. The Euro-Christian civilization is clearly against the unity of Islam. The state mercenary armies of the Muslim countries are the curse to Islam and the source of internal *fitnah*. Does the sight of companies with ill-clad, demoralized, poorly trained, and poorly equipped soldiers at the checkpoints in the streets of Syria, Jordan, Egypt, and Pakistan present a picture of an army protecting Islam from its enemy? The picture is that of *fitnah* and oppression of Muslims by the regimes of these countries. They prevent free movement of the citizens in their legitimate quest for freedom and work. The mercenary armies of Islam are the armies of occupation in the land of Islam.

The largest army on the earth: Imagine a country with the largest land base, with coasts rimmed by thousands of miles of blue water oceans, with a vast number of rivers flowing from hundreds of snowcapped mountains through its deserts, grasslands, fertile valleys, and plains into rich deltas, lakes, and oceans bursting with marine life and other resources—a land blessed by Allah with resources never equaled in history, peopled with devout, hardworking populations who know how to utilize such resources in the service of Allah and His creatures. Again, see in your mind's eye an army, the largest in history of mankind, keeping this land, its borders and resources, its oceans and skies, its people and wealth secure from marauders who have traditionally raided other lands for their resources.

These defense forces compose of an army of six million men in about 300 infantry and mechanized divisions equipped with 30,000 tanks and armored vehicles, an air force of 3,580 aircraft of varying vintage, and a naval force equipped with 230 coastal and oceangoing ships equipped with armaments bought from the West and Russia. There are also 60 submarines in the armada. These armed forces are also equipped with short- and medium-range missiles tipped with about 100 nuclear bombs. The country has a budding arms-manufacturing industry producing low- and medium-technology weapons. The annual budget of the combined forces is $150 billion, of which $50 billion annually goes to Western countries to purchase their discarded and obsolete weaponry. The West then uses these funds to refurbish its own arsenal with the latest high-tech weapons.

You might have guessed that we are talking about the combined might of the Islamic world at the beginning of the twenty-first century. This army has never won any battle of significance since the war for the Gallipoli Peninsula about a century ago. These armed forces have not defended in any significant manner the Islamic world since the disintegration of the Ottoman Empire. The wars of independence of Islamic lands from the colonial rule in India, Iran, Iraq, Syria, Egypt, Morocco, and Algeria were fought by the masses with civil disobedience and jihadi guerrilla warfare. The largest army in the world, the state-organized mercenary army of Islam, has failed to safeguard people from *fitnah* and oppression in Palestine, Afghanistan, Iraq, Lebanon, Kashmir, Sinkiang, Kosovo, Bosnia, Mindanao, Chechnya, and the other Muslim peoples of Russia.

The Muslim armies and security services are the source of *fitnah*, oppression, and treachery to the *momineen*, resisting the tyranny of the circle of evil of the *Munafiqeen* and the *Mutaffifeen*. What went wrong? The Muslim army of the twentieth and twenty-first centuries has its guns pointed inward toward its own people, whereas the external borders of Islam are guarded and patrolled by the naval fleets of America and United Europe. The Muslim state armies should be fighting the *fitnah*, treachery, and oppression by enemies of Allah and Islam—the *kafirun*, the *mushrikun*, the *Munafiqeen* and the *zalimun*, who have usurped and plundered the resources of the believers for the last two hundred years. Instead, the Muslim armies and security forces are themselves the source of *fitnah*, oppression, and treachery to the *muttaqeen*, resisting the tyranny of the circle of evil of the *Munafiqeen* and the *Mutaffifeen*. Clear examples are the armed and security forces of Reza Shah Pahlavi of Iran, the mullahs of Iran, Saddam Hussein of Iraq, the Taliban of Afghanistan, military dictators of Pakistan, the Saudi family of Arabia, Suharto of Indonesia, the Assads of Syria, Anwar Sadat and Hosni Mubarak of Egypt, Gaddhafi of Libya, the military tyrants of Algeria, and the corrupt royalty of Morocco. This is a clear testimony that the believers of the covenant of Allah and those who control the mercenary armies of Islam have not surrendered to the will of the same Allah and do not strive in His path. In fact, the armies of the Muslim states are the perpetrators of tyranny and *fitnah*.

3. The *Fitnah* of the Rulers of Islam: Islam is a religion of voluntary submission of man to the will of Allah after a considered conviction that Allah is the only reality and that everything else springs out of that reality. Allah has given every man the freedom of choice to submit or not to His will. There is no compulsion in matters of the *din*. Yet there are humans who by force of arms compel other humans to submit to their will. They demand obedience through imprisonment, torture, and murder. Every Muslim state in this day is a police state. Every Muslim ruler abuses his authority to plunder and debase the lands of Islam.

The Muslim states are governed by self-appointed kings, dictators, or politicians who are divorced from their *din* and their people, the believers. They belong to and serve the interests of the circle of evil.

There is a clear reason for the glaring weakness of the state-run armies of the Muslim nation-states. The Muslim states are governed by kings, dictators, and politicians whose only interest is the maintenance of their power over their people.

4. The External *Fitnah* of the Circle of Evil: Two hundred years ago, the circle of evil began its control of the world's wealth through conspiracy, subterfuge, and secrecy by undermining the stability of countries through war, strife, and discord and by undermining governments through the creation of confusion in the financial markets. The Western armies and intelligence services are the foot soldiers of the circle of evil, and the rulers both of the East and the West are their pawns and puppets to be manipulated at will for the purpose of control of the power and wealth of the world.

The circle of evil is the external *fitnah* whose intent is to destroy Islam. Its intent has always been to corrupt, divide, and control the wealth of the Islamic land through the manipulation of its rulers who were initially placed in positions of power by the circle with the help of Western armies, intelligence, and diplomacy. The weakness of the nation-state mercenary armies of the modern Islamic states clearly arises from the nonfulfillment of Allah's injunctions in the covenant. Faith in Allah's promise and His power, unity of the *ummah*, justice, and struggle to end *fitnah* and tyranny are essential actions ordained in the covenant. When an individual believer reneges in the fulfillment of his covenant with Allah, he only does it to the detriment to his own soul. However, such an action on the part of the community and its appointed leaders leads to the undermining, enslavement, and impoverishment of the whole Islamic community for many generations.

The foundation of the regimes of the imperial families of the Arabian Peninsula, Jordan, Brunei, and Morocco and the imperial occupation governments of Hosni Mubarak of Egypt and the generals of Pakistan are supported by the external *fitnah*—the British, US, and NATO armed forces, intelligence, and diplomatic services in opposition to the aspirations of their own people. In return, these regimes provide services to the circle of evil to subvert, undermine, and weaken the neighboring Islamic and Arab countries of Iran, Afghanistan, Iraq, Syria, Libya, Algeria, Sudan, and Mauritania. The *ummah* is saddled with the curse and the *fitnah* of priesthood, mercenary armies of Muslim states, and their corrupt rulers.

The Eighteenth Commandment of Allah

Be Quick in the Race for Forgiveness from Your Lord, Restrain Anger, and Pardon All Humans

Fear the Fire, which is prepared for those who reject Faith;

And obey Allah and the Rasool; that you may obtain mercy.

Be quick in the race for forgiveness from your Lord, and
for a Garden whose measurement is that of the heavens
and of the earth, prepared for the righteous.

Those who give freely whether in prosperity, or in adversity,
those who restrain anger, and pardon all humans, for Allah loves
those who do beautiful deeds. (Ali 'Imran 3:130–34, Koran)

Among Allah's names are *ar-Rahman* (the Beneficent), *ar-Rahim* (the Merciful), and *al-Ghafoor* (the Forgiving). His mercy overtakes His punishment and anger.

Say: "O my Servants who have transgressed against their souls! despair not of the Mercy of Allah: for Allah forgives all sins: for He is Oft-Forgiving, Most Merciful. (Az-Zumar 39:53)

Every human action in daily life reaches back into the divine reality that everything in the universe is governed by tawhid, yet Allah has granted humans a freedom of choice, which can upset the balance in the creation, balance of justice, and balance of atmospheric elements and of environmental pollution and cause destruction of animal species and of populations, cities, and agriculture through human actions. The covenant tells people why they should be Allah's servants and explains which path they should follow to become His vicegerents. It makes clear that human activity is deeply rooted in the Real, and this has everlasting repercussions in this world and in the hereafter.

The wholesome (*salihun*) are the ones who live in harmony with the Real (*Haqq*) and establish wholesomeness (*saalihaat*) through their words and deeds throughout the world. In contrast, the corrupt (*mufsidun*) destroy the proper balance and relationship with Allah and His creation. *Fasid* are the corrupt, the evil, and those who do wrong.

Allah measures out good and evil, the wholesome and the corrupt. Humans have enough freedom to make their own choices; if they make the choice to do beautiful and wholesome deeds, (*saalihaat*) motivated by faith (*iman*) and God-wariness (*taqwa*), they please Allah and bring harmony and wholesomeness to the world, resulting in peace, justice, mercy, compassion, honor, equity, well-being, freedom, and many other gifts through Allah's grace. Others choose to do evil and work with corruption (*mufsidun*), destroying the right relationship among the creation, causing hunger, disease, oppression, pollution, and other afflictions. In the universal order, corruption is the prerogative of humans, and vicegerency gives them the freedom to work against the Creator and His creation. Only the misapplied trust can explain how moral evil can appear in the world. When humans choose wrong and corrupt actions, they displease Allah. Allah loves those who do what is beautiful, not those who do what is ugly:

> When he turns his back, he hurries about the earth to work corruption there and destroy the tillage and the stock. Allah loves not corruption. (Al-Baqarah 2:205, Koran)

Allah loves doing what is beautiful, and because of His love for those who do the beautiful, He brings them near to Himself, and His nearness is called Allah's mercy:

> Work not corruption in this world after it has made wholesome and call upon Allah in fear and hope. Surely the mercy of Allah is near to those who do what is beautiful. (Al-A'raf 7:56, Koran)

The covenant of Allah presents us with the scope of the freedom of choice that humans have in doing what is wholesome and beautiful or what is corrupt and ugly and in the human role among the creation that distinguishes right activity, right thought, and right intention from their opposites. It reminds us of how the scales of Allah's justice, the two hands of Allah—His mercy and His wrath—are reflected in the human domain, where people have been appointed Allah's vicegerents. Deeds of goodness and wholesomeness are associated with mercy, paradise, and the beautiful. Evil and corruption is rewarded with wrath, hell, and the ugly.

To err is human. Allah is most forgiving to those who have erred and repented. Above all, Allah's mercy knows no bounds. The Koran and the teachings of the blessed *nabi* guide those who seek the path of Allah. Allah says:

O my Servants who have transgressed against their souls! Despair not of the Mercy of Allah: for Allah forgives all sins: for He is Oft-Forgiving, Most Merciful." Turn you to your Lord (in repentance) and bow to His Will before the Penalty comes on you: after that you shall not be helped. (Az-Zumar 39:53, Koran)

Allah, in His Mercy, has laid down guidelines for the punishment of transgressors. For transgressors and sinners, there is Allah's wrath with life constricted in this world and the next. If they repent, Allah forgives them. The Koran constantly emphasizes repentance and reform of the individual and Allah's mercy and grace. Allah's mercy knows no bounds. *'Adl* (justice) is a divine attribute defined as "putting every object in the right place." When the transgressor repents and mends his ways and does not repeat the wrongdoing and the wrong and evil has been put in the right place and replaced with good, Allah bestows His mercy. The community's obligation is to pardon and help educate and reform the individual. Allah advises every individual to restrain from anger and resentment. Anger is a smoldering volcano quietly burning the human from the inside, robbing his tranquility and peace. Forgiveness restores peace and brings nearness to Allah.

For the unrepentant transgressor, the penalty is prescribed in the Koran. Never is the gate to Allah's mercy closed. The key to this gate is repentance and a walk in Allah's straight path.

The Nineteenth Commandment of Allah

Take Not Life, Which Allah Has Made Sacred

Life is sacred. Allah forbids the taking of life unless it is by way of justice (jihad against *fitnah*, tyranny, and oppression) or when ordained by the law of equality or punishment for murder, in which case the

Koran recommends clemency. Allah's covenant forbids individual believers and their community from killing and taking life. The same injunction applies to the ruler or the *amri minkum* appointed by the believers. War against Muslims and other people for acquisition of territory and wealth is forbidden, and anyone who wages such a war disobeys Allah. Anyone who, in disobedience to the covenant of Allah, slew a person is guilty of slaying the whole human race. Persecution, punishment, imprisonment, and murder of innocent citizens who strive in the cause of Allah is a heinous crime that amounts to *fitnah*. Rulers and their bureaucracy that perpetrate such crimes are answerable to the families of the victims as proclaimed by the blessed *nabi* in the covenant of Yathrib:

> The pious believers follow the best and the most upright guidance. Whoever is convicted of killing a believer deliberatively but without righteous cause shall be liable to the relatives of the killed. Until the latter are satisfied, the killer shall be subject to retaliation by each and every believer.

> If anyone slew a person - unless it be for murder or for spreading mischief in the land - it would be as if he slew the whole people: and if any one saved a life, it would be as if he saved the life of the whole people. (Al-Ma'idah 5:32, Koran)

> Take not life, which Allah hath made sacred, except by the way of justice or law: This He commands you, that you may learn wisdom. (Al-An'am 6: 151–53)

The Twentieth Commandment of Allah

Devour Not Usury, Doubled and Multiplied, Allah Will Deprive Usury of All Blessing

Forbidden is the practice of usury to the Muslims. Also forbidden is making money from money. Money, in its present form, is only a medium of exchange, a way of defining the value of an item but in itself has no value and therefore should not give rise to more money by earning interest through deposit in a bank or loaning it to someone else. The human endeavor, initiative, and risk involved in a productive venture are much more important than the money used to finance it. Money deposited in a bank or hoarded is potential capital rather than capital. Money becomes capital only when it is invested in a venture. Accordingly, money loaned to a business as a loan is regarded as a debt of the business, and it is not capital; as such, it is not entitled to any return, such as interest.

Muslims are encouraged to spend (purchase necessities or spend in the way of Allah) or invest their money and are discouraged from keeping their money idle. Hoarding money is unacceptable. Allah's commandments in His covenant with the believers in the following three *ayahs* exhort Muslims to (a) spend, after their needs are met, in charity; (b) devour not in usury; and (c) hoard not gold and silver.

> They ask thee how much they are to spend (in charity); say: "What is beyond your needs." Thus, doth Allah make clear to you His Signs: in order that you may consider. (Al-Baqarah 2:222, Koran)

> Allah will deprive usury of all blessing but will give increase for deeds of charity; for He loves not creatures ungrateful and wicked. (Al-Baqarah 2:275–76, Koran)

> And there are those who hoard gold and silver and spend it not in the Way of Allah: announce unto them a most grievous penalty. (Al-A'raf 9:34, Koran)

The haraam, usurious monetary system of the world:

> And let not those who covetously withhold of the gifts which Allah hath given them of His Grace, think that it is good for them: nay, it will be the worse for them; soon shall the things which they covetously withheld be tied to their necks like a twisted collar, on the Day of Judgment. To Allah belongs the heritage of the heavens and the earth; and Allah is well-acquainted with all that ye do. (Qur'an 3:180 Ali 'Imran).

Proliferation of wealth through creation of fiat money in the twentieth century and the creation of capital through lending money on interest have corrupted the Muslim communities and their governments. In the Islamic system, money is based on the value of labor needed to produce a commodity, and this money is only a medium of exchange. Introduction of the Western monetary system to the Muslim countries has corrupted the Islamic trade and commerce as well as way of life. The giving of zakat and other charities creates equity in society and circulates the total wealth within the community over a period of forty years. Every rich man is a boon to society as he circulates his wealth within his community. In Islam, there should be no billionaires as the dispensation of mandatory zakat will deplete the cycle of acquisition and cause the graph of prosperity to even out in the *ummah*. Yet the cult of acquisition based on usury is doubling the number of billionaires in the Arabian Peninsula every year.

Cult of money and acquisition: The cult of money and acquisition is very secretive. *Sama* in the Koran signifies the universe and *ardh* man's domain on the earth pertaining to his social and economic world. Allah is the Lord of the heavens and the earth and what is in between. The divine laws under which the universe functions so meticulously and smoothly should also apply to the economic life of man so that he might achieve a balanced, predictable, equitable, and just financial life. *Sama* is the source of Allah's benevolence to humanity and of His universal laws that govern human subsistence and sustenance on the earth (*ardh*), controlling man's economic life in this world. Allah's kingdom over the heavens and the earth sustains man's economic life and directly influences on man's conduct and his obedience to Allah's covenant.

Allah's grace and bounty showers the earth to nurture the whole of Allah's creation. There is enough in this grace to feed, shelter, clothe, educate, and nurture humanity and protect the rest of Allah's creation. Fewer than five hundred of the world's richest men control 5 percent of the world's wealth. Five percent of mankind has positioned itself to deprive 95 percent of humanity and the rest of Allah's creation of His beneficence. Their nets, positioned under the tree of life, catch most of the fruit before it falls to the earth to benefit the rest of Allah's creatures.

The cult of money of the *Mutaffifeen* controls the world's economy through deceit, force, and subterfuge. Fewer than five thousand families who all know one another hold on to most of the world's wealth. Through a secret network of corporations, secret societies, religious cults, and international organizations, they control the natural resources of this world, and they plan to keep it that way. Through their minions in political, religious, financial, academic, and military and intelligence service organizations, they control the world's affairs to suit their own plan. They control the world's finest real estate and hoard gold. In today's world, such wealth is dormant, but it is held as a hedge in the future control of the world. The power play of the *Mutaffifeen* lies in the following:

1. **Usury.** The total debt of the governments and peoples of the world far exceeds the ownership of wealth by the people of the world. The *Mutaffifeen* bankers have indebted the world by creating paper money out of nothing and then lending it out to governments and the people, who will never be able to escape the debt cycle as, in the bigger picture, there is never enough wealth in the world to pay back the principal and interest. Thus, governments and the people will never be able to pay off the debt and will continue to pay the interest in perpetuity. With increasing debt, the interest continues to rise to thousands of billion dollars every year. All that money ends up in a few hands that control the governments in a very subtle, secretive way. The governments and the people of the world today are indebted to the tune of over one hundred trillion dollars. In other words, goods and services worth the nominal value of one hundred trillion dollars have changed hands with the help of "make-believe printed paper money" borrowed from a group of men who do not own the money they lent.

Private owners of central banks issue fake notes that run the world's economy. These *Mutaffifeen* receive an estimated five trillion dollars for their services every year in what is commonly called "interest payment." Through secret organizations, the *Mutaffifeen* artificially create crisis to scare citizens and governments. A powerful image of an enemy with an infinite ability of destruction and doom is created through the media and politics. The presidents and politicians are then seen rushing around the world, trying to stop the terrorists from destroying the just and innocent civilizations.

The 9/11 implosion was created to cause chaos, fear, and uncertainty among the citizens. After creating such catastrophic crisis, the instruments of the secret society's satanic Illuminati and Freemasons—the circle of evil—struck. The blueprint for the creation of Pax America drawn up by a group of people working within the Pentagon on behalf of the *Mutaffifeen* was brought out in a timely fashion, pushing for American occupation of Afghanistan and Iraq. The blueprint written in September 2000 was based on an earlier document recommending the maintenance of American bases in Saudi Arabia and Kuwait to keep American control over Arab oil. The minions of the *Mutaffifeen* were already discussing "going after Iran and Syria" after war in Afghanistan and Iraq.

Wars are planned by the *Mutaffifeen* to facilitate borrowing by the governments. Within a few months, the *Mutaffifeen* had indebted the Americans and the British governments by $553 billion. This was additional to the previously incurred debt of $8 trillion owed by the Americans and the British governments. This debt will never be paid back. Nevertheless, Americans and the British people will continue to pay $350 billion in interest year after year in perpetuity. In lieu of this debt, the American and British soldiery, naval forces, secret services, and diplomats will continue to be beholden to the *Mutaffifeen*. They will be used to prod, convince, and bully the rest of the world into accepting ever-evolving schemes of deceit and extortion. Whether the Americans and the British people like it or not, they will be forced to do the devil's work for the coming century.

With this amount of debt and budgetary deficit, the United States was at the verge of bankruptcy when three airplanes mysteriously crashed into the Twin Towers and the Pentagon on September 11, 2001. There is compelling evidence that those in authority were aware of the impending attack on the American targets yet did nothing to stop them. American Airlines flight 77 flew with great precision and dropped 7,000 feet in 2½ minutes, flying so low, taking utility poles, and clipping trees to its target, the Pentagon, while traveling at 530 miles per hour. This high-precision flight could not have been executed by desert Arabs or Afghans who had only flown Cessna and Piper Cherokee propeller planes in a flight school. Some of these pilots allegedly had not even mastered "touch and go" procedures. The pilots and the crew on board were all able bodied and strong and could not have been cowed down by hijackers brandishing mere box cutters. Surely, some of the passengers would have resisted.

There is little doubt that the 9/11 episode was a well-orchestrated, well-planned, and technically high-precision job undertaken by skilled people in collaboration with those within the aviation authority, the air force, the FBI, the immigration department, and a centralized group of planners with international intelligence connections. Who did it? The answer lies in the fact about who benefited from this tragedy.

Three days after the World Trade Center attack, Congress approved $410 billion spending bill. Half the money went to military spending, $15 billion to bail out the airline industry, $100 billion for New York City cleanup, $79 billion for the Iraq and the Afghan War, $87 billion for the Iraq War, and another $750 million for lost revenue to New York City. The Federal Reserve loaned another $150 billion to the insurance companies. That makes $412 billion dollars of debt.

This money is to be paid by the American people to the Federal Reserve bank, which in turn is owned by private banks. The private banks do not owe allegiance to anyone but to their own greed and avarice. The interest on this money amounting to $10 billion annually is owed in perpetuity at the current 5 percent interest compounded daily. The Americans pay an additional $370 billion in interest on their national debt to the same bankers annually in perpetuity. It is thus clear that a group of people benefit from wars and catastrophes;

they create in secrecy, in intricate coordination with other secret groups to promote such tragedies. By the middle of October 2006, over $333 billion have gone up in smoke in Afghanistan and Iraq.

Four secret societies—the Council on Foreign Relations, the Bilderberg Group, the Illuminati, and the Trilateral Commission—rule the United States and influence the international and financial policies of the Americas, Europe, and to some extent the whole world. The Americans are under the impression that they elect their president democratically, who in turn runs the government according to the people's wishes. Nothing could be farther from the truth.

The Council on Foreign Relations has about three thousand members who join the council only by invitation by a corps of unnamed, faceless persons. Although the members meet regularly, the planning and decision-making is the function of a supersecretive inner circle that compartmentalizes the information provided to the members. Each member is only told what he essentially needs to know as part of his function. Only the inner circle is aware of the whole picture.

The Council on Foreign Relations picks presidential candidates for both the Republicans and the Democrats years ahead of the election. The candidates, nurtured in the philosophy of the CFR, are obedient to the dictates of the CFR. The CFR then backs both the candidates through its mastery of the media and with money and organization, which they control. The news media is totally under the control of the secret societies, and the people are only told what the CFR wants them to know. The elections take the air of a highly publicized rooster fight, with emotions running high for and against each candidate. On the morning of his victory, the winning candidate is presented by the CFR with the list of the names of his cabinet. The cabinet carries out the policies of the CFR. Almost all the people in the cabinet are chosen from among the three thousand members of the CFR.

2. **Trade.** Since the end of the Cold War, the United States and the European Union has launched a trade war against the poor economies of the world. To be precise, it is the continuation of the colonial war on the assets of the poor nations that Europe launched with its naval and maritime fleets on the shores of Africa and Asia in the seventeenth century. This war was interrupted for about forty years when there was no free trade and the economies of the two rival groups were disconnected. Within each rival block, economies interacted through foreign aid in a competition for the hearts and minds of the Third World. There was, at that time, more give than take by the rival superpowers of the opposing powers.

This new trade war is being launched not by the poor economies that have suffered during the last three hundred years but by the countries that have reaped all the benefits of trade over the centuries through deceitful practices. When rich nations continue to squeeze every unfair advantage out of the trading system that has been proved to be deceitful, over the last three centuries, the world economy will soon plunge into a deep depression, chaos, and anarchy. The poor suffer more from economic depressions, and the rich, although cushioned by their wealth and power, suffer in political repercussions, wars, and terror.

The believers of Allah seeking fairness, justice, and equality for all should be aware of these unsavory facts of the world economy. For trade and commerce to be fair and beneficial to all, the trade among nations has to be:

1. free from ideology and politics,
2. equality and fairness in terms of trade,
3. full global employment and equality of wages per hour worked,
4. neutral gold and commodity currency to be used as the media of exchange in trade.

Countries generate wealth through the utilization of the skills of their manpower producing their mineral, industrial, and agricultural products and services. *Surplus trade produces capital for domestic and social development.* Because of the dollar hegemony, all foreign investment funds of developing nations are diverted to the export sector where US dollar can be earned. *The dollar trade surpluses go to hold large dollar reserves to support the exchange rate of their currencies.* The Third World economies cannot use their surplus trade earnings for domestic development and social programs because they are forced to use their huge dollar reserves to support the value of their currencies.

Exports of manufactured goods by low-wage developing nations during the last thirty years have increased from 25 percent in 1965 to 75 percent. *In the meanwhile, agricultural exports of developing nations have fallen from 50 percent to less than 10 percent.* Most developing countries have gained little from the increase in their manufactured goods trade because most of its profit was sucked up by foreign capital investors. For instance, a shirt manufactured in Bangladesh for Walmart pays fifty cents to workers in Bangladesh, two dollars go toward expenses, and twenty dollars lands in profit to the foreign capital. The key cause of unemployment in developing countries is collapse of trade in agricultural products, exacerbated by massive government subsidies provided to farmers by the USA and the European Union. The collapse of agriculture in developing countries means collapse of their economy and upheaval of the social structure by demographic shift of populations to the cities.

Purchasing power parity measures the disconnection between exchange rates and local prices. Exchange rates are dependent on *usury,* interest rates, and haram investment in stocks and interest-bearing bonds. A dollar investor can earn the same interest rate in a foreign economy with purchasing power parity of four. For example, because of the purchasing power parity between the US dollar and the Chinese yuan, the local wages in China have to be four times (75 percent) lower than the wages in the USA. However, the law of one price says that identical goods should sell for the same price in two separate markets when there are no transportation costs and differential taxes applied in those markets. Nevertheless, in international trade, the law of one price does not apply to labor. Foreign capital producers seek to manufacture their goods in lowest-wage locations and sell their goods in highest-price markets. This is the incentive of outsourcing. *The cross-border "one price" applies only to certain products such as oil.* Thus, in economies like Egypt, China, Pakistan, or Bangladesh with a *purchase power parity* of four, a rise in oil prices will cost them four more times in other goods than the cost in the USA or the European Union. The larger the *purchase power parity* between the local currency and the dollar, the more severe is the tyranny of dollar hegemony on forcing down the wage differentials.

The Bretton Woods Conference at the end of the Second World War established the US dollar, at that time a solid currency backed by most of the world's gold, as a benchmark currency for financing international trade, with all other currencies pegged to it at fixed rates that changed only infrequently. The fixed exchange rate was designed to keep trading nations honest and to prevent them from running perpetual trade deficits. The Bretton Woods Agreement was conceived when cross-border flow of funds was not considered necessary or desirable for financing world trade. Not a single Muslim state was invited to participate in this conference. Since 1971, the dollar has changed from gold-backed currency to a *global reserve monetary instrument* that the United States can produce by fiat. The United States produces this instrument by printing notes out of ink and paper that cost nothing to produce. The United States had frittered away all its gold reserves in twenty-five years after the Second World War by incurring both current account and fiscal deficits. First, it exhausted its gold and then incurred a debt that stands at eight trillion dollars today. This debt is financed with fiat money, *printed paper.*

1. World trade under the dollar hegemony is a game in which the USA prints paper dollars, and the rest of the world produces the real goods that the US make-believe paper money can buy.
2. Islam's sixty or so nations along with other underdeveloped countries, through global trade, compete in exports to earn the needed fiat dollars to service their foreign debts and to accumulate enough dollar reserves to sustain the exchange value of their domestic currencies in foreign exchange markets.
3. To prevent attacks by manipulative American and European speculators on their currencies, the world's central banks must acquire and hold fiat dollar reserves in corresponding amounts of market pressure on their currencies in circulation. The higher the market pressure to devalue a particular currency, the more dollar reserves its central banks must hold. This provides a built-in support for a strong dollar that, in turn, forces all central banks to acquire and hold more dollar reserves, making it even stronger.
4. Critical commodities, mostly oil, are denominated in dollars because only dollars can buy oil. This is the price the USA extracted from oil-producing countries for US tolerance of oil-producing cartels since 1973. This has caused an unprecedented growth of dollars in circulation around the world. This US capital account surplus, in turn, finances the US trade deficit of two billion dollars every day. Moreover, any asset, regardless of its location in the world, that is denominated in dollars is a US asset in essence. When oil is denominated in dollars, the US essentially owns the world's oil for free. Thus, all Muslim oil denominated in fiat dollars becomes a US asset. Sixty percent of the world's currency

reserves are denominated in dollars; therefore, they constitute as an American asset. The dollar is a fiat currency, printed from paper and ink at almost no cost to the Americans. And the more paper money the USA prints, the higher the price of US assets will rise.

5. Compelling developing economies to trade to accumulate surplus in US dollars subjects these economies to perpetual low wages, weak domestic consumption, and reduced investment for development projects.

The USA can print dollars at will and with impunity. The dollar is fiat money that is not backed by gold, US productivity, or US export prowess. The whole world's total gross national product is thirty trillion dollars. The US gross national product amounts to about ten trillion dollars measured in US currency. The United States government has frittered away all its gold reserves and other assets. Consequently, it has been forced to borrow from the rest of the world eight trillion dollars to maintain its style of living and governance. And the people of the United States had to borrow another thirty-three trillion dollars to maintain their style of living. The Americans owe to themselves and to the rest of the world more than the value of the whole world's gross wealth. In other words, according to conventional wisdom, the US economy is bankrupt and should have gone into receivership years ago and treated in the same manner as Egypt and the Ottoman Empire in the late nineteenth century, when trustees were appointed to supervise their treasuries.

The US dollar is bankrupt and is incapable of being used as the world's trading currency. However, the dollar is backed by US military power. Any threat to the US hegemony and to the dollar hegemony is swiftly dealt with the might of world's only superpower. The US military budget has gone up from $310 billion in 2001 to $421 billion in 2005.

The US trade and fiscal deficit stands at over 6 percent of its GDP, and its military budget is 4 percent of GDP. In other words, the US trading partners are forced to subsidize one and a half times the annual cost of the US military, which in turn systemically undermines world peace and stability. In plain language, robbery and gangsterism controls the world through force and deceit. It is through propaganda, force, and fraudulent international institutions that the world has been duped into believing that the worthless US dollar is gold.

While the deception lasts, the house of cards will stand. The slaves that prop the shaky walls of the house of cards are the usurious central banks, the Arab petrodollars, the thriving Chinese export trade, the drug trade, and the long-suffering Third World poor. Once the people of the world recognize the dupery, the present world order will collapse on itself, and the world will be rid of tyranny of the dollar hegemony, colonialism, and the one-thousand-year-old crusade against Islam. Unfortunately, the world will fall into turmoil and instability until a new system arises from the ashes of the old one.

During the 1991 presidential election campaign, Bill Clinton and his Democrats produced figures that revealed the obscene fact that 1 percent of Americans own 40 percent of the wealth of the United States. They also said that if you eliminated home ownership and only counted businesses, factories, and office buildings, then the top 1 percent owned 90 percent of all the commercial wealth of the United States. Moreover, the top 10 percent, they said, owned 99 percent of the wealth[8].

A corps of several thousand determined families among the top 1 percent of the American treasure holders form the patrician class, akin to the old Roman aristocracy. Under the facade of democracy, the common folk (the plebeians) live under the illusion that they

8 Henry C. K. Liu "US Dollar Hegemony Has Got to Go," Asia Times, April 11, 2002.

run the American administrations, elected by them every four years. In fact, the elections are farcical. The fact is that secret councils of the patricians determine the candidates who will run for presidency and, subsequently, the members of the president's cabinet and their government's fiscal and foreign policies.

The corps of patricians of old money, European money, and the new Jewish money determine the financial stakes around the world and control the world's oil, minerals, agriculture, trade, and commerce through usury. In fact, these few thousand patrician families of immense wealth gotten through usury control the president, armed forces, intelligence services of the United States, Federal Reserve bank, and other institutions of the government; and through them, they influence the policies of international organizations such as the United Nations, IMF, the World Bank, WTO, and NATO. They determine when to send their legions and praetorian guards, the marines, to the outlying posts to conquer and plunder new lands and bring back gold, oil, minerals, and other wealth. While 1 percent of the US population (the filthy rich patricians) drains 90 percent of North America's wealth into their coffers, the common folk (the plebeians), brainwashed with patriotism and propaganda, live under the illusion of belonging to God's chosen people in a land of opportunity, justice, truth, and milk and honey. With their wits dimmed by the daily barrage of falsified images by the news media and by their government, the plebeians (90 percent of common Americans) willingly pay the perpetual interest on the debt of forty trillion dollars accumulated by their patrician class in their quest for the world's wealth.

The world's total gross national product amounts to thirty trillion dollars. Fewer than eight hundred European and American men own and control three trillion dollars' worth of this wealth. In other words, eight hundred men from the Western world control 10 percent of the world's wealth. With wealth comes the control of the world's economies.

Usury and hoarding of wealth:

Devour not usury, doubled, and multiplied; Be in taqwa of Allah (fear Allah) that you may prosper.

Forbidden is the practice of usury to the Muslims. Forbidden is also making money from money. Money, in its present form, is only a medium of exchange, a way of defining the value of an item but in itself has no value and therefore should not give rise to more money by earning interest through deposit in a bank or loaning it to someone else. The human endeavor, initiative, and risk involved in a productive venture are much more important than the money used to finance it. Money deposited in a bank or hoarded is potential capital rather than capital. Money becomes capital only when it is invested in a venture. Accordingly, money loaned to a business as a loan is regarded as a debt of the business and is not capital; and as such, it is not entitled to any return, such as interest.

Muslims are encouraged to spend (purchase necessities or spend in the way of Allah) or invest their money and are discouraged from keeping their money idle. Hoarding money is unacceptable. Allah's commandment in His covenant with the believers, in the following three *ayahs*, exhorts Muslims to:

a) spend in charity after their needs are met,
b) devour not in usury and Allah will deprive usury of all blessing,
c) hoard not gold and silver.

???

They ask thee how much they are to spend (in charity); say: "What is beyond your needs." Thus, doth Allah make clear to you His Signs: in order that you may consider. (Al-Baqarah 2:222, Koran)

Allah will deprive usury of all blessing but will give increase for deeds of charity; for He loves not creatures ungrateful and wicked. (Al-Baqarah 2:275–76, Koran)

And there are those who hoard gold and silver and spend it not in the Way of Allah: announce unto them a most grievous penalty. (Al-A'raf 9:34, Koran)

An Islamic government is forbidden to lend or borrow money from institutions such as international banks, World Bank, or the International Monetary Fund on interest as both usury and interest are expressly forbidden. Banking based on fiat money is also forbidden. The value of money is diluted by the creation of new money out of nothing; the property rights of savers and those who have been promised future payments, such as pensioners, are violated. This is stealing. The trappings of money system and banking have been compared to that of a cult; only those who profit from it understand its inner workings. They work hard to keep it that way.

The central banks print notes adorned with signatures, pictures, and seals of a president or a queen; counterfeiters are severely punished; governments pay their expenses with them; populations are forced to accept them; they are printed like newspaper in such vast quantity, representing an equal worth to all the treasures of this world, all the resources above and under the ground, all assets of populations, and their work and labor to fabricate every item that has ever been manufactured. Yet these notes cost nothing to make. In truth, this has been the greatest hoax, the worst most crime against humanity, a swindle of proportions never seen by humanity before.

As we have found, the Koran forbids usury, gambling, speculation, and hoarding of gold and silver. The Koran advocates trade and spending on good things in life, on the kith and kin, and to provide wealth in the cause of Allah. The modern economic system is entirely alien to the teachings of the Koran and is full of pitfalls and trappings laid down by Satan. The Dar es Salaam has slid downhill, submerged into the quicksand of make-believe economy. Every successful businessperson and trader are forced to operate in the pagan, sinful system of economy. Here is the solution for a successful economic system as laid down in the covenant of the Koran:

- Elimination of usury and interest in the Dar es Salaam.
- Elimination of fiat money and elimination of banking based on money created out of nothing with a printing press. There will be no more lending of nine times of the bank deposit to create capital and wealth. It is a fraudulent Western practice based on trickery. Such a practice constitutes an institutionalized theft, supported by state and international institutions.
- Creation of a unitary currency for the united Islamic state. Gold dinars and silver dirhams based on the measures established by Umar ibn al-Khattab, the second caliph. A currency bureau, an arm of the state of Dar es Salaam, will be charged with the minting and circulation of the currency.
- Dar es Salaam's trading relations with the rest of the world involving drastic changes. All commodities utilized within the state will be produced within the country, and the *ummah* will be independent of foreign trading systems. The commodities for export—oil, minerals, and raw and manufactured

goods—will be sold against gold and in gold-based currency. Fiat currency and paper and printed money will be abolished unless it is backed by gold.

- Labor of every human in the Islamic state measured in a standardized index per hour worked. This index will be uniform for every worker around the world. Pricing of commodities in international trade will be based on this index of equal value for all human labor internationally.

The Koran says:

> Those that spend of their goods in charity by night and by day, in secret and in public, have their reward with their Lord: on them shall be no fear, nor shall they grieve.
>
> Those who devour usury will not stand except stands the one whom the Satan by his touch has driven to madness. That is because they say: "Trade is like usury," but Allah hath permitted trade and forbidden usury. Those who after receiving direction from their Lord, desist, shall be pardoned for the past; their case is for Allah to judge; but those who repeat (the offence) are Companions of the Fire; they will abide therein (forever).
>
> Allah will deprive usury of all blessing but will give increase for deeds of charity; for He does not love ungrateful and wicked creatures. (Al-Baqarah 2:274–76, Koran)
>
> Those who believe and perform wholesome deeds, establish regular prayers and regular charity have rewards with their Lord. On them shall be no fear, nor shall they grieve.

Fear Allah and give up what remains of your demand for usury, if you are indeed believers. If you do it not, take notice of war from Allah and His Rasool: but if you turn back, you will still have your capital sums.

Deal not unjustly, and you shall not be dealt with unjustly.

If the debtor is in a difficulty, grant him time until it is easy for him to repay. But if you remit it by way of charity, that is best for you. (Al-Baqarah 2:277-80, Koran)

Devour not usury, doubled and multiplied; Be in taqwa of Allah (fear Allah) that you may prosper.

Fear the Fire, which is prepared for those who reject Faith; and obey Allah and the Rasool; that you may obtain mercy.

Be quick in the race for forgiveness from your Lord, and for a Garden whose measurement is that of the heavens and of the earth, prepared for the righteous.

Those who give freely whether in prosperity, or in adversity; those who restrain anger, and pardon all humans; for Allah loves those who do beautiful deeds (Al -muhsinun). (Ali 'Imran 3:130-34, Koran)

There are indeed many among the priests and clerics who in falsehood devour the substance of men and hinder them from the way of Allah. And there are those who bury gold and silver and spend it not in the way of Allah: announce unto them a most grievous penalty.

On the Day when heat will be produced out of that wealth in the fire of Hell, and with it will be branded their foreheads, their flanks, and their backs, "This is the treasure which you buried for yourselves: taste then, the treasures which you buried!" (At-Tawbah 9:34–35, Koran)

The Twenty-First Commandment of Allah

We Have Enjoined on Man Kindness to His Parents: Kill Not Your Children on a Plea of Want; We Provide Sustenance for You and for Them

The Koran repeatedly commands the believers to do what is beautiful, and it promises that those who perform beautiful deeds will be brought under the sway of Allah's gentle, merciful, and beautiful names. Human qualities gain their reality from the most beautiful divine qualities. When humans turn to Allah, their beautiful qualities become indistinguishable from Allah's own qualities.

> To Allah belongs all that is in the heavens and on earth; so that He rewards those who do ugly, according for what they have done, and He rewards those who do beautiful with the most beautiful. (An-Najm 53:31, Koran)

The first beautiful act that believers perform after tawhid is doing what is beautiful and good to their parents, those who brought them into existence. It is parents who provide the means that Allah employs in creating people, nurturing and educating them, and making them beautiful and God fearing. Allah takes credit for His creation, which is the requirement of tawhid. Allah expects his creatures to act appropriately toward His intermediaries of creation. Only in this manner can humans expect that other creatures, including their own children, will act beautifully toward them.

Respect and care of the parents is a fundamental act in Islamic society to maintain the cohesion of the family structure. The family is the underlying unit of the structure of the community that forms the support group for children, adults, and the elderly among the family; the neighbors, the kin, and the communal structure around the mosque; and schools.

Infanticide and its modern version, abortion, and the taking of life of both human and animals are forbidden by the Koran. Allah has made life sacred. And avoid *Fahasha*, the shameful deeds that set the human down a slippery slope of the ugly and evil.

Worship none but Allah; treat with kindness your parents and kindred, and orphans and those in need; speak fair to the people; be steadfast in prayer; And practice regular charity. (Al-Baqarah 2:82, Koran)

Say: "Come, I will rehearse what Allah hath (really) prohibited you from": join not anything as equal with Him; be good to your parents; kill not your children on a plea of want - We provide sustenance for you and for them - come not nigh to shameful deeds, whether open or secret; take not life, which Allah hath made sacred, except by way of justice and law: thus doth He command you, that you may learn wisdom. (Al-An'am 6:151, Koran)

Take not with Allah another object of worship; or thou wilt sit in disgrace and destitution Thy Lord hath decreed that you worship none but Him, and that you be kind to parents. Whether one or both of them attain old age in thy life, say not to them a word of contempt, nor repel them, but address them in terms of honor. And, out of kindness, lower to them the wing of humility, and say: "My Lord! bestow on them thy Mercy even as they cherished me in childhood." (Al-Isra 17:22, 24, Koran)

We have enjoined on man kindness to his parents: in pain did his mother bear him, and in pain did she give him birth. The carrying of the (child) to his weaning is (a period of) thirty months. At length, when he reaches the age of full strength and attains forty years, he says: "O my Lord! grant me that I may be grateful for Thy favor which Thou hast bestowed upon me, and upon both my parents, and that I may work righteousness such as Thou may approve; and be gracious to me in my issue. Truly have I turned to Thee and truly do I bow (to Thee) in Islam." (Al-Ahqaf 46:15, Koran)

The Twenty-Second Commandment of Allah

You are Forbidden to Treat Women With Harshness; on the Contrary, Treat Them on a Footing of Equality, Kindness, and Honor

You are forbidden to take women against their will. Nor should you treat them with harshness, on the contrary treat them on a footing of equality kindness and honor.

Allah has granted each believer, man and woman, equality; right to freedom; right to practice his faith in accordance with his beliefs since, in Islam, there is no compulsion in matters of religion; right to life, which includes mental, physical, and emotional well-being; right to safeguard one's property; right to intellectual endeavors, acquisition of knowledge, and education; right to make a living; and right to free speech and action to enjoin good and forbid evil. In enjoying his freedoms, the individual ensures that his activities do not impinge on the similar rights of others.

Equality of men and women: Fifty percent of the population of the believers (the women) has been excluded from mainline Islam by the priests, mullahs, jurist-scholars, and Hadith scholars against the commandments of the Koran. Women were regarded as inferior beings in most pre-Islamic cultures, including the Arabs, Persians, Greeks, Romans, and Hindus. Their status was not any higher among the Turkish and the Mongol tribes of Central Asia. In Judaism, women were forbidden from the inner sanctuary of the temple; and in early Pauline Christianity, their position was relegated to the entrance or outside the church at prayer time.

Islam brought dignity and grace to the status of women—the mothers, wives, and daughters. Women had their rights established and their social status elevated as equal to that of men. They attended prayer services at the Prophet's Mosque; they held regular and frequent discourse with the *nabi* of Allah on religious, women's, and family issues. They participated in battles alongside their men. Women worked outside their homes. The first person to convert to Islam, Khadijah, was a successful international trader and owned an import and export business, dealing in goods from India, Persia, Africa, Yemen, and the Byzantine Empire. She employed several men to assist her in her business. Other women memorized the Koran and taught other Muslims. A'ishah gave regular talks and discourses on religious matters. Other women led the ritual prayers and *dhikr-e-Allah* gatherings. The ulema and other followers of the Hadith collections of the third century over the last one thousand years have betrayed Allah and His *rasul* by excluding women from congregation prayers, businesses, public and social affairs, and most importantly education.

The Muslim communities have betrayed Allah and His *rasul* concerning their obligations to their women—their mothers, wives, sisters, and daughters. Allah's covenant applies equally to every individual within the community, both men and women. Allah has elevated the rank and dignity of the children of Adam, both men and women, with special favors above that of most of His creation, including the angels. *The dignity and favors promised by Allah include six special values—safeguards of faith, life, intellect (education), property, lineage, and freedom of speech and action.*

The Koran addresses men and women who submit to Allah, who believe, who are devout, who speak the truth, who are righteous, who are humble, who are charitable, who fast and deny themselves, who guard their chastity, and who remember Allah much and promises them a great reward and forgiveness for their transgressions. In this address, Allah treats individual men and women equitably with a promise of similar reward for their good acts. In Allah's eyes, all men and women who do good deeds carry an equal favor with Him.

Allah admonishes both the believing men and women to lower their gaze and guard their chastity. He also admonishes women to dress modestly and not display their adornments outside of their immediate family environment. Allah commands believers to turn all together toward Him so that they may prosper. This can happen only when the believers, men and women, turn to Allah collectively as a community in a mosque as was customary during the lifetime of the *nabi* of Allah.

According to the Koran, men and women are autonomous and answerable to Allah for their own deeds and actions, and only they as individuals are rewarded or punished for their deeds. In a community, men as a group or the state has no sanction from the Koran to enforce any restrictions on the freedom of righteous and believing women. To every man and to every woman, Allah has bestowed rights to freedom, faith, life, intellect, property, and education. The authority of a ruler who denies these basic freedoms to men or women is openly disputable. The individual obeys the ruler on the condition that ruler obeys the Koran and Allah's covenant.

The Koran addresses men and women equally, subjecting them together to similar obligations of submission to Allah, regular prayer, giving in charity, modesty in dress and behavior, righteousness, humility, chastity, worship, truthfulness, remembrance of Allah, and being kind and just. Allah blessed mankind (*insan*), both men and women, with dignity, justice, and equality and promised them with the same rewards as well as obligations. "Be steadfast in prayer and practice regular charity" is an ongoing and repetitive theme in the Koran. Allah calls those who believe, both men and women, to hasten to the congregation prayer on Friday, the day of assembly.

> O you who believe! (Men and women) When the call
> is proclaimed to prayer on Friday, the Day of Assembly
> hasten earnestly to the Remembrance of Allah and leave off
> business and traffic that is best for you if you but knew!
>
> And when the Prayer is finished, then may you disperse through the
> land, and seek of the Bounty of Allah: and celebrate the Praises of
> Allah often: that you may prosper. (Al-Mumtahinah 62:9–10, Koran)

Women attended obligatory prayers, *jum'ah* prayers, and Eid prayers in the Prophet's Mosque. Whenever the apostle of Allah finished his prayers with *Taslim,* the women would get up first, and he would stay in his place for a while before getting up. The purpose of his stay was that the women might leave before the men who had finished their prayer.

Soon after the *nabi* died, there occurred an enormous expansion of the Islamic domain. Women, for a while, enjoyed their newly won freedom and dignity given by Islam and proclaimed by the blessed *nabi* Muhammad. Soon afterward, the Arabs reached an unprecedented level of prosperity and began to accumulate large harems, wives, concubines, female slaves, and servants. These women were increasingly confined to their quarters and not allowed to go out unchaperoned. Subsequently, the architecture of the Middle East dwellings changed to suit the new circumstances. The courtyard of the house had high walls, and the only entrance was where the master of the house sat. The master of the harem was so jealous of the chastity of his women that he employed eunuchs as servants and guards in his house. The institution of eunuchs was a peculiar Middle Eastern practice related to the institution of the harems of the elite.

The trampling of the women's rights was and is a betrayal of the blessed *nabi* Muhammad's emancipation of women. As more Arabs, Romans, Persians, Hindus, Turks, and Mongols embraced Islam, they brought with them their peculiar bias against women and female infants. The Islamic emancipation of women was ignored; women were confined within their houses, covered head to foot in cloth, denied spiritual growth, and denied access to education and to places worship. Shamefully, the scholars and the ulema encouraged this state of affairs. Women were gradually discouraged from praying in the mosque and were excluded from congregational worship. Women were deprived of education and knowledge of Islam; consequently, their children grew up in ignorance. The first school is in the cradle, and this is the school Muslim children were denied. *Thus, over the centuries, the Muslims have betrayed the* rasul *of Allah and disobeyed His covenant.*

Pre-Islamic Arab and other cultures regarded women as their chattel and possession. Abduction and rape of opponents' women was a favored pastime of those victorious in battle to humiliate the vanquished. Thus, the birth of a female child was regarded as a matter of shame, which led to the practice of infanticide. This practice was forbidden earlier on during the prophet's mission. However, the primordial masculine instinct resurfaced in the new Muslim. His subconscious shame and embarrassment of the female in his household was sublimated into a gentler and socially acceptable alternative. As the Koran points out, he chose to retain the female child on sufferance and contempt rather than bury it in the dust. And the Koran points out, "*What an evil choice they decide on!*" The shame and cultural burden in some of Muslim societies is so intense that the female infant is buried in the coffin of yashmak (burka) in the confines of the brick walls of her house. She is not killed off physically but nevertheless killed intellectually and spiritually by withholding the intellectual and spiritual sustenance that Allah has provided for her.

> Indeed Lost are those who slay their children, foolishly and without knowledge, and have forbidden that which Allah has provided for them, and inventing lies against Allah. They have indeed gone astray and heeded no guidance. (Al-An'am 6:140, Koran)

> When news is brought to one of them, of the birth of a female child, his face darkens, and he is filled with inward grief! With shame does he hide himself from his people, because of the bad news he has had! Shall he retain it on sufferance and contempt, or bury it in the dust? Ah! What an evil choice they decide on? (An-Nahl 16:58–59, Koran)

In a just and moral society, women should have all the freedoms bestowed on them by the covenant of Allah. Women should themselves arise and demand their God-given birthright to freedom and equality. They should have an intellectual awakening to assert their rights.

Women in communal worship: Allah blessed mankind (*insan*), both men and women, with dignity, justice, and equality and promised them with the same rewards as well as obligations. "Be steadfast in prayer and practice regular charity" is an ongoing and repetitive theme in the Koran. Allah calls those who believe, both men and women, to hasten to the congregation prayer on Friday, the day of assembly.

The whole world is the place of prostration, and every place where Allah is remembered is aglow in Allah's *nur*. Every place of prostration and Allah's remembrance has Allah's presence and light. The believing men and women approach the Lord in His *taqwa* in awe and gratitude, supplicating in His presence, aware that He is there and they see Him; however, if they do not see Him, they are aware that He sees them and is sentient of their prayer, gratitude, and supplication. Allah calls on all believers, men and women, to salat:

> O you who believe! Bow down, prostrate yourselves, and adore your Lord; and do good; that you may prosper. And strive in His cause as you ought to strive, (with sincerity and under discipline). He has chosen you and has imposed no difficulties on you in religion. (Al-Hajj 22:77–78, Koran)

> Those who do wholesome deeds, establish regular prayers and regular charity have rewards with their Lord. On them shall be no fear, nor shall they grieve. (Al Baqarah 2:280, Koran)

> Seek help with patience, perseverance, and prayer. Allah is with those who patiently persevere. (Al-Baqarah 2:153, Koran)

When Allah calls on all believers, men and women, to salaat, to remember and praise Him, the believers purify themselves by washing their faces and their hands to the elbows, wipe their heads, and wash their feet to the ankles. If they are unclean, they purify themselves by bathing. They then approach their Lord, submit to Him, and renew their covenant with Him. Salaat, *dhikr*, recitation, fasting, *taqwa* of Allah, and *furqan* are the beams of light (*nur* of Allah) that maintain the believer's connection with the divine light. Islam (submission, prostration) is the direct link between the believer and Allah.

The believer asks, and Allah gives. The believer loves Allah, and Allah loves him in return. The believer asks for the straight path, and Allah shows him the way. The believer prays to Allah, and Allah showers His mercy and grace on him. The believer remembers Allah, and Allah responds to those who praise Him, thank Him, and ask Him. The believer in every case is the human, a man and a woman. Allah addresses both man and woman in equality. And Allah reassures them:

On you there shall be no fear, nor shall you grieve.
Seek help with patience, perseverance and prayer.
Allah is with those who patiently persevere.

Yet when Allah calls the believers to prayer, *some believers are indeed afraid, and on some, there is indeed fear and grief.* Places of prostration in the Islamic world are masculine preserves, men's clubs. Believing, upright women, if not totally forbidden, are indeed discouraged from praying in the mosques by men, those who control the entrances. Such actions amount to *fitnah* and oppression of women by these men. The mosques that do permit women to pray have separate entrance for them and a segregated and sometimes unclean, uncomfortable, unventilated prayer room for women and children. The khutbah and the prayers are inaudible. When Allah calls on the believers, he addresses both men and women together in unison. And in Allah's house, the Kaaba, there are men with canes and women with paddles who hit and scream at women and crippled old people who stray from the orders of the Saudi controllers of the house of Allah. Such men and women of ignorance bring shame on the devout believers of Allah.

Allah made tribes and nations from a single pair of man and woman so that humans communicate and come to know one another. Allah honors those humans who have *taqwa* of Allah and the ones who are righteous. The acts of good works and righteousness recognized in the Koran are to show compassion, to be merciful and forgive others, to be just, to protect the weak, to defend the oppressed, to be generous and charitable, to be truthful, to seek knowledge and wisdom, to be kind, to be peaceful, to love others, and to perform beautiful deeds.

Oppression and tyranny that deprives an individual believer, man or woman; a community of believers; or their nation (the *ummah*) of their God-given rights is *fitnah* as described in the Koran. The perpetrators of such tyranny and oppression cannot belong to the fellowship of Allah, the fellowship of the covenant of Allah, nor the fellowship of the blessed *Nabiien* of Allah. Allah commands the believers to fight such tyranny till there is no more *fitnah*, treachery, and oppression and there prevails justice and faith in Allah all together everywhere. Yet in the Muslim world, there are men who, instead of showing compassion to the weak, deprive women of their right to worship in the houses of Allah in equality with men. In Islam, there is no compulsion in matters of religion. Such actions of compulsion amount to *fitnah* and oppression of women by these men. And the believers are commanded by Allah to fight the perpetrators of *fitnah* and tyranny.

> We created you from a single pair of a male and a female, and made you into nations and tribes, that you may know each other. Verily the most honored of you in the sight of Allah is the one with taqwa of Allah, the most righteous of you. And Allah is All Knowing, All Aware. (Al-Hujurat 49:12–13, Koran)

The earliest Muslims gathered for prayers in a makeshift mosque partly open to the elements. The *rasul* of Allah, the *nabi* of Islam, led the prayers for everyone to see and hear. The men prayed behind the *nabi*, followed by rows of children and women, who occupied the back rows of the Prophet's Mosque, where they could be seen and heard by the rest of the congregation in the same small room. In between the prayers, men and women were able to mingle, and the blessed *nabi* was accessible to each person if any man or woman wanted a conversation or had questions.

Direct visual contact between the blessed *nabi,* as the imam who led the prayers, and those who attended the prayers seems to have been an important element in the Friday khutbah. On Fridays, the blessed *nabi* preached the khutbah, leaning on his staff. And the men, women, and children sat in front of him, their faces raised toward him, and they listened as they watched him.

The idea that the mosque is a privileged place, a collective space where the community debates important matters before making decisions, is the fundamental concept of Islam that provides the community autonomy and a voice through consultation and consensus. Everything passes through the mosque. The mosque, in the history of Islam, became the school for indoctrination of new converts. It became the nerve center of the community for ritual prayer, community organization, and socialization. In the mosque, worshippers came to know and bonded with one another. This is where the Ansar became the brethren of the Muhajirun.

The mosque became established as the place where dialogue between the leader and the people took place. Here, the teacher, the *nabi*, taught and preached; and the populace, both men and women, came to listen to him. The apparently simple decision to install a minbar in the mosque was treated by the *nabi* as a matter that concerned all Muslims. The *nabi* used to say the Friday prayers standing, leaning against a palm trunk. Not every person could see the *nabi* clearly, and the believers urged the him to take his place on a platform at the time of prayer so that everybody could see him. Within a few months, the number of Muslims had grown considerably. 'Why not build a pulpit like I have seen in Syria?" suggested a companion. The *nabi* asked those present for their advice on the question, and they agreed to the suggestion. A Medina carpenter cut a tree and built a pulpit with a seat and two steps up to the seat. Thus, the congregation—men in front, children in the middle, and women at the back—was able to see and hear the blessed *nabi* when he taught in the mosque.

That women are discouraged from worshipping in the mosque because they "distract" men from their spiritual pursuit and that women stimulate men's sexual urges rest on sham premise. Islam is a religion of reform and self-control. The covenant has established strict guidelines and boundaries over the believer's behavior both in private and in public.

> For men and women who surrender unto Allah, for men and women who believe, for men and women who are devout, for men and women who speak the truth, for men and women who persevere in righteousness, for men and women who are humble, for men and women who are charitable, for men and women who fast and deny them selves, for men and women who guard their chastity, for men and women who remember Allah much, for them Allah has forgiveness and a great reward. (Al-Ahzab 33:35, Koran)

> Say to the Believing men that they should lower their gaze and guard their modesty: That will make for greater purity for them: And Allah is acquainted with all that they do.

> And say to the Believing women that they should lower their gaze and guard their modesty; that they should not display their adornments except what is ordinarily obvious. That they should draw a veil over their bosom and not display their adornments. (Except to the immediate family) And that they should not strike their feet in order to draw attention to their hidden adornments.

And O you Believers! Turn you all together Toward
Allah that you may prosper. (An-Nur 24:30-31)

O you Believers! Turn you all together toward
Allah that you may prosper.

[And this could only occur in prayer in a place of prostration.]

The believers, men and women are protectors one of another

[meaning that men and women work as team to protect
their mutual spiritual and earthly interests].

they enjoin what is just and forbid what is evil.

[This is a clear indication that men and women
together promote a just and moral community.]

They observe regular prayers, practice regular
charity, and obey Allah and His Rasool.

[Again, Allah urges both men and women to establish
regular salat, practice regular charity, and obey Allah's
covenant as given to the blessed *nabi* in the Koran.]

On them will Allah pour His mercy, for Allah is exalted in power, wise.

[The believers who turn to Allah together in prayer, work to protect
one another, promote a just and moral society, establish regular prayer,
give in charity, and obey Allah's covenant will bathe in His mercy.]

Oh, you who believe! Guard your souls, If you follow (right)
guidance, No hurt can come to you from those who stray;
The goal of you all is to Allah, It is He who will show you
the truth of all that you do. (At-Tawbah 9:71, Koran)

The above *ayah* of the Koran has defined the boundaries of behavior for both men and women for all times to come. It tells men and women to lower their gaze in modesty. Could it be clearer? And then Allah tells both men and women:

> It is not fitting for a Believer, man, or woman, when a matter has been decided by Allah and His Messenger, to have any option about their decision: if anyone disobeys Allah and His Messenger, he is indeed on a clearly wrong Path. (Al-Ahzab 33:36, Koran)

The innate self of man, the *nafs*, has the ability to perform good and evil. Life is a chain of emotions, intentions, and actions. *Taqwa* of Allah drives away the temptations and cravings from man's *nafs*. Only Satan's temptations will lead a man to *Fahasha* and fulfillment of his lust.

Every being is responsible for his own emotions, intentions, and actions. Every man has been bequeathed control over his own *nafs*. Life is but a trial of one's deeds on which men will be judged for their own actions. And women, likewise, will be judged for their own. The argument that men lose self-control over their lust in public places assumes that Muslim men have no more control over their animal instincts than a dog or a donkey. Through such reasoning, men abdicate moral responsibility over their own actions and behavior. Men must assume responsibility for their own emotions, intentions, and actions.

The Taliban and the Wahhabi solution to manipulate the environment to make women fade away behind brick walls and veils, to keep men's erectile responses in check, raises important questions about men's control over their own *nafs*. What does this say about men's capacity to take full responsibility for their own spirituality and actions? To what understanding of humanity are the men entitled to control the houses of worship?

> The Believers, men, and women are protectors one of another: they enjoin what is just and forbid what is evil: they observe regular prayers, practice regular charity, and obey Allah and

His apostle. On them will Allah pour His mercy: for Allah is Exalted in Power, Wise. (At-Tawbah 9:71, Koran)

To every man and woman, Allah has bestowed equal rights to freedom, faith, life, intellect, property, education, and freedom of speech and action, enjoining what is right and forbidding what is wrong.

The Twenty-Third Commandment of Allah

Crave Not Those Things of Which Allah Has Bestowed His Gifts More Freely on Some Than Others

Crave not those things of what Allah has bestowed His gifts more freely on some than others, men are assigned what they earn and women that they earn.

Allah created the earth and then bestowed on man His favors to extract sustenance from it. He also created the sun, moon, and stars to create a just equilibrium and harmony in the universe. The sun provides energy for the growth, sustenance, and well-being of humans, plants, and animals. Over the centuries, man began to extract more than his personal needs from the earth. When the boom of economics, trade, and commerce began, man's craving and greed kept pace, creating cycles of imbalance, disharmony, wars, poverty, tyranny, and injustice throughout the globe. The breakdown of equilibrium and harmony in the universe caused by craving and greed blemished the human virtue, and consequently, animal and plant life suffered through disappearance of species. In the race for control, acquisition, and hoarding of the world's wealth, nations and men polluted the rivers, oceans, and land, threatening the future of life on the earth. Man disobeyed Allah's universal laws and covenant.

According to the Koran, economics and the observance of the moral code of the covenant of Allah go hand in hand, and they cannot be separated from each other:

He has created the heavens and the earth for just ends far
is He above having the partners they ascribe to Him!

He has created man from a sperm-drop; and behold
this same (man) becomes an open disputer!

And cattle He has created for you (men): from them you derive
warmth, and numerous benefits, and of their (meat) you eat.

And you have a sense of pride and beauty in them
as you drive them home in the evening, and as you
lead them forth to pasture in the morning.

And they carry your heavy loads to lands that you could
not (otherwise) reach except with souls distressed: for
your Lord is indeed Most Kind, Most Merciful.

And (He has created) horses, mules, and donkeys,
for you to ride and use for show; and He has created
(other) things of which you have no knowledge.

And unto Allah leads straight the Way, but there are ways that
turn aside: if Allah had willed, He could have guided all of you.

It is He Who sends down rain from the sky. From it you drink, and
out of it (grows) the vegetation on which you feed your cattle.

With it He produces for you corn, olives, date palms, grapes, and every kind of fruit: verily in this is a Sign for those who give thought.

He has made subject to you the Night and the Day; the Sun and the Moon; and the Stars are in subjection by His Command: verily in this are Signs for men who are wise.

And the things on this earth which He has multiplied in varying colors (and qualities): verily in this a Sign for men who celebrate the praises of Allah (in gratitude).

It is He Who has made the sea subject, that you may eat thereof flesh that is fresh and tender, and that you may extract there from ornaments to wear, and You see the ships therein that plough the waves, that you may seek (thus) of the bounty of Allah and that you may be grateful.

And He has set up on the earth mountains standing firm, lest it should shake with you; and rivers and roads; that you may guide yourselves.

And marks and signposts; and by the stars (Men) guide themselves. Is then He Who creates like one that creates not? Will you not receive admonition?

If you would count up the favors of Allah, never would you be able to number them; for Allah is Oft-Forgiving, Most Merciful. (An-Nahl 16:3–18, Koran)

Sama in the Koran signifies the universe and *ardh* man's domain on the earth pertaining to his social and economic world. Allah is the Lord of the heavens and the earth and what is in between. The divine laws under which the universe functions so meticulously and smoothly should also apply to the economic life of man so that he might achieve a balanced, predictable, equitable, and just financial life. *Sama* is the source of Allah's benevolence to humanity and of His universal laws that govern human subsistence and sustenance on the earth (*ardh*), controlling man's economic life in this world. Allah's kingdom over the heavens and the earth sustains man's economic life and directly affects man's conduct and his obedience to Allah's covenant.

Ayahs in Sura An-Nahl are explicit. Allah created the heavens and the earth for just ends, to bring peace, harmony, equilibrium, and justice to the universe. He is Allah, the One, Lord of creation. He sends water from the heavens for the sustenance of life on the earth—life of humans, plants, and animals. Allah sends sunshine to the earth to provide warmth and light to sustain human, plant, and animal life. Allah fashioned the moon and stars to create equilibrium in the universe, every object in its intended place, revolving in its fixed orbit in perfect harmony and balance. Allah knows the secrets and the mysteries of the heavens and the earth, the so-called sciences, and the knowledge of particles, elements, cells, mitochondria, chromosomes, gravity, black holes, only an infinitesimal portion of which he revealed to man, yet man is arrogant and boastful.

Allah speaks to the believers:

> Squander not your wealth among yourselves in egotism and conceit: Let there be trade and traffic amongst you with mutual goodwill nor kill or destroy yourselves: for verily Allah hath been Most Merciful to you. If any do that in rancor and injustice, soon shall we cast them into the fire: and easy it is for Allah. If you abstain from all the odious and the forbidden, Allah shall expel out of you all evil in you and admit you to a Gate of great honor.

And crave not those things of what Allah has bestowed His gifts more freely on some than others, men are assigned what they earn and women that they earn. But ask Allah of His bounty. Surely Allah is knower of everything. (An-Nisa 4:29-32)

Land and the resources of life belong to Allah, who bestowed it to man and woman, His regents on the earth. The covenant of Allah expects man to tend Allah's garden for all His creatures, men and beasts, and to conserve the resources of the world for future generations. Whatever is left over beyond one's needs should go to meet the necessities of the rest of humanity, starting with one's *qurba* (near and dear) and then the community, followed by the surrounding communities. The land does not belong to kings, states, governments, tribal chiefs, military, aristocracy, timars, or *iqtas*. Land cannot be owned by individuals or families nor inherited. Land belongs to Allah for the use of His creatures.

In return for all of Allah's favors, He commands the following:

- Justice (*'adl*). Justice, fairness, honesty, integrity, and evenhanded dealings are a prerequisite of every Muslim's conduct when dealing with others whether socially or in business transactions.
- Doing what is good and what is beautiful (*ihsan*). This attribute includes every positive quality such as goodness, beauty, and harmony. Human beings have an obligation to do what is wholesome and beautiful in their relationship with Allah and His creatures.
- Providing for those near to you (*qurba*) and kith and kin. Help them with wealth, kindness, compassion, humanity, and sympathy.
- Rejection of *Fahasha,* all evil deeds, lies, false testimony, fornication, selfishness, ingratitude, greed, and false belief.

- Fulfillment of the covenant of Allah. Whosoever does beautiful and righteous deeds will be given new life and rewarded with greater wages by Allah.

> Allah commands justice, the doing of good, and liberality to kith and kin, and He forbids all shameful deeds, and injustice and rebellion: He instructs you, that you may receive admonition.

> Fulfill the Covenant of Allah when you have entered into it and break not your covenant after you have confirmed it, indeed you have made Allah your surety; for Allah knows all that you do. (An-Nahl 16:90–91, Koran)

> Whoever works righteousness, man, or woman, and has Faith, verily, to him will We give a new Life, a life that is good and pure, and We will bestow on such their reward according to the best of their actions. (An-Nahl 16:97, Koran)

Tawhid, the main pillar of Islam, signifies that man's economic life depends wholly on Allah's laws of the universe and that their relationship to those who believe is through obedience to the covenant of Allah. Allah maintains in the Koran that there is no creature on the earth whose sustenance is not provided by Allah.

> No creature moves on earth that Allah does not nourish. He knows its essential nature and its varying forms; every detail has its place in the obvious plan. (Hud 11:6, Koran)

How are the people in need provided for their sustenance and daily needs? All wealth belongs to Allah, who bestows it on some people more than others. This wealth is given in trust, whereby the possessor is obliged to give the surplus in Allah's cause to his kin, to the widows and orphans, and to the needy first in his community and then in the other communities around him. Wealth is to be shared so that not a single individual of the *ummah* or indeed in the world should go hungry or without health care, education, and shelter.

It is not righteousness that you turn your faces towards East or West; but it is righteousness to believe in Allah and the Last Day, and the Angels, and the Book, and the Rasools; to spend of your substance, out of love for Him, for your kin, for orphans, for the needy, for the wayfarer, for those who ask, and for the ransom of slaves; to be steadfast in prayer, and practice regular charity, to fulfill the covenants which you have made; and to be firm and patient, in pain (or suffering) and adversity, and throughout all periods of panic. Such are the people of truth, the God-fearing. (Al-Baqarah 2:71, Koran)

And when they are told, "Spend you of (the bounties) with which Allah has provided you," The Unbelievers say to those who believe: "Shall we then feed those whom, if Allah had so willed, He would have fed, Himself. You are in nothing but manifest error. (Ya-Sin 36:47, Koran)

Alms are for the poor and the needy, and those employed to administer the funds; for those, whose hearts have been (recently) reconciled (to the truth); for those in bondage and in debt; in the cause of Allah; and for the wayfarer: (thus is it) ordained by Allah, and Allah is full of knowledge and wisdom. (At-Tawbah 9:60, Koran)

In the above two verses, the clear indication is that man is given bounty by Allah. In return, his obligation is to distribute the surplus after his needs have been met to the needy. The Koran specifies that the charities be disbursed to the *fuqara* (the poor who ask), to *al masakin* (the poor and the needy who do not ask), to zakat administrators, to those who spread the light of Islam to those inclined, for the freedom of those in bondage, to those in debt, for the cause of Allah, and for the wayfarer who treads the path in Allah's service.

In the covenant between the individual believer and Allah, the individual surrenders to Allah his life and belongings in return for His guidance, a place in paradise in the hereafter, and peace with prosperity in this world. Every believer according to his or her covenant with Allah has the obligation to extend the benefits that Allah has provided them to those who did not receive the same benefits. Such acts of generosity will be rewarded by Allah with a place in *Jannat* (place of peace and plenty) in the afterlife. Life of *Jannat* is to be attained in this world also, provided the compact with Allah is adhered to. The believer is Allah's instrument who will fulfill His promise to Adam that

> none will remain without food or clothes and none
> will suffer from heat or thirst. (Koran 20:118)

In the verses below, Allah has promised those who believe and obey His Covenant a reward for their acts of charity. He will double the harvest of their labors, forgive their sins, and provide them His bounties, nor shall they have fear or grieve. Fear and grief arise from misfortunes, which cause anxiety and depression. Allah's promise, therefore, safeguards the believers from misfortunes.

And to those devouring usury, Allah will deprive them of all blessings. Obeying Allah's covenant provides *Jannat* in the hereafter and a life of *Jannat*, peace, and plenty in this world. It also brings balance, harmony, and stability to the economic life of the world in that it meets the necessities of each individual and eliminates unnecessary suffering.

O you who believe! Do no render in vain your charity by reminders of your generosity or by injury, like him who spends his wealth to be seen of men, but he does not believe in Allah nor in the Last Day. His likeness is the likeness of a smooth rock on which is a little soil; on it falls heavy rain, which leaves it bare. They will not be able to do anything with what they have earned. And Allah does not guide the disbelieving people.

And the likeness of those who spend their substance, seeking to please Allah and to strengthen their souls, is as a garden, high and fertile; heavy rain falls on it but makes it yield a double increase of harvest, and if it receives not heavy rain, light moisture suffices it. And Allah is seer of what you do. (Al-Baqarah 2:264–65, Koran)

Men and women live in small communities. These small communities form a fellowship and a brotherhood that looks after its own need, and such a need may be of sustenance, clothing, shelter, knowledge, well-being, spirituality, understanding, protection, justice, or just simple reassurance. And such assistance is extended to the surrounding communities till it reaches the far-flung communities of the *ummah*. Each basic community owns the land in its surrounds, tilled and administered by the community as a whole for the well-being of the community in justice and in harmony according to the covenant of Allah. The Islamic economic system is based on capitalism in the production of wealth and socialism in its expenditure with the difference that individuals are free and able to make wealth but are responsible for the needs of their kith and kin and their neighbor. The state has little role in the welfare system. The land owned by the community may be assigned to individuals or may be tilled communally for the mutual benefit of the whole community, producing food and paying for schools hospitals, roadways, municipal services, and so on. The community is meant to be self-sufficient economically for all its needs and responsible for the welfare of every individual for his nutrition, clothing, shelter, health, schooling, and old-age provision.

Economic Principles of the Covenant of Allah: The covenant of Allah in the Koran has laid down principles and guidelines for the well-being of the economic life of the believers. Obeying the principles will bring peace, harmony, spiritual enlightenment, and economic prosperity. Disobeying means misery, ruin, and Allah's wrath.

First Principle: Land and sources of production are not the personal property of individuals. *Ardh* is the source of life and means of sustenance and production of food and resources and therefore must remain available to the community of Islam, the *ummah.* Allah created *ardh* and *sama* and has power over everything in them and all that is in between. To Allah belongs the heaven and the earth and what is in between them. Allah's kingdom over the heavens and the earth sustains man's economic life and directly affects man's conduct and his obedience to Allah's covenant.

In *ayahs* of Sura An-Nahl, Allah clearly mentions all the comforts He has provided man for the sustenance of life and for his economic well-being. Allah created cattle for humans for warmth, food, and transport; horses, mules, and donkeys for riding and show. With the moisture from the skies, He produces for man corn, olives, date palms, grapes, and every type of fruit. Allah made good things for humans in different colors and quantities so that man celebrates the praises of Allah in gratitude. Allah made the sea subject to humans so they may eat fresh and tender seafood, obtain beautiful ornaments from the ocean, sail their ships, and plow the oceans around the world. From the cattle, Allah produces milk, pure and wholesome to drink; and from the fruit of the date palm and vine, you get food and drink and from the bees, honey of varying colors that heals ailments.

Historically, land was there for man and beasts to roam around freely and spread through the world. Later, tribes and communities laid claims on pieces of land they needed for their needs with some extra surrounding area for their security. At the beginning of the Islamic era, productive land and water resources were owned by tribes for the use of their clan members. After the message of the Koran was established, the clans, the tribes, the former kingdoms, and the nations amalgamated to form the community of Islam, the *ummah,* which in principle owned the title to the land and resources with theoretical tenancy. The ownership of land by the *ummah* began to change with the downfall of the Abbasid caliphate.

From 1040 to 1200 CE, with the collapse of the central authority, there were many regional power struggles that allowed for the breakdown of the eastern Iranian frontiers against nomadic invasions. Central Asian nomads searching for pasturage in the tenth, eleventh, and twelfth centuries spilled over into the region north of the Aral Sea and into Transoxania and Afghanistan. From contact with settled peoples, trade, and the activities of the missionaries, these Turkish peoples began to convert to Islam. Their chieftains became acquainted in the ways of agriculture, trade, city administration, and imperial conception of rule and order. Most of the useful land in the Islamic states was taken over by the Turkish chiefs and soldiers for their own use and for the advancement of their own political power.

The Seljuk decline opened a way for the third phase in the history of the region from 1150 to 1350. This was a period of further nomadic invasion from inner Asia, culminating in the devastating Mongol invasions and the establishment of Mongol regimes over most of the Middle East. With every change of the ruling class, the land and resources shifted from the peasantry to the tribal chiefs and the soldiery. To the west, the slave military forces in Egypt and Syria consolidated the Mamluk regime, with land being distributed among the new elite.

The final phase was the Timurid period, 1400–1500. The Mongol period was succeeded by new times, troubles, and conquest by Timur, also known Tamerlane. This era of repeated nomadic invasions brought demographic changes in the ethnic and religious identity of populations. A new Turkic-speaking population migrated into Transoxania, the Hindu Kush mountain range, Iran, the Caucasus, Anatolia, and Mesopotamia. Turkish settlement led to the Islamization of northeastern Iran, Armenia, and Anatolia both by settlement of newcomers and by the conversion of existing populations.

To consolidate their power, control of provinces was delegated to the family members and the nomadic chieftains. *Iqta* lands were assigned to the military leaders. The result was usurpation of power at both the provincial and local levels, with the formation of microregimes funded by the resources of the land and heavy taxation of the peasants.

The Ottoman cavalry were recruited from among Turkish warriors. They were not garrisoned as a regular army, but they were provided with land grants and timars (Arabic equivalent of *iqtas*) throughout the empire. The timar holders provided local security and served in Ottoman campaigns. The timar system was based on an old-fashioned feudal pattern. The Ottomans also used the resources of the land to maintain their control over the empire and toward their new conquests. The timar holders exploited the peasants and the subject population.

The subject population belonged to a lesser order of existence. Common people, Muslim and non-Muslim, were considered the *reava* (flocks) to be shorn in the interests of the political elite. The Ottomans operated on the principle that the subjects (*reava*) should serve the interests of the state; the economy was organized to ensure the flow of tax revenues, goods in kind, and the services needed by the government and the elites. The populace was systematically taxed by maintaining a systematic record of the population, households, property, and livestock.

All the lands in the empire were owned by the ruler; some lands (*tapulu*) were on perpetual lease to the peasants who had the right to assign that right to their male descendants, and *mukatalu* lands were leased to a tax collector in return for a fixed payment for a lease. In the fifteenth century, the Ottomans had conceded to Turkish military rulers and Muslim religious rulers the ownership right to the land. In the course of the next century and a half, the sultans dispossessed the local notables and reassigned the tax rights to the *timar* holders appointed by the sultan. Ottoman policies were inimical to accumulation of private property. Large private fortunes were regularly confiscated by the state. The Ottoman economic policy on taxation and trade was based on fiscalism that was aimed at accumulation of as much bullion as possible in the state treasury, which was primarily used for the expenditure of running the Topkapi court and the continuous ongoing wars in the West.

The ownership of land in the Islamic world is not owned or distributed according to the covenant of the Koran, causing the present unequal distribution of wealth, poverty, deprivation, and degradation of a large part of the Islamic society. Land, therefore, belongs to Allah, who bestowed it to man and woman, His regents on the earth.

Second principle: All surplus money and resources should not remain with individuals. They shall be used for the benefit and uplift of the community.

> They ask thee how much they are to spend (in charity); say: "What is beyond your needs". Thus, doth Allah make clear to you His Signs: in order that you may consider. (Al-Baqarah 2:222, Koran)

Third principle: Wealth and commodities should not be hoarded. Surplus wealth is to be spent for the needs of the community as prescribed by Allah.

> O you who believe! There are indeed many among the priests and clerics, who in falsehood devour the substance of men and hinder (them) from the Way of Allah. And there are those who bury gold and silver and spend it not in the Way of Allah: announce unto them a most grievous penalty. (At-Tawbah 9:34, Koran)

Fourth principle: Wealth shall be spread through the community (the *ummah*) and shall not be impounded, stolen, and looted by conquerors, tribes, rulers, classes, and the *Mutaffifeen* (dealers in fraud) as practiced in the un-Koranic Muslim societies of the present times.

> What Allah has bestowed on His Rasool from the people of the townships, belongs to Allah, to His Rasool and to the near of kin and orphans, the poor, and the homeless, in order that it may not merely make a circuit between the wealthy among you. So, take what the Rasool assigns to you, and deny yourselves that which he withholds from you. And fear Allah, for Allah is strict in Punishment. (Al-Hashr 59:7 Koran)

Fifth principle: No one shall subsist on the earnings of others, and except for those who are incapacitated, everyone shall work. Everyone, man and woman, shall also contribute their labor and sweat toward the well-being of the *ummah*.

The Koran calls the people who stint as *Mutaffifeen*, those who get the full measure from others but stint when measuring for others. They lead an easy life from the earnings of others. The Koran mentions three such groups. One group consists of people who "take with an even balance and give less than what is due."

Woe to those that deal in fraud, those who,
from others exact full measure,
But when measuring or weighing for others, give less than due.
Do they not think that they will be called to account,
on a Mighty Day, A Day when (all) mankind will stand before
the Lord of the Worlds? (Al-Mutaffifin 83:1–6, Koran)

Another group comprises those who inherit money, land, and property, and they use that wealth to accumulate more and more without ever giving back to the needy. The third group gobbles up the earnings of others:

O you who believe! There are indeed many among the priests, the clerics and leaders who in falsehood devour the substance of men and hinder (them) from the Way of Allah. And there are those who bury gold and silver and spend it not in the Way of Allah: announce unto them a most grievous penalty. (Al-A'raf 9:34, Koran)

The Koran pronounces:

- Squander not your wealth among yourselves in egotism and conceit: Let there be trade and traffic amongst you with mutual goodwill nor kill or destroy yourselves: for verily Allah hath been Most Merciful to you. If any do that in rancor and injustice, soon shall we cast them into the fire: and easy it is for Allah. If you abstain from all the odious and the forbidden, Allah shall expel out of you all evil in you and admit you to a Gate of great honor.

  And crave not those things of what Allah has bestowed His gifts more freely on some than others, men are assigned what they earn and women that they earn. But ask Allah of His bounty. Surely Allah is knower of everything. (An-Nisa 4:29–32, Koran)
- You who believe! not your wealth or your children divert you from the remembrance of Allah. If any act thus, the loss is their own. And give freely, out of which We have bestowed on you, before death

should come to each of you and he should say, "O my Lord! Why didst Thou not give me respite for a little while? I should then have given generously and be among the righteous. But to none does Allah give respite when his time has come; and Allah is well acquainted with all that you do. (Al-Munafiqun 63:9–11, Koran)

- O you who believe! among your wives and your children are some that are contenders of your obligations: so, beware! But if you forgive them and overlook their faults, verily Allah is Most - Forgiving, Most Merciful. Your riches and your children may be but a temptation: Whereas Allah! With Him is an immense reward. So be in taqwa of Allah and fear Allah as much as you can; listen and obey; and spend in charity for the benefit of your own souls. And those saved from their own greed are the ones that prosper. If you loan to Allah a beautiful loan, He will double it for you, and He will forgive you: for Allah is both Appreciative (Shakoor) and Magnanimous (Haleem), Knower of what is hidden and what is manifest, Exalted in Might, Full of Wisdom. (At-Taghabun 64:14–18, Koran)
- And spend something (in charity) out of the substance which We have bestowed on you, before Death should come to any of you and he should say, "O my Lord! Why didst Thou not give me respite for a little while? I should then have given (largely) in charity, and I should have been one of the doers of good." (Al-Munafiqun 63:9–11, Koran)

The Twenty-Fourth Commandment of Allah

Deal Not Unjustly, and You Shall Not Be Dealt with Unjustly

- O you who believe! Fear Allah and speak always the truth that He may direct you to righteous deeds and forgive you your sins: he that obeys Allah and His Rasool have already attained the highest achievement. (Al-Ahzab 33:69–73, Koran)
- Stand firm for justice as witness to Allah, be it against yourself, your parents, or your family, whether it is against rich or poor, both are nearer to Allah than they are to you. Follow not your caprice lest you

distort your testimony. If you prevaricate and evade justice Allah is well aware what you do. (An-Nisa 4:135, Koran)

- you who believe! Stand firmly for Allah as a witness of fair dealing. Let not the malice of people lead you to iniquity. Be just, that is next to worship. Be with taqwa of Allah, fear Allah. Allah is well aware with what you do. (Al-Ma'idah 5:8, Koran)
- Betray not the trust of Allah and His Rasool. Nor knowingly misappropriate things entrusted to you. (Al-Anfal 8:27, Koran)
- If you have taqwa of Allah, and fear Allah, He will grant you a Criterion to judge between right and wrong and remove from you all misfortunes and evil and forgive your sins. Allah is the bestower of grace in abundance. (Al-Anfal 8:29, Koran)
- Be in taqwa of Allah, fear Allah, and be with those who are true in word and deed. (At-Tawbah 9:119, Koran)
- Deal not deal unjustly, and you shall not be dealt with unjustly. (Al-Baqarah 2:277–80, Koran)
- Whenever you give your word speak honestly even if a near relative is concerned.
- And come not near the orphan's property, except to improve it, until he attains the age of full strength, (Al-An'am 6:151–52, Koran)
- And give full measure and full weight with justice. No burden We place on any soul but that which it can bear. (Al An'am 6:151–52, Koran)
- If an impostor (fasiq) comes to you with any news, ascertain the truth, lest you harm people unsuspectingly and afterwards become full of remorse for what you have done. And know that amongst you is Allah's Rasool: were he in many matters to follow your desires, you would certainly fall into misfortune: but Allah has bestowed on you the love of iman (faith) and has made it beautiful in your hearts, and he has made abhorrent to you disbelief, wickedness, and disobedience to Allah: such indeed are those who are righteous (rashidun). (Al-Hujurat 49:6–10)

Justice (*'adl*) is a divine attribute defined as "putting all things in the right place." The opposite of *'adl* is *zulm,* which in Koranic terms means "wrongdoing." *Wrongdoing* is a human attribute defined as "putting things in the wrong place." *Zulm* is one of the common terms used in the Koran to refer to the negative acts employed by human beings.

Wrongdoing is the opposite of justice, and justice is to put everything in its right place and every act of the humans to be performed as prescribed by Allah. Hence, wrongdoing is to put things where they do not belong. *Zulm* (injustice) is to, for example, associate others with Allah. Others do not belong in the place for the divine; it is to place false words in place of the truth and to put someone else's property in place of your own. Other examples are taking a life against the divine commandments, replacing people's liberty with oppression, waging war instead of peace, and usurping people's right to govern themselves.

The Koran repeatedly stigmatizes humans of wrongdoing. When it points out who is harmed by injustice, wrongdoing, or *zulm*, the Koran always mentions the word *nafs* or self. People cannot harm Allah. By being unjust or doing wrong or by putting things in the wrong place, people harm themselves. They distort their own natures, and they lead themselves astray. Whom can one wrong? It is impossible to wrong or do injustice against Allah since all things are His creatures and do His work. Hence, wrongdoing and injustice is an activity against people and Allah's creation.

Allah has prescribed His covenant to humans for the good of human beings. People, tribes, and nations are being helped since Allah leads them into accord, harmony, and justice, which in turn create peace in the world. Allah has laid out all the basic principles for justice in His covenant for humans to live in harmony. Those who refuse to follow His commandments are therefore ungrateful and hence *kafirs.* Thus, they are wrongdoers (*zalimun*) and only harm themselves. Of the 250 verses where the Koran mentions *zulm* or *zalimun*, it mentions the object of wrongdoing in only 25 verses. In one verse, the object of wrongdoing are *people:*

> The blame is only against those who oppress men with wrongdoing and insolently transgress beyond bounds through the land, defying right and justice: for such there will be a Penalty grievous. (Ash-Shura 42:42, Koran)

In a second verse, the object of wrong and injustice is the signs of Allah:

> The weighing that day will be true. He whose scales are heavy, are the prosperous. Those whose scale are light, they have lost themselves for wronging Our Signs. (Al-A'raf 7:8–9, Koran)

Allah reveals His signs in nature and in scriptures so that the people may be guided. By disobeying these signs, they wrong only themselves.

In the remaining 23 verses in which the object of wrongdoing is mentioned, the wrongdoers are said to wrong only themselves.

> And We gave you the shade of clouds and sent down to you Manna and quails, saying: "Eat of the good things We have provided for you:" (but they rebelled); to Us they did no harm, but they wronged their own souls. (Al-Baqarah 2:57 and Al-A'raf 7:160, Koran)

> Verily Allah will not deal unjustly with humans in anything: it is the human who wrongs his own soul. (Yunus 10:44, Koran)

> And We wronged them not, but they wronged themselves. (Hud 11:101, Koran)

> If anyone does evil or wrongs his own soul but afterwards seeks Allah's forgiveness, he will find Allah Oft-Forgiving, Most Merciful. (An-Nisa 4:110, Koran)

The Koran admonishes:

> Deal not unjustly and you shall not be dealt with unjustly. (Al-Baqarah 2:278, Koran)

The Betrayal of the Covenant of Allah by "Muslims": The Justice System: The blessed *nabi* said, *"The Qur'an, consists of five heads, things lawful, things unlawful, clear, and positive precepts, mysteries, and examples. Then consider that is lawful, which is there declared to be so, and that which is forbidden as unlawful; obey the precepts, believe in the mysteries, and take warning from the examples."* The only purpose of the Sharia is to ensure that the laws are just and that justice is done. Sharia should ensure human dignity, equality, justice, consultative government, a state where there is realization of lawful benefits to people, prevention of harm, removal of hardship, and education of individuals by inculcating in them self-discipline, patience, restraint, and respect for rights of others. Sharia is a system under which there is restitution of all wrongs and imbalances in society. When the law and the justice system do not fulfill these requirements, they cannot be deemed to be according to Allah's laws and does not fulfill the requirements of Sharia.

When the rulers of Islam, the caliphs, sultans, kings, emirs, colonial rulers and their Muslim successors, politicians, and dictators imposed themselves over Muslim societies, they threw aside the authority of the Koran and the Sharia. They enlisted as their supporters and helpers people who perpetrated *fitnah* and oppression over the believers. The tribal rulers brought their eunuch and slave armies, and the colonial capitalists brought their banks, merchants, and civil servants. Out of this chaos evolved the indigent babu, sahib, and effendi class of pashas, beys, deputy commissioners, tax collectors, moneylenders, and the new brown capitalist class emulating their earlier white masters. This new class fraternized with the drawing room politicians and the *darbari* mullahs to form the new ruling elite of Islam in the late twentieth century. The captains and colonels in their colonial-era khaki uniforms charged into the foray to grab power in the land of Islam. This scum—a blend of colonial servants, politicians, merchants, mullahs, and the subservient colonial colonel class—became the rulers of Islam for the next sixty years. For them, the knowledge of Allah and the Koran was too unbecoming for their lifestyles.

Secularism became the name of the game, and the Western institutions defined the rule of the play. Capitalistic colonialism continued to rule Islam through these new proxy rulers. Without the love of Allah and of their people, they fell victim to the desires and cravings of their newfound power and wealth. They have continued to suck the lifeblood out of their land and their nation. The post-twentieth-century governance is the extension of the un-Islamic ruling arrangement of the nomadic Mongol and Turkish tribal formations that gave birth to the Ottoman, Safawid and the Mogul Empires. The new ruling class is imbued with the culture of *fitnah*, parasitism, and corruption that their class had inflicted on the *ummah* in the previous centuries. The conquerors grabbed their reward of gold and real estate from the conquered people. The power to pillage and snatch passed down step by step from the highest in the hierarchy to the meanest, sucking their victims of everything but the barest means of survival. This class carried their wealth of guild and precious stones in their proverbial turban and saddle, building no infrastructure nor institutions for the benefit of their people.

The subject population belonged to a lesser order of existence. All commoners were considered to be flocks to be shorn for the interests of the elite. The small community and village organizations were left under the control of the tax collector, the landlord, or the clerical and priestly leaders. These leaders were part of a feudal, religious, and military fraternal hierarchy of state functionaries responsible to the sultan and the imperial authorities. These leaders assisted the state in collecting taxes and enforcing social discipline. The sultans operated on the principle that the subjects should serve the interests of the state. The economy was organized to ensure the maximum flow of tax revenues, goods in kind, and all the services required by the sultans, emirs, and elites. The populace was systematically fleeced through the maintenance of a systematic record of the population, households, property ownership, and livestock.

The sultan owned all the lands of the Muslim empires: some lands, estates, and the *tapulu* were on perpetual lease to the peasants, and *mukatalu* lands were leased to a tax collector in return for a fixed payment for the lease. The economic policy on taxation and trade was aimed at accumulation of as much bullion as possible in the sultan's treasury. The Muslim rulers did not see trade policy or scientific and technological development as means of creating wealth. Rather, they sought wealth from conquered and annexed territories. The rulers and their religious, feudal, and military helpers were above the law—the law of the Sharia and the laws of the land. The laws of the Koran and Sharia were meant to control the flock but not the shepherd.

In the postcolonial era, power was handed down to the opportunist emirs and sheikhs in the Arab world and to politicians and bureaucrats in countries such as Pakistan and Egypt. The intelligence services of Britain and USA discovered that it was simpler to bribe, sweet-talk, and manipulate the simple Bedouin and the colonel class than the nationalist and wily politicians. It was by no sheer coincidence that all Islamic states gradually came to be run by sheikhs and military dictators acceptable to the West. The West required influence in the lands of the Muslims, and there were legions of willing Muslims bidding to be hired.

During the previous two hundred years, the Muslim society underwent a slow but perceptible change. In the late twentieth century, the believers found an alien culture in their midst. This alien society comprised constables, lance corporals, captains, session judges, deputy commissioners, inspectors, barristers, brigadiers, and an assortment of people with colonial-sounding titles who had in an earlier period greased the smooth running of the colonial empire by imitating their colonial masters and intimidating the natives. After the wars of liberation, Muslims found that the same people had reinvented and organized themselves into cadres of senior civil servants, police commissioners, army generals, ministers of the government, governors, and presidents.

The culture and society of the *ummah* bifurcated into two divergent groups. The tiny minority comprising the alien class of policemen, civil servants, judiciary, and soldiers trained in the colonial mode of governance became emboldened sufficiently to believe that they were the new ruling class of Islam and had the divine right to intimidate, direct, punish, and control the remaining majority. They put their beliefs into practice and began to seize and extort the wealth and property of the citizens at checkpoints, courthouses, roadsides, airports, shopping areas, and all the other public and private places. Their position provided them an assured authority to arrest, interrogate, imprison, and torture any citizen who infringed on their pleasure. The members of this privileged class had been initiated and indoctrinated to believe in their supremacy over the common folks in the same manner as the previous white-skinned colonial masters.

At the bottom, the common citizens scrape for their meager earning, beholden to their new masters in a culture of graft and corruption. Citizens are expected to bribe and grease their way through the maze of official hierarchy for the services of the lowly peon all the way up to the ranks of the mighty prime ministers and presidents. Their offices have little traps set as in the game of Monopoly, where the humble citizens are required to make offerings before they can have any official work done. Bribery and theft of public and private wealth goes on in open view. When walking down the streets, the offices, and the parliament buildings of Cairo, Islamabad, Lahore, and Amman, one wonders whatsoever happened to those with the *taqwa* of Allah. Where have they all gone?

The one and a half billion believers are in the clutches of this alien class of people who look like and pretend to be *Muslim*, yet their actions impose *zulm* and *fitnah* on the believers. Through their actions, *fitnah* has become rooted in the body politics of Islam; *fitnah* is embedded in the social fabric of Islam. *Zulm* and *fitnah* are implanted in the way Muslims treat their mothers, sisters, wives, and daughters; they have roots in the way Muslims treat other Muslims. And above all, the priesthood of Islam, the mercenary armies of Muslim states, and the rulers of Muslim states are the greatest purveyors of *zulm* and *fitnah*. Muslim rulers and their mercenary armies are the instruments of occupation of *zulm* and *fitnah* over the *ummah*. Such "Muslims" and their rulers plunder their kin and the community without shame or embarrassment. Some lead a life of self-deception, delusion, and hypocrisy, which drive a wedge among the body of the *ummah*.

Cleansing of the *muttaqeen* begins with the knowledge that Islam abhors *zulm*, *fitnah*, oppression, and tyranny. Those who call themselves *Muslim* and, in turn, inflict *zulm* and *fitnah* on Muslims cannot be the people of the fellowship of Allah. That *fitnah* is set in the covetousness and cravings of those who disobey Allah's commandments, and inflicting *zulm* and *fitnah* on the believers of Allah belie their belief in Him. Thus, such people cannot be a part of the *ummah*, the fellowship of Allah.

> Stand firmly for Allah as a witness of fair dealing. Let not the malice of people lead you to iniquity. Be just, that is next to worship. Be with taqwa of Allah, fear Allah.

Allah has granted each believer, man and woman, rights and freedoms. In enjoying his freedoms, the individual ensures that his activities do not impinge on the similar rights of others.

> The blame is only against those who oppress humans, (insan: men and women) with wrongdoing and insolently transgress beyond bounds through the land, defying right and justice: for such there will be a Penalty grievous. (Ash-Shura 42:42, Koran)

The Twenty-Fifth Commandment of Allah

Knowledge: Travel through the Earth and See How Allah Did Originate Creation; So Will Allah Produce a Later Creation

- O you who believe! Allah will exalt in rank those of you who believe and who have been granted Knowledge.
- Proclaim! And thy Lord is Most Bountiful, He Who taught (the use of) the Pen, Taught man that which he knew not. O my Lord! Enrich me in knowledge.

When Muslims forget Allah and they fail in their knowledge of His word and ignore their covenant with Allah, they suffer the consequences of their ignorance.

When you are told to make room in the assemblies, spread out and make room: ample room will Allah provide for you. And when you are told to rise up, for prayers, Jihad or other good deeds rise up: Allah will exalt in rank those of you who believe and who have been granted Knowledge. And Allah is well acquainted with all you do. (Al-Mujadila 58:11, Koran)

He Who taught (the use of) the Pen, Taught man that which he knew not. (Al-'Alaq 96:4–5, Koran)

Is one who worships devoutly during the hours of the night prostrating himself or standing (in adoration), who takes heed of the Hereafter, and who places his hope in the Mercy of his Lord, (like one who does not)? Say: "Are those equal, those who know and those who do not know? It is those who are endued with understanding that receive admonition. (Az-Zumar 39:9, Koran)

All knowledge comes to humans through humanity's openness to God. Humans accept the concept of God as the Creator of everything that is. He wills, and it is. He is beyond human comprehension, and His divine systems do not conform to the human concepts of creed and dogma. Allah, God the Creator, created the galaxies, worlds, stars, sun, moon, little atoms, protons, neutrons, and tiny particles that show the complexity of His genius. Allah, the Lord of creation, sends water from the heavens for sustenance of life on the earth. Allah directs sunshine to the earth to provide warmth and light to sustain human, plant, and animal life. Allah formed sun, moon, and stars to create equilibrium in the universe, every object in its intended place, revolving in its fixed orbit in perfect harmony and balance. Allah created the secrets and the mysteries of the heavens and the earth, the so-called sciences, and the knowledge of particles, elements, cells, mitochondria, chromosomes, gravity, and black holes, only a minute portion of which he revealed to man.

Allah clearly provided humans a mind to wonder at His infinitesimal wisdom. Yet man is conceited and arrogant to believe that God is driven by man-created creed, testament, dogma, Sunna, and Sharia. Allah does not require a shrine, temple, *shakan*, tent, or talisman to live in. His presence is everywhere. He is present in the smallest particle (*nuqta*) and in the greatest expanse. He is accessible to each and every object that He has created. Every object obeys Allah's will except for man. Man has been given a free will. The covenant of Allah presents us with the scope of the freedom of choice that humans have in doing what is wholesome and beautiful or what is corrupt and ugly and in the human role among the creation that distinguishes right activity, right thought, and right intention from their opposites. It reminds us of how the scales of Allah's justice—the two hands of Allah, His mercy and His wrath—are reflected in the human domain, where people have been appointed Allah's vicegerents. Deeds of goodness and wholesomeness are associated with mercy, paradise, and the beautiful. Evil and corruption is rewarded with wrath, hell, and the ugly.

Allah the Divine is open to the most miniscule of beings. From the vastest of expanse to the minutest of particle, there is a connection with Allah, the Cherisher and the Nourisher of the universe. Within this communion of the Divine with the creation passes the Spirit of Allah into His creatures. The human lays his heart and mind open to Allah in submission to receive His Spirit and guidance.

In the space and the emptiness of the universe, there flow currents and whispers of wind and energy. These winds of silence, light, and sound carry the divine whisper, and in this sound is Allah's knowledge. His knowledge descends into the believer's receptive heart in peace, silence, and tranquility. When the angels and the Spirit descend with Allah's guidance, the eyes perceive the most beautiful divine light, the ears hear the softest tinkle of the bell, the nose smells the fragrance of a thousand gardens, and the skin feels the most tranquil of the gentle breeze. When this happens, the soul has seen nirvana; man is in communion with Allah. This is the knowledge of Allah. And this is the knowledge of certainty.

Allah sent thousands of prophets to mankind to teach humanity precepts and knowledge of His straight path of unity, truth, and goodness. Over thousands of years, these precepts and principles spread around the world through civilizations till mankind, as a whole, began to comprehend the knowledge of one universal God, the Creator of every particle and every being in the whole universe. Man listened and occasionally regressed into his inherent paganism, greed, selfishness, and egotism. Allah bestowed on man a vicegerency on the earth, a mind, free will, and a covenant. Allah then announced that there were to be no more prophets. The era of prophecy had ended. Man, in stages, had received the knowledge required to live in submission to Allah's will (*islam)* in peace and harmony on the earth, have faith in the divine Master (*iman*), and perform wholesome and beautiful deeds (*ihsan*) in accordance with the divine laws, which were sent down as a guidance to every human community for a life of truth justice, goodness, and peace. Such knowledge consisted of the following:

Unity: There is one absolute Being from which all stems; the universe of galaxies and all the living things in the universe are all connected to one another and cannot be separated from that absolute Being. Everything alive—humans, animals, plants, and microorganisms—is created by the absolute Being, all nurtured with the same organic matter, all breathing the same air; and in turn, their physical self disintegrates to the same elements, which then return to the earth and the universe. In this cycle of creation and disintegration, the only permanence is of the Real, the Absolute. All else is an illusion and a mirage. One moment humans are flesh and blood, in the next dust blown away by the wind. Nothing is left behind—no riches, no honor, no ego, and no pride. What is left, however, is an account of your deeds, upon which one day you will be judged. Deeds of goodness and wholesomeness are rewarded with mercy, paradise, and the beautiful. Evil and corruption is rewarded with wrath, hell, and the ugly.

Mind: The human is bestowed with a mind and free will. The mind has the ability to perceive ideas and knowledge from the Divine and from the signs of Allah. The whisper of the Divine, the rustle of the wind, the light of God (*nur*), the fragrance of God's creation, and the sensation of the Divine touch all inspire the human mind with an endless stream of ideas and knowledge. Man has been granted the ability to process his thoughts and given knowledge with a free will.

The verse of the light encompasses the totality of the knowledge and guidance that God sent to man through His prophets. The pagan in the human confused God's message and instead began to worship the *rasul*. With the end of the era of prophecy, man has the freedom to open his heart to the light of Allah and to learn to recognize the presence of God within himself in his own heart.

Allah is the Light of the heavens and the earth. The parable of His Light is as if there were a Niche and within it a Lamp: the Lamp enclosed in Glass; the glass as it were a brilliant star: lit from a blessed Tree, an Olive, neither of the East nor of the West, whose Oil is well-nigh luminous, though fire scarce touched it: Light upon Light! Allah guides whom He will to His Light: Allah sets forth Parables for men, and Allah is the font of all Knowledge, and knows all things. Lit is such a light in houses, which Allah hath permitted to be raised to honor and celebrate His name. In them He is glorified in the mornings and in the evenings, over and over again. (An-Nur 24:35-36, Koran)

The parable of divine light is the essence of the belief in one universal God for the whole humankind. Allah is the light of the heavens and the earth, and His light bestows life, love, grace, and mercy on His creatures. Allah loves His creation. Allah' s *nur* illuminates the hearts of those who love Him, trust Him, and open their heart in submission to Him. Those hearts glow with the light, Spirit, and knowledge of Allah with the brilliance of a star—the star lit from divine wisdom, the tree of knowledge, and the knowledge of Allah's signs. For those who believe, Allah is within, and the believer is aglow with Allah's love—light upon light, light seen from the heavens and the earth. The dwellings in which Allah is glorified in the morning and in the evening over and over again are aglow with His light of love and mercy.

Allah has granted the knowledge and wisdom of *furqan* and *taqwa* to the believers who have opened their hearts and minds to Him. Man has been granted the freedom of choice in doing what is wholesome and beautiful or what is corrupt and ugly. It is only man among the creation that has been given the knowledge to distinguish right activity, right thought, and right intention from their opposites. This knowledge reminds man of the scales of Allah's justice; the two hands of Allah, His mercy and His wrath, are reflected in the human domain, where people have been appointed Allah's vicegerents. Deeds of goodness and wholesomeness are associated with mercy, paradise, and what is beautiful. Evil and corruption is rewarded with wrath, hell, and what is ugly.

The fundamental knowledge is the "knowledge of certainty" (*ilm al-yaqin*, Koran 102:5).

The lure of wealth enthralls you.

Until you reach the graves.

But aye, then shall you know.

Again, aye then in the end shall you know.

Nay, were you to know with the knowledge of certainty.

You shall surly see the hellfire!

Surely you shall see it with the eye of certainty.

Then, shall you be questioned that Day about the pleasures (of wealth). (Koran 102:1–8)

This type of certainty results from human capacity for logic and reasoning and the appraisal of Allah's presence in the world, Allah's signs. The knowledge of certainty is rational and discursive, a point that the Koran acknowledges when it admonishes human beings to

Say: "Travel through the earth and see how Allah did originate creation; so will Allah produce a later creation: for Allah has power over all things." (Al-'Ankabut 29:20, Koran)

It is He Who gives life and death, and to Him (is due) the alternation of Night and Day: will you not then understand? (Al-Mu'minun 23:80)

Over time and under the influence of contemplation and spiritual practice, the knowledge of certainty may be transformed into a higher form of knowledge of Allah that the Koran calls the "eye of certainty" (*ain al-yaqin*, Koran 102:7). This knowledge is acquired by spiritual intellect, which believers in the East locate metaphorically in the heart. Once the heart and the mind are open to Allah in submission, they form the niche in which glows the divine light and the Spirit and wisdom of Allah in man. Once opened, the heart receives knowledge as a type of divine light or illumination (*nur*) that leads the believer toward the remembrance of Allah. Just as with the knowledge of certainty, with the eye of certainty, the believer sees Allah's existence through His presence in this world. With the eye of certainty, what lead the believer to the knowledge of Allah are not the arguments to be understood by the rational intellect but by theophanic appearances (*bayyinat*) that strip away the veils of worldly phenomenon to reveal the divine reality underneath.

The third and most advanced type of knowledge builds on the transcendent nature of knowledge itself. The highest level of consciousness is called the "truth of certainty" (*haqq al-yaqin*).

> But truly Revelation is a cause of sorrow for the Unbelievers.
> But verily it is Truth of assured certainty. So, glorify the name
> of thy Lord Most High. (Al-Haqqah 69:50–52, Koran)

This multidimensional conception of knowledge comprehends a reality that lies hidden within the unique world yet can be revealed by the human mind and the vision of the spiritual intellect through the signs of Allah that are present in the world itself. In the Koran, Allah calls humanity:

> So I do call to witness what you see
>
> And what you see not,
>
> This is a Message sent down from the Lord of the Worlds.
>
> But verily it is Truth of assured certainty. (Al-Haqqah 69:38–39, 43, 51)

The Twenty-Sixth Commandment of Allah

Let There Arise out of You a Band of People Inviting to All That Is Good, Enjoining What Is Right, and Forbidding What Is Wrong

Let there arise out of you a band of people inviting to all that is good, enjoining what is right, and forbidding what is wrong: they are the ones to attain happiness. (Ali 'Imran 3:103–5, Koran)

The Koranic principle of enjoining good and forbidding evil is supportive of the moral autonomy of the individual. This principle authorizes the individual to act according to his or her best judgment in situations in which his or her intervention will advance a good purpose. The following saying of the blessed *nabi* also supports individual action by a believer:

If any one of you sees an evil, let him change it by his hand, and if he is unable to do that, let him change by his words, and if he is still unable to do that let him denounce it in his heart, but this is the weakest form of belief.

This principle assigns to the individual an active role in the community in which he or she lives. *The Koran annunciated the principle of free speech fourteen hundred years ago.* Believing men and women are reminded that they are the best of people, a witness over other nations. Such a responsibility carries with it a moral burden of an exemplary conduct of one who submits to the divine truth and whose relationship with Allah is governed is by *taqwa*, the consciousness of humankind's responsibility toward its Creator. The believer has the responsibility of acting in accordance with the three types of knowledge—the knowledge of certitude, the eye of certitude, and the truth of certitude. With that knowledge and faith, the believer is well equipped to approach others to enjoin what is right and forbid what is wrong. This moral autonomy of the individual, when bound together with the will of the community, formulates the doctrine of infallibility of the collective will of the *ummah*, which is the doctrinal basis of consensus.

Each believer carries a moral burden of knowing what is good and living the path of that goodness. The guidance to the path is in Allah's covenant. Fulfilling Allah's covenant equips man with the exemplary conduct that enables him to be a witness over other people. On this journey in this world, man is presented with Allah's covenant as his guide, *taqwa* of Allah as his shield against evil, and *furqan* as Allah's compass to the straight path of righteousness. If the human accepts the path of Allah and follows His covenant as his guide, *taqwa* of Allah as his shield against evil, and *furqan* as Allah's compass to the straight path, he becomes a believer and of the righteous.

The way to righteousness is through Allah's guidance and covenant in the Koran. Every little bit of devotion makes the *nur* of Allah glow in the heart till the believer is connected with Allah and begins to follow His path. This communion between the believer and Allah becomes exclusive. Submission establishes the link between them. The believer asks, and Allah gives. The believer loves Allah, and Allah loves him in return. The believer asks for the straight path, and Allah shows him the way. The believer praises Allah, and Allah showers His mercy and grace upon him. The believer remembers Allah, and Allah responds to those who praise Him, thank Him, and ask Him.

Allah's *din* is divine. Allah is *Haqq*, and all truth emanates from Him. The Koran is Allah's word on the earth and the expression of *haqq*. *Haqq* is the reality and the truth; *batil* refers to something that is imaginary or false. When humans add dogma and creed to Allah's *din*, it is not *haqq*. In matters of din, what is not absolute truth is not *haqq*. What is not *haqq* is *batil* (false or fabricated). What is not truthful cannot be a witness over Allah's word and *din*. Therefore, all human additions to the *din* of Allah do not constitute the truth. Therefore, every human fabrication to the *din* after the completion of *wahiy* is *batil* or falsehood.

A just and moral society:

> Let there arise out of you a band of people inviting to all that is good, enjoining what is right, and forbidding what is wrong.

Let every believer take control of his home and his *din*. And let every community of the *ummah* take charge of its affairs and return to the governance on the basis of tawhid, truth, justice, and equality for all. The precepts of the covenant of Allah ensure human dignity, equality, justice, consultative government, a state where there is realization of lawful benefits to the people, prevention of harm, removal of hardship, and education of individuals by inculcating in them self-discipline, patience, restraint, and respect for rights of others. It is a system under which there is restitution of all wrongs and imbalances in society.

The Islamic society as envisioned in the Koran and the Sunna is a just and a moral society in which every individual, from the highest to the lowest, from the first to the last, has equal, unimpeded, and unquestioned right to freedom; right to practice his faith in accordance to his beliefs as, in Islam, there is no compulsion in matters of religion; right to life, which includes mental, physical, and emotional well-being; right to safeguard one's property; right to intellectual endeavors, acquisition of knowledge, and education; right to make a living; and right to free speech and action to enjoin good and forbid evil. In enjoying his freedoms, the individual ensures that his activities do not impinge on the similar rights of others.

Jihad is the struggle of the individual man on his way from the path of ignorance to the path of Allah. Man hears Allah's call through the noise and the commotion of the world and, through the eye of his soul, lets the *nur* of Allah into the niche of his heart. Allah's call is to obedience, goodness, and selflessness. Man bows down his head on the ground in submission and in humility to his Lord. The Lord guides, and the believer follows. The believer has faith in his Allah, and Allah holds his hand. Allah shows His believer the way to goodness, and the believer performs wholesome deeds. The *nur* of Allah glows in the believer's heart, and the believer accepts Allah in his heart. Submission establishes a link between the believer and Allah. Allah commands, and the believer follows.

The *nafs,* unlike the Freudian ego, is capable of both good and bad. The *nuqta* of the *nafs* or the self, when magnified a million times, becomes visible as a shiny disk, a mirror. The *fitra* of the *nafs* is to shine like a mirror with Allah's *nur.* When man walks the path of Allah in *taqwa* of Him with the knowledge that Allah is with him, watching him and guiding him, Allah's *nu*r shines on the *nafs,* keeping it pure and safe.

However, when man's desires, cravings, and ego overpower his love and obedience for Allah, the shiny mirror of his *nafs* becomes obscured by the smoke of his cravings. Man loses sight of the *nur* of Allah and falls into error and decadence. The effort required to keep focus on Allah's *nur* and the *taqwa* of Allah is the inner jihad. And this jihad is the effort involved in being conscious of Allah's commandments when Allah calls on His believers with the words *O you who Believe* and commands them to acts of faith and goodness in seventy-five verses of the Koran. Obedience to every such command is jihad. The expression *in the path of Allah*, of course, is the path of right conduct that Allah has set down in the Koran. Jihad is simply the complement to *islam*, the surrender to the will of Allah. The surrender takes place in Allah's will, and it is His will that people struggle in His path. Hence, submission and surrender to Allah's will demands struggle in His path.

Once the believer has purified himself with Allah's *nur*, he has prepared himself for the *outer jihad*. When the believer has purified his own *nafs* and soul with submission to Allah (*islam*), having faith in the only reality *(iman)*, and by performance of wholesome deeds in the name of Allah (*ihsan*), he is ready to teach and show humanity the way to Allah. The believer is ready to fulfill Allah's command:

> Let there arise out of you a band of people inviting to all that is good, enjoining what is right, and forbidding what is wrong: they are the ones to attain happiness. (Ali 'Imran 3:103–5, Koran)

The Twenty-Seventh Commandment of Allah

Do Not Say to Another Muslim, "You Are Not a Believer."

> When you go forth in the cause of Allah be careful to discriminate and say not to the one who greets you with alaikum o salaam, "Though art not a believer".
>
> Would you covet perishable goods of this life when there are immeasurable treasures with Allah? You were like the person who offered you salutation before Allah conferred on you His favors. Therefore, carefully investigate for Allah is well aware of all that you do. (An-Nisa 4:94, Koran)

Every believer's journey into Islam cannot be the same and uniform. A lot depends on the cultural background, education, and intellectual biases of the individual. The first principle of faith is tawhid, the assertion that God, Allah, is one and that there is only a single worthy object of worship, Allah. All other subjects of worship are false. To serve anything else is to fall into error, misguidance, and sin of *shirk*.

The Koranic notion of religious belief (*iman*) as dependent on knowledge is actualized in practice in the term *islam*. The term *islam* signifies the idea of surrender or submission. Islam is a religion of self-surrender; it is the conscious and rational submission of dependent and limited human will to the absolute and omnipotent will of Allah. The type of surrender Islam requires is a deliberate, conscious, and rational act made by a person who knows with both intellectual certainty and spiritual vision that Allah, who is the subject of Koranic discourse, is reality itself. The knower of God is a Muslim (fem. *Muslimah*), "one who submits" to the divine truth and whose relationship with God is governed by *taqwa*, the consciousness of humankind's responsibility toward its Creator.

However, consciousness of God alone is not sufficient to make a person a Muslim. Neither is it enough to be merely born a Muslim or to be raised in an Islamic cultural context. The concept of *taqwa* implies that the believer has the added responsibility of acting in accordance with three types of knowledge—*ilm al-yaqin*, *ain al-yaqin*, *and haqq al yaqin* (knowledge of certainty, eye of certainty, and truth of certainty). The believer must endeavor at all times to maintain himself or herself in a constant state of submission to Allah. By doing so, the believer attains the honored title of "slave of Allah" (*abd Allah,* fem. *amat Allah*), for he recognizes that all power and agency belongs to God alone. Thus, the believer surrenders to the will of Allah through his own deliberate, conscious, and rational act, and he knows with both intellectual certainty and spiritual vision that Allah is the reality. After submission to the will of Allah, observation of the five pillars by the believer opens the way for him or her to understand *ihsan* and perform good deeds for humanity:

> Those who believe, do deeds of righteousness, and establish regular prayers and regular charity, will have their reward with their Lord: on them shall be no fear, nor shall they grieve. (Al-Baqarah 2:277, Koran)

Every individual is at a different stage of their life's journey. Only Allah is the Judge and the Knower of the hidden and the manifest. Only He knows what is in a person's breast.

The Twenty-Eighth Commandment of Allah

Avoid Suspicion and Spy Not on Each Other nor Speak Ill behind Each Other's Backs

> Avoid suspicion, for suspicion in some cases is sin; and spy not on each other, nor speak ill of each other behind their backs. Would any of you eat the flesh of his dead brother? No, you would abhor it. Be in taqwa of Allah, fear Allah: for Allah is Forgiving, Most Merciful. (Al-Hujurat 49:12–13)

Allah gave humans the trust of vicegerency over the earth with the stipulation that they acknowledge Him as their Lord and worship Him and thank Him for His benevolence. As part of the trust, people are free to make their choices about their actions. Allah does not force them to make the correct choices without taking the trust away from them, and if He took the trust away, they could no longer be humans.

Along with the vicegerency came acquisition of wealth, land, and women. Acquisition of wealth breeds greed, covetousness, and hoarding of wealth. The prospect of loss of such acquisitions produces insecurity and constant watchfulness. Paranoia has a forceful impact on the society of man. Assumptions, suspicions, and suppositions lead to quarrels among people, wars between nations, and thus a breakdown of the world order. Deceit and falsehood cause suspicion and lack of trust among people and nations. As a consequence, nations spend billions in expensive and intricate spy and security agencies, using spying equipment on the ground, in the air, and in space to obtain information on other nations. People and police spy on people and each other, and cities are full of cameras tracking the movement of citizens.

The same insecurity of people's psyche gives rise to resentment, jealousy, and mistrust, leading to feuds and social disruption. Truth dissipates paranoia and suspicion, which are by-products of insecurity and fear that accompany acquisition and hoarding of wealth. Believers who are secure in their trust of Allah and of the *ummah* have nothing to fear.

The Twenty-Ninth Commandment of Allah

Do Not Ridicule Other Believers nor Revile Each Other with Wicked Names

> Let not some folk among you ridicule others: it may be that they are better than you are: nor let some women mock others: it may be that the others are better than them: nor defame or revile each other by offensive names: ill-seeming is wicked name calling for the one who has believed; and those who do not desist are indeed wrong doers. (Al-Hujurat 49:11, Koran)

The covenant of Allah forbids suspicion, spying on each other, backbiting, and ridiculing other believers. The heart is like a shining mirror. Troublesome deeds are like the smoke that will obscure the mirror, and then you will not be able to see the light and the reality of Allah. You are then veiled from His reality. To understand the reality of Allah, you have to uncover ignorance and darkness so as to see the light and the reality. Some of the properties of this smoke and darkness are arrogance, ego, pride, envy, vengeance, lying, gossiping, backbiting, and many other unwholesome traits. To rid of these evils and odious traits, one has to polish the mirror of the heart. This cleansing of the heart is done through acquisition of understanding and knowledge and by acting on this knowledge to fight against one's ego by ridding oneself of multiplicity of being by achieving unity with Allah. When the heart becomes alive with the light of unity and it is with that light, the eye of the clean heart will see the reality of Allah's attributes.

The Thirtieth Commandment of Allah

Secret Counsels Are Only Inspired by Satan so That He May Cause Grief to the Believers

When you hold secret counsel, do it not for iniquity and hostility, and disobedience to the Rasool; but do it for righteousness and self-restraint; and fear Allah, to Whom you shall be brought back.

Secret counsels are only inspired by the Satan, in order that he may cause grief to the Believers; but he cannot harm them in the least, except as Allah permits; and on Allah let the Believers put their trust. (Al-Mujadila 58:9-10, Koran)

No believer, individual, community, or ruler shall make a compact on behalf of the *ummah* or part of it in secret with the unbelievers. Islam regards secret pacts with enemies and hostile actions against one's own people as an act of treason. During the period the *nabi* was in Medina, there were some people who professed Islam and at the same time conspired with the enemy, the *kafirun*, against their fellow Muslims. The Koran has the following description of the fate of the *Munafiqeen:*

> Of the people there are some who say: "We believe in Allah and the Last Day;" but they do not really believe.
>
> Fain would they deceive Allah and those who believe, but they only deceive themselves, and realize it not!
>
> In their hearts is a disease; and Allah has increased their disease: and grievous is the penalty they incur, because they are false to themselves.
>
> When it is said to them: "Make not mischief on the earth," they say: "Why, we only want to make peace!"
>
> Of surety, they are the ones who make mischief, but they realize (it) not. (Al-Baqarah 2:8–12, Koran)
>
> Allah will throw back their mockery on them, and give them rope in their trespasses; so, they will wander like blind ones to and fro.
>
> These are they who have bartered guidance for error: but their traffic is profitless, and they have lost true direction.
>
> Their similitude is that of a man who kindled a fire; when it lighted all around him, Allah took away their light and left them in utter darkness. So, they could not see. Deaf, dumb, and blind, they will not return to the path. (Al-Baqarah 2:15–18, Koran)

Time and again, we find shame and ignominy brought to Islam by professional rulers of Islam who sat on the throne with the help of mercenary armies and ruled the believers against the dictates of the law, the Koran, and the covenant of Allah. Knowledge of Islam's flawed history is essential to prevent the rule of traitors in the future. To know the past is to forecast the future. When the believers celebrate their heroes, they must also commemorate their traitors so that the history of Islam's ignominies do not repeat itself. Freshening of such painful memories is an essential part of *ummah's* maturity into righteousness and greatness. Islam's history is laden with stories of covetous adventurers who, for little personal gain or a purseful of gold, stabbed the *ummah* in the back.

1095 CE: The Crusades: The One-Thousand-Year War

November 25, 1095, is a milestone in the history of Europe and Christendom. On this day at the Council of Clermont, Pope Urban II—addressing a vast crowd of priests and knights and poor folk—declared a holy war against Islam. For Europe, this was a defining moment, and this event has ongoing repercussions until today in the Middle East. This holy war, begun in the twilight of the eleventh century, is still ongoing under various guises and forms into the beginning of the twenty-first century. NATO troops in Afghanistan, Kosovo, Bosnia, and Iraq (the coalition) are the legacy of the Council of Clermont, now called the Council of Europe, and NATO.

The pope declared the race of Seljuk Turks who had recently converted to Islam to be barbarians. They had swept into Anatolia and seized lands from the Christian empire of Byzantium. The pope declared that the Turks were an accursed race that was utterly alienated from

God who had not entrusted their spirit to God[9]. Killing these godless monsters was a holy act; it was a Christian duty to "exterminate this vile race from our lands."[10] Once they had purged Asia Minor of this Muslim filth, the knights would engage in a still holier task. They would then march to the holy city of Jerusalem and liberate it from the infidel. It was shameful that the tomb of Christ should be in the hands of Islam.

Since that time, there has been a constant onslaught against Islam by the West. When the Euro-Christian states were not fighting against one another, they grouped together in a pack to attack the Muslim states. On the surface for the public consumption, they fought for their religion to destroy the infidel, but the true motive underlying the thousand-year war was always economic exploitation of the East by the top echelons of the Euro-Christianity. The thousand-year incursions of exploitation have changed its stance every so often that the historians have lost the truth between the Crusades; Venetian trade; voyages of discovery; slave trade; colonialism; racism; economic subversion of the natives; piracy in the open seas; maritime ambushes and robbery of coastal cities; plunder of mineral, agriculture, and human resources; opium trade; capitalism; socialism; communism; world wars; globalization of world trade in the hands of few nations; and finally the control of oil.

When Damascus fell to the British troops in September 1918, Gen. Edmund Henry Allenby made it a point to visit the tomb of the great warrior Salah al-din Yusuf ibn Ayyub, the liberator of Jerusalem. Upon approaching the grave of the sultan, he kicked it with his riding boot and uttered, "Finally, the Crusades have been avenged." Allenby, the

---

9 Robert the Monk, *Historia Iherosolimitana.* Quoted by August C Krey, *The First Crusade: The Accounts of Eye Witnesses* (Princeton and London, 1921).

10 Fulcher and Chartres, *History of the Expedition to Jerusalem, 1095–1127,* trans. Rita Ryan (Knoxville, 1969), 66.

Christian conqueror of Damascus, had remembered Pope Urban's one-thousand-year-old call to arms against Islam.

1492 CE: The Fall of Spain

When the *Muwahhid* dynasty ended, more than half of the northern part of Spain and all the western provinces were in Christian hands. Muslim Spain had come under anarchy once again. Muslim territories were broken into small fragments, each at war with the other. Every Muslim chief invited Christian troops against another and offered them some cities and forts in return for their military help. This depravity of Muslim rulers was very pleasing and encouraging to the Christians. By the middle of thirteenth century, many Muslims in Spain had become subject to Christians either by conquest or treaty. Such Muslims were called Mudejares. They had preserved their religion and the laws but had begun to forget Arabic and begun to adopt Romance tongue.

The Nasrid sultans were embroiled in their dynastic quarrels that have been a perpetual curse of the Muslim sultans. The final ruin of the Muslim kingdoms was hastened by the irresponsible move by Sultan Abu al-Hasan 'Ali, who refused to pay customary tribute to Ferdinand and commenced hostilities by attacking Castilian territory. Ferdinand in 1482, in a surprise attack, took Al-Hammah, which stood at the foot of the Sierra de Alhama, and guarded the southwestern entrance of the Granadan domain. At this time, a son of Abu al-Hasan—Abu 'Abd Allah Muhammad—instigated by his mother, Fatima, raised the banner of rebellion against his own father. Fatima took revenge against her royal husband for his attachment and attention toward a Christian concubine and her children. Supported by the garrison, Abu 'Abd Allah in 1482 seized Alhambra and made himself master of Granada.

In the following year, Abu 'Abd Allah—whose name became corrupted to Boabdil in Spanish—had the temerity to attack the Castilian town of Lucena, where he was beaten and taken captive. Abu al-Hasan 'Ali reinstated himself to the Granadan throne, where he ruled till 1485, when he abdicated in favor of his brother Muhammad XII, nicknamed al-Zaghall. Ferdinand and Isabella saw a perfect tool in their prisoner Abu 'Abd Allah in their plan for destruction of Islam and its presence in Spain. Supplied with Castilian men and money, Abu 'Abd Allah in 1486 occupied part of his uncle's capital and once more plunged Granada into a destructive civil war. In the meantime, the Castilian army was advancing. Town after town fell before it. Malaga was captured in the following year, and its Muslim inhabitants were sold in slavery. The noose was getting tighter around the doomed capital. Al-Zaghall made a few unsuccessful stands against the armies of Ferdinand and was defeated. Abu 'Abd Allah fought alongside the Christian armies of Ferdinand against his uncle.

No sooner had al-Zaghall been disgracefully disposed of by his nephew than Abu 'Abd Allah was ordered by Ferdinand to vacate the city and surrender Granada to Isabel and Ferdinand. Abu 'Abd Allah refused to comply. In the spring of 1491, Ferdinand with an army of ten thousand horses marched on Granada and occupied all the land around it. He destroyed crops and farms in a blockade to starve the population into submission. When winter came, extreme cold and heavy snow barred all access to the outside world. Food became scarce, and the population starved. In December 1491, the hardships of the people had reached their extreme, and the garrison agreed to surrender. The following terms for the surrender were agreed. Abu 'Abd Allah and his officers and people would take an oath of obedience to the Castilian sovereigns. The Castilians entered Granada on January 2, 1492, and supplanted a cross on the crescent on the towers of the fortress.

The sultan Abu 'Abd Allah, with his queen, richly dressed, left his red fortress, never to return. As he rode away, he turned to take a last look at his capital, sighed, and burst into tears. His mother, till then his evil genius, turned to him with the words *"You do well to weep like a woman for what you could not defend like a man."* The rocky eminence where he took his sad farewell look is still known by the name *El ultimo suspiro del Moro* (the last sigh of the Moor).

Ferdinand and Isabella failed to abide by their terms of capitulation. A campaign of forced conversion of Muslims was inaugurated in 1499. All books in Arabic were burned in a bonfire of Arabic manuscripts in Granada. In 1501, a royal decree was issued that all Muslims in Castile and Leon should either convert to Catholicism or leave Spain. In 1526, Muslims of Aragon were confronted with the same alternatives. In 1556, Phillip II promulgated a law requiring the remaining Muslims to abandon at once their language, worship, institutions, and in 1609 manner of life. The final order of expulsion of all Muslims from Spain was signed by Phillip III, resulting in forcible deportation en masse of all Muslims from Spanish soil. Some half a million Muslims landed on shores of Africa or took ships to distant lands of Islam. Between the fall of Granada and the first decade of the seventeenth century, it is estimated that three million Muslims were banished or executed.

1757–1761: The Battle of Plassey

In the history of Islam, there are defining moments when the actions of an individual's greed left a lasting impact on the freedom of the Muslim community, lasting over several hundred years. Abu 'Abd Allah's avariciousness in conjunction with Isabella and Ferdinand dealt the death blow to seven hundred years of Islamic civilization in Spain and the death and expulsion of three million Muslims from Spain.

Half a world away to the East in 1757, the French and the English had been jockeying for primacy for the control of trade of the Indian peninsula. The Europeans had brought a powerful navy with guns, which the Indians could not match. A small number of well-trained Europeans and European-trained Indian mercenary infantrymen armed with muskets could load and fire with synchronized rapidity that could produce enough firepower to halt a conventional Indian cavalry charge. Armed with this knowledge, the English set out to control revenue-bearing Indian real estate and land. Added to their weapons was skill to divide, rule, and bribe Indian Muslim noblemen. The covetousness of these noble grandees lost Muslim India.

The English had made Calcutta a wealthy trading post and submitted considerable revenues to the nawab of Bengal. The English provided refuge to some rebels, and the nawab of Bengal Siraj al-Dawlah, a grandson of a previous Mogul governor, demanded their return. When he received no response, Siraj attacked Calcutta and drove the English out. Siraj suddenly found himself master of Calcutta with an assortment of Englishmen, women, and children who failed to get away with the remaining English who had made a panic-stricken dash to the ships and sailed away. Unharmed, the group was lodged overnight in the detention cell of the fort built by the English for their prisoners. How many were detained is not certainly known, but the next morning, only twenty-three staggered out. Dehydration and suffocation had tragically accounted for possibly fifty lives.[11]

The tragedy was apparently unintended. Nevertheless, Siraj was held responsible. Clive, the commander of the British garrison, was thirsting for revenge. Seven months later in 1757, he marched back to the Hugli River and retook Calcutta. He continued the hostilities and marched up the river to Murshidabad, Siraj's capital. In the meantime,

---

[11] John Keay, *India: A History* (Harper Collins) 389–91.

Siraj's army took up a defensive position at Plassey. Siraj had a well-trained army of fifty thousand. Against him were three thousand British troops with slightly superior artillery. Had the battle been fought, the odds were clearly in Siraj's favor.

Clive had little hope of victory and rested his hopes entirely on the treachery of the dignitaries of the Muslim army. He had already negotiated a secret pact with Mir Ja'far, Siraj's commander in chief and a relative. Mir Ja'far deserted with more than half of Siraj's army and joined Clive. Siraj had to run for his life. Clive personally placed Mir Ja'far on the throne of Bengal. British arms had put Ja'far on the throne, and now the British palms waited his greasing. For the British services, Mir Ja'far paid out over £1,250,000 ($3 billion in today's money) from the Bengal treasury, of which over £400,000 was paid to Clive in the form of revenue-bearing estates. The demands of the British for more revenue continued to increase. When in 1760–61 Mir Ja'far refused to comply with the British demands, he was promptly replaced on the throne by the British with his son-in-law.

The circle of evil of the *Munafiqun*, hungry for power and wealth, collaborated with the evil of the West in their hunt for power and gold. Mir Ja'far opened the gates of Muslim India to the British for subjugation and plunder that lasted another two hundred years. The British now discovered that revenue rights were much more profitable than the profits of trade. The revenue receipts from the Indian farmer would quickly eliminate the need to finance imports from India with export of bullion from Britain. In Bengal and later in the rest of India, relieving the ruling princes of revenue rights became a standard practice of the British. In the wake of Plassey, the British traders fanned out into Bengal, Bihar, and beyond to acquire monopoly rights over choice export commodities of saltpeter, indigo, cotton, and opium and over the lucrative internal trade in sea salt. Acquisition of Bengal enabled the British to siphon off the Indian revenue direct from the Indian peasant to the stately homes of Britain, the foundation of English wealth and power. This wealth was the engine of the industrialization of England, Germany, and the USA, while India was systematically impoverished.

1907–1925: Traitors Within: The Shame of Islam

In July 1908, army units of the Ottoman Army in Macedonia revolted against Sultan Abdulhamid II and demanded a return to constitutional rule. Again, on April 2, 1909, troops loyal to the revolution marched from Macedonia and took the capital, Istanbul. The Young Turks were aided in their march onto Constantinople by the Central Powers, especially by the *Neue Freie Presse* of Vienna. And three days later, Sultan Abdulhamid was deposed.

On the twenty-seventh of April 1909, 240 members of the Ottoman senate, under pressure from the nationalist Young Turks, agreed to remove Abdulhamid from power. The appearance of four people in the sultan's office—an Arab, a Turk, a Jew, and a Christian—who came to remove him from power was a premonition of the dismemberment of the Islamic world with treachery of the Arabs and the Turks in collusion with Jews and Christians. The caliphate effectively came to an end with the fall of Abdulhamid.

Foreign powers took advantage of the political instability in Istanbul to seize portions of the Ottoman Empire. Austria annexed Bosnia and Herzegovina immediately after the 1908 Turkish revolution, and Bulgaria proclaimed its complete independence. Italy proclaimed war in 1911 and seized Libya. After a secret pact, Greece, Serbia, Montenegro, and Bulgaria invaded and defeated Ottoman forces in Macedonia and Thrace in October 1912.

After a series of disasters, in January 1912 in a coup d'état,[12] the most authoritarian elements of the Young Turks movement took control of the Ottoman government. Kamil Pasha was driven from power, and Nazim Pasha was murdered by Enver Bey. The leadership of the Committee of Union and Progress emerged as a military dictatorship with power concentrated in the hands of the triumvirate of Mehmet Talat Pasha, Ahmet Cemal Pasha, and Enver Bey. Enver, as war minister, was acknowledged as the leader of the group in the government.

On January 13, 1913, Talat and Enver hastily collected about two hundred followers and marched to the Sublime Porte, where the ministers were meeting. Nazim Pasha, hearing the uproar, stepped into the hall, courageously faced the crowd with a cigarette in his mouth and hands thrust in his pockets, and said in good humor, "Come, boys, what is this noise about? Don't you know it is interfering with our deliberations?" The words had hardly left his mouth when he fell dead. A bullet had pierced his heart. The mob led by Enver and Talat then forced their way into the council chamber. They forced Kamil Pasha, the grand vizier, to resign his post by threatening him with the fate that had befallen Nazim.

Assassination became the method by which these conspirators usurped supreme power. So assassination continued to be the instrument by which they kept their hold on power. The Young Turks destroyed Abdulhamid's regime to restore a democratic constitutional government; instead, they created a reign of terror. Men were arrested and deported by the score, and hangings of opponents became a common occurrence.

Early in January 1914, Enver—then only thirty-two years old—became war minister. Enver's elevation to the ministry of war was

12 John Ridley-Dash, *The Demise of Ottoman* (Girne American University, 1995).

virtually a German victory. He immediately instituted drastic reorganization of the armed forces. By March 1914, Germans—with the help of Talat, Enver, and Cemal—had tightened their hold on Turkey. Liman von Sanders was first made the head of the first army corps and then the inspector general of all the Turkish armed forces. Another German general, Bronsart von Schellendorf, was appointed the chief of staff, and scores of German officers held commands of first importance. And the Turkish politician Enver Pasha, an outspoken thirty-four-year-old champion of Germany, was minister of war. The kaiser had almost completed his plans to annex the Turkish Army to his own.

Enver secretly signed a treaty of Turko-German alliance on August 2, 1914. Only five people in Turkey knew of this treaty, which brought on the final disintegration of the Ottoman Empire. The puppet grand vizier Said Halim, Talat, and Cemal were convinced by Enver of the wisdom of supporting the Germans in case the war broke out. Enver Pasha chose to ally Turkey with the Central Powers by citing Germany's earlier victories in the war. Thus, the Ottoman Empire joined the Central Powers to form a triple alliance without the knowledge of the cabinet, the parliament, the army generals, and the Ottoman populace. The empire was ruled by three collaborators and puppets of Germany, traitors to Islam, to the Muslims in Turkey, and to the whole *ummah*. They acted secretly as collaborators, with a foreign government working toward the destruction and disintegration of the only free Islamic state.

Two German warships, the battleship *Goeben* and the cruiser *Breslau*, that were caught in a neutral Turkish port when the war broke out in Europe were handed to the Ottoman Navy. In October, they were put out to sea, flying the Ottoman flag with German officers and crew, and shelled Odessa and other Russian ports. Enver Pasa, as the Ottoman war minister, gave secret orders in a sealed envelope to

Admiral Souchon, the commander of the Turko-German fleet, only to be opened when the fleet was deep in the Black Sea. The orders read:

War minister Enver Pasha to Admiral Souchon

October 25, 1914.

The entire fleet should maneuver in the Black Sea. When you find a favorable opportunity, attack the Russian fleet. Before initiating the hostilities, open my secret orders given to you personally this morning. To prevent transport of material to Serbia, act as already agreed upon. Enver Pasha. (Secret Order): The Turkish fleet should gain the mastery of the Black Sea by force. Seek out the Russian fleet and attack her wherever you find her without declaration of war.

Enver Pasha

Souchon now had a surprise for Enver. Rather than causing an incident at sea, the admiral attacked simultaneously the Russian ports of Sebastopol, Theodosia, Novorossiysk, and Odessa on the morning of October 29. This action, in effect, declared a war on Russia and its allies Britain and France. Once again, Enver acted secretly at the behest of Germany. He did not consult his coconspirators, Talat or Cemal, before ordering the attack on Russia or the declaration of war against the Western allies. He kept his cabinet colleagues, the parliament, and the people of the empire in the dark, who on the morning of October 29, 1914, were surprised to find themselves at war.

The conspiracies, utter stupidity, and lust for power of three men—Talat, Cemal, and Enver—led to the dismemberment of the Ottoman Empire. For another one hundred years, this land of Islam was to know no peace. It became prey for the circle of evil of the Euro-Christian, Jew, and Arab conspirators.

1914–Present: The Hashemites: From Common Traitors to Kings of Arabs

According to some sources, Sharif Hussein's son Abdullah had made contacts with the British consul general in Egypt, Lord Kitchener, as early as 1912, if not 1913.[13] Kitchener established a line of communication with Hussein's family through Hussein's representative, Muhammad al-Faruqi. Kitchener's letters to Hussein contained statements pledging British support in the event of an Arab uprising against the Turks, promising an independent Arabia after the war. In January 1915, Lord Kitchener was replaced by Sir Henry McMahon. In the ensuing correspondence, Hussein set forth a list of demands calling on the British government to support the independence of "Arab countries" within an area bounded on the north by the Mersin-Adana line and the thirty-seventh parallel, on the east by the Persian frontier and the Persian Gulf, on the south by the Indian Ocean (excepting Aden), and on the west by the Red and Mediterranean Seas. Hussein also requested the establishment of an Arab caliphate to supplant the Turkish sultan. In exchange for these concessions, Hussein offered economic preference to Great Britain and a defensive alliance.

In reply, McMahon dispatched on October 24 a letter that more precisely outlined the territorial parameters within which the British were prepared to recognize Arab independence. These boundaries corresponded roughly with those asked by Hussein earlier with several important differences; in view of Britain's established position and interests, the vilayets of Basra and Baghdad were excluded. Also excluded were the areas of Syria, west of the district of Damascus, Homs, Hama, and Aleppo, as well as districts of Mersin and

---

[13] Bruce Westrate, *The Arab Bureau: British Policy in the Middle East, 1916–1920* (Pennsylvania State University Press, 19920.

Alexandretta. Hussein's response on November 5 accepted the exclusion of Mersin and Alexandretta but objected to the exception of what essentially were Lebanon and the coastal Latakia area. Hussein was willing to accept the British claim to the two Mesopotamian vilayets in exchange for monetary compensation, pending the region's eventual return to Arab rule. In his letter on December 14, McMahon held firm to his stance on the Syrian littoral, citing prior French interests precluding the inclusion of the area to the Arab zone.

Hussein was never promised personal rule of the territory in question; an Arab caliphate was only obliquely referred in the correspondence. Hussein did not make any attempt to clarify the position taken by the British before he led a revolt against his caliph, sultan, country, and coreligionists under the protection of an alien, infidel, colonial, expansionist power with the full knowledge that parts of the Islamic state—including Syria, Lebanon, Palestine, and Iraq—would pass from Islamic rule to an economic and colonial subjugation of a non-Muslim power. For the sake of his own hunger for power, he used his holy prophetic bloodline to break up the united Islamic state when what its people most needed was a moral and just leadership to steer the state into the path of Allah. He could have drawn on his authority, knowledge, and influence to correct what was wrong in the *ummah* rather than subvert it. He appealed to an infidel power for his own personal elevation to the position of caliph, the spiritual and the temporal leadership of the whole Islamic nation.

At that time, there was another player in the treason game with the British. He was the young Bedouin tribal leader 'Abd al-'Aziz (Ibn Saud). He was a master of the *ghazzu,* raiding other tribes to steal their women, camels, sheep, and grain. He was backed by the religious zealots of the Wahhabi sect, who had little regard for life and sought death in the hope of martyrdom and ascent to heaven. Bedouin sheikhs frowned on *ghazzu* as an unwholesome and dishonorable activity. The heads of major Bedouin tribes who claimed hegemony over large tracts of land did not practice it. The way of robbery and plunder as practiced by 'Abd al-'Aziz was contrary to all Koranic teaching and Arab traditions of generosity to the vanquished. 'Abd al-'Aziz prided himself on never taking any prisoners; he murdered all the men of the raided tribe to prevent future retaliation.

Ibn Saud's political emergence began in 1902, when he reclaimed Riyadh[14], the city where his family had been local sheikhs, appointed by local emirs. His first merciless act was to terrorize the population by spiking the heads of his enemies and displaying them at the gates of the city. His followers burned twelve hundred people to death. While conducting a raid, he and his followers were very much in the habit of taking young maidens back as slaves and as gifts to friends. This was how Ibn Saud lived at the turn of the century before he became a king when he was mere head of a small tribe.

The third player was Lawrence. Thomas Edward Lawrence was the illegitimate child of an illegitimate child. His father was Thomas Chapman and his mother, Thomas Chapman's family governess, was the offspring out of wedlock of an English mother and a Norwegian father. In 1913 and 1914, Lawrence worked on a geographical survey of the Negev desert under the archaeological rubric of the Palestine Exploration Fund. Lawrence acquired a great deal of vital cartographic and geographic data for the British intelligence before the venture was terminated by the Turkish authorities in early 1914. When the war began, he found himself as an intelligence officer on the staff of Lord Horatio Herbert Kitchener with David Hogarth, his mentor, a key figure in the British administration in the Middle East. Hogarth later became the head of the Arab Bureau, planning and executing the so-called Arab Revolt.

---

[14] Said K. Aburish, *The Rise, Corruption, and Coming Fall of the House of Saud* (St. Martin's Griffin, New York).

Kitchener, the British consul general in Egypt, was in secret contact with Abdullah, son of Sharif Hussein of Mecca, who at the time was a member of Parliament in Istanbul. Sharif Hussein ibn Ali was Turkish-appointed governor of Mecca as a caretaker of the holy Muslim shrines of Mecca. Kitchener's strategy was to establish a channel of communication with Hussein to take advantage of the situation in the event of war with Turkey as the Arab lands were critical to the British position in India and Egypt. Winston Churchill underlined the strategic importance of the Persian Gulf oil and the huge refinery at Abadan and made clear the intention of the British government to become the owners and the controllers of the gulf oil required by the British navy. This vital priority led to the occupation of Basra in 1914 and later the invasion of Mesopotamia.

In June 1916, supported by Abdullah, Faisal, and his other sons, Hussein proclaimed the Arab Revolt against the sultan and the caliph of the Ottoman Empire. For Hussein and sons, it was an act of treason—treason against their religion, treason against their people, and treason against their sovereign to whom they had sworn allegiance and loyalty. Faisal, who was a serving officer in the Ottoman Army, deserted his post in Syria to join the revolt. It proved to be a dud. Hussein, it turned out, had no following at all. Muslims did not respond to his call nor did the Arabs. Under his banner, or rather the one that a British official designed for him, those who rallied under him were closer to one thousand rather than one hundred thousand, and they were Bedouin tribesmen and not soldiers. And those who did join were bribed with British gold.

In the make-believe world of Lawrence, Faisal ibn Hussein the commoner became Prince Faisal, the field commander of the Arab armies of under one thousand men; and at Faisal's request, Lawrence was assigned to be the British liaison officer with him. With such untrained and undisciplined band of men in Faisal's army, a frontal attack on the Ottoman troops would be suicidal. Some Bedouin men had qualms against fighting face-to-face against fellow Muslims. Over half the Ottoman Army was ethnically Arab. Lawrence, therefore, believed that Faisal's Bedouins would be better employed in fighting a guerilla war than in trying to fight a conventional one. Their object was to take the city of Medina, which lay to the north and blocked Faisal's force from riding to Palestine, where the Middle East war was to be fought.

Faisal's men raided a single-track railway from the Ottoman Palestine, which was the only source of reinforcement and supply to Medina's defenders. A British officer, Herbert Garland, taught Faisal's Bedouins how to dynamite the railroad. Garland, Lawrence, and other British officers went on to dynamite it repeatedly. The campaign failed. The Ottoman Muslim forces repaired the railway after each attack and kept it running. Medina never fell to Faisal or to the British. The Ottoman Muslim garrison held on till the end of the war, blocking the land road to Palestine. The Arab and Muslim defenders of Medina and Asir stood their ground to the last day of the war.

June 1916 was a historical moment when, for the first time in the history of Islam since the Battle of Badr in the first year of hijra, the combined forces of the *kafireen* and *Munafiqeen* attacked the city of the *nabi* of Islam, though unsuccessfully. This attack introduced the combined evil dominion of the *Mutaffifeen*, *kafireen*, and *Munafiqeen* to the heartlands of Islam for the next century to come.

Medina continued to stand in Faisal's way, and had Lawrence not thought of a way around it, using the Red Sea route, Hussein's revolt would have stayed bottled up in the Hejaz desert. Now that Lawrence had secured a port in Palestine, General Allenby sent boats to bring Faisal and about a thousand Bedouin followers from Ragheb on the Red Sea to Aqaba. Faisal arrived in Aqaba as a conqueror, and so the world was told by the British media and by Prime Minister Lloyd George's secretariat. In Aqaba, Faisal was reinforced by about twenty-five hundred men, Auda abu Tayi's Bedouins, and some Arab deserters from the Ottoman Army. All together, they formed a camel cavalry corps that harassed the Turkish flank when Allenby's Egypt- based army invaded Palestine and marched into Syria.

Faisal's camel corps presented a pretense that Syria was liberated by the Arabs themselves. In fact, there were a million British troops (*comprising mostly colonial Indian soldiers*) fighting in the Middle East in 1918 and only thirty-five hundred Husseini troops, and on the face of it was a British war of conquest over the Arabs and not a war of liberation for the Arabs. The British on May 9, 1916, in a secret convention, had already promised Arab Syria to the French (Sykes-Picot Agreement) and on November 2, 1917, in the Balfour Declaration, gave away Arab Palestine to the Jews. The Lawrence-Hussein-sons puppet show was being cleverly orchestrated from London. Each one of the players understood their role and the reward for their part except Hussein and sons. The ambiguous language, willful face-to-face lies, secret agreements, double dealings, deception, flattery, and bribery as a skill and art had become the trademark of perfidious English diplomacy over the previous one hundred years. The Arabs and the Bedouins had their own share of guile and cunningness; they were, however, no match for the Anglos as the next one hundred years were to reveal. And the Arab leaders never learned.

For his treachery, Sharif Hussein received his first reward in gold sovereigns in March 1916, a shipment in the amount of £53,000, three months before he announced his revolt. Commencing on August 8, 1916, the official allowance was set at £125,000 a month, a sum that was frequently exceeded at Hussein's demand. For example, in November 1916, £375,000 in gold sovereigns was dispatched to Hussein by the British for hajj expenses. The money was to have been used by Hussein to pay his armies and to bribe the sheikhs and the tribes into joining his revolt. The payments were broken down into five categories representing the four armies under the command of Hussein's sons and an allotment for the upkeep of the mosque at Kaaba and for hajj facilities as well as for the operation of Hussein's government in Mecca and Jeddah. Forty thousand pounds was allocated to Faisal, £30,000) to Abdullah, £20,000 each for Ali and Zeid, and £15,000 for expenses at Mecca and Jeddah.

The year 1916 must have been the lowest point in the history of Islam. It was surrounded by powerful enemies around the world, and inside, it was being destroyed by self-serving traitors at the very heart of the faith, the Kaaba. For the first time in the history of Islam, the very upkeep of the Holy Mosque of Mecca and the Kaaba and the hajj expenses were being paid for by the *kafireen* at the behest of the *Munafiqeen* under the claim of their lineage from the holy prophet. While claiming their bloodline, they forgot the teachings of the Koran and the example of the prophet.

The British were unable to make all the payments from their London treasury, so in the spring of 1917, the British drew gold out of the rapidly diminishing Egyptian treasury. The source of gold in the Egyptian treasury was the sweat and blood of the Egyptian peasant. Hussein had insisted that he needed additional £75,000 monthly to meet his bloated payroll. The Egyptian peasants were in double jeopardy as they not only had to pay in taxes for Hussein's misadventure but also had to provide free labor of one hundred thousand men for the transport of troops, equipment, and supplies to the British Expeditionary Force of General Allenby from Egypt to Palestine. The British-controlled Egyptian treasury by June 1917 had only £200,000 in reserve that was available for Hussein. To meet Hussein's demand for additional cash, there was a scramble for alternative source for money. Silver was scarce in India, and agriculture goods were too dear in Egypt. Hussein demanded that the total payment be made in gold; however, he was eventually forced to accept shipments of fiat Indian paper rupees and goods in lieu of precious metals.

1902–Present: The Saudis: From Desert Thugs to Kings of Arabs and Servants of the *Kafireen*

The Ottomans with German finance and technology planned a railway from Berlin through the Ottoman Empire to end in the Persian Gulf at Kuwait, which was the only deepwater harbor in the region. The railway threatened the growing British influence in the region, and the British quietly preempted the German move by signing an agreement with Sheikh Mubarak al-Sabah of Kuwait. The gist of the agreement signed on January 23, 1899, stated that the sheikh would not receive the agent or representative of any other power without the sanction of the British government, nor would he cede, sell, lease, mortgage, or give for occupation any part of his territory to any other power without British permission. There was in the treaty no mention of the establishment of a protectorate over Kuwait, although the British Crown assumed that to be the case. Britain then appointed a resident political officer in Kuwait a year after signing of the treaty.

Ibn Saud, a homeless and hungry tent-dwelling Bedouin youth living in Kuwait, was looking for adventure and a sponsor. At least on two occasions, he wrote to the Ottoman sultan offering his services; however, he was turned down. The British were looking for influence and contacts in the interior of Arabia and had sent several intelligence agents in the form of explorers. The first British contact with 'Abd-al-'Aziz probably occurred soon after the political agent had established himself in Kuwait in 1901. By 1904, 'Abd-al-'Aziz was already in the pay of the British and, until 1911, continued to receive small amounts of money. The British scouts had recognized him as potentially useful and kept him in reserve in case hostilities broke out against the Turks.

'Abd-al-'Aziz certainly had a mysterious source of support when he raided Riyadh with equipment and camels and with a number of men, which were thought to be beyond his means. After he captured Riyadh, relative peaceful equilibrium of the desert was disturbed by the young Bedouin tribal leader Ibn Saud. He was a master of the *ghazzu,* raiding other tribes to steal their camels, sheep, and grain. He was backed by the religious zealots of the Wahhabi sect, who had little regard for life and sought death in the hope of martyrdom and ascent to heaven. Bedouin sheikhs frowned on *ghazzu* as an unwholesome and dishonorable activity, and the heads of major Bedouin tribes who claimed hegemony over large tracts of land did not practice it. The way of robbery and plunder as practiced by 'Abd-al-'Aziz was contrary to all Koranic teachings as well as Arab traditions of generosity to the vanquished. 'Abd-al-'Aziz (Ibn Sa'ud) prided himself on never taking any prisoners; he murdered all the men of the raided tribe to prevent future retaliation. Ibn Sa'ud used much of the money from the British to sponsor colonies of the Ikhwan brotherhood, fanatics of the Wahhabi sect to which Ibn Sa'ud belonged. The Ikhwan formed the backbone of Ibn Saud's conquering army, whose savagery wreaked havoc across Arabia.

Ibn Sa'ud had no formal education. His literary talent, if any, was extremely restricted; and therefore, his worldview was limited by his own experience of the life of a Bedouin and the tribal code, which had barely changed for fourteen hundred years. His resting place was a tent or the starlit sky. Food and water were scarce, security and refuge were with the family, clan, and tribe. Intertribal disputes and feuds were frequent and were settled by the sword; raiding the neighboring tribes for their goods and animals was a sport. Killing another Muslim and looting his property in a *ghazzu* was perfectly acceptable and did not cause remorse. Slavery was practiced and prevalent; women were nonentities and not worthy of equality with men. 'Abd-al-'Aziz once boasted that he had never had a meal with a woman and that he never looked at the face of the woman with whom he made love. Yet he had been married to over a hundred women and had a similar number of concubines and sex slaves.

Religion and spirituality were judged through the narrow tunnel vision of Wahhabi men of religion in a nomadic social setting where neither the Koran nor other religious texts were available to the common man. Any person not following the narrow edicts of the Wahhabi sect of Islam was automatically a heretic and therefore an infidel and punishable by public flogging, amputation, or beheading. Armed with these moral values and ethics 'Abd-al-'Aziz set out to conquer Arabia with the financial and military assistance of the British. His first victims were the Ibn Rashids of the Ottoman-controlled part of the Arabian Peninsula. The defeat of the Ibn Rashids was, in effect, a British victory. Sir Percy Cox, a British resident in the Persian Gulf, wrote, "With Ibn-Saud in Hasa (the Gulf Coast of Arabia) our position is very much strengthened." Percy Cox openly encouraged Ibn Sa'ud to attack the remaining territory of the Ibn Rashids to divert them from reinforcing Turkish troops against the British.[15] Ibn Sa'ud had constant British financial aid, arms, and advisers, initially William Shakespeare and Percy Cox and later Harry Saint John Philby.

After they helped him to master eastern Arabia in 1917, the British found another use for Ibn Sa'ud. In 1924, Hussein declared himself

---

[15] *Kuwait Political Agency: Arabic Documents 1899–1949*, May/June 1917: Correspondence between Ibn Sa'ud and Sir Percy Cox. Sir Percy urges Ibn Sa'ud to take Ha'il, since Ibn Rashid's position is weakened, and the area is under threat from his enemies to the north. Ibn Sa'ud replies that Ha'il is not in danger as Ibn Rashid has no enemies to the north and that those enemies he does have are not in a position to act. He tells Sir Percy that he is ill informed and should send an Arab specialist to Ibn Sa'ud's camp to learn about the natural and political conditions in Arabia.

caliph of Islam without the consent of the British. Abdullah being entrenched in Amman and Faisal in Baghdad and the elevation of Sharif Hussein to the leadership of whole Islam threatened Britain's growing interests in the Middle East. These interests included strategy to continue to divide and rule the Middle East through subservient local notables. Although Hussein's sons were pliable and obedient to these imperialistic plans, Hussein demanded that Britain live up to its promises to grant Arab's independence and a free hand in all the Arab countries. He objected to British plans to provide Jews with a national home in Palestine. Ibn Sa'ud started his thrust into Hejaz; although the British ostensibly cut off the arms supplies to both sides, most historians believe that the British continued to supply small but crucial amounts of money and arms to Ibn Sa'ud and his merciless Ikhwan. Some of the military equipment used by Ibn Sa'ud was expensive and could not have been obtained without outside help and could not have been used without instructors. At the time, statements by British officials do point to the British hand in Ibn Sa'ud's attack on Mecca. Arthur Hirtzel—a Jew, head of the British India Office at that time—expressed the need for Ibn Sa'ud to establish himself in Mecca.

In 1925, Hejaz fell to Ibn Sa'ud's Ikhwan army. The most advanced and settled part of Arabia with a long history of contact with the outside world, constitutional government, with established institutions, and established justice system fell to an anarchist, tribal army of religious fanatics. If the British secret planners had wanted to destroy and divide the heart of Islam, they could not have chosen a more competent and effective allies. Ibn Sa'ud's Ikhwan soldiers killed hundreds of males, including children; pillaged homes of the conquered populace for money, gold, and valuable objects; murdered non-Wahhabi religious leaders; and destroyed whole towns. Tolerance of others' beliefs was against Wahhabi and Ikhwan teachings and traditions. They committed massacres in At Ta'if, Bureida, and Al

Huda. They tried to destroy the tomb of the prophet and remove the domes of the major mosques. They also desecrated the Sunni graveyards of Mecca. They carried out genocide against Shias of eastern Arabia.

The Ikhwan forces of Ibn Sa'ud indulged in mass killings of mostly innocent victims, including women and children. Ibn Sa'ud's cousin Abdallah bin Mussallem bin Jalawi beheaded 250 members of the Mutair tribe, and Ibn Sa'ud himself set an example for his followers by personally beheading 18 rebels in a public square of the town of Artawaya. The Shammar tribe suffered 410 deaths, the Bani Khalid 640, and the Najran a staggering 7,000. Ibn Sa'ud used massacres to subdue his enemies No less than a 400,000 people were killed and wounded in the Saudi campaign to subdue the Arabian Peninsula. The Ikhwan did not take prisoners and mostly killed the vanquished. Well over a million inhabitants of the territories conquered by Ibn Sa'ud fled to Kuwait, Egypt, Iraq, Jordan, and Syria. By the time Ibn Sa'ud and his family had subdued the country, they had carried out 40,000 public executions and 350,000 amputations, respectively 1 and 4 percent of the estimated population of 4 million.[16]

To summarize the brutality and the insensitivity of Ibn Sa'ud's regime, one has to understand the degree of devastation of the country, which he proudly named after himself in 1932. At the turn of the twentieth century, the population of the territory that became Saudi Arabia was an estimated 3.5 million. By the time, 'Abd al-'Aziz established his control over the kingdom, a million inhabitants had fled the country, 400,000 were killed or wounded, 40,000 were beheaded in public squares, and 350,000 had their limbs amputated for opposing the Saudi regime. Thus, to accommodate 'Abd al-'Aziz in his newfound kingdom, an estimated 30 percent of the population chose exile,

---

[16] Aburish, *House of Saud*, 24–27.

13 percent were killed in war or beheaded in public squares, and 10 percent had their limbs amputated. This left only 47 percent of the population of able-bodied men women and children in the kingdom. Assuming that of the 2.5 million people remaining after the ones who fled the country, 1,250,000 were male and the same number were females, both adult and children, and again assuming that most of the people killed, executed, and dismembered were males, then we are forced to assume that by mid-1930s, the total population of males in Saudi Arabia was only 810,000, of whom 460,000 were able bodied and the remaining 350,000 amputees, mutilated by the state. The ratio of able-bodied men to women was almost 1:3. This would explain the destitution of Saudi Arabia before the discovery of oil when most of the able-bodied, educated, cultured, and enterprising men was eliminated, leaving uneducated Bedouins to run the country. This also explains why after each man took four wives, still, there were plenty of women left to marry. In a culture where women had equality with men, suddenly, women were the underdog, unable to resist the inequity. This would also explain the need for foreign workers to man most jobs in the kingdom and why the Saudis have not been able to raise a large enough army, having to depend on the Americans for the defense of their country.

In the hot wind and sand-blown desert, this genocide and iniquity went unnoticed by the world, while similar crimes later during the century in Nazi Germany caused public outcry. It was so because it was a Muslim carrying out genocide against Muslims in the name of Islam with the British-supplied arms for the greater glory of the British Empire. Lord Crewe, a British minister, had proclaimed, "What we want is not a united Arabia, but a disunited Arabia split into small principalities under our suzerainty."[17] With ongoing turmoil within his own kingdom and skirmishes with Hejaz and later with Jordan, Iraq, and Yemen, Ibn Sa'ud afforded Britain the comfort of keeping the Arabs and Muslims divided. This protected its commercial and political interests by opposing a unified Muslim state.

1915 to Present: Creation of Israel, a State for the Jews on the Land of Islam

Alfred Milner, son of a university lecturer, was born in Bonn, Germany, in 1854. After childhood in Germany, he came to England and completed his education at the Oxford University. George Joachim Goschen, who was the chancellor of the Exchequer, brought Milner into the British establishment as his private secretary. On Goschen's recommendation, Milner was appointed undersecretary of finance in Egypt in 1890 and was responsible for the taxation of the Egyptian population to pay off the Egyptian debt to the Jewish bankers.

Cecil Rhodes and Milner were members of a secret society that was patterned on the organization of Jesuits. It was also based on political, personal, and family relationship built over a long period. Financial backing came informally from the fortunes of Cecil Rhodes, the Rothschilds, and other Jewish bankers. There was, by the turn of the century, an acceptance of social mixing among the moneyed Jews and the British aristocracy. Among the first initiates to the Round Table

[17] Speech to the conservative Middle East Council, Bournemouth, October 5, 2004. The ambassador of the custodian of the Two Holy Mosques to the United Kingdom and Ireland, Prince Turki Al-Faisal, in a forthright speech during the Conservative Party's annual conference, linked the sources of current terrorism to a disaffection and "sense of injustice that can be traced back to the World War I." Quoting Lord Crewe who said, "What we want is not a united Arabia, but a weak and disunited Arabia, split into little principalities as far as possible under our suzerainty but incapable of coordinated action against us." Prince Turki described the division of the Middle East among the Western powers as like "portioning out cake."

were Rhodes, Lord Rothschild, Milner, Grey, Balfour, Lord Rosebery (Lord Rothschild's son-in-law), and Alfred Beit, a Jewish business genius who handled all of Rhodes's business affairs. Among others to join later was Winston Churchill, who as well as his father, Randolph, before him had been allowed to live a life of opulence, thanks to the benevolence of Lord Rothschild.

The Round Table was originally a major fief within the great nexus of power, influence, and privilege controlled by the Cecil family. The method used to control the center of power was penetrating the fields of politics, education, and journalism; recruitment of men of ability chiefly from All Souls College at Oxford; and linking these men to Cecil and the Round Table block by matrimonial alliances and then granting them positions of power and titles. Milner had recruited Leo Amery, a secret Jew, when he was still at Oxford. Amery was an eminent scholar and, at the time, was regarded as the chief imperial theorist. He served as the *London Times* chief war correspondent during the Boer War and into the period leading to the Great War. Milner actively supported his effort to be elected to Parliament in 1906.

David Lloyd George appointed Milner to his war cabinet in 1916 as secretary of war. Milner, a Jew in league with Cecil Rhodes and Lord Nathaniel (Natty) Rothschild, had intrigued to instigate the Boer War in 1902 to establish British control over the whole of southern Africa. The aim was to exploit extensive mineral wealth of that region. After becoming the secretary of war, Milner brought Leo Amery, another Jew albeit a secret one, as the secretary of the war cabinet. Milner had maintained his contacts with the Rothschilds; in 1912, he had helped Natty Rothschild unify the divided Jewish community of London, less than one spiritual head, Chief Rabbi Joseph Herman Hertz.[18]

---

[18] Niall Ferguson, *The House of Rothschild* (Penguin Books), 259.

British cabinet minister Herbert Samuel, a Jew, wrote a memorandum "The Future of Palestine" in 1915, when Palestine was still a Turkish possession. He argued that Palestine should become a British protectorate, "into which the scattered Jews in time swarm back from all quarters of the globe, in due course obtain home rule, and form a Jewish Commonwealth like that of Canada and Australia." Lord Walter Rothschild, Natty Rothschild's successor as the leader of the British Jews, bent the ears of the prime minister, Lloyd George, and his foreign secretary for a declaration about Palestine. Balfour suggested that "they submit a declaration for the cabinet to consider." The declaration was written by Milner and revised several times. The final version was drafted by Leo Amery, which read,

> *His Majesty's Government view with favor the establishment in Palestine a national home for the Jewish people and will use their best endeavors to facilitate the achievement of this object, it being clearly understood that nothing shall be done which may prejudice the civil and religious rights of existing non-Jewish communities in Palestine, or the rights and political status enjoyed in any other country.*

The British cabinet approved the declaration, which was addressed to Lord Walter Rothschild and signed by the foreign secretary Balfour. The Balfour Declaration, as this Jewish Magna Carta came to be known, gave birth illegitimately to the state of Israel. The document was written by Lord Alfred Milner, a Jew; it was revised and finalized by Leo Amery, another Jew, at the behest of Lord Walter Rothschild. And it was addressed to Lord Walter Rothschild, the leader of the Jews of London, for the purpose of the creation of a state for the Jews in the name of the British government on a land that did not belong to the Jews or to the British. In fact, this was an agreement among a group of conspirators belonging to a secret organization that had a long history of fraud and extortion to grab the world's wealth.

In this case, the plotters made full circle in their relationship. Lord George Joachim Goschen, a German Jew, patronized Alfred Milner, another German Jew, and brought him into the English establishment and introduced him to the Rothschilds. Milner, in turn, brought Leo Amery, a secret Jew, into the war cabinet, and they together wrote the Balfour Declaration for the Lord Rothschild. To complete the circle, George Goshen's daughter Phyllis Evelyn Goschen married Francis Cecil Balfour, Foreign Secretary Balfour's son, on August 31, 1920. From among the same group of conspirators, Herbert Samuel was appointed the high commissioner to Palestine to establish Jewish immigration; Rufus Isaacs (as Lord Reading) was appointed viceroy of India with authority over the affairs over Iraq, Persian Gulf, Palestine, and Arabia.

From this time, Zionists became the allies of the British government, and every help and assistance was forthcoming from each government department. Space was provided for the Zionists in Mark Sykes's office with liaison to each government department. The British government provided financial, communication, and travel facilities to those working in the Zionist office. Mark Sykes, who had negotiated the Sykes-Picot agreement giving Syria to the French, was now working for the Zionists, offering them a part of the same territory. In the meantime, through secret communications, the British, USA, France, Italy, and Vatican had all come to a secret understanding of establishment of a Jewish nation in Palestine. The Balfour Declaration was the culmination of secret negotiations and maneuverings among these powers whose price would be paid to the international Jewry for financial and intelligence support in the war against the Germans and the Turks.

The Koran speaks of the deceivers thus:

O you who believe! Take not for friends Unbelievers rather than Believers: do you wish to offer Allah an open proof against yourselves? (An-Nisa 4:144)

Allah, in the covenant, also reminds the believers repeatedly not to take the *kafirun* (infidels), Jews, and Christians as their *awliya* (friends and protectors) in place of believers. They are friends and protectors unto one another. He who among believers turns to them is one of them. Allah does not guide those who are unjust and evildoers (*zalimun).* He from among the believers who turns to them is from among the *kafirun*, *Munafiqeen*, *mushrikun*, and *zalimun.*

1921-1970: Treaty of Versailles: The Shame of Muslims, the *Munafiqeen*, the Traitors among Us

Faisal's camel corps presented a pretense that the Arabs themselves liberated Syria. In fact, there were a million British troops fighting in the Middle East in 1918 and only thirty-five hundred Husseini troops, and on the face of it was a British war of conquest over the Arabs and not a war of liberation for the Arabs. The British, on May 9, 1916, in a secret convention, had already promised Arab Syria to the French (Sykes-Picot Agreement) and on November 2, 1917, in the Balfour Declaration gave away Arab Palestine to the Jews. The Lawrence-Hussein-sons puppet show was being cleverly orchestrated from London. Each one of the players understood their role and the reward for their part except Hussein and sons. The ambiguous language, willful face-to-face lies, secret agreements, double dealings, deception, flattery, and bribery as a skill and art had become the hallmark of perfidious English diplomacy over the previous one hundred years. The Arabs and the Bedouins had their own share of guile and cunningness; they were, however, no match for the Anglos and the Franks as the next one hundred years were to reveal. And the Arab leaders never learned.

For his treachery, Sharif Hussein started to receive his reward in gold sovereigns from March 1916 onward, three months before he announced his revolt. The total shipments were in the amount of £1,928,000. The payments were broken down into five categories representing the four armies under the command of Hussein's sons and an allotment for the upkeep of the mosque at Kaaba and for hajj facilities as well as for the operation of Hussein's government in Mecca and Jeddah. Forty thousand pounds per month was allocated to Faisal, £30,000 to Abdullah, £20,000 each for Ali and Zeid, and £15,000 for expenses at Mecca and Jeddah.

The year 1916 must have been the lowest point in the history of Islam. At that time, it was surrounded by powerful enemies around the world; and inside, in its very heart, the Kaaba, it was being destroyed by traitors to Islam. For the first time in the history of Islam, the very upkeep of the Holy Mosque of Mecca, the Kaaba, and the hajj expenses were being paid for by the *kafireen* at the behest of the *Munafiqeen* under the claim of their lineage to the holy prophet. While claiming their bloodline, they forgot the teachings of the Koran and the example of conduct set by the prophet.

The covenant of Allah states:

- When you hold secret counsel, do it not for iniquity and hostility, and disobedience to the teachings of the Rasool; but do it for righteousness and self-restraint; and fear Allah, to Whom you shall be brought back.
- The Satan inspires secret counsels, in order that he may cause grief to the Believers; but he cannot harm them in the least, except as Allah permits; and on Allah let the Believers put their trust.

No believer, individual, community, or ruler shall make a compact on behalf of the *ummah* or part of it in secret with the unbelievers. Islam regards secret pacts with enemies and hostile actions against one's own people as treason. During the blessed prophet's lifetime in Medina, some people professed Islam yet conspired with the *kafirun* against their fellow Muslims. The Koran has the following description of these *Munafiqeen*.

- Fain would they deceive Allah and those who believe, but they only deceive themselves, and realize it not! In their hearts is a disease; and Allah has increased their disease: and grievous is the penalty they incur, because they are false to themselves. When it is said to them: "Make not mischief on the earth," they say: "Why, we only want to make peace!" Of a surety, they are the ones who make mischief, but they do not realize. (Al-Baqarah 2:8–12)
- Allah will throw back their mockery on them, and give them rope in their trespasses; so, they will wander like blind ones to and fro. They have bartered guidance for error: but their traffic is profitless, and they have lost true direction. Their similitude is that of a man who kindled a fire; when it lighted all around him, Allah took away their light and left them in utter darkness. So they could not see. Deaf, dumb, and blind, they will not return to the path. (Al-Baqarah 2:15–18)

1973–1979: Betrayal of the Covenant: Treason

Anwar Sadat and the Egyptian Army won partial victory over the Jewish state of Israel in 1973. The victory made Sadat a hero in the eyes of many Arabs, if not equal to then almost comparable to the great Arab hero Gamal Abdel Nasser. Puffed up by success and sycophancy from the likes of Henry Kissinger, Sadat forgot his own roots and began to take advice and comfort from Kissinger and the Israeli lobby in Washington. Against the advice of his closest advisers and the leaders of other Arab countries, he made a secret trip to Israel and addressed the Knesset, the Israeli parliament. Under the American tutelage and patronage, he abandoned his Arab allies, negotiated, and signed a peace treaty with many secret appendices with Israel at the expense of the Palestinians and Syrians. Therefore, all Palestine and the Golan Heights are under Israeli occupation. The Arabs are disunited and in disarray. Sadat sold out Egyptian sovereignty, the Islamic nation, and the holy Islamic places in Jerusalem for four billion dollars a year. Sadat took Jews and Christians as his *awliya* and willfully disobeyed the covenant that every Muslim, if he was a believer, has pledged to obey. He also disobeyed the provisions of the covenant of Yathrib and the prophet's teaching:

> Just as the bond to Allah is indivisible, all the believers shall stand behind the commitment of the least of them. All believers are bonded one to another to the exclusion of other men. This Pax Islamica is one and indivisible. No believer shall enter a separate peace without all other believers whenever there is fighting in the cause of God, but will do so only on the basis of equality and justice to all others. In every expedition for the cause of God we undertake, all parties to the covenant shall fight shoulder to shoulder as one man. All believers shall avenge the blood of one another when anyone falls fighting in the cause of God.

Once again, the *Yahudi-Salibi* ingenuity used a *Munafiq* to sow the seeds of discord in the Islamic world.

1980–2007: Saddam Lured into War with Iran: The Circle of Evil

In 1980, Iraq's Saddam Hussein was suddenly a big-time international "player" invited to the gaudy palaces of the Saudi Arabian monarchy. But there was an ulterior motive behind the flattering invitation.

Saddam's army was the new protector of the petro-rich against the Iranian hordes.[19]

In summer 1980, Iraq's wily president, Saddam Hussein, saw opportunities in the chaos sweeping the Persian Gulf. Iran's Islamic revolution had terrified the Saudi princes and other Arab royalty who feared uprisings against their own corrupt lifestyles. Saddam's help was sought too by CIA-backed Iranian exiles who wanted a base to challenge the fundamentalist regime of Ayatollah Ruhollah Khomeini. And as always, the Western powers were worried about the Middle East oil fields. Because of geography and his formidable Soviet-supplied army, Saddam was suddenly a popular fellow.

On August 5, 1980, the Saudi rulers welcomed Saddam to Riyadh for his first state visit to Saudi Arabia, the first for any Iraqi president. The Saudis obviously wanted something. At those fateful meetings, amid the luxury of the ornate palaces, the Saudi royal family encouraged Saddam Hussein to invade Iran. The Saudis also passed on a secret message about President Carter's geopolitical desires.

During that summer of 1980, President Carter's failure to free fifty-two American hostages held in Iran was threatening his political survival. This multisided political intrigue shaped the history from 1980 to the present day. Iraq's invasion of Iran in September 1980 deteriorated into eight years of bloody trench warfare that killed and maimed an estimated one million people. This war generated billions of dollars in profits for the West and their well-connected arms merchants.

Haig's Talking Points

Robert Parry in his article in the Consortium on December 31, 2002, states that he gained access to the Iran-Contra investigation

[19] Robert Parry, Consortium, December 31, 2002.

documents, including papers marked secret and top secret, that apparently had been left behind by accident in a remote Capitol Hill storage room.

> *Those papers filled in twenty years of missing pieces of the intrigue that led to the Iraqi invasion of Iran. The papers clarified President Reagan's early strategy for a clandestine foreign policy hidden from Congress and the American people. One such document was a two-page Talking Points prepared by Secretary of State Alexander Haig for a briefing of President Reagan.*

Marked top secret/sensitive, the paper recounted Haig's first trip to the Middle East in April 1981.

In the report, Haig wrote that he was impressed with bits of useful intelligence that he had learned. Both Egypt's Anwar Sadat and Saudi prince Fahd explained that Iran was receiving military spares for US equipment from Israel. This fact might have been less surprising to President Reagan, whose intermediaries allegedly collaborated with Israeli officials in 1980 to smuggle weapons to Iran behind President Carter's back.

But Haig followed that comment with another stunning assertion. It was also interesting to confirm that President Carter gave the Iraqis a green light to launch the war against Iran through Fahd. In other words, according to Haig's information, Saudi prince Fahd, later King Fahd, claimed that President Carter, apparently hoping to strengthen US hand in the Middle East and desperate to pressure Iran over the stalled hostage talks, gave clearance to Saddam's invasion of Iran. If true, Jimmy Carter, the peacemaker, had encouraged a war. Haig's written report contained no other details about the green light. The paper represented the first documented corroboration of Iran's long-held belief that the United States backed Iraq's 1980 invasion.

The Iraqi invasion did make Iran more desperate to get US spare parts for its air and ground forces. Yet the Carter administration continued to demand that the American hostages be freed before military shipments could resume. But according to house task force documents that Parry found in the storage room, the Republicans were more accommodating.

Secret FBI wiretaps revealed that an Iranian banker, the late Cyrus Hashemi who supposedly was helping President Carter on the hostage talks, was assisting Republicans with arms shipments to Iran and peculiar money transfers in fall 1980. Hashemi's elder brother, Jamshid, testified that the Iran arms shipments via Israel resulted from secret meetings in Madrid between the GOP campaign director William J. Casey and a radical Islamic mullah named Mehdi Karroubi.

For whatever reasons, on Election Day 1980, President Carter still had failed to free the hostages, and Ronald Reagan won in a landslide. Within minutes of President Reagan's inauguration on January 20, 1981, the hostages finally were freed. In the following weeks, the new Reagan administration put in place discreet channels to Middle East powers as Haig flew to the region for a round of high-level consultations. Haig met with Iraq's chief allies, Saudi Arabia and Egypt, and with Israel, which was continuing to support Iran as a counterweight to Iraq and the Arab states.

On April 8, 1981, Haig ended his first round of meetings in Riyadh. After Haig's return to Washington, his top secret talking points fleshed out for President Reagan the actual agreements that were reached at the private sessions in Saudi Arabia, as well as at other meetings in Egypt and Israel. "As we discussed before my Middle East trip," Haig explained to President Reagan, "I proposed to President Sadat, Israel's Prime Minister Menachem Begin and Crown Prince Fahd that we establish a private channel for the consideration of particularly sensitive matters of concern to you. Each of the three picked up on the proposal and asked for early meetings."

Haig wrote that, upon his return, he immediately dispatched his counselor, Robert Bud McFarlane, to Cairo and Riyadh to formalize those channels. He held extremely useful meetings with both Sadat and Fahd, Haig boasted. These early contacts with Fahd, Sadat, and Begin solidified their three countries as the cornerstones of the administration's clandestine foreign policy of the 1980s with

- the Saudis as the moneymen,
- the Israelis as the middlemen,
- and the Egyptians as a ready source for Soviet-made equipment.

Although President Carter had brokered a historic peace treaty between Egypt and Israel, Sadat, Begin, and Fahd had all been alarmed at signs of US weakness, especially Washington's inability to protect the Shah of Iran from ouster in 1979. Haig's talking points captured that relief at President Carter's removal from office. "It is clear that your policies of firmness toward the Soviets have restored Saudi and Egyptian confidence in the leadership of the US," Haig wrote for the presentation to his boss.

Both Fahd and Sadat went much further than ever before in offering to be supportive. Haig said Sadat offered to host a forward headquarters for the rapid deployment force, including a full-time presence of US military personnel. Sadat also outlined his strategy for invading Libya to disrupt Mu'ammar al-Gaddhafi's intervention in Chad. Haig reported that Prince Fahd was also very enthusiastic about President Reagan's foreign policy. Fahd had agreed in principle to fund arms sales to the Pakistanis and other states in the region, Haig wrote. The Saudi leader was promising too to help the US economy by committing his oil-rich nation to a position of no drop in production of petroleum. "These channels promise to be extremely useful in forging compatible policies with the Saudis and Egyptians," Haig continued. "Both men value the 'special status' you have conferred on them and both value confidentiality."

In the following years, the Reagan administration would exploit the special status with all three countries to skirt constitutional restrictions on executive war-making powers. Secretly, the administration would tilt back and forth in the Iran-Iraq War between aiding the Iranians with missiles and spare parts and helping the Iraqis with intelligence and indirect military shipments. According to a sworn affidavit by a former Reagan national security staffer, Howard Teicher, the administration enlisted the Egyptians in a secret Bear Spares program that gave the United States access to Soviet-designed military equipment. Teicher asserted that the Reagan administration funneled some of those weapons to Iraq and also arranged other shipments of devastating cluster bombs that Saddam's air force dropped on Iranians troops.

In 1984, facing congressional rejection of continued CIA funding of the Nicaraguan contra rebels, President Reagan exploited the special status again. He tapped into the Saudi slush funds for money to support the Nicaraguan contra rebels in their war in Central America. The president also authorized secret weapons shipments to Iran in another arms-for-hostages scheme, with the profits going to off-the-shelf intelligence operations. That gambit, like the others, was protected by walls of deniability and outright lies.

When Parry interviewed Haig several years ago, he asked him if he was troubled by the pattern of deceit that had become the norm among international players in the 1980s. "Oh, no, no, no, no!" he boomed, shaking his head. "On that kind of thing? No. Come on. Jesus! God! You know, you'd better get out and read Machiavelli or somebody else because I think you are living in a dream world! People do what their national interest tells them to do and if it means lying to a friendly nation, they are going to lie through their teeth."

But sometimes the game playing did have unintended consequences. In 1990, a decade after Iraq's messy invasion of Iran, an embittered Saddam Hussein was looking for payback from the sheikhdoms that he felt had egged him into war. Saddam was especially furious with Kuwait for slant drilling into Iraq's oil fields and refusing to extend more credit. Again, Saddam was looking for a signal from the US president, this time George Bush. When Saddam explained his confrontation with Kuwait to US ambassador April Glaspie, he received an ambiguous reply, a reaction he apparently perceived as another green light. Eight days later, Saddam unleashed his army into Kuwait, an invasion that required five hundred thousand US troops and thousands more dead to reverse.

This document is a window into the workings of the circle of evil, the agents of Euro-Christianity, Zionism, and *Munafiqeen* that are out to destroy Islam. Saddam, Fahd, Sadat, Begin, and the agents of the West started a chain reaction in 1980 that set off the Iran-Iraq War, the Israeli invasion of Lebanon, the Iraqi invasion of Kuwait, the subsequent multination invasion of Iraq, the UN embargo of Iraq, the NATO invasion of Afghanistan, the ongoing occupation of Iraq, the second Israeli war against Lebanon, and the ongoing occupation and massacre of the Palestinians.

During the last forty-one years, the turmoil initiated by Saddam, Fahd and his Saudi clan, and Sadat in collaboration with the West and Israel has killed more than seven million Muslims—Arabs, Iranians, Afghans, Libyans, and Syrians. Many more millions have been made homeless. Five nations have been decimated and totally ruined. Millions have sought shelter in foreign lands. This circle of evil, in the last forty years, has prevented Islam from freeing itself from the clutches of slavery of the West.

1979–1991: Saddam, the Servant of the *Kafireen*, Traitor to Islam

Saddam Hussein replaced al-Bakr as president of Iraq in July 1979. The bloodbath that followed eliminated all potential opposition to him. Saddam was now the master of Iraq with no one around him daring to question his actions. Two actions that he initiated led the Islamic community to disastrous disunity and debt. He attacked his fellow Muslims, Iran in 1980 and Kuwait in 1990.

The Iran-Iraq War turned out to be a battle between two egomaniac personalities, each with a Messiah complex, with neither of them willing to call a truce and a halt to the hostilities. The result was emaciation and bleeding of both countries to near bankruptcy. The Iraqi troops launched a full-scale invasion of Iran on September 22, 1980. France supplied high-tech weapons to Iraq, and the Soviet Union was Iraq's largest weapon supplier. Israel provided arms to Iran, hoping to bleed both the nations by prolonging the war. At least ten nations sold arms to both warring nations to profit from the conflict.

The United States followed a more duplicitous policy toward the warring parties to prolong the war and cause maximum damage to both of them. The United States and Iraq restored diplomatic relations in November 1984. Washington extended a $400 million credit guarantee for the export of US goods to Iraq. The CIA established a direct Washington-to-Baghdad link to provide the Iraqis with faster intelligence from US satellites.[20] The satellite data provided to Iraqis was some factual and some misleading information. Casey, the CIA

[20] Stephen Engelberg, "Iran and Iraq Got Doctored Data, US Officials Say," *New York Times*, Jan. 12, 1987, A1, A6.

director, was urging Iraqi officials to carry out more attacks on Iran, especially on economic targets.[21]

The US policy toward Iran was two faced as it followed two tracks at the same time. On the one hand, the US government carried out a covert program to undermine the government of Iran[22]. Starting in 1982, the CIA provided $100,000 a month to a group in Paris called the Front for the Liberation of Iran, headed by Ali Amini, who had presided over the reversion of Iranian oil to foreign control after the CIA-backed coup in 1953. The United States also provided support to two Iranian paramilitary groups based in Turkey, one of them headed by Gen. Bahram Aryana, the Shah's army chief.[23] The United States also carried out clandestine radio broadcasts into Iran from Egypt, calling for Khomeini's overthrow and urging support for Bakhtiar. Simultaneously, the United States pursued the second track of clandestinely providing arms and intelligence information to Iran in 1985 and 1986. In 1984, Washington launched Operation Staunch in an effort to dry up Iran's sources of arms supplies by pressuring US allies to stop supplying arms to Iran. While Washington was pretending to be neutral in the war and trying to make everyone else stop selling arms to Iran, the United States made secret arms transfers to Iran and encouraged Israel to do the same.[24] The United States provided intelligence to Iranians, which was a mixture of factual and

---

21 Bob Woodward, *Veil*, 480.

22 The Tower Commission, *President's Special Review Board* (Bantam Books, New York), 294–95.

23 Leslie H. Gelb, "US Said to Aid Iranian Exiles in Combat and Political Units," *New York Times*, March 7, 1982, A1, A12.

24 Leslie Gelb, "Iran Said to Get Large-Scale Arms from Israel, Soviets and Europeans," *New York Times*, March 8, 1982, A1, A10; Anthony Cordesman, *The Iran-Iraq War*, 31.

bogus information. The USA did, however, provide full critical data to Iran before its critical victory in the Fao Peninsula in February 1986.

The Iran-Iraq War was not between good and evil. Islam forbids fighting among the Muslims and forbids murder and the taking of life unless it is in the cause of justice. Saddam Hussein launched a murderous war to regain a few square miles of territory that his country had relinquished freely in 1975 border negotiations. There were one and a half million Muslim casualties in this senseless fraternal war. The war ended in a cease-fire that essentially left prewar borders unchanged. The covenant of Allah not only forbids such an internecine war but also provides a mechanism for dispute resolution. Instead of condemning the aggressor, the Arab states sided with Saddam Hussein, providing him with funds for further bloodletting. Saddam Hussein used banned chemical weapons against fellow Muslims, the Iranians and Kurds. The eight-year-long war exhausted both countries. The primary responsibility for the prolonged bloodletting must rest with the governments of the two countries, the ruthless military regime of Saddam Hussein and the ruthless clerical regime of Ayatollah Khomeini in Iran. Whatever his religious convictions, Khomeini had no qualms about sending his followers, including young boys, to their deaths for his own greater glory. This callous disregard for human life was no less characteristic of Saddam Hussein.

Saudi Arabia gave $26 billion and Kuwait $10.0 billion to Iraq to fuel the war and the killing of Muslims by Muslims. Saddam Hussein also owed the Soviets, USA, and Europe $40 billion for the purchase of arms. The cost of war to the Iranians was even greater. The rest of the world community sold arms for eight and a half years and watched the bloodletting. The USA sold arms and information to both sides to prolong the war strategically and to profit and gain influence and bases in the Gulf countries. Ayatollah Khomeini, in particular, was a hypocrite in dealing with Israel in secret, especially when his public pronouncements were venomously anti-Israel.

Iran, Iraq, and all the Arab states of the Persian Gulf took Western countries, the Soviet Union, and Israel as their *awliya* in contradiction to the commandments of the covenant. The ayatollah and his clerics should have known and understood their obligations to Allah and to their people as spelled out in Allah's covenant. The uncontrolled Arab-Iranian hostility left a deep, festering wound in the body of the nation of Islam. The West made gains by setting up permanent bases in Saudi Arabia, Oman, the United Arab Emirates, Bahrain, Qatar, and Kuwait. This is the land that Muhammad, the blessed messenger of Allah, freed from the infidels, only to be handed over to infidels by the *Munafiqeen.*

1990–2006: Saddam Opens the Gateway of Islam to the *Kafireen*

On August 2, 1990, Saddam Hussein was into mischief again. He invaded and occupied Kuwait. The sheikh of Kuwait and his family fled to Saudi Arabia. A coalition of Arabs, NATO, and many other countries carried a massive bombardment of Baghdad and other parts of Iraq on January 17, 1991, destroying the military installations, industrial units, and civilian infrastructure of Iraq. On February 24, 1991, American-led forces launched a ground offensive into Iraq and defeated the Iraqi Army. A United Nations resolution placed Iraq under an embargo till Iraq gave up all its biological and chemical weapons and also all nuclear weapon-making material.

After the Kuwait war at the invitation of King Fahd, the USA has continued to maintain large operational army and air force bases and command and control facilities that enable them to monitor all air and sea traffic as well as all civilian and military communications in the Middle East. Bahrain, in the meantime, has become the headquarters of the naval fleet command. Qatar has the longest runways in the Middle East and host to the United Stated Central Command Center. The Middle East, at the beginning of the twenty-first century, is under the absolute military and economic grip of the USA and NATO. The circle of evil—the *Yahudi*, *Salibi*, and *Munafiqeen*—continues to dominate the lives of the Muslims.

1992–Present: The American Empire: The Circle of Evil

After Saddam Hussein's Iraq was thoroughly trounced by the United States and its NATO and Arab allies in February 1991, the Western countries used their power in the United Nations Security Council to set up an embargo on Iraq. No food, medicines, or equipment for use in the reconstruction of the destroyed power and water purification plants was allowed into Iraq. Over the following twelve years, over half a million Iraqi children died and five million children suffered from malnutrition and disease. Iraq suffered from depravation and disease created by the United Nations, a world body established to bring about peace and reduce suffering in the world. Eventually, when the UN did start the oil-for-food program, the funds were skimmed by the United Nations to pay for war reparations, and the food aid meant for the victims of the embargo did not always get to them.

The New American Century

Iraq was thoroughly humiliated and defeated in February 1991. This was considered by the Americans to be a magnificent victory. In fact, the war was between a war-weary Iraq, with a population of eighteen million people, and a coalition of the world's most developed countries and the wealthy Arabs. The Arabs supplied over a hundred billion dollars and all the air, land, and naval bases to fight this war. After its humiliating defeat in Vietnam, the USA had avoided any frontal assault on any country till the war on Iraq. Actually, the Americans had been bold enough to attack two ministates, Granada and Panama, which had only parade ground armies and won hands down.

In early 1990s, emboldened with these victories and by the fall of Soviet Russia from internal decay, a group of Republican politicians founded the Project for the New American Century. They planned and conspired to take the White House and the two other branches of government as well. They began to lay on the drawing board their vision about how the United States should move in the world when the time came.

Donald Rumsfeld, Dick Cheney, James Woolsey, Paul Wolfowitz, Richard Perle, Bill Kristol, James Bolton, Zalmay M. Khalilzad, William Bennett, Dan Quayle, and Jeb Bush led the Project for the New American Century. They were representing ideas and ideologies of faceless, influential, wealthy individuals and corporations that helped them set up think tanks and provided them funds to buy up media outlets—newspapers, magazines, TV networks, radio talk shows, and cable channels. Through the inside manipulations of the governor of Florida, Jeb Bush, and through the friendship of Dick Cheney with his fishing pal, justice of the Supreme Court Antonin Scalia, George W. Bush was selected the president of the United States. The new president was a foreign policy novice and described by some as intellectually incurious who had struggled with alcoholism all his life.

In our age, we have people who think that they can get the best both the worlds by compromising their nations and Islam's interests with the enemy. Beyond what has been stated, more than their diplomatic, economic, and military strength is the power provided to United States, Britain, and Israel by the traitors of Islam. They constitute the other half of the circle of evil that is destroying Islam. They pretend to be Muslims. They pray, they fast, and they go for the hajj pilgrimage. Their fingers robotically sift through their prayer beads. Allah has bestowed on them so much wealth and power that their next one hundred generations will be able to live lavishly off their wealth. They love the luxury of their private Gulf Stream jets and granite places with silken rugs and gold plumbing fixtures. Dozens of attendants rush to their raised brow. Are they happy? Moreover, are they in peace with Allah's grace upon them? No. Wealth and power is not enough; they want more of it.

The Circle of Evil among the Muslims: Nine countries collectively have acted as the Muslim part of the circle of evil. They are Egypt, Pakistan, Bahrain, Kuwait, Qatar, United Arab Emirates, Oman, Jordan, and Saudi Arabia. In the Afghanistan and Iraq invasions of 2002–2006, an estimated 260,000 Muslim men, women, and children were killed and hundreds of thousands injured and millions made homeless by bombing. Two sovereign Islamic nations have been decimated, their state structure shattered, and economies annihilated. It would take at least thirty years to rebuild these nations and rehabilitate their citizens. The loss was not to the Taliban or to Saddam Hussein. The loss is to the unity of the *ummah*, the unity that has been ordained in the covenant with Allah. Who will assist in the destruction of Islam perpetrated by a secret cabal of *Yahudi-Salibi* conspirators in Washington? In the twenty-first century, treason is hard to hide.

Pakistan: Pakistan's illegitimate dictator Musharraf, who had stolen the government by force of arms, craved for legitimacy. Power corrupts, and absolute power corrupts absolutely. Any power and wealth acquired with *harramma* will continue to be maintained with *harramma*. Those who promote disunity of the *ummah* are promised severe retribution. Disobedience of the covenant of Allah is haram and is cursed. Haram will breed more haram and Allah's wrath. It reminds us of how the scales of Allah's justice, the two hands of Allah—His mercy and His wrath—are reflected in the human domain, where people have been appointed Allah's vicegerents. Deeds of goodness and wholesomeness are associated with mercy, paradise, and the beautiful. Evil and corruption is rewarded with wrath, hell, and the ugly.

The other "Muslims" who perpetrate evil association with the *kafireen* are princes and kings of Arabia, the land of Islam, Allah's blessed prophet, and the holy shrines of Mecca and Medina. Bahrain, Kuwait, Qatar, United Arab Emirates, Jordan, Oman, and Saudi Arabia united with the evil to destroy the lives of 50 million Muslims in Iraq and Afghanistan and the faith of 1.5 billion believers. Although *Bahrain* is a constitutional monarchy, it is run like a family enterprise by the Al Khalifah family. In 1992, the sheikh gave himself the title of king. The king, the crown prince, the commander in chief, the prime minister, the defense minister, housing minister, the interior minister, the oil and development minister, and the foreign ministers are related through blood and marriage, and they all are kith and kin of the Al Khalifah family, afraid to share governance with their 724,000 subjects. This family has carved most of Bahrain's agriculturally fertile land for their own private use. Members of the Al Khalifah family control over 80 percent of the agriculture land in Bahrain. They have allocated themselves virtually all the coastal land. Thirty-three percent of all oil revenue goes to the members of the Al Khalifah family; the instruments of the state are run on the rest. Two percent of the population owns 90 percent of the wealth of the islands. To safeguard the wealth and position of this family, the Al Khalifah clan has secret treaties with the United States to protect the family from their subjects and from their neighbors. They act as the springboard for the United Stated Army, Marines, and Navy in their two invasions of Iraq and Afghanistan and in the ongoing hostilities against Iran.

The Al Khalifah family has permitted the American Fifth Fleet to be based in Bahrain. The Fifth Fleet, for over thirty years, has menaced the Persian Gulf and has worked against the freedom of Iran and Iraq.

Kuwait, an oil-rich patch of desert, was carved out of the Basra district of the Ottoman Empire through the connivance of the British to circumvent the German plan to build railways from Berlin through the Ottoman Empire to Kuwait in the Persian Gulf. Kuwait, being the only deepwater harbor on the western edge of the Persian Gulf, provided the British with a supply and refueling center for its navy. It has continued to be subservient to the *kafireen* to maintain the Sabah family's power and riches. The Sabah family, like other Arab monarchies, runs their country as a family incorporation, all ministries being run by the family. Most of the country's wealth reverts to the royal family.

2003 to Present: Muslim Complicity in the Invasion of Iraq

Bahrain, Kuwait, Qatar, United Arab Emirates, Oman, Jordan, Pakistan, and Saudi Arabia willingly provided Britain and the United States facilities for overflight, air operations, basing, port facilities, and facilities to preposition equipment for the Iraq invasion. It should come as no surprise to Muslims around the world that the Saudi royal family directly participated in the American invasion of Iraq and the slaughter of about 260,000 Iraqis and in the destruction of Iraq's infrastructure.

Treason amongst Us: On Friday, November 15, 2002, the Saudi ambassador Prince Bandar bin Sultan came to the Oval Office to see Pres. George W. Bush. Dick Cheney and Condoleezza Rice were also there. Bandar had been a long-term fixture in Washington, having served during four American presidencies. He had a ready access to American presidents, particularly the first President Bush, and the Bush family regarded him as a member of the family, where the prince had acquired the name Bandar Bush. On the same token, the Saudis had reputedly invested $1.4 billion in the Bush family, and the American president could safely be named George Bush Ibn Sa'ud. In this relationship, the Saudis do the American bidding in the Middle East, and the Americans protect the royal family interests and investments. In spite of this deep relationship and $3 trillion Saudi investment and support to the American economy, the Saudis do not have the resolve and will to use their clout to solve the Palestinian problem.

Bandar handed the president a private letter from Prince Abdullah, the de facto ruler of Saudi Arabia, and provided an English translation of the text. The text, in summary, congratulated the president's victory achieved by the Republican Party under his leadership. It stated that Prince Bandar was authorized to convey and discuss his message to the president face-to-face. As instructed Bandar then said formally, "Since 1994, we have been in constant contact with you at the highest level regarding what needs to be done with Iraq and Iraqi regime. Now, Mr. President, we want hear from you directly on your serious intention regarding this subject so we can adjust and coordinate so we can make right policy decision."[25]

In 1994, King Fahd had proposed to President Clinton a joint US-Saudi covert action to overthrow Saddam, and Crown Prince Abdullah in April 2002 had suggested to Pres. George Bush that they spend up to $1 billion in a joint operation with the CIA. "Every time we meet, we are surprised that the United States asks us to give our impression about what can be done regarding Saddam Hussein," Bandar said, suggesting that the repeated requests caused them to "begin to doubt how serious America is about the issue of regime change. Now tell us what you are going to do."

[25] Bob Woodward, *Plan of Attack* (Simon & Shuster), 228–30.

Bandar read, "If you have a serious intention, we will not hesitate so that our two military people can then implement and discuss in order to support the American military action or campaign. This will make Saudi Arabia a major ally for the United States."

President Bush thanked the ambassador and said that he always appreciated the crown prince's views; he was a good friend and a great ally. Bush added that when he made up his mind on the military option, he would contact the crown prince before his final decision.[26]

On January 11, 2003, Dick Cheney invited Prince Bandar bin Sultan, the Saudi ambassador, to his West Wing. Present on this occasion were Defense Secretary Don Rumsfeld and Joint Chief of Staff Chairman Gen. Richard Myers. The American defense officials appraised Bandar, a foreigner, of their battle plans against Iraq, even before Colin Powell, the US secretary of state, knew of them. General Meyers unfurled a large map of the area and explained the first part of the battle plan. The plan involved a massive bombing campaign over several days. The United States would drop on Iraq four times the bombs that destroyed it during the forty-two days of the Gulf War. And during those days, Americans dropped more bombs on Iraq than were dropped by all the combatants during the Second World War. Bandar was informed that his fellow Arab and Muslim Iraqis were to be exploded, incinerated, and blown to bits with four times the explosives than had ever been used on this planet previously. Special forces, intelligence teams, and air strikes would be launched through the five-hundred-mile Saudi border with Iraq.

The next day, Bandar met George W. Bush. The Saudis wanted an assurance that, this time, Saddam would be totally finished, and the president reminded the ambassador of his briefings from "Dick, Rummy, and General Meyers," in which they had assured Bandar that,

---

[26] Woodward, *Plan of Attack*, 228–30.

this time, Saddam indeed would be toast.[27] Bandar flew to Riyadh and provided a verbatim report of the battle plan to Crown Prince Abdullah. Abdullah advised Bandar to maintain strict secrecy till they could figure out their next move.

On Friday, March 14, 2003, Bandar was shown into the Oval Office; Cheney, Rice, and Card were there. Bandar was unshaven, he had put on weight, and the buttons on his jacket were straining. He was tired, nervous, and excited. He was sweating profusely. "What's wrong with you?" the president asked Bandar. "Don't you have a razor to shave with?"

"Mr. President," Bandar replied, "I promised myself I would not shave until this war starts."

"Well, then, you are going to shave very soon."

"I hope so," Bandar said. "By the time this war starts, I will be like bin Laden." He then indicated a long beard of a foot or two.

On Wednesday, March 19, 2003, at 7:30 p.m., Condoleezza Rice told Bandar, "The president has asked me to tell you that we are going to war. At about 9:00 p.m., all hell will break loose."

"Tell him he will be in our prayers and hearts," Bandar said. "God help us all."

Bandar then called Crown Prince Abdullah in a prearranged code in reference to an oasis, Roda outside Riyadh. "Tonight the forecast is there will be heavy rain in the Roda," Bandar said from his car phone to Saudi Arabia.

Abdullah asked, "Do you know how soon the storm is going to hit?"

Bandar replied, "Sir, I don't know, but watch TV."

The American air campaign against Iraq was essentially managed from inside Saudi Arabia, where American military commanders

---

[27] Ibid., 263–68.

operated an air command center and launched refueling tankers, F-16 fighter jets, and sophisticated intelligence-gathering flights, according to American officials.[28] Senior officials from both countries told the Associated Press that the royal family permitted widespread military operations to be staged from inside the kingdom during the invasion of Iraq.

Between 250 and 300 air force planes were staged from Saudi Arabia, including AWACS, C-130s, refueling tankers, and F-16 fighter jets, during the height of the war, the officials said. Air and military operations during the war were permitted at the Tabuk air base and the Arar regional airport near the Iraq border. "We operated the command center in Saudi Arabia. We operated aeroplanes out of Saudi Arabia, as well as sensors and tankers," said Gen. T. Michael Moseley, a top air force general who was the architect of the campaign. During the war, US officials held a media briefing about the air war from Qatar although the air command center was in Saudi Arabia—a move designed to prevent inflaming the Saudi public.

When the war started, the Saudis allowed cruise missiles to be fired from navy ships across their airspace into Iraq. The Saudis provided tens of millions of dollars in discounted and free oil, gas, and fuel for American forces. During the war, a stream of oil delivery trucks, at times, stretched for miles outside the Prince Sultan air base, said a senior US military planner. The Saudis were influential in keeping down the world oil prices during the run-up to the Iraq War by pumping 1.5 million barrels a day. The Saudis kept Jordan supplied with cheap oil for its support in the Iraq War. Although King Abdullah of Jordan had met with the leaders of Turkey, Syria, and Egypt and made well-publicized statements against the war on Iraq, he had secretly committed to support the American war effort against

[28] "New Details on Saudi Help in Iraq War," Associated Press, April 25, 2004, http://wwwfoxnews.com/story/0,933,118084,00.html.FoxNews.

Iraq. American troops and intelligence services operated from inside the Jordanian borders in their invasion of Iraq.

Saddam Hussein was a traitor to Islam and a tyrant and deserved humiliation. However, at the eve of the war, he contacted Egypt for asylum. The Egyptians, at the behest of the Americans, refused. Prince Bandar had been informed directly by Hosni Mubarak. Yet Iraqis were attacked and the country decimated.[29]

The Saudis, Egyptians, and other Arab rulers were aware of the magnitude of the planned air attack on the Iraqi people. The invasion of Iraq ostensibly was to depose Saddam and his regime. Saddam tried to abdicate, leave Iraq, and sought asylum in Egypt. Yet the Arab rulers let the invasion go unchallenged and, in fact, assisted a *kafir* power to occupy a sovereign Muslim country. They allowed 260,000 Iraqis to be blown to bits and hundreds of thousands of civilians to be maimed. Eighty percent of the population lost their jobs. The country was decimated. The infrastructure had been blown into stone age, and the desert had been poisoned with radioactive waste from spent ammunition for thousands of years to come.

Islam is a religion of peace, truth, justice, and harmony. Conflict and war is only permitted by the covenant of Allah in self-defense and to fight *fitnah*, treachery, oppression, and injustice.

2001 to Present: After Eighty-Seven Years, History Repeats Itself: More Traitors(1914-2001).

Enver Pasa secretly signed a treaty of Turko-German Alliance on August 2, 1914. Only five people in Turkey knew of this treaty, which brought on the final disintegration of the Ottoman Empire. The puppet grand vizier Said Halim, Talat, and Cemal were convinced by Enver of the wisdom of supporting the Germans in case the war

[29] Woodward, *Plan of Attack*, 312.

broke out. Enver Pasa chose to ally Turkey with the Central Powers by citing Germany's earlier victories in the war. Thus, the Ottoman Empire joined the Central Powers to form a triple alliance without the knowledge of the cabinet, the parliament, the army generals, and the Ottoman populace. The empire was ruled by three collaborators and puppets of Germany, traitors to Islam, to the Muslims in Turkey, and to the whole of the *ummah*. They acted secretly as collaborators, with a foreign government working toward the destruction and disintegration of the only free Islamic state.

Two German warships, the battleship *Goeben* and the cruiser *Breslau*, that were caught in a neutral Turkish port when the war broke out in Europe were handed to the Ottoman Navy. In October, they were put out to sea, flying the Ottoman flag with German officers and crew, and shelled Odessa and other Russian ports. Enver Pasa, as the Ottoman war minister, gave secret orders in a sealed envelope to Admiral Souchon, the commander of the Turko-German fleet, only to be opened when the fleet was deep in the Black Sea. The orders read:

> *War minister Enver Pasha to Admiral Souchon*
>
> *October 25, 1914.*
>
> *The entire fleet should maneuver in the Black Sea. When you find a favorable opportunity, attack the Russian fleet. Before initiating the hostilities, open my secret orders given to you personally this morning. To prevent transport of material to Serbia, act as already agreed upon. Enver Pasha. (Secret Order): The Turkish fleet should gain the mastery of the Black Sea by force. Seek out the Russian fleet and attack her wherever you find her without declaration of war. Enver Pasha*

The admiral attacked simultaneously the Russian ports of Sebastopol, Theodosia, Novorossiysk, and Odessa on the morning of October 29. The first cannon shot from the Turkish fleet, in effect, declared a war on Russia and its allies Britain and France. Once again, Enver acted secretly at the behest of Germany. He did not consult his coconspirators, Talat and Cemal, before ordering the attack on Russia or the declaration of war against the Western allies. He kept his cabinet colleagues, the parliament, and the people of the empire in the dark, who on the morning of October 29, 1914, were surprised to find themselves at war.

The conspiracies, utter stupidity, and lust for power of three men—Talat, Cemal, and Enver—led to the dismemberment of the Ottoman Empire. For another one hundred years, this land of Islam was to know no peace. This land of Islam became the prey of the circle of evil of the Euro-Christian, Jew, and Arab conspirators.

The New American Century: The *Yahudi-Salibi* Conspiracy

At the end of the twentieth century, American planners formulated a new doctrine for the deployment of American might. It reads:

> *Unites States will rule the world. United States will turn into the Centre of global empire. Washington will decide the fates of governments divide up riches of foreign economies and impose democracy in American sense of the world. With overwhelming military superiority United States will prevent new rivals to from rising up to challenge it on world stage. United States will have dominion over friends and foes alike. United States will be the bully on the block. If required, its armed forces will use preemptive overwhelming military force. It will prevent and discourage development of nuclear programs in other countries.*
>
> *In American view, Iran, Iraq, and North Korea are the axis of evil, and the destruction of their military and economic prowess is a priority.*

Wars and military adventures benefit from coalitions, but the United States must determine and control all missions and lead the fights. United States will not only be the most powerful but must be powerful to deter the emergence of rival powers.

After the wane of the Soviet Union, there was no threat to the security of the United States and its people; therefore, the American people demanded reduction in the defense expenditure. The defense industry and the financial institutions demanded continuing spending on armaments and defense industry to keep the economy running. America needed a threat to replace the Soviet Union. Inexplicably, this threat suddenly appeared from the caves in the Hindu Kush Mountains of Afghanistan. From a cave lit with a kerosene lantern in Tora Bora, on September 11, 2001, a man called Osama bin Laden directed and launched four massive airliners full of innocent passengers, which crash-landed into the Twin Towers of the World Trade Center and the Pentagon. The US Air Force shot down the fourth plane on the way to the White House. Three thousand people died. This catastrophe shook America and the world.

The Pentagon boosted its budget in increments from $260 billion to $480 billion over a period of twenty months. To the surprise of most people who were not aware, almost all the planners of the new American century were Jews. The conspirators Abram Shulsky, Robert Martinage, Paul Wolfowitz, Lewis Libby, James Lasswell, Mark Lagon, Phil Meilinger, Robert Kilebrew, William Kristol, Steve Rosen, Robert Kagan, Dov Zakheim, Fred Kagan, Donald Kagan, Devon Gaffney Cross, Stephen Cambone, Elliot Cohen, Alvin Bernstein, and Richard Perle are all Jews, and most of these men have spent some part of their life in Israel. They hold Israeli citizenship and are active in promoting pro-Israeli and anti-Arab and anti-Muslim causes. A few are right-wing Christian Zionists. All are committed to Israel and the Likud Party of the former Israeli prime minister Sharon.

This Jewish-Israeli transplant in Washington and the Christian right movement want to decisively shift the balance of power in the Middle East in favor of Israel so that it could effectively impose peace terms on Palestinians and Syrians, divide and fragment Arab and Muslim countries, and impose American/Israeli hegemony and economic and military control over the Middle East. They want to demonstrate to the world that America does have the will and power to disarm any rogue state that attempts to acquire weapons of mass destruction. They also want to demonstrate to any future rival powers that America could invade the Persian Gulf and deny any rival supplies of oil. In other words, comply with the American/Israeli wishes or else.

To achieve these objectives, the conspiring hawks planned to dominate the oil-rich arch of Islam extending from Syria on the Mediterranean to Afghanistan in the Hindu Kush Mountains. They planned to set up military bases in Iraq and link those to bases in Central Asia, Horn of Africa, Persian Gulf, and the Mediterranean.

The planning of invasion of Iraq and its execution were carried out secretly by a group of Jews working inside the Pentagon, namely, Paul Wolfowitz, Richard Perle, Douglas Feith, and Paul Nitze. In July 2001, at the Group of Eight summit held in Genoa, Italy, plans were discussed for the ouster of the Taliban from power. Wolfowitz, Perle, and Nitze were the people pushing for the American occupation of Afghanistan and Iraq. Bush's cabinet intended to take military action to take control of the Persian Gulf whether or not Saddam Hussein was in power. The blueprint written in September 2000 was supported by an earlier document written by Wolfowitz and Libby recommending maintaining American bases in Saudi Arabia and Kuwait to keep American control over the Arab oil. Another member of this team was the propagandist William Kristol, a Council on Foreign Relations (CFR) member.

Donald Rumsfeld (secretary of defense) and Paul Wolfowitz (deputy secretary of defense) set up a secret bureau within in the Pentagon. The Office of Special Plans (OSP) in the Pentagon dealt with the Middle East. Douglas Feith headed the Near East South Asia Center (NESA). Retired intelligence officers from the State Department, the Defense Intelligence Agency, and the Central Intelligence Agency had long charged that this office exaggerated and doctored the intelligence from Iraq and the Middle East before passing it along to the White House. Key personnel who worked in the OSP and NESA under the control of Douglas Feith were part of a broader network of Jews and Zionists who worked with similar Bush political appointees scattered around the American national security network. Their assignment was to move the country to war, according to the retired lieutenant colonel Karen Kwiatkowski. Kwiatkowski was assigned to NESA from May 2002 through February 2003.[30] Other political appointees who worked with them were William Loti, Abram Shulsky, Michael Rubin, David Schenker, Michael Makovsky, and Chris Lehman.

Along with Feith, all the political appointees have a common close identification with Ariel Sharon and the Likud Party in Israel. This group works closely with Richard Perle, John Bolton, Michael Wurmser, and Elizabeth Cheney. There are published reports that this group works with a similar group in the Israeli prime minister Ariel Sharon's office in Jerusalem. The OSP and the NESA personnel are already discussing and planning "going after Iran and Syria" after the war in Afghanistan and Iraq. Political plans of the Likud Party and the Council for Foreign Relations work on behalf of the Jewish finance

---

[30] Jim Lobe, "Pentagon Now Home to Neoconservative Network," *Dawn*, Aug. 9, 2003.

and defense industry to facilitate borrowing by the governments. It is amazing how in banking and wars Jewish names keep coming up.

In the arch of Islam, Iran is the keystone; and Syria, Iraq, Afghanistan, and Pakistan constituted the western and eastern halves of the arch. If Iran fell, the whole Muslim world would come tumbling down into the American lap. The planners decided to work on the weakest link of the chain. Afghanistan and Iraq had been devastated by twenty-five years of war, and Iraq had further been bled through the United Nations sanctions. Once Iraq and Afghanistan had been decimated and removed from the arch, then Iran and Syria would come tumbling down too.

After the fall of the Soviet Empire, the world was settling down to a slumber of peace, and the people of the world looked forward to a disarmed world. The planners of the new American century wanted an event so overwhelming and catastrophic that would propel the American people's psyche into a prolonged period of perpetual warfare. The assistance for such an event came from a very unsuspecting source.

Pakistan: The *Munafiq* Connection

Gen. Pervez Musharraf, in a bloodless coup d'état on October 12, 1999, ousted the elected Pakistani government, arrested the prime minister Nawaz Sharif, and installed his own military regime. Accusing the previous government of corruption and ruining the economy, Musharraf promised to bring economic progress and political stability, eradicate poverty, build investor confidence, and restore democracy as quickly as possible. Two years later, none of these promises had been fulfilled. The economy was on a knife-edge, and there was growing, popular discontent with falling living standards and lack of basic democratic rights. The regime was under fire not only from the political opposition but also from its supporters in the ruling military elite. The schisms in the military reflected the pressure that the regime was under both domestically and internationally.

While the USA and other major powers tacitly accepted the coup, they had become increasingly critical of Musharraf's failure to carry out the economic measures demanded by the International Monetary Fund and his failure to crack down on Islamic fundamentalism. The USA had effectively blocked IMF loans and had not lifted economic sanctions imposed on Pakistan after its 1998 nuclear tests. The USA also demanded that Musharraf put pressure on the Taliban regime in Afghanistan to hand over Osama bin Laden, whom the USA blamed for the terrorist bombing of US embassies in Kenya and Tanzania.

Musharraf's junta confronted serious debt problems as a result of the IMF's repeated delays in disbursing one and a half billion dollars in loans. Without the IMF's backing, Pakistan had been unable to reschedule its thirty-eight billion dollars in foreign loans and was at the risk of defaulting on repayments of five billion dollars of its loans that were due by the end of the year. According to official records, Pakistan's foreign exchange reserves were down to a bare one-third of a billion dollars.

To impose its policies, the military regime resorted to an outright repression, making a mockery of its claims of returning Pakistan to democracy by 2002. All the evidence pointed to a regime with a rapidly dwindling base of support. Its only answer to protests and opposition was more repression and seeking respite from foreign sources.

There was evidence that Musharraf's junta was secretly cooperating and cozying up with the US military and intelligence services and covertly helping the USA in its operations in Afghanistan. With CIA backing and with the injection of massive amounts of US military aid, Pakistan's Inter-Services Intelligence (ISI) had, in the 1980s and 1990s, developed into a major intelligence network wielding enormous power over all aspects of Pakistani civilian and military life. The ISI had a staff of military and intelligence officers, bureaucrats, undercover agents, and informers estimated at 150,000.[31] With this active collaboration with the CIA, the ISI continued to perform covert intelligence operations in the interests of the United States in Afghanistan and Central Asia. The ISI had directly supported and financed a number of terrorist organizations, including al-Qaeda. This cooperation with the al-Qaeda began as an extension of American interest in the region, and it could not have continued without the consent and the knowledge of the CIA.

The Sequence of Events

April 4, 2000. ISI director Gen. Mahmood Ahmed visited Washington. He met officials at the CIA and the White House. In a message meant for both Pakistan and the Taliban, US officials told him that al-Qaeda had killed Americans and "people who support those people will be treated as our enemies." However, no actual action, military or otherwise, was taken against either the Taliban or Pakistan.

May 2001. CIA director Tenet made a quiet visit to Pakistan to meet with Pres. Pervez Musharraf in May 2001. While in Islamabad, Tenet had an "an unusually long meeting" with General Musharraf. He also met with his Pakistani counterpart, ISI director Lt. Gen. Mahmood Ahmed.

July 2001. The BBC's George Arney reported on September 18 that American officials had told former Pakistani foreign secretary Niaz

---

[31] Ahmed Rashid, "The Taliban: Exporting Extremism," *Foreign Affairs*, November-December 1999. See also Michel Chossudovsky, Who is Osama bin Laden, Global Outlook, No. 1, 2002.

Naik in mid-July of plans for military action against the Taliban regime: "Mr. Naik said US officials told him of the plan at a UN-sponsored international contact group on Afghanistan which took place in Berlin. Mr. Naik told the BBC that at the meeting the US representatives told him that unless Bin Laden was handed over swiftly America would take military action to kill or capture both Bin Laden and the Taliban leader, Mullah Omar." The wider objective, according to Mr. Naik, would be to topple the Taliban regime and install a transitional government of moderate Afghans in its place, possibly under the leadership of the former Afghan king Zahir Shah. "Mr. Naik was told that Washington would launch its operation from bases in Tajikistan, where American advisers were already in place. He was told that Uzbekistan would also participate in the operation and that 17,000 Russian troops were on standby. Mr. Naik was told that if the military action went ahead it would take place before the snows started falling in Afghanistan, by the middle of October at the latest."

July 2001. The FBI confirmed in late September 2001, in an interview with ABC News, that the 9/11 ringleader, Mohammed Atta, had been financed from unnamed sources in Pakistan in July 2001:

> *As to September 11th, federal authorities have told ABC News they have now tracked more than $100,000 from banks in Pakistan, to two banks in Florida, to accounts held by suspected hijack ringleader, Mohammed Atta. As well... "Time Magazine" is reporting that some of that money came in the days just before the attack and can be traced directly to people connected to Osama bin Laden. It's all part of what a successful FBI effort has been so far to close in on the hijacker's high commander, the money men, the planners and the mastermind.*[32]

[32] Statement of Brian Ross reporting on information conveyed to him by the FBI, ABC News, September 30, 2001.

The FBI had information on the money trail. They knew exactly who was financing the terrorists. Less than two weeks later, the findings of the FBI were confirmed by Agence France-Presse and the *Times of India*, quoting an official Indian intelligence report. According to these two reports, the money used to finance the 9/11 attacks had allegedly been "wired to WTC hijacker Mohammed Atta from Pakistan, by Ahmad Umar Sheikh, at the instance of ISI Chief General Mahmood Ahmad."[33]

July 2001. At the Group of Eight summit held in Genoa, Italy, plans were discussed for the ouster of the Taliban from power. Wolfowitz, Perle, and Nitze were the people pushing for the American occupation of Afghanistan and Iraq. Bush's cabinet intended to take military action to take control of the Persian Gulf whether or not Saddam Hussein was in power. The blueprint written in September 2000 was supported by an earlier document written by Wolfowitz and Libby recommending maintaining American bases in Saudi Arabia and Kuwait to keep American control over the Arab oil.

Late August 2001. Barely a couple of weeks before September 11, Rep. Porter Goss, together with Sen. Bob Graham and Sen. Jon Kyl, were on a top-level intelligence mission in Islamabad. They held meetings with Pres. Pervez Musharraf and with Pakistan's military and intelligence brass, including the head of Pakistan's Inter-Services Intelligence, Gen. Mahmood Ahmed. Porter Goss, a Florida Republican and former CIA operative, was chairman of the House Intelligence Committee. He also chaired, together with Sen. Bob Graham, the Joint Senate House Committee on the September 11 attacks.

Amply documented, Porter Goss had an established personal relationship to the head of ISI, Gen. Mahmood Ahmed, who

[33] *Times of India*, Delhi, October 9, 2001.

according to the *Washington Post* "ran a spy agency notoriously close to Osama bin Laden and the Taliban" (May 18, 2002).

According to the Council on Foreign Relations, the ISI had over the years supported a number of Islamic terrorist organizations while maintaining close links to the CIA:

> *Through its Inter-Services Intelligence agency (ISI) Pakistan has provided the Taliban with military advisers and logistical support during key battles, has bankrolled the Taliban, has facilitated trans-shipment of arms, ammunition, and fuel through its territory, and has openly encouraged the recruitment of Pakistanis to fight for the Taliban.*
>
> *Pakistan's army and intelligence services, principally the Inter-Services Intelligence Directorate (ISI), contribute to making the Taliban a highly effective military force In other words, up to and including September 11, 2001, extending to December 2001, the ISI had been supporting Taliban network.*

And that was precisely the period during which Porter Goss and Bob Graham established a close working relationship with the ISI chief, Gen. Mahmood Ahmed. The latter had, in fact, "briefed" the two Florida lawmakers at ISI headquarters in Rawalpindi, Pakistan:

> *Senator Bob Graham's first foreign trip as chairman of the Senate Intelligence Committee, in a late-August 2001, with House intelligence Chairman Goss and Republican Senator Jon Kyl of Arizona, focused almost entirely on terrorism. It ended in Pakistan, where (ISI Chief) General Mahmood Ahmed's intelligence agents briefed them on the growing threat of al Qaida while they peered across the Khyber Pass at an obscure section of Afghanistan, called Tora Bora. The Americans also visited General Ahmed's compound and urged him to do more to help capture Osama bin Laden. The general hadn't said much, but the*

group had agreed to discuss the issue more when he visited Washington on September 4, 2001.

September 4, 2001: General Mahmood Ahmad arrives in the US on an official visit.

September 4-9, 2001: He meets his US counterparts including CIA Head George Tenet. Official sources confirm that he met Tenet this week. He also held long parleys with unspecified officials at the White House and the Pentagon. But the most important meeting was with Marc Grossman, U.S. Under Secretary of State for Political Affairs.

September 4, 2001. Gen. Mahmood Ahmed arrived in the USA on an official visit.

September 4–9, 2001. He met his US counterparts, including CIA head George Tenet, according to official sources. He also held long parleys with unspecified officials at the White House and the Pentagon. But the most important meeting was with Marc Grossman, US undersecretary of state for political affairs.

September 9, 2001. The leader of the Northern Alliance, Gen. Ahmad Shah Masoud was assassinated on the ninth of September 2001. The ISI, headed by General Ahmed, was allegedly involved in ordering the assassination of General Masoud. Ahmad Shah Masoud was the last hurdle in the Northern Alliance's cooperation with the USA in the coming invasion of Afghanistan. The kamikaze assassination took place two days before the attacks on the Twin Towers and the Pentagon during Gen. Mahmood Ahmed's official visit to Washington (September 4–13, 2001). The official communiqué of the Northern Alliance pointed to the involvement of the ISI.

September 10, 2001. According to Pakistani journalist Amir Mateen in a revealing article published one day before the 9/11 attack[34]:

> *ISI Chief Lt-Gen. Mahmood's week-long presence in Washington has triggered speculation about the agenda of his mysterious meetings at the Pentagon and National Security Council. Officially, he is on a routine visit in return to CIA Director George Tenet's earlier visit to Islamabad. Official sources confirm that he met Tenet this week. He also held long parleys with unspecified officials at the White House and the Pentagon. But the most important meeting was with Marc Grossman, U.S. Under Secretary of State for Political Affairs. One can safely guess that the discussions must have centered around Afghanistan. and Osama bin Laden. What added interest to his visit is the history of such visits. Last time Ziauddin Butt, Mahmood's predecessor, was here, during Nawaz Sharif's government, the domestic politics turned topsy-turvy within days.*

Morning of September 11, 2001. The three lawmakers Bob Graham, Porter Goss, and Jon Kyl and General Mahmood *all met in a top-secret conference room on the fourth floor of the US Capitol.* Also present at this meeting were Pakistan's ambassador to the USA Maleeha Lodhi and several members of the Senate and House intelligence committees. According to Graham's copious notes, they discussed "poppy cultivation" before they discussed terrorism. But then the Americans pressed Ahmed even harder to crack down on al-Qaeda. And then:

> *9:04 -- Tim gives note on 2 planes crash into World Trade Center, NYC.* (*Washington Post*, May 4, 2003)

---

[34] Amir Mateen, "ISI Chief's Parleys Continue in Washington," *News*, September 10, 2001.

However, at no time since 9/11 had Rep. Porter Goss and his Senate counterpart, Bob Graham (chairman of the Senate Intelligence Committee), acknowledged the role of Pakistan's ISI in supporting al-Qaeda. In fact, quite the opposite. One year after the attacks, the former head of the ISI continued to be described as a bona fide intelligence counterpart supportive of the US "war on terrorism." In an interview in the *New York Times* on the first anniversary of 9/11, Sen. Bob Graham described his August 2001 encounter with General Ahmed:

> I had just come back a few days before September the 11th from a trip [to] Pakistan and [a] meeting with President Musharraf and with the head of the Pakistani intelligence service. While we were meeting with the head of the intelligence service, a general whose name was General Ahmed, he had indicated he would be in Washington in early September, we -- Porter Goss, myself -- had invited him to meet with us while he was there. It turned out that the meeting was a breakfast the day of September the 11th.

The head of the ISI arrived in the USA on the fourth. Graham stated in the interview that he got back a few days before 9/11, which suggested that the Goss-Graham mission could well have returned to Washington on board the same military plane as General Ahmed.

> *So, we were talking about what was happening in Afghanistan, what the capabilities and intentions of the Taliban and Al Qaida were from the perspective of this Pakistani intelligence leader, when we got the notices that the World Trade Center towers had been attacked.*

September 12–13 2001: At 10:00 a.m. a day after the devastating terrorist attacks on New York's World Trade Center and Pentagon headquarters in Washington, Gen. Mahmood Ahmed, ISI chief, arrived at the State Department for an emergency meeting with the US deputy secretary of state, Richard Armitage. "General, we require your country's full support and cooperation," Armitage told Pakistan's spymaster and member of the triumvirate that ruled the country. "We want to know whether you are with us or not, in our fight against terror." The meeting was adjourned for the next day after the general had assured Armitage of Pakistan's full support.

"We will tell you tomorrow what you are required to do," Armitage said as they left the room.

Meanwhile at 1:30 p.m., Colin Powell spoke to President Musharraf on the phone. "The American people would not understand if Pakistan did not cooperate in this fight with the United States," Powell said candidly as one general to another. President Musharraf promised to cooperate fully with the United States.

It was 12:00 p.m. on September 13, 2001, when General Mahmood returned to the State Department for the second meeting. "This is not negotiable," said Armitage as he handed over a single sheet of paper with seven demands that the Bush administration wanted him to accept.

The general glanced through the paper for a few seconds and replied, "They are all acceptable to us."

The swift response took Armitage by surprise. "These are very powerful words, General. Do you not want to discuss with your President?" he asked.

"I know the president's mind," replied General Mahmood.

A visibly elated Armitage asked General Mahmood to meet with George Tenet, the CIA chief, at his headquarters at Langley. "He is waiting for you," said Armitage.

The American demands, to which General Mahmood acceded to in no time, required Pakistan to abandon its support for the Taliban regime and provide logistical support to the American forces. The list of demands included the following:

1. Stop al-Qaeda operations on the Pakistani border and intercept arms shipments through Pakistan and all logistical support for bin Laden.
2. Give blanket overflights and landing rights for US planes.
3. Provide access to Pakistan's naval bases, airbases, and borders.
4. Give immediate intelligence and immigration information.
5. Curb all domestic expression of support for terrorism against the United States and its friends and allies.
6. Cut off fuel supply to the Taliban and stop Pakistani volunteers going into Afghanistan to join the Taliban.
7. Break diplomatic relations with the Taliban and assist the USA to destroy bin Laden and his al-Qaeda network.

September 13, 2001. General Ahmed met Sen. Joseph Biden, chairman of the Senate Foreign Relations Committee.

The Decision to go to War: At meetings of the National Security Council and in the so-called war cabinet on September 11, 12, and 13, CIA director George Tenet played a central role in persuading Pres. George Bush to launch the "war on terrorism."

September 11, 2001, 3:30 p.m. A key meeting of the National Security Council (NSC) was convened, with members of the NSC communicating with the president from Washington by secure video.[35] In the course of this NSC videoconference, CIA director George Tenet fed unconfirmed information to the president. Tenet stated that

[35] *Washington Post*, January 27, 2002.

"he was virtually certain that bin Laden and his network were behind the attacks.[36]"

The president responded to these statements quite spontaneously, off the cuff, with little or no discussion, and with an apparent misunderstanding of their implications. In the course of this videoconference (which lasted for less than an hour), the NSC was given the mandate by the president to prepare for the "war on terrorism." Very much on the spur of the moment, the green light was given by videoconference from Nebraska. In the words of President Bush, "We will find these people. They will pay. And I don't want you to have any doubt about it."[37]

4:36 p.m. (one hour and six minutes later). Air Force One departed for Washington. Back in the White House, that same evening at nine, a second meeting of the full NSC took place, together with Secretary of State Colin Powell, who had returned to Washington from Peru. The NSC meeting (which lasted for half an hour) was followed by the first meeting of the so-called war cabinet. The latter was made up of a smaller group of top officials and key advisers.

9:30 p.m. At the war cabinet, "Discussion turned around whether bin Laden's Al Qaida and the Taliban were one and the same thing. Tenet said they were."[38]

11:00 p.m. By the end of that historic meeting of the war cabinet, the Bush administration had decided to embark on a military adventure that began the war on Afghanistan and Iraq. Astonishingly, within a course of forty-eight hours, the military junta of Pakistan took an about-turn to become a lynchpin in the US-led military operation in

---

[36] Ibid.

[37] Ibid.

[38] Ibid.

Afghanistan that ousted the Taliban regime. The speed of the quick about-turn surprised even the American authorities.

Events after September 11 during the week in Washington and Islamabad provided an interesting insight into the ad hoc and arbitrary decision-making process of military dictatorships on crucial national security and foreign policy issues. Like the policy to support the Taliban regime, the decision to surrender the country's sovereignty was also taken just by two generals. There were no consultations at any level when President Musharraf abandoned support for the oppressive and reactionary regime in Afghanistan, gave the American forces complete access to Pakistani territory, and assisted in the invasion of an ally and an independent Muslim state. A similar sequence of events had occurred in the history of Islam when, eighty-seven years earlier, Enver Pasa secretly signed a treaty of Turko-German Alliance on August 2, 1914.

On the evening of September 12, General Musharraf received a phone call from General Mahmood in Washington, who briefed him about his meeting with Armitage. Later, US ambassador Wendy Chamberlain met with him and conveyed a formal message from the American leaders for cooperation. The president assured her of Pakistan's full support.

As it occurred in Turkey eighty-seven years earlier, in Pakistan, there was no consultation with political leaders on the paradigm shift in the strategic discourse of the nation. General Musharraf took his handpicked, unelected cabinet into confidence, almost three days after his ISI chief had already signed on the dotted line to the US demands. He told the ministers that the decision to cooperate with the United States was necessary to safeguard Pakistan's nuclear assets and its Kashmir policy.

General Musharraf did not find it hard to convince his cabinet, but it was not so simple when it came to his corps commanders and members of his military junta. At least seven senior officers, including Lieutenant General Mahmood, who had earlier in Washington signed on the dotted line, showed reservations on the decision to pull out support for the Taliban regime. The people of Pakistan and the owners of the land were astonished when they found themselves involved in a long war on behalf of the *kafireen* against their own countrymen in Waziristan and against other Muslims in Afghanistan.

Musharraf acted swiftly and fired the dithering general Mahmood and the other reluctant generals who disagreed with him. Through a series of purges at the top level, General Musharraf consolidated his position with the new commanders backing him fully on the new policy on Afghanistan. The shift in Pakistan's Afghan policy and the decision to support the United States brought minor economic and political benefits to General Musharraf's regime. From a pariah state, Pakistan became the center of focus of the international community. Never before had so many head of states traveled to Pakistan as they did in the few weeks after September 11. Pakistan was, once more, the USA's strategic partner.

According to senior American sources, the US-led coalition could not have achieved its swift success in Afghanistan without the ISI's intelligence support. The agency, which had been deeply involved with the Taliban movement from its inception, guided the American forces in the bombing and massacre of the Taliban, its brainchild. For this treachery Musharraf's junta extracted paltry economic aid and concessions from the USA and other Western countries. Pakistan sold its honor for a $1 billion loan write-off and $600 million in budgetary support and debt rescheduling. Pakistan was sold for $1.6 billion. Musharraf sold the heritage of each Pakistani man, woman, and child for $US10 per head, equivalent to five hundred Pakistani rupees.

Munafiqeen in Pakistan assisted a *kafir* power to occupy two sovereign Muslim countries, Afghanistan and Iraq. They allowed 260,000 Afghans and Iraqis to be blown to bits and hundreds of thousands of civilians to be maimed. Eighty percent of the population lost their jobs. The countries were decimated. Their infrastructure had been blown into stone age, and the desert and the mountains had been poisoned with radioactive waste from spent ammunition for thousands of years to come.

Yet this is not the end. And yet to come is the invasion of Iran, Libya, and Syria. Do the Saudis, Pakistanis, and the Egyptians feel that they will be spared of this fate, when the *kafireen* will decide to go for them?

Carefully Planned *Yahudi-Salibi-Munafiq* Intelligence Operation

The 9/11 attacks on New York and Washington were carefully planned intelligence operations. The 9/11 terrorists did not act on their own volition. The suicide hijackers were instruments of a carefully planned international intelligence operation. The evidence confirmed that al-Qaeda was the brainchild of the CIA and supported by Pakistan's military intelligence, the Inter-Services Intelligence. And the ISI, in turn, was an arm of the CIA in South Asia and owed its existence to the CIA. The ISI is the foreign flag of the CIA.

The spontaneity of the discovery of the culprits and the instant declaration of war against the Taliban and al-Qaeda is a play written long time ago by the authors of the new American century in which the actors recited the long-memorized lines. The prologue was the act in which the Twin Towers exploded in a haze of smoke and dust, a real smoke screen of deception and lies foreshadowing what was yet to come.

The ISI and the CIA began planning the massacre of the Twin Towers in April 2000. Such a gigantic explosive event was meant to be shown live on every television screen around the world to arouse sympathy for America as the victim and repulsion against the perpetrators of the ghastly event. It was the opening scene of America's war against the world.

The evidence showed an intense collusion and collaboration between the president of Pakistan and his top intelligence staff and the senior American officials, the overseers of US intelligence services from the House and the Senate of the United States, and the director of the CIA. And Mahmood Ahmed traveled to the United States for the final fine-tuning of the planned operation between his men and the US side. There is little doubt that the 9/11 episode was a well-orchestrated, well-planned, and technically high-precision job undertaken by skilled people in collaboration with those within the aviation authority, the air force, the FBI, the immigration services, and a centralized secret group of planners with international intelligence connections with the CIA, ISI, and others. And finally, the perpetrators sat down all together to watch the results of their handiwork in a top secret room on the fourth floor of the US Capitol. Mahmood's presence in Washington was to ensure that the Pakistani intelligence chief delivered all that he had promised and did not crawl out of his part of the bargain.

In this conspiracy of the circle of evil, over three thousand innocent men and women lost their lives. And it was just the opening shot in a long war against humanity.

> If anyone slew a person - unless it be for murder or for spreading mischief in the land - it would be as if he slew the whole people: and if anyone saved a life, it would be as if he saved the life of the whole people. (Al-Ma'idah 5:32, Koran)

> Take not life, which Allah hath made sacred, except by the way of justice or law: This He commands you, that you may learn wisdom. (Al-An'am 6:151–53, Koran)

The covenant of Muhammad written in Medina is the first constitution of Dar es Salaam. The covenant is a brief summary of the covenant of the Koran underlining the fundamental obligations of the individual believers to their community in times of conflict.

The Muslims constitute one Ummah to the exclusion of all other men.

All believers shall rise as one man against anyone who seeks to commit injustice, aggression, crime, or spread mutual enmity amongst the Muslims even if such a person is their kin.

Just as the bond to Allah is indivisible, all the believers shall stand behind the commitment of the least of them. All believers are bonded one to another to the exclusion of other men.

The believers shall leave none of their members in destitution without giving him in kindness that he needs by the way of his liberty.

This Pax Islamica is one and indivisible. No believer shall enter a separate peace without all other believers whenever there is fighting in the cause of God, but will do so only on the basis of equality and justice to all others.

In every expedition for the cause of God we undertake, all parties to the covenant shall fight shoulder to shoulder as one man.

All believers shall avenge the blood of one another when any one falls fighting in the cause of God. No believer shall slay a believer in retaliation for an unbeliever, nor shall he assist an unbeliever against a believer. Whoever is convicted of killing a believer deliberatively but without righteous cause shall be liable to the relatives of the

> killed. Until the latter are satisfied, the killer shall be subject to retaliation by each believer. (The Covenant of Muhammad)

During the last two hundred years, Muslims have lost in the battlefield in every conflict against the West; and in doing so, they have been subjected to humiliation and colonization lasting more than a century. Why did that happen? Muslim communities are beset with traitors and *Munafiqeen*. They look like Muslims, dress like Muslims, and pray like Muslims. They frequently go for *umrah* and hajj, yet for a price, they disobey every article of the covenants of Muhammad and of the Koran. For the price of a kingdom and a fiefdom, they betray their *din* and the *ummah*.

During the last three centuries, the Muslim states had had many external enemies whose motives were varied. All of them used disgruntled Muslim princes, noblemen, and tribes with the temptation of wealth and territory in fostering their aim. Once the conquering armies managed to gain a stranglehold on the Muslim territory, the traitors were discarded like rags once their usefulness was over. Yet in Muslim history, there had never been shortage of such traitors. In recent history, those who invited and aided the infidels in the occupation of the lands of Islam are the generals of the Pakistan Army, Northern Alliance of Afghanistan, Kurds of Iraq, the Shias of Iraq, the Saudi royal family, the Jordanian royals, and the sheikhs of Qatar, Kuwait, Bahrain, United Arab Emirates, and Oman. The result is the occupation of Afghanistan and Iraq, with the resulting loss of life of over 260,000 believers in Afghanistan and Iraq in the years 2002–2006. The loss of life of over 1 million Iraqis caused by the United Nations sanctions was also aided and abetted by the rulers of the Arabian Peninsula, Turkey, Jordan, and Iran. In fact, all the Islamic states combined are in no better position now to solve their problems of defense, disunity, infighting, poverty, illiteracy, and poor world image than they had in 1909, when Caliph Abdulhamid was deposed by their ilk. When the Koran says the following, it might as well have been addressed to the present rulers of Islam:

> When the Hypocrites come to thee, they say, "We bear witness that thou art indeed the Rasool of Allah". Yes, Allah knows that you are indeed His Rasool, and Allah bears witness that the Hypocrites are indeed liars.
>
> They have made their oaths a screen (for their hypocrisy), thus they obstruct (men) from the Path of Allah: truly evil are their deeds.
>
> That is because they believed, then they disbelieved: so, their hearts are sealed, therefore they understand not.
>
> When you look at them, their figures please you, and when they speak, and you listen to their words, they are as worthless as decayed pieces of wood propped up. They panic that every shout is against them. They are the enemies, beware of them. Let the curse of Allah be on them! How they are perverted! (Al-Munafiqun 63:1–8, Koran)

How apt and fitting are Allah's words with regard to rulers of Islam. You see them sitting on their grandiose gold-covered chairs with thick velvet cushions, dressed in silken robes with gold embroidery, attending meetings of the Arab League and the Organization of Islamic Cooperation. We say, "Wow, these are our princes of Islam, all of them meeting to seek ways and means of our deliverance from tyranny and oppression." After their hard and difficult deliberations, they speak out gently in soft tones of their anguish and concern about the state of the *ummah*. Their words are as worthless as a rotten, hollow, and crumbling log unable to support the truth. Their hypocrisy and lies have dogged the *ummah* year after year for the last three hundred years. They are insecure and panic stricken in case the believers seek justice and retribution. The Koran says,

> These hypocrites are the enemies, beware of them. Let the curse of Allah be on them! How they are perverted!
>
> When you look at them, their figures please you, and when they speak, and you listen to their words, they are as worthless as decayed pieces of wood propped up. They panic that every shout is against them. They are the enemies, beware of them. Let the curse of Allah be on them! How they are perverted!

We have seen in this chapter that there is a distinct circle of evil that does Satan's bidding. A circle of smart financiers, usually Jews, spins the web of the devil or sets the trap using the Christian armies to snare the Muslims. There are traitors among the Muslims, the *Munafiqeen*, who finally snap shut the trapdoor. Throughout the history of man, this story has been repeated over and over again. The trap can be set only with deception and guile.

On the eve of the Iraq War while the Jews in the Pentagon were planning and the Pentagon and the White House were carrying on the troop deployment, the whole world knew what was happening. The Arab kings, the third dimension of the evil, were doing the bidding of the *kafireen*; the only people being fooled were the Arab and Muslim people. Yet the people who drove the fuel tankers to the air bases, the Saudi and Jordanian armies, the diplomats, and the news reporters knew the game plan. If anyone was deceived by Bandar and Abdullah and their royal kin, they wanted to be deceived.

In this day and age of paper and pen and electronic communication, every believer has access to the guidance of Allah and their covenant with Him. In Islam, there are no professional kings or rulers, nor are there professional politicians. Today the whole world knows of the *fitnah*, corruption, dishonesty, *Fahasha*, treachery, and disobedience to the covenant of Allah by the Muslim ruling classes and politicians.

> The professional kings and rulers of Islam cannot rule unless the Believers want to be ruled by them. The *Munafiqeen* and the *Fahishah* cannot be the guardians of *Beit el Allah* and the guardians of the rites of Hajj unless the Muslims allow them. If 'Muslims' follow the lead of the Munafiqeen, disobey the Covenant, and do evil they themselves become tainted by the same evil. Every Believer is reminded by his Covenant to invite others to all that is good and right and forbid what is wrong.

> Let there arise out of you a band of people inviting to all that is good, enjoining what is right, and forbidding what is wrong: they are the ones to attain happiness. (Ali 'Imran 3:103–5, Koran)

The Koranic principle of enjoining good and forbidding what is evil is supportive of the moral autonomy of the individual. This principle authorizes the individual to act according to his or her best judgment in situations in which his or her intervention will advance a good purpose. The following saying of the blessed prophet supports individual action by a believer:

> If any one of you sees an evil, let him change it by his hand, and if he is unable to do that, let him change by his words, and if he is still unable to do that let him denounce it in his heart, but this is the weakest form of belief.

This principle assigns to the individual an active role in the community in which he or she lives. *The Koran annunciated the principle of free speech fourteen hundred years ago.* Believing men and women are reminded that they are the best of people, witnesses over other nations. Such a responsibility carries with it a moral burden of an exemplary conduct of one who submits to the divine truth and whose relationship with Allah is governed is by *taqwa*, the consciousness of humankind's responsibility toward its Creator. With that knowledge and faith, the believer is well equipped to approach others to enjoin what is right and forbid that is wrong. This moral autonomy of the individual, when bound together with the will of the community, formulates the doctrine of infallibility of the collective will of the *ummah*, which is the doctrinal basis of consensus.

When the blessed prophet died, he left behind the Koran, the *din*, and the Dar es Salaam. The blessed prophet wisely did not nominate a successor to his spiritual and worldly legacy. The believers all together inherited the Koran, the *din*, and the Dar es Salaam till the end of time. Allah addresses individual believers, both men and women, in His covenant, guiding them to the conduct of this spiritual and worldly legacy of the prophet. Every believer has the autonomy of their conduct of their spiritual and the earthly affairs. Humans have enough freedom to make their own choices: if they make the choice to do beautiful and wholesome deeds (*saalihaat*) motivated by faith (*iman*) and God-wariness (*taqwa*), they please Allah and bring harmony and wholesomeness to the world, resulting in peace, justice, mercy, compassion, honor, equity, well-being, freedom, and many other gifts through Allah's grace. Others choose to do evil and work corruption (*mufsidun*), destroying the right relationship among the creation, causing *fitnah*, hunger, disease, oppression, pollution, and other afflictions. In the universal order, corruption is the prerogative of the humans, and vicegerency gives the humans the freedom to work against the Creator and His creation. Allah measures out the good and the evil, the wholesome and the corrupt. Allah commands the humans to be righteous.

In the commandments of the covenant, Allah addresses individual men and women who in unity form a community, the *ummah*. Nevertheless, the emphasis of the guidance is to the individual believer for his and her own conduct. The concept of a covenant also symbolizes the relationship between humans, among Allah's creatures, and the rest of His creation. They all share one God, one set of guidance and commandments, the same submission and obedience to Him, and the same set of expectations in accordance with His promises. They all can therefore trust one another since they all have similar obligations and expectations. In view of the Koran, humans, communities, nations, and civilizations will continue to live in harmony and peace so long as they continue to fulfill Allah's covenant.

The Thirty-First Commandment of Allah

Forbidden to You Are Intoxicants and Gambling

Forbidden to you are intoxicants and gambling, dedication of stones and divination by arrows. These are an abomination and Satan's handiwork; they hinder you from prayer and remembrance of Allah, and place enmity and hatred amongst you. Abstain from them so that you may prosper. (Al-Ma'idah 5:90–91, Koran)

Today the world is bedeviled with evils that consume people and deprive them of self-control and motivation to lead a life of purpose and usefulness for themselves, their families, and their fellow humans. The urge for immediate gratification and relief from the stresses of daily life sends people scurrying to alcohol and drugs. In the Western world, a tenth of the adult population is addicted to alcohol or drugs, and another half are habitual users of intoxicants. One in every three families carries the burden of an addicted dear one. In the Muslim world, although alcohol is the lesser substance of abuse, marijuana, cocaine, hashish, and khat use is rampant. Tobacco, a substance of extreme addiction but of mild intoxicant properties, is the weed of popular use. A fifth of the world's workforce is underproductive and disabled physically and intellectually because of intoxication and addiction.

The covenant of the Koran fourteen hundred years ago forbade humans from the use of intoxicants in an effort to save mankind from self-destruction. All forms of gambling—including lotteries, slot machines, betting, card playing, and entertainment in casinos—are all forbidden. The covenant says,

> These are an abomination and Satan's handiwork; they hinder you from prayer and remembrance of Allah, and place enmity and hatred amongst you. Abstain from them so that you may prosper.

The Thirty-Second Commandment of Allah

Forbidden to You Are the Carrion, Blood, and Flesh of Swine and Any Other Food on Which Any Name Besides That of Allah Has Been Invoked

> Eat of good things provided to you by Allah and show your gratitude in worship of Him. Forbidden to you are the carrion, blood, and flesh of swine, and on any other food on which any name besides that of Allah has been invoked. If forced by necessity, without willful disobedience or transgressing due limits, one is guilt less. Allah is Most Forgiving and Most Merciful. (Al-Baqarah 2:172–73, Koran)

Allah, in His generosity and mercy, has permitted the believers to eat of all good things provided by Him. Expressly forbidden is to eat unclean food, which constitutes four things: carrion, blood, flesh of swine, and animals slaughtered in the name of any other than Allah. Fourteen hundred years ago, in the sparse and the hot desert of Arabia, the Koran established the first ever public health dietary regulations to prevent disease and epidemics. It was not till the eighteenth century when the rest of the world became aware of the diseases caused by bacteria and parasite in the food. More importantly, Allah makes the believer aware of the sanctity of life:

Take not life, which Allah hath made sacred,

Allah permits slaughter of animals for food in His name. The believer asks Allah for His mercy for himself and for the animal. With this comes the believer's awareness of his connection with Allah and with His creation, and this connection reminds the believer of his responsibility to Allah's creatures.

The Thirty-Third Commandment of Allah

Make Not Unlawful the Good Things That Allah Has Made Lawful to You

Make not unlawful the good things, which Allah hath made lawful to you. Commit no excess; Allah loves not people given to excess. Eat of things that Allah has provided for you, lawful and good. Be in taqwa of Allah, fear Allah in whom you believe. (Al-Ma'idah 5:87, Koran)

Allah has, in very explicit words, laid out in His covenant the acts forbidden to the believers:

1. *Shirk*: Join not anything in worship with him.
2. Mistreatment of parents: Be good to your parents.

3. Kill not your children (infanticide and abortion) on a plea of want, We provide sustenance for you and for them.
4. Come not near shameful deeds *fahasha*, whether open or secret.
5. Take not life, which Allah hath made sacred, except by way of justice and law.
6. Stealing: Come not near to the orphan's property, except to improve it, until he attains the age of full strength. The term 'orphan' may also include other helpless citizens who may be subject to oppression.
7. Cheating: And give measure and weight with justice; (do not cheat) no burden do We place on any soul, but that which it can bear. (Al-An'am 6:151–53, Koran)
8. Lying and falsification: whenever you speak, speak always the Truth, even if a near relative is concerned.
9. Violation of Allah's covenant: Fulfill the Covenant of Allah: thus, doth He command you, that you may remember. Verily, this is My Way leading straight: follow it; follow no other paths: they will scatter you about from His Path; thus, doth He command you, that you may be righteous. (Al An'am 6:151–53, Koran)
10. Intoxicants.
11. Gambling.
12. Dedication of stones.
13. Divination by arrows.

    These are an abomination and Satan's handiwork; they hinder you from prayer and remembrance of Allah, and place enmity and hatred amongst you. Abstain from them so that you may prosper. (Al-Ma'idah 5:90–91, Koran)
14. Carrion.
15. Blood.
16. Flesh of swine.
17. Any other food on which any name besides that of Allah has been invoked. (Al-Baqarah 2:172–73, Koran)

18. Usury (*riba*): Devour not usury double and multiplied: Be in taqwa of Allah, that you may prosper. (Ali 'Imran 3:130, Koran)
19. It is not lawful for you to take women against their will, nor should you treat them with harshness. On the contrary treat then with honor and kindness. (An-Nisa 4:19, Koran)
20. Any actions that infringe on the unity of the ***ummah*** and the nation of Islam: And hold fast, all together, by the Rope, which Allah stretches out for you, and be not divided among yourselves. You were enemies and He joined your hearts in love, so that by His Grace, you became brethren and a community. Thus, does Allah makes His Signs clear to you that you may be guided. Be not like those who are divided amongst themselves and fall into disputations after receiving clear signs: for them is a dreadful penalty.

These twenty actions have been forbidden (haram) by the covenant of Allah.

And Allah commands:

> Make not unlawful the good things, which Allah hath made lawful to you. Commit no excess; Allah loves not people given to excess. Eat of things that Allah has provided for you, lawful and good. Be in taqwa of Allah, fear Allah in whom you believe. (Al-Ma'idah 5:57, Koran)

Islamic scholar-jurists frequently quote various Hadith and proclaim many aspects of the daily life of pious and observant believers as haram. Such actions include listening to music, women's education, women's role in congregational prayers, and other mundane activities such as kite flying, tourism, pursuit of Western education, and use of modern technology.

Music: Music is part of the human soul. Every child, when happy, springs up to a melody and dance to the rhythm. When the blessed *nabi* received the revelation from Allah, at times, it appeared in the form of a tinkle or the chimes of a bell, and the words of the revelation blossomed in Blessed Muhammad's mind. The Koran, when recited in rhythmic Arabic, produces a heavenly song of Allah's revelation. Singing Allah's *dhikr* with or without instrument or music has a powerful and profound effect on the listener's soul, which reflects divine beauty. Listening to mere wind chimes makes one aware of the divine origin of the sounds of the wind, the rustle of trees, and the sound of running water in rivers, falls, and oceans. Allah bequeathed man the ability to produce the most beautiful sounds in His remembrance and to celebrate life and Allah's grace toward mankind.

Fulfillment of Allah's covenant bestows peace and tranquility to the soul and happiness and contentment on the believer. Islam is not a religion of doom, gloom, sorrow, and melancholia but a *din* of celebration of Allah's blessings and of performance of beautiful deeds for His sake. To show contentment, peace, harmony, happiness, and proper balance of things in life is to express *shukr*, gratitude to Allah for His mercy and grace. Man is blessed with the sense of sight, sound, small, taste, and touch to recognize the *haqq* of Allah, the absolute Truth, in Allah's signs. The sight perceives Allah's *nur*, the ears note the resonance of Allah's melody in the rustle of the wind and the birdsong, the tongue tastes the flavor of Allah's bounty, the nose smells the fragrance of Allah's garden, and the skin feels the touch of Allah's creation around us.

Allah does not deprive humans of His divine gift of harmony and song; on the contrary, He urges them to recite the Koran in slow, rhythmic tones, to celebrate the praises of Allah often, and to glorify Him in the morning and at night. It is Allah and His angels who also send their blessings on the believers so "He may lead the Believers out of the depths of darkness into light." Celebration of Allah's praises and glorifying Him means to rejoice and to be happy. The word *celebrate*, therefore, has the connotation of a happy occasion, which includes song and music.

Confinement of believing and devout women is not a mandate of Allah's covenant nor is covering women from head to toe. Acquiring knowledge and education is incumbent on every believer, man and woman. Muslim ulema frequently ignore Allah's admonition:

> Make not unlawful the good things, which Allah hath made lawful to you. Commit no excess; Allah loves not people given to excess. (Al-Ma'idah 5:57, Koran)

The Thirty-Fourth Commandment of Allah

When You Make a Transaction Involving Future Obligations, Write It Down in Presence of Witnesses

> When you make a transaction involving future obligations, write it down in presence of witnesses, or let a scribe write it down faithfully. Let the party incurring the liability dictate truthfully in the presence of two witnesses from among your own men and if two men are not available then a man and two women, so that if one of them errs then the other one, can remind him. Disregard not to put your contract in writing, whether it be small or large, it is more suitable in the eyes of Allah, more suitable as evidence, and more convenient to prevent doubts in the future amongst yourselves. (Al-Baqarah 2:282–83, Koran)

The Thirty-Fifth Commandment of Allah

Respect Other People's Privacy: Enter Not Houses Other Than Yours until You Have Asked Permission and Invoked Peace upon Those in Them

Enter not houses other than yours until you have asked permission and invoked peace upon those in them. If you find none in the house whom you seek enter not unless permission is granted. If you asked to leave go back, it is best for you that makes for greater purity for you. Allah knows all that you do. (An-Nur 24:27, Koran)

The four walls of every person's home are his circle of privacy, within the confines of which he or she has freedom from intrusion by outsiders, be it the neighbor or the state. The residents of the home are protected from physical intrusion or intrusion with electronic devices. This dwelling is the basic autonomous unit of the Islamic state that amalgamates with other such units to form a community. The communities, with some complexity, join other communities to form the state. What is important is that the residents of each dwelling have their seclusion protected by the mandate of the covenant of the Koran. Importantly, each one of the believers in this dwelling is an inheritor of the blessed *nabi's* legacy, the Koran, the *din*, and the Dar es Salaam. Each one, therefore, has a voice in the administration of the common affairs of the community.

The Thirty-Sixth Commandment of Allah

This Day I Have Perfected Your Religion for You

- We have made the (Qur'an) easy in your own tongue, that with it you may give glad tidings to the righteous, and warnings to people given to contention. Therein is proclaimed every wise decree, by command, from Our Presence, for We are ever sending Revelations, as a Mercy from your Lord. We have explained in detail in this Qur'an, for the benefit of mankind, every kind of similitude.

- This day have those who reject faith (kafaru) given up all hope of compromising your faith, fear them not but only fear Me. This day have I perfected your religion for you, bestowed on you with My blessings, and decreed Islam as your religion. (Al-Ma'idah 5:3, Koran)

- Ha Mim. By the Book that makes matters lucid; We revealed it during the blessed night, verily We are always warning against Evil. Therein is proclaimed every wise decree, by command, from Our Presence, for We are ever sending revelations, as a Mercy from your Lord: for He is the hearer and knower. The Lord of the heavens and the earth and all that is in between them, if you have an assured faith. There is no god but He: it is He Who gives life and death, the Lord and Cherisher, your Lord and Lord of your forefathers. (Ad-Dukhan 44:1-8, Koran)

- So, have We made the (Qur'an) easy in your own tongue, that with it you may give glad tidings to the righteous, and warnings to people given to contention. But how many (countless) generations before them have We destroyed? Canst thou find a single one of them (now) or hear (so much as) a whisper of them? (Taha 19:97, Koran)

- We have explained in detail in this Qur'an, for the benefit of mankind, every kind of similitude: but man is, in most things, contentious. And what is there to keep back men from believing, now that guidance has come to them, nor from praying for forgiveness from their Lord, but that (they ask that) the ways of the ancients be repeated with them,

> or the Wrath be brought to them face to face? (Al-Kahf 18:54–55, Koran)

The blessed *nabi* of Allah, Muhammad, proclaimed to the world on the mount of Arafat Allah's *wahiy* (message) on the last Friday, the ninth day of *Zul-hajj* in the tenth year of hijra (631 CE), "*This day have I perfected your religion for you.*"

> This day have those who reject faith (kafaru) given up all hope of compromising your faith, fear them not but only fear Me. This day have I perfected your religion for you, bestowed on you with My blessings, and decreed Islam as your religion. (Al-Ma'idah 5:3, Koran)

On that day, the *din* of Islam was complete, and all man-made innovations after that were just novelties; anyone indulging in such innovations was making a sport of his religion. The people, men and women, who obey and fulfill their covenant with Allah are the believers, the *muttaqeen*. They are the believers of Allah, and the Koran is revealed to the world through the prophethood of Blessed Muhammad. The believers follow the Koran and Allah's covenant; for their *din*, Allah only suffices them. They are not Shias or Sunnis, nor do they belong to any other sect. They are believers of Allah.

The Koran establishes a universal order based on the divinely ordained values of life. Were every human to fulfill the covenant of the Koran, the world shall be at peace forever, and justice would prevail. By following the *Hadith collections* of the third-century hijra, *Muslims* have relegated their faith from a divinely ordained order to a human set of values, misleading themselves and deviating others from Allah's path. According to the Koran, *iman* is not just belief but also, in fact, knowledge. *Iman* is the conviction that is based on reason and knowledge. The Koran does not recognize belief that involves blind acceptance. Islam does include acceptance of certain things that cannot be explained by perception through human senses. Our reason and thinking will compel us to recognize the existence of such things. *Iman*, according to the Koran, signifies conviction based on full mental acceptance and intellectual satisfaction. *Iman* gives a person inner contentment, a feeling of *amn* (same common root). Thus, *iman* means to believe in something and to testify to its truthfulness, to have confidence in that belief, and to bow down in obedience.

There are five fundamental facts stated in the Koran that a believer must accept. *Iman* in

1. Allah,
2. the law of *mukafat* and the afterlife,
3. angels, (*malaika*),
4. the revelations,
5. the *rasuls*.

Belief in Allah means not only to profess obedience to Him and His Covenant but also to show it in one's actions and to be always in *taqwa* of Allah. Belief in the law of *mukafat* means to have conviction that every action of the human has an inescapable consequence of reward or retribution. Angels are not the winged creatures depicted in children's literature. They are heavenly forces that carry out laws of Allah governing the universe. They bow to Allah since they follow his orders. They also bow to humans because we are able to study, understand, and manipulate the laws of nature for the benefit of mankind. Belief in revelations and *rasuls* implies that human intellect alone cannot safely reach the final destination without divine guidance in the form of *wahiy*, revelation, delivered by the *rasuls* to mankind. This guidance is to the whole humankind sent through many *rasuls*.

The Muslim tradition began with *Ibrahim*, our father (Abraham of the Bible). The believers have a belief system and a course of action to witness over and spread the message to mankind that began with *Ibrahim* and was completed with *Muhammad.* Whereas the message of *wahiy* is divine and universal for all human races, the message of Hadith collections of the third century hijra is human and transcends only parts of the Arabian Peninsula, Iran, and the Indian subcontinent, mainly embraced by unlettered populations and Hadith scholars.

The Thirty-Seventh Commandment of Allah

After His Submission to the Will of Allah, the Believer Must Fulfill the Covenant He Has Made with Allah; with This Compact of Submission, the Believer Is Obligated to Perform Wholesome and Beautiful Deeds

The covenant of the Koran is a total belief system of an individual based upon total submersion of one's personality with Allah with total awareness and *taqwa* of Him at all times through observance of the thirty-seven commandments of Allah's covenant. This communion is not only with Allah but also, through Him, with other humans and Allah's creation, both alive and inanimate. The phrase *amilu al saalihaat* (to do good, to perform wholesome deeds) refers to those who persist in striving to set things right, who restore harmony, peace, and balance. Other acts of good works recognized in the covenant of the Koran are to show compassion, to be merciful and forgive others, to be just, to protect the weak, to defend the oppressed, to be generous and charitable, to be truthful and to seek knowledge and wisdom, to be kind, to be peaceful, to love others, and to perform beautiful deeds.

On those who believe and do good, will
[Allah] Most Gracious bestow love,

There are fifty such verses in the Koran that remind the believers of the rewards of righteous deeds. The following are some of the *ayahs* in the Koran mentioning the righteous deeds.

Alladhina aaminu wa 'amilu al saalihaat.[39]

But those who believe and work righteousness. They are Companions of the Garden: therein shall they abide (forever). (Al-Baqarah 2:82, Koran)

Those who believe, do deeds of righteousness, and establish regular prayers and regular charity, will have their reward with their Lord: on them shall be no fear, nor shall they grieve. (Al-Baqarah 2:277, Koran)

As to those who believe and work righteousness, Allah will pay them in full their reward; but Allah loves not those who do wrong (zalimeen). (Ali 'Imran 3:57, Koran)

But those who believe and do deeds of righteousness, We shall soon admit to Gardens, with rivers flowing beneath, their eternal home, and therein shall they have companions pure and holy: We shall admit them to shades, cool and ever deepening. (An-Nisa 4:57, Koran)

But those who believe and do deeds of righteousness, We shall soon admit them to Gardens - with rivers flowing beneath - to dwell therein forever. Allah's promise is the truth, and whose word can be truer than Allah's? (An-Nisa 4:122, Koran)

---

[39] Koran 2:25; 2:82, 277; 4:57, 122; 5:5; 7:42; 10:9; 11:23; 13:29; 14:23; 18:2, 88, 107; 19:60, 96; 20:75, 82, 112; 21:94; 22:14; 23:50, 56; 24:55; 25:70–71; 26:67; 28:80; 29:7, 9, 58; 30:15, 45; 31:8; 32:19; 34:4, 37; 38:24; 41:8; 42:22–23, 26; 45:21, 30; 47:2, 12; 48:29; 64:9; 65:11; 84:25; 85:11; 95:6; 98:7; 103:3.

If any do deeds of righteousness, - be they male or female - and have faith, they will enter Heaven, and not the least injustice will be done to them. (An-Nisa 4:124, Koran)

But to those who believe and do deeds of righteousness, He will give their due rewards, and more, out of His bounty: but those who are disdainful and arrogant, He will not punish with a grievous penalty; nor will they find, besides Allah, any to protect or help them. (An-Nisa 4:173, Koran)

To those who believe and do deeds of righteousness hath Allah promised forgiveness and a great reward. (Al-Ma'idah 5:9, Koran)

On those who believe and do deeds of righteousness there is no blame for what they ate (in the past), when they guard themselves from evil, and believe, and do deeds of righteousness - (or) again, guard themselves from evil and believe - (or) again, guard themselves from evil and do good. For Allah loves those who do good. (Al-Ma'idah 5:93, Koran)

But those who believe and work righteousness - no burden do We place on any soul, but that which it can bear - they will be Companions of the Garden, therein to dwell (forever). (Al-A'raf 7:42, Koran)

To Him will be your return, of all of you. The promise of Allah is true and sure. It is He Who began the Creation, and its cycle, that He may reward with justice those who believe and work righteousness; but those who reject Him will have draughts of boiling fluids, and a Penalty grievous, because they did reject Him. (Yunus 10:4, Koran)

Those who believe, and work righteousness, their Lord will guide them because of their Faith: beneath them will flow rivers in Gardens of Bliss. (Yunus 10:9, Koran)

But those who believe and work righteousness, and humble themselves before their Lord, they will be Companions of the Garden, to dwell therein forever! (Hud 11:23, Koran)

For those who believe, and work righteousness is every blessedness, and a beautiful place of (final) return. (Ar-Ra'd 13:29, Koran)

Islam and Sharia (Islamic law) are concerned with everyday activities of the believer, differentiating right from wrong and guiding the individual along the correct path. *Islam* defines sin as "breaking the commandments of Allah" and *good works* as "following Allah's instructions and following the blessed *nabi's* conduct."

Iman adds a dimension to the understanding of human activity in that every human action in daily life reaches back into the divine reality that everything in the universe is governed by tawhid, yet Allah has granted humans a freedom of choice, which can upset the balance in the creation, the balance of justice, and the balance of atmospheric elements and of environmental pollution and lead to the destruction of animal species, populations, cities, and agriculture through human actions. It tells people why they should be Allah's servants and explains which path they should follow to become His vicegerents. It makes clear that human activity is deeply rooted in the Real, and this has everlasting repercussions in this world and in the hereafter.

Ihsan adds to *islam* and *iman* a focus on people's intention to perform good and wholesome deeds on the basis of awareness of Allah's presence in all things. According to the Koran, doing wholesome deeds, along with faith, will yield paradise.

Whoso does wholesome deeds, be it male or female,
and has faith, shall enter the garden, therein provided
for without reckoning. (Ghafir 40:40, Koran)

Those who have faith and do wholesome deeds, them we shall admit
to gardens through which rivers flow. (An-Nisa 4:57, 122, Koran)

Another fifty verses in the Koran mention that people who perform beautiful deeds and have faith shall inherit the garden. The Koran uses the word *saalihaat* for beautiful and wholesome deeds and the word *salihun* for wholesome people. The root word for both *saalihaat* and *salihun* means "to be beautiful, sound, wholesome, right, proper, and good." Another word used in the Koran about thirty times is *islah*, which means "establishing wholesomeness." In modern times, the word *islah* has been used to mean "reform." The word *sulh* is used in the Koran once to mean "peace and harmony in family relationships." In modern times, the word *sulh* has come to mean "peace in the political sense." While the Koran calls the wholesome people as *salihun*, it employs the opposite, *fasid*, for the corrupt, ruined, evil, and wrong. The wholesome are the ones who live in harmony with the Real (*Haqq*) and establish wholesomeness through their words and deeds throughout the world. In contrast, the corrupt (*mufsidun*) destroy the proper balance and relationship with Allah and His creation. *Fasid* means "corrupt, evil, and wrong."

Allah measures out good and evil, the wholesome and the corrupt. Humans have enough freedom to make their own choices; if they make the choice to do beautiful and wholesome deeds (*saalihaat*) motivated by faith (*iman*) and god-wariness (*taqwa*), they please Allah and bring harmony and wholesomeness to the world, resulting in peace, justice, mercy, compassion, honor, equity, well-being, freedom, and many other gifts through Allah's grace. Others choose to do evil and work with corruption (*mufsidun*), destroying the right relationship among the creation, causing hunger, disease, oppression, pollution, and other afflictions. In the universal order, corruption is the prerogative of humans, and vicegerency gives humans the freedom to work against the Creator and His creation. Only misapplied trust can explain how moral evil can appear in the world. Modern technology; scientific advancement; nuclear, chemical, and biological weapons of mass destruction; genetic engineering of plants, animals, and humans; and exploitation of nonrenewable resources of the earth has made self-destruction of the human race and all life on the planet a distinct and imminent possibility.

> Corruption has appeared on the land and in the sea because what people's hands have earned, so that He may let them taste some of their deeds, in order that they may turn back from their evils. (Ar-Rum 30:41, Koran)

When humans choose wrong and corrupt actions, they displease Allah. Allah loves those who do what is beautiful, not those who do what is ugly:

> When he turns his back, he hurries about the earth to work corruption there and destroy the tillage and the stock. Allah loves not corruption. (Al-Baqarah 2:205).

Allah loves doing what is beautiful, and because of His love for those who do the beautiful, He brings them near to Himself, and His nearness is called Allah's mercy:

> Work not corruption in this world after it has made wholesome and call upon Allah in fear and hope. Surely the mercy of Allah is near to those who do what is beautiful. (Al-A'raf 7:56, Koran)

The covenant of the Koran presents us with the scope of the freedom of choice that humans have in doing that is wholesome and beautiful or what is corrupt and ugly and in the human role among the creation that distinguishes right activity, right thought, and right intention from their opposites. It reminds us of how the scales of Allah's justice—the two hands of Allah, His mercy and His wrath—are reflected in the human domain, where people have been appointed Allah's vicegerents. Deeds of goodness and wholesomeness are associated with mercy, paradise, and the beautiful. Evil and corruption is rewarded with wrath, hell, and the ugly.

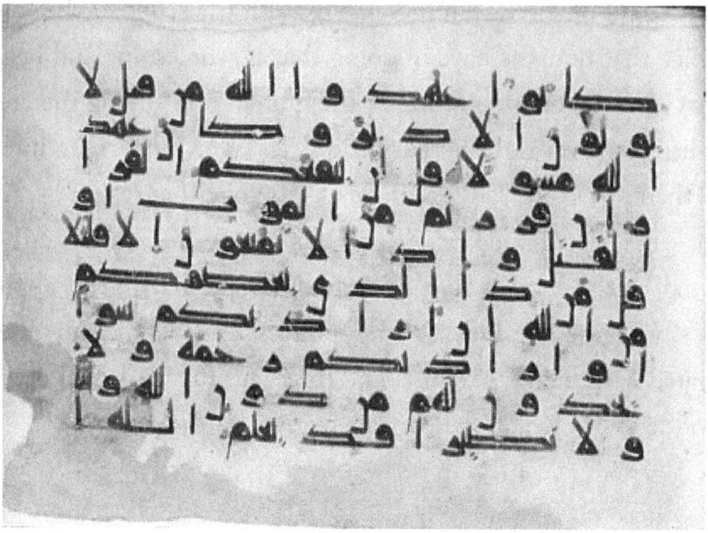

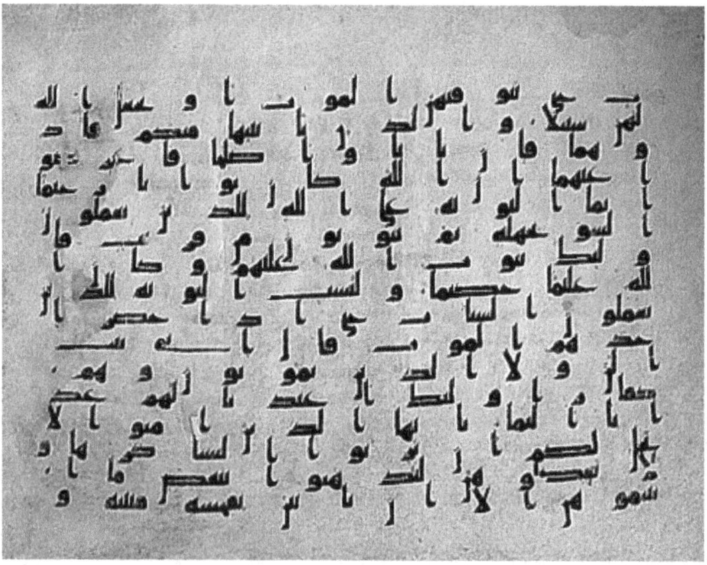

Kufic manuscripts from second century AH. These two manuscripts on parchment are written in the Kufic script called *al-mishaq al-mujud*. The writing is in black ink with red used for short vowels. The *fatha* is indicated by a superscript dot to the right of the letter, and two perpendicular dots to indicate *fatha tanwin*. A dot under the letter indicates *kasrah* with two dots for *kasrah tanwin*. Located in the King Faisal Center for Research and Islamic Studies.

Chapter Seven

The New Islamic Century

The new Islamic century, the fifteenth-century hijra, began on November 19, 1979. It will end in November 2076. The believers woke up from their deep despair at the turn of the fourteenth-century hijra, conscious of their responsibilities to Allah, to their community, and to Allah's creation. The nineteenth and twentieth centuries of the Common Era were disastrous for Islam and its believers. For the disasters of the last two hundred years, Muslims universally have continued to blame everyone except themselves for their situation they are in.

Muslims are the authors of their own demise. By deposing the sultan and the caliph Abdulhamid on the twenty-seventh of April 1909, the Young Turks—a party of Westernized Turks, Jews, and Christians indoctrinated in Western political thought and Masonic intrigue—effectively put an end to the Islamic sovereignty over Muslim lands after a continuous tradition of thirteen hundred years. Ottoman sultans were not the perfect rulers; according to the covenant of the Koran, their station did represent the unity of the *ummah*, and they were a beacon of light to which the Muslims of India, Indonesia, and Africa looked at in their own fight for freedom. Sultan-Caliph Abdulhamid—a linguist, poet, astute statesman, devout Muslim, and patriot—endeavored to transform the Ottoman Empire into a modern industrial, commercial, and militarily strong nation. He succeeded in paying off the country's debts, embarked on the modernization of the educational system, and modernized the military. Another fifty years of peace and tranquility would have transformed the Muslim nation. That was not to be. Alas, what he could not combat was the coalition of traitors within and the enemies without. The appearance of four people in his office on the twenty-seventh of April 1909—an Arab, a Turk, a Jew, and a Christian—who came to remove him from power was a premonition of the dismemberment of the Islamic world with the treachery of Arabs and Turks in collusion with Jews and Christians. The caliphate effectively came to an end with the fall of Abdulhamid.

The handover of the of Islamic sovereignty and the socioeconomic future of the Middle East to the capitalistic European civilization and Euro-Christianity for the next one hundred years was presided over by two families. One family carried out its treason under the guise of its descent from the blessed *nabi*. The second one harvested the plunder of oil wealth under the banner of the Koran and *shahadah*.

Such people caused the division and subjugation of Islam. They are motivated by their cravings for power and hunger for wealth. The believers have been warned of them. The Koran speaks of them thus:

> They have made their oaths a screen for their misdeeds, thus they obstruct men from the Path of Allah: truly evil are their deeds. That is because they believed, then they rejected Faith: so a seal was set on their hearts: therefore they understand not. When you look at them, their exteriors please thee; and when they speak, you listen to their words. They are as worthless as rotten pieces of timber propped up, unable to stand on their own. They think that every cry is against them. They are the enemies; so beware of them. The curse of Allah be on them! How are they deluded away from the Truth! (Munafiqun 63:4)

It is not only the Koran that makes the believers aware of the tricks of such people. The blessed *nabi* Jesus spoke of them in these terms:

> Jesus said, "Beware of false prophets, which come to you in sheep's clothing, but inwardly they are ravenous. You shall know them by their fruits. Do men gather grapes of thorns, or figs of

thistles? Even so every good tree brings forth good fruit, but a corrupt tree brings forth evil fruit. "A good tree cannot bring forth evil fruit; neither can a corrupt tree bring forth good fruit." Every tree that brings forth bad fruit is hewn down and cast into the fire. Therefore, by their fruits shall you know them."

The Dar es Salaam

Pax Islamica

But Allah does call.

To the Abode of Peace: Dar es Salaam

He does guide whom He pleases.

To a way that is straight. (Yunus 10:25, Koran)

Dar es Salaam is the abode of peace that Allah has promised to His righteous servants who follow His straight path. Dar es Salaam is the home of the *ummah*, which extends in the east from the Muslim populations of the Philippines to the Atlantic coast of Africa; and in the north, its domains extend from the Muslim population of Russia to those of Indonesia to the south. Every country with a majority of Muslims constitutes the geographic domain of Islam, the abode of peace. Every believer within and outside the domain of Islam has the right to the citizenship of the Dar es Salaam and shall enjoy all the benefits and the obligations that go with such citizenship. Every home and place of worship of believers everywhere on the earth constitute a piece of the Dar es Salaam. There is neither a border nor frontiers in the Dar es Salaam.

Through the fulfillment of the covenant of Allah, the *ummah* is now ready to roll over artificial borders and barriers dividing the

Dar es Salaam, to assume its *executive sovereignty* over the land of Islam, and to establish the governance of the *ummah* in accord with the covenant of Allah through justice, consultation, and consensus of the community. The greatest miracle of Islam is the revelation and preservation of the divine word, the Koran. The next greatest miracle is survival and continuing expansion of the *ummah* through centuries of tyrannical and turbulent sultanic and colonial rule. In spite of the alien systems of governments of sultans and dictators founded on self-aggrandizement and personal power, the common people and the community of Islam have continued to receive nurturing and spiritual enlightenment through love of Allah and His blessed *nabi*. Holy men, sages, Sufis, and other humble religious teachers have continued to nurture the love of Allah in the heart of the people. They have sought to teach unity, *taqwa*, and knowledge of Allah in humility and sincerity.

Insignificant raindrops fall on parched land singly and disappear forever; however, same raindrops coalesce in strength to form little streams and then little rivulets and join together to become mighty rivers flowing farther, dropping into powerful and majestic waterfalls, yet again joining other rivers, lakes, and more hill torrents to end up in mighty oceans ever increasing in size, in length, in depth, and in power, at all times obedient to the will of Allah. An insignificant human without faith is like a drop of water on parched land. Yet the same human, a believer strengthened by his covenant with Allah, joins others with the covenant to form a little community that, in communion with Allah and in unity, becomes the *ummah* of believers around the world, a powerful united people witnessing over other nations, with Allah and His *nabi* witnessing over them. At the turn of the twenty-first century, there are more believers than ever in the history of mankind. These believers of Allah are in Islam and in other religions. It is the obligation of every Muslim to commune with every believer of Allah in the brotherhood of the people of *haqq*.

The house of Islam, the Dar es Salaam, is spread over territories of the *ummah* whose boundaries were demarcated by the un-Koranic conquering sultans and the colonial West in their sweep of plunder of the Muslim world. In the land of the believers, these artificial borders do not exist. They are the figment of the imagination of the un-Koranic rulers, their armies, and their intelligence services.

The *ummah* is one community in one land, the abode of peace, the Dar es Salaam, ordained by Allah. For the believer, there are no borders between Muslim communities. Our land is one land: Afghanistan, Albania, Algeria, Bahrain, Bangladesh, Benin, Bosnia, Brunei, Burkina Faso, Cameroon, Chad, Chechnya, Comoros, Djibouti, Egypt, Ethiopia, East Turkistan, Gabon, Gambia, Guinea, Guinea-Bissau, Guyana, Indonesia, Iran, Ivory Coast, Iraq, Jordan, Kashmir, Kazakhstan, Kosovo, Kuwait, Kyrgyzstan, Lebanon, Libya, Malaysia, Maldives, Mali, Mauritania, Morocco, Mindanao, Mozambique, Niger, Nigeria, Oman, Pakistan, Palestine, Qatar, Saudi Arabia, Senegal, Sierra Leone, Somalia, Sudan, Suriname, Syria, Tajikistan, Tanzania, Togo, Tunisia, Turkey, Turkmenistan, United Arab Emirates, Uzbekistan, and Yemen.

Muslim homes and mosques in Russia, China, India, Kenya, Serbia, Macedonia, and the rest of the world constitute little patches of the Dar es Salaam, where the laws of Allah are supreme. Any Muslim everywhere around the world represents the *ummah*. Every believer, through his covenant with Allah, is bound to the Dar es Salaam and to his community.

In the tempest and turmoil of the last three hundred years, the believers were swept away and blown into many nations and communities lost to one another in many oasis separated by vast deserts. Individually, the believers prospered and grew into vast families. Each nation had strengths that they could not pass on to others. The winds of adversity had obscured the pathways and connections of one nation to the other with the desert sand, while others in frailty and weakness were unable to seek help. Now the believers—fortified with the *nur*, knowledge, and signs of Allah—have overcome the adversity of separation and disconnection.

Allah's Guidance and Commandments to the *Ummah*: The covenant of Allah is enshrined in the Koran. Every believer, upon his submission to Allah, makes a compact with Allah to obey His covenant. The covenant of the blessed *rasul* of Allah (Covenant of Yathrib) affirms the covenant of Allah and pronounces the criterion of conduct of the *ummah* and that of the Islamic state, the Dar es Salaam. These two covenants form just basis of the code of conduct of each believer and their community. Together, they constitute the constitution of the Islamic state not to be tampered with by ordinary humans, whether they come under the guise of kings, sultans, sheikhs, presidents, generals, or ordinary citizens.

The Covenant of Allah: The Covenant of the Koran

- Verily those who pledge their allegiance unto you, (O Muhammad) swear it unto none but Allah; the Hand of Allah is over their hands. Thereafter whosoever breaks his Covenant does so to the harm of his own soul, and whosoever fulfils his Covenant with Allah, Allah will grant him an immense Reward. (Al-Fath 48:10, Koran)
- He is Allah, there is no Deity but He, Knower of the hidden and the manifest. He is the Rahman (the Most Gracious), the Rahim, (Most Merciful.)
- He is Allah; there is no Deity but He,

  The Sovereign, the Pure and the Hallowed,

Serene and Perfect,

The Custodian of Faith, the Protector, the Almighty,

The Irresistible, the Supreme,

Glory be to Allah; He is above all they associate with Him.

He is Allah, the Creator, the Sculptor, the Adorner of color and form. To Him belong the Most Beautiful Names: whatever so is in the heavens and on earth, Praise and Glory Him; and He is the Almighty and All-Wise. (Al-Hashr 59:18–24, Koran)

- Allah. There is no god but He, the ever Living, the One Who sustains and protects all that exists. No slumber can seize Him or sleep.

  His are all things in the heavens and on earth. Who is there to intercede in His presence except as He permits?

  He knows what happens to His creatures in this world and in the hereafter. Nor do they know the scope of His knowledge except as He wills.

  His Throne extends over the heavens and the earth, and He feels no fatigue in guarding and protecting them.

  He is the Most High, Most Great. (Al-Baqarah 2:255, Koran)

- Say, Come I will recite what your Lord has prohibited you from: Join not anything in worship with Him.

  Be good to your parents: kill not your children because of poverty, We provide sustenance for you and for them.

  Come not near to shameful deeds (sins and illegal sexual activity) whether open or secret.

  Take not life, which Allah hath made sacred, except by the way of justice or law: This He commands you, that you may learn wisdom.

  And come not near the orphan's property, except to improve it, until he attains the age of full strength.

  And give full measure and full weight with justice. No burden We place on any soul but that which it can bear.

Whenever you give your word speak honestly even if a near relative is concerned.

And fulfill the Covenant of Allah. Thus, He commands you that you may remember.

Verily, this is My Way leading straight: follow it: follow not (other) paths for they will separate you from His path. This He commands you that you may remember. (Al-An'am 6:151–53, Koran)

- Believe in Allah, His Rasool, and the Book that He has sent to His Rasool and the Scriptures that He sent to those before him. Any who deny Allah, His angels, His Books, His Rasools, and the Day of Judgment has gone far far astray. (An-Nisa 4:136, Koran)
- Bow down, prostrate yourself and serve your Lord, and do wholesome deeds that you may prosper. Perform Jihad, strive to your utmost in Allah's cause as striving (jihad) is His due. He has chosen you and Allah has imposed no hardship in your endeavor to His cause. You are the inheritors of the faith of your father Abraham. It is He who has named you Muslims of the times before and now, so that Allah's Rasool may be an example to you and that you are an example to mankind. (Al-Hajj 22:77–78, Koran)

But Allah doth call to the Abode of Peace.

Dar es Salaam

He doth guide whom He pleased to a Way that is straight.

To those who do right and in abundance neither darkness nor shame shall cover their faces!

They are the heirs of Paradise, they will abide therein forever. (Yunus 10:25, Koran)

It is not righteousness that you turn your faces towards East or West; but it is righteousness to believe in Allah and the Last Day, and the Angels, and the Book, and the Rasools; to spend of your substance, out of love for Him, for your kin, for orphans, for the needy, for the wayfarer, for those who ask, and for the ransom of slaves;

to be steadfast in prayer, and practice regular charity, to fulfill the Covenant which you have made; and to be firm and patient, in pain (or suffering) and adversity, and throughout all periods of panic. Such are the people of truth, the God-fearing. (Al-Baqarah 2:177, Koran)

Verily fellowship of yours is a single brotherhood, and I am your Lord and Cherisher: therefore, serve Me (and no other). (Al-Anbiya 21:92, Koran)

And hold fast, all together by the rope which Allah (stretches out for you).

And be not divided amongst yourselves.

And remember with gratitude Allah's favor on you:

For you were enemies and He joined your hearts in love,

So that by His grace, you became brethren and a community.

Let there arise out of you a band of people enjoining what is right and forbidding what is wrong. They are the ones to attain felicity.

Be not like those who are divided amongst themselves,

And fall into disputations after receiving clear signs.

For them is a dreadful penalty. (Ali 'Imran 3:103–5, Koran)

You are the best of the peoples evolved for mankind,

Enjoining what is right, forbidding what is wrong, and believing in Allah. (Ali 'Imran 3:110, Koran)

Thus, have We made of you an Ummah of the center,

That you might be witness over other nations,

And the Rasool a witness over yourselves.

And We appointed the Qibla.

To which thou wast used,

Only to test those who followed.

The Rasool from those

Who would turn their heels. (Al-Baqarah 2:143, Koran)

Whoever submits his whole self to Allah, and is a doer of good,

Has grasped indeed the most trustworthy handhold,

And with Allah rests the end and decision of [all] affairs. (Luqman 31:22, Koran)

Take not the Jews and the Christians for your friends and protectors,

They are but friends and the protectors to each other.

And he amongst you that turns to them is of them.

Verily Allah does not guide the people who are unjust and evil. (Al Ma'idah 5:51, Koran)

Oh, you who believe!

Take not for friends and protectors those who take your religion for a mockery or sport,

Whether among those who received the scripture before you, or among those who reject faith. (Al-Ma'idah 5:57, Koran)

O you who believe!

Take not infidels (kafireen) for Awliya (friends and protectors) in place of believers. Would you offer Allah a clear warrant against yourselves? (An-Nisa 4:144, Koran)

O you who believe! Take not for friends and protectors (Awliya those who take your religion for mockery, whether from amongst people of the book or from amongst the kafireen. Be in taqwa of Allah, fear Allah if you have faith indeed. (Al-Ma'idah 5:57, Koran)

Your (real) friends are Allah, His Rasool and the Fellowship of Believers, those who

Establish regular prayers and regular Charity and they bow down humbly in worship.

As to those who turn for friendship to Allah, His Rasool and the fellowship of Believers, it is

the Fellowship of Allah that must certainly triumph. (Al-Ma'idah 5:55-56, Koran)

Oh, you who believe obey Allah and obey the Rasool,

And those charged with authority among you. If you differ in any thing

among yourselves, refer it to Allah and His Rasool if you do believe in Allah, and the last Day.

That is the best, and the most suitable for the final determination. (An-Nur 4:59, Koran)

And the firmament has He raised high,

And He has setup the balance of Justice, in order that you may not transgress due balance.

So, establish weight with justice and fall not short in the balance.

Of those We have created are people who direct others with truth and dispense justice therewith. (Al-A'raf 7:181, Koran)

Those who hearken to their Lord and establish regular prayer.

Who conduct their affairs by mutual consultation.

Who spend out what we bestow on them for sustenance.

And those who when an oppressive wrong is inflicted on them, are not intimidated but defend themselves. (Ash-Shura 42:38-39, Koran)

The recompense for an injury is an injury equal thereto (in degree): but if a person forgives and makes reconciliation, his reward is due from Allah: for (Allah) loves not those who do wrong. (Ash-Shura 42:42, Koran)

There is no compulsion in religion: Truth stands out clear from error,

Whoever rejects evil and believes in Allah hath grasped the most trustworthy Handhold, which never breaks. And Allah hears and knows all things. (Al-Baqarah 2:254–57, Koran

For men and women who surrender unto Allah,

For men and women who believe,

For men and women who are devout

For men and women who speak the truth,

For men and women who persevere in righteousness,

For men and women who are humble,

For men and women who are charitable,

For men and women who fast and deny them selves

For men and women who guard their chastity,

For men and women who remember Allah much,

For them Allah has forgiveness and a great reward.

For men and women who surrender unto Allah,

For men and women who believe,

For men and women who are devout

For men and women who speak the truth,

For men and women who persevere in righteousness

For men and women who are humble,

For men and women who are charitable,

For men and women who fast and deny themselves,

For men and women who guard their chastity,

For men and women who remember Allah much,

For them Allah has forgiveness and a great reward. (Al-Ahzab 33:35, Koran)

It is not fitting for a Believer, man, or woman, when a matter has been decided by Allah and His Messenger, to have any option about their decision; if anyone disobeys Allah and His Messenger, he is indeed on a clearly wrong Path. (Al-Ahzab 33:36, Koran)

Say to the:

Believing men that they should lower their gaze and guard their modesty: That will make for greater purity for them: And Allah is acquainted with all that they do. And say to the Believing women that they should lower their gaze and guard their modesty; That they should not display their adornments except what is ordinarily obvious, That they should draw a veil over their bosom and not display their adornments.

(Except to the immediate family)

And that they should not strike their feet in order to draw attention to their hidden adornments.

And O you Believers!

Turn you all together Toward Allah that you may prosper. (An-Nur 24:30-31)

The Believers, men, and women are protectors, one of another: they enjoin what is just, and forbid what is evil: they observe regular prayers, practice regular charity, and obey Allah and His Rasool. On them will Allah pour His Mercy: for Allah is Exalted in power, Wise. (At-Tawbah 9:71, Koran)

Fight in the cause of Allah those who fight you but do not transgress limits: for Allah loves not transgressors and slay them wherever you catch them, And turn them out from wherever they have turned you out for tyranny and oppression are worse than slaughter.

But fight them not at the Sacred Mosque, unless they (first) fight you there but if they fight you, slay them. Such is the reward of those who suppress faith. But if they cease, Allah is oft Forgiving, Most Merciful. And fight them on until there is no more tyranny or oppression,

And there prevail justice and faith in Allah: but if they cease let there be no hostility except to those who practice oppression. (Al-Baqarah 2:190–93, Koran)

Those who devour usury will not stand except as stands one whom the Satan by his touch hath driven to madness. That is because they say: Trade is like usury, But Allah hath permitted trade and forbidden usury. Those who after receiving direction from their Lord, Desist, shall be pardoned for the past: their case is for Allah to (judge); But those who repeat (the offence) are the companions of fire; They will abide therein (forever). Allah will deprive usury of all blessing, However, will give increase for the deeds of charity: For He does not love those who are ungrateful and wicked. (Al-Baqarah 2:275–76, Koran)

And eat not up your property among yourselves for vanities, nor use it as a bait for judges, with intent that you may eat up wrong fully and knowingly some of other people's property. (Al-Baqarah 2:188, Koran)

Oh you who believe! Guard your souls, if you follow right guidance, No hurt can come to you from those who stray; The goal of you all is to Allah, It is He who will show you the truth of all that you do.[40]

[40] Al-Baqarah 2:143, 156, 177, 188, 190–92, 275–76, 278, 279; Ali 'Imran 3:103–5, 110; An-Nisa 4:59; Al-Ma'idah 5:51, 57, 105; Al-A'raf 7:181; At-Tawbah 9:71; Yunus 10:25–26; Al-Anbiya 21:92; An-Nur 24:30–31; Luqman 31:22; Al-Ahzab 33:35; Ash-Shura 42:38–39; Ar-Rahman 55:79.

The Covenant of Yathrib: The Covenant of the Blessed *Rasul* of Allah, Muhammad

In the name of Allah, the compassionate, and the merciful.

1. No believer shall slay a believer in retaliation for an unbeliever, nor shall he assist an unbeliever against a believer. This is a covenant given by Muhammad to the believers.
2. They constitute one Ummah to the exclusion of all other men.
3. The believers shall leave none of their members in destitution without giving him in kindness that he needs by the way of his liberty.
4. No believer shall take as an ally a freedman of another Muslim without the consent of his previous master. All believers shall rise as one man against anyone who seeks to commit injustice, aggression, crime, or spread mutual enmity amongst the Muslims even if such a person is their kin.
5. Just as the bond to Allah is indivisible, all the believers shall stand behind the commitment of the least of them. All believers are bonded one to another to the exclusion of other men.
6. This Pax Islamica is one and indivisible. No believer shall enter a separate peace without all other believers whenever there is fighting in the cause of God but will do so only on the basis of equality and justice to all others. In every expedition for the cause of God we undertake, all parties to the covenant shall fight shoulder to shoulder as one man. All believers shall avenge the blood of one another when anyone falls fighting in the cause of God.
7. The pious believers follow the best and the most upright guidance.
8. Whoever is convicted of killing a believer deliberatively but without righteous cause shall be liable to the relatives of the

killed. Until the latter are satisfied, the killer shall be subject to retaliation by each and every believer.

9. Any Jew who follows us is entitled to our assistance and the same rights as any one of us, without injustice and partisanship. As the Jews fight on the side the believers, they shall spend their wealth on equal par with the believers. The Jews are an Ummah alongside the believers. The Jews have their religion and the Muslims theirs. Both enjoy the security of their populace and clients except the unjust and the criminal amongst them. The unjust and the criminal destroy only himself and his family.
10. None of the Jewish tribes may go to war without the permission of Muhammad, though none may be prevented from taking revenge for a wound inflicted upon them. Whosoever murders anyone will have murdered himself and the members of his family, unless it be the case of the man suffering a wrong, for God will accept his actions. The Jews shall bear their public expenses and so will the Muslims. Each shall assist the other against any violator of this covenant. Their relationship shall be one of mutual advice and consultation, and mutual assistance and charity rather than harm and aggression. Assistance is due to the party suffering an injustice not to one perpetrating it.
11. Yathrab shall constitute a sanctuary to the parties of this covenant. Whatever the difference or dispute between the parties to this covenant remains unsolved shall be referred to God and to Muhammad. The Jews are entitled to the same rights as this covenant has granted to other parties together with the goodness and charity of the latter. Allah is the guarantor of the piety and the goodness that is embodied in this covenant. The people in this covenant come to the assistance of one another against any aggressor.
12. Allah is the guarantor of the truth and goodwill of this covenant Allah grants his protection to whosoever acts in piety, charity, and goodness.

Covenant of Allah and the Dar es Salaam

The covenant of Allah has established a simple code of conduct for the believers to follow in their daily lives. The same conduct applies to the community of Islam, the *ummah*, and their state. Muslims disobey the covenant at their peril.

The Chain of Authority: Allah addressed the believers and ordained a chain of authority in the management of their affairs: "*Obey Allah and obey the Rasool, and those charged amongst you with authority in the settlement of your affairs. If you differ in anything among yourselves, refer it to Allah and His Rasool (The Qur'an and the Prophet's teachings).*" The sovereignty of the Islamic state belongs exclusively to Allah, whose will and command binds the community and state. The dignified designation in the Koran of the community as vicegerent of Allah on the earth makes the Muslim community, the *ummah*, a repository of the "executive sovereignty" of the Islamic state.

The community as a whole, after consultation and consensus, grants people among themselves the authority to manage its affairs (*ulil amri minkum*). Those given authority act in their capacity as the representative (*wakil*) of the people and are bound by the Koranic mandate to obey Allah and the *rasul* in the management of the affairs of the *ummah*. They are also bound by the Koranic mandate to consult with the community. The community, by consultation and in consensus, has the authority to depose any person charged with authority, including the head of state, in the event of gross violation of Allah's law. The believers will, from time to time, choose their *wakil* to manage the affairs of the Dar es Salaam. Such affairs will be administered on the basis of the commandments of Allah in accordance with His covenant.

This Pax Islamica is one and indivisible. No believer shall enter a separate peace without all other believers whenever there is fighting in the cause of Allah but will do so only on the basis of equality and justice to all others. In every expedition for the cause of Allah, all parties to the covenant shall fight shoulder to shoulder as one man. All believers shall avenge the blood of one another when anyone falls while fighting for the cause of Allah. All Muslims are one brotherhood, one *ummah*, in one land, all servants of one Allah, the First and the Last, fulfilling His covenant, witnessed over by Allah's *rasul*—an *ummah* that witnesses over other nations.

The Roll of Islam in the Twenty-First Century: The miracle of the twenty-first century is that, in spite of warfare, turmoil, and *fitnah*, Islam is the fastest-spreading religion in the world. Three large regions of spiritual osmosis and spiritual regeneration are in India, sub-Saharan Africa, and the Euro-Christian world of Americas and Europe. The Koran is the most recited book every day in the world. Islam continues to influence other beliefs toward the belief in one universal God. Because of Islam's silent influence in the contemporary world, there are now more believers in the unity of God among Jews, Christians, Hindus, Buddhists, and other religions than any other time in history.

As in the times past, in the present, the believers of the *ummah wast*, the *ummah* of the middle path, seek their salvation in communion with Allah. The believers march in the path of Allah, the path of moderation guided by their covenant with Him in silence, peace, fortitude, and humility. The *ummah* is the best of the peoples evolved from mankind, enjoining what is good and forbidding all that is evil. The blessed *nabi* delivered the message of peace and love to the world. He came as an inspiration, a beacon of light, a bearer of glad tidings, to invite humanity to Allah's grace and mercy. Strengthened by this inspiration, when Islam advances, the world gains tranquility, love, and knowledge. With the role of Islam, there is truth, honesty, justice, equality, and prosperity for all. The precepts of the covenant of Allah ensure human dignity, equality, justice, consultative government, a state where there is realization of lawful benefits to people, prevention of harm, and removal of hardship. The covenant of Allah educates individuals by inculcating in them self-discipline, patience, restraint, and respect for the rights of others.

The believers constitute one *ummah* to the exclusion of all other men. Just as the bond with Allah is indivisible, all believers shall stand in commitment with the least of them. All believers shall rise as one against anyone who seeks to commit injustice, aggression, or crime or spread mutual enmity among the Muslims. The believers shall leave none of their members in destitution without giving him in kindness and liberty what he needs. In every expedition in the cause of Allah, the *ummah* undertakes to fight shoulder to shoulder as one man. All believers shall avenge the blood of one another when anyone falls fighting in the cause of God. Whoever is convicted of killing a believer deliberatively but without righteous cause shall be liable to the relatives of the killed. Until the latter are satisfied, the killer shall be subject to retaliation by each and every believer.

When one and a half billion people of Islam ignore Allah's commandments, they bring on themselves *fitnah* and oppression of the *Munafiqeen.* Life of delusion and self-deception in search of the material things of the world brings on *fitnah,* oppression, and loss of hope. Allah helps those who help themselves. When people choose to be led by falsehood to live in disunity, disharmony, and subjugation, they have no hope. Hope is in Allah and in His covenant. Hope is in tawhid, truth, and justice for humanity. When the believers among the one and a half billion Muslims practice their *din* in the path of Allah, goodness in the world outweighs all evil, and there is peace in the world. There is no hunger, war, or oppression. There is hope, and Allah's *din* reigns supreme.

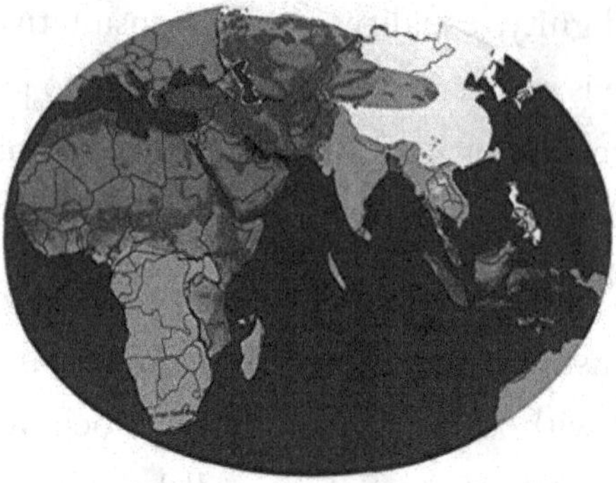

The Dar es Salaam

Seven Simple Steps to Freedom: In Islam, life is a chain of good intentions and good deeds:

1. Submission to Allah is in tawhid, which is the proclamation of the unity of the believer with Allah and the communion of believers in one *ummah* under the grace of the one merciful Lord, Allah. This unity is proclaimed in every call to prayer (*adhan*) five times a day from sunrise to sunset around the world day after day. And in this communion, Allah declares, "*Your real friends are Allah, His Rasool and the Fellowship of Believers, those who establish regular prayers and regular charity. And they bow down humbly in worship. As to those who turn for friendship to Allah, His Rasool and the fellowship of Believers, it is the Fellowship of Allah that must certainly triumph.*"
   This unity is ordained by Allah. To enforce this unity of the *ummah*, each Believer must determine his intention with an action. This action is to show the power and the resolve of the *fellowship of Allah* to those opposed to the unity of Islam, the *Munafiqeen* and the *kafireen*. Each believer will raise the standard of the *ummah* over his home, his mosque, and every Muslim institution everywhere in the world.

This standard is the crescent and the star of Islam over the background of blue sky, the sign of the universe of Allah. This is the standard of the Dar es Salaam. This standard represents tawhid and the precepts of the covenant of Allah that ensure human dignity, equality, justice, consultative government, a state where there is realization of lawful benefits to people, prevention of harm, removal of hardship, and education of every individual by inculcating in him self-discipline, patience, restraint, and respect for rights of others. It is a standard under which there is restitution of all wrongs and imbalances in society. The show of the standard of the Dar es Salaam is a reminder to the believers of Allah's promise that His fellowship will certainly triumph.

2. Each believer will act to ensure that his kin, his neighbors, his fellow citizens, his government, his leaders, the media, the universities, all Islamic organizations, political parties, and parliaments reaffirm their oath of obedience to the following declaration of Allah:

> Verily fellowship of yours is a single brotherhood, and I am your Lord and Cherisher: therefore, serve Me and no other.

> And hold fast, all together by the rope which Allah (stretches out for you). And be not divided amongst yourselves; And remember with gratitude Allah's favor on you: For you were enemies and He joined your hearts in love, So that by His grace, you became brethren.

> Enjoining what is right and forbidding what is wrong. Let there arise out of you a band of people, inviting all that is good.

Be not like those who are divided amongst themselves,
And fall into disputations after receiving clear signs For
them is a dreadful penalty. (Ali 'Imran 3:103–5, Koran)

You are the best of the peoples evolved for mankind, Enjoining
what is right, forbidding what is wrong, and believing in Allah.

Thus, have We made of you an Ummah of the center, that
you might be witness over other nations, And the Rasool
a witness over yourselves. And We appointed the Qibla to
which you were used to only to test those who followed
the Rasool from those who would turn their heels.

Whoever submits his whole self to Allah, and is a doer
of good, has grasped indeed the most trustworthy
handhold. And with Allah rests the end and decision
of [all] affairs. (Al-Baqarah 2:143, Koran)

And following the reaffirmation their faith in Allah and their oath to obey the His declaration, every believer will declare and affirm the political unity of the Islamic world by the twenty-seventh of April 2034, the 125th anniversary of the forced abdication of the last genuine caliph, Abdulhamid.

3. One and a half billion believers, the fellowship of Allah, have the resolve, authority, and power to physically remove the un-Koranic rulers who oppose the unity of the *ummah*. The believers will peacefully march through their palaces and offices to remove from places of authority all vestiges of *fitnah*, treachery, and oppression. Fewer than fifty families responsible for the decadence in the governance of the *ummah* represent the circle of evil in the Islamic state. With the *ummah's* resolve, these fifty or so families will be made to step down from their

positions of authority and relinquish their ill-gotten assets to the people.

4. One and a half billion believers, the fellowship of Allah, have the authority, power, and resolve to physically remove all Western and foreign military bases and intelligence services from the lands of Islam. The believers will peacefully march through the offices, barracks, hangars, ammunition dumps, armories, and installations of all foreign military bases and remove from there all vestiges of *fitnah,* treachery, and oppression. Opposition to such eviction will meet the peril of fire of thousands of remotely controlled aerial, terrestrial, and maritime explosive vehicles that will vaporize the power of the un-Koranic external *fitnah* and its agents from the land of Islam.
5. All pacts, treaties, and agreements, both covert and open, signed by Muslim rulers with the Western powers have been extinguished with the invasion of Afghanistan and Iraq. Today all such treaties are void and shall be extinguished.
6. The organizations of the *ummah* and the existing Islamic states will coordinate the following:
    a. Establish a rapid deployment mobile expeditionary force of believers under a unified command from the armies of all Islamic states to fight *fitnah,* conspiracy, and aggression against every part of Islam. This force will defend every inch of the land of Islam from *fitnah* and oppression. This force will comprise a mechanized army of one million men and women with one thousand frontline aircraft and modern naval fleets in all Muslim waters. They will defend all the land, seas, and oceans of Islam.

b. Train and arm a volunteer mobile commando force of twelve million *mujahideen* men and women organized in three hundred autonomous armies with their own armor, air force, and ships. Their loyalty will be to Allah and the precepts of His covenant and the Dar es Salaam.
c. Establish a unified foreign policy for all Islamic lands under a unified organization. All current treaties and pacts signed will automatically extinguish. Relations and agreements with the rest of the world will be renegotiated under the name of the one unified state of the Dar es Salaam.
d. Establish a unified currency supported by gold. No fiat money will be accepted in trade. Usury will be abolished and banking and trade reorganized. Pricing of products for trade and commerce will be based on a just and standardized unit of hourly work performed by every human around the world.
e. The Dar es Salaam, the Islamic union, will exit the Western-controlled United Nations and its subsidiary organizations and sponsor the formation of a new world organization based on justice and equality rather than power and riches. This world organization will represent the people of the world rather than nations. It will be run by the people for the well-being of the peoples of the world. The Dar es Salaam will exit the World Bank, the International Monetary Fund, the World Trade Organization, and the Breton Woods Agreement. New agreements will be negotiated with the Euro-Christian, Chinese, Hindu, and African

civilizations on the basis of equality and justice for all the people of the world.

f. Organize unified intelligence services to defend the Dar es Salaam.

7. A unified structure of governance of the Dar es Salaam shall be established based on the precepts of the covenant of Allah.

Within one year of the of the renewal of Islam's world order, establishment of the structure of Dar es Salaam's governance will take place. In Islam, there are no professional or hereditary rulers. And in Islam, there are no priests and no politicians.

Every believer inherits the Koran, the law, and the blessed nabi's *legacy.* And each believer is the guardian and the executor of the law. In Allah's Dar es Salaam, men constitute 750 million individuals of the *ummah*, and women constitute the other 750 million. And between them, they form one solid, united *ummah.* Together in partnership, men and women have produced the progeny of Adam to carry out the divine and omnipotent will of Allah. The Koran addresses all believers, both men and women, together:

> And you Believers (men and women)! Turn you all together towards Allah, that you may attain prosperity.

The Dar es Salaam constitutes the following territories of the *ummah*: Afghanistan, Albania, Algeria, Bahrain, Bangladesh, Benin, Bosnia, Brunei, Burkina Faso, Cameroon, Chad, Chechnya, Comoros, Djibouti, Egypt, Ethiopia, East Turkistan, Gabon, Gambia, Guinea, Guinea-Bissau, Guyana, Indonesia, Iran, Ivory Coast, Iraq, Jordan, Kashmir, Kazakhstan, Kosovo, Kuwait, Kyrgyzstan, Lebanon, Libya, Malaysia, Maldives, Mali, Mauritania, Morocco, Mindanao, Mozambique, Niger, Nigeria, Oman, Pakistan, Palestine, Qatar, Saudi

Arabia, Senegal, Sierra Leone, Somalia, Sudan, Suriname, Syria, Tajikistan, Tanzania, Togo, Tunisia, Turkey, Turkmenistan, Uganda, United Arab Emirates, Uzbekistan, and Yemen. Other Muslim domains within the boundaries of countries of Russia, China, India, Serbia, and Macedonia will have an extraterritorial association with the Dar es Salaam through their large Muslim populations.

Every Muslim, whether residing in or outside the bounds of the Dar es Salaam, is a member of the *ummah* and has the right and the obligation to the citizenship of the Dar es Salaam. Equally, every non-Muslim residing within the bounds of the Dar es Salaam who has sworn allegiance to the state will have the same citizenship rights and obligations, as well as all freedoms prescribed by the Koran to the Muslims, in short absolute and complete equality. (Document of Yathrib: First Year of Hijra)

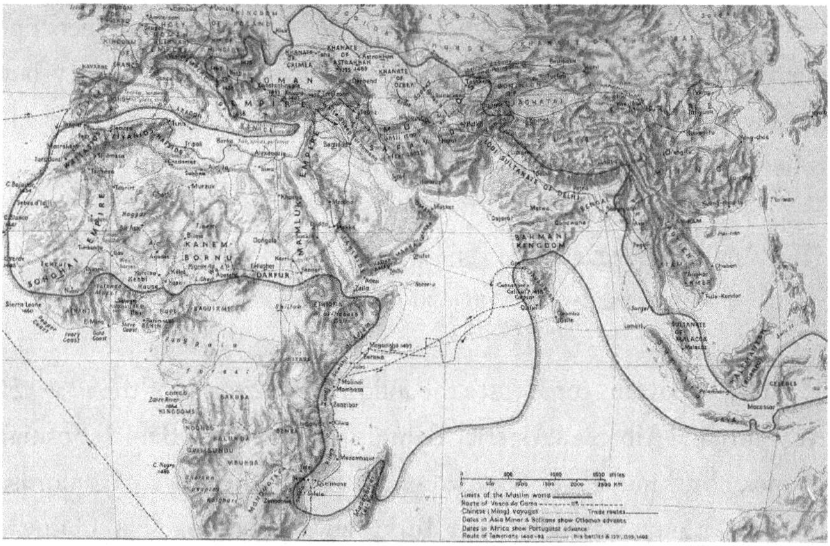

The extent of the Islamic world at the advent of the European awakening in the fifteenth century CE.

Electoral College of the *Ummah*

At the grassroots level, the *ummah* has been, through divine guidance, a democratic society governing itself justly in consultation and consensus through its own intrinsic resources. Historically, however, it was denied the means of a participatory democratic system of government at higher levels by ongoing upheavals in their lands caused by marauding armies in search of power and booty. The democratic and the humane social system at the basic level could not be transformed into a viable democratic political order of consultation and consensus at the governing level because of the tribal, feudal, and sultanic monarchial order of the ruling classes. For over one thousand years, the rulers and their governments were cut off from the people. Troops and civil servants came from the tribal formations, slaves, and *devsirme* classes. Land and revenue-bearing estates were allocated to the military commanders and revenue agents, and the people were merely sharecroppers. Such un-Koranic feudalism has continued to exist in all Islamic lands. Allah has proclaimed a code of conduct for the Muslim *ummah* in His covenant in the Koran. Without fulfilling the whole covenant of Allah, all acts of submission, faith, and worship become meaningless and are of little consequence.

The Ummah.

Verily this brotherhood of yours is a single brotherhood, and I am your Lord and Cherisher. Therefore, serve Me and no other, and hold fast, all together the Rope which Allah stretches out for you and be not divided amongst yourselves. And remember with gratitude Allah's favor on you, For you were enemies and He joined your hearts in love,

So that by His Grace, you became brethren. Let there arise
out of you a band of people inviting to all that is good,
enjoining what is right, and forbidding what is wrong.

Be not like those who are divided amongst themselves and
fall into disputations after receiving clear signs; for them
is a dreadful penalty. (Qur'an 3:103-105 Ali Imran).

You are the best of the peoples evolved for mankind, enjoining
what is right, forbidding what is wrong, and believing in Allah.

Thus, have We made of you an Ummah of the center, that you are
witness over other nations, and the Rasool a witness over yourselves.

Whoever submits his whole self to Allah, and does wholesome and
good deeds, has grasped indeed the most trustworthy handhold,

And with Allah rests the end and decision
of all affairs. (Al-Baqarah 2:143)

Allah is the Sovereign of the universe. The sovereignty of the Dar es Salaam rests with the Muslim *ummah*, which is the aggregate of individual believers who do the bidding of Allah. For the aggregate to believe in and to comply with the divine commandments, the individual has to be reformed and taught his responsibilities as the member of a divinely ordained indivisible brotherhood, the fellowship of Allah. The responsibilities of the individual believer are as follows:

- His and her own conduct in spiritual and worldly matters as commanded by Allah.
- His and her accountability to kith and kin, neighbors, and community.

- His and her duty to the solidarity, prosperity, intellectual enlightenment, liberty, justice, and unity of the *ummah.*
- To invite all that is good, to enjoin what is right, and to forbid what is evil.
- To ensure that his *ulil amri minkum* receives proper advice and acts in consultation and that all decisions regarding the *din* and the *ummah* are made in consultation and consensus.
- To take steps to stop corruption, mismanagement, and abuse of authority among the state functionaries employed on his behalf.

Insignificant raindrops fall on parched land singly and disappear forever; however, the same raindrops coalesce in strength to form little streams and then little rivulets and then join together to become mighty rivers flowing further, dropping into powerful and majestic waterfalls, yet again joining together with other rivers, lakes, and more hill torrents, to end up in mighty oceans ever increasing in size, in length, in depth, and in power yet at all times obedient to the will of Allah. Similarly, an insignificant man without faith is like a drop of water on parched land. Yet the same man, a believer, strengthened by his covenant with Allah, joins others with the covenant to form a little community that, again, with other communities in unity with Allah form a single united *ummah* of all the Muslims around the world, a powerful, united people witnessing over other nations, with Allah and His prophet witnessing over themselves.

Ummah el Nuqta

The primary unit of the *ummah* is the *ummah el nuqta*, consisting of about one thousand adults over the age of fifteen years, comprising around five hundred families of a neighborhood. The *nuqta* is an autonomous, self-help neighborhood administered by the members of the community in consultation and with consensus. This community ensures the well-being of every member of the community in matters of sustenance, spiritual and worldly education, health, housing, clean water, waste disposal, social planning, and development. The *nuqta* community ensures that none of its members go without food, shelter, health care, and education.

a) The *ummah el nuqta* will, in mutual consultation and consensus, select or elect from among themselves an *ulil amri minkum*, a *sheikh al nuqta* and a committee of four members—*mushirs*, two men and two women—to administer the affairs of the *nuqta* every two years for a tenure of four years. The *sheikh al nuqta* will run the affairs of the community and will act as the chairperson of the committee. The *sheikh al nuqta* will run the day-to-day affairs of the community with the help of his committee with ongoing consultation with the community, and all decisions will be arrived at through community consensus. The *sheikh al nuqta* may be a man or a woman in accord with the community's will. The *mushirs* will represent their community on various administrative boards related to education, health, transport, and municipal affairs and in matters of interest to the community at the next higher level of the administration, the *ummah el haraf.*
b) The *sheikh al nuqta* will be responsible for the civic discipline and law and order within the community. He will mediate any disputes within the community and will act as a magistrate at the community level. The community will police itself without interference from the outside except at the request of the committee.
c) Each *nuqta* community will aim for the highest possible standard of public health, education, health care, housing, and nutrition for its members. It will promote universal

literacy for its members within a short period of four years, to be achieved with the maximum effort on the part of each member, assisting one another. Such mutual assistance will also be carried out in matters of education, trade, business, and housing and in every other matter of civic and social concern within the community.

d) The community will appoint a scholar as a spiritual guide or an imam for a designated period, whose appointment may or may not be renewed at the end of that period according to the community's will. The imam will provide spiritual guidance to those seeking it, as well as religious services to the community.

e) As with the sheikh and the *mushirs*, the tenure of the imam will depend on his character, ability, and performance.

f) The state government will provide funding for the administration of *ummah el nuqta*. Community welfare and developmental projects will be funded from the zakat and *sadaqah* contributions and government funds in tax money.

g) Individual families, cooperative associations, and women's groups within the *nuqta* will utilize their dormant and nonproductive wealth to create industry, jobs, and productivity within their community. It is estimated that an average couple in the Middle East owns one hundred grams of gold ornaments, the rich own several kilograms of gold, and the poor own no gold; nevertheless, the average amount is estimated to be about a hundred grams per couple. The *nuqta* community (500 families × 100 g = 50 kg) will have access to 50 kg of gold for investment, converting a dormant hoard into a personal and a community asset.

Ummah el Haraf

One hundred *nuqta* communities will get together and authorize the next level of administration, the *ummah el haraf,* which will run the rural communities comprising about one hundred thousand adults or twenty-five thousand families. Some communities may merge where geographic or ethnic interests dictate such a merger. One *mushirs* from the *ummah el nuqta* will represent his or her community on the *ummah el haraf* executive council, and another representative will sit on the *ummah el haraf* planning committee charting out the future course of the communities. In urban areas and cities, similar arrangements will constitute a city municipality executive council and city municipality planning council. The two *mushirs* from the *ummah el nuqta* will represent their community in the two *ummah el haraf* councils, the executive and the planning. Care will be taken to balance gender equality of the members on the councils. The *mushirs* sitting on the executive and planning committees of the *ummah el haraf* will, in consultation with their communities, select the *sheikh el haraf* from among themselves as the head of the *ummah el haraf.* The *sheikh* will be the chairperson of both the executive and the planning councils.

a) The *mushirs*, along with experts from a variety of disciplines, will sit on various committees dealing with hospitals, schools, highways, finance, police, water, garbage disposal, planning, business, commerce, and so on. Recognizing the sovereignty of the *ummah*, the sheikh and the *mushirs* will consult the community before coming to any decisions, which will be made in consensus with the community. The decision-making will of necessity be slow and will require the assent of the community. The planning council will look at the needs of the community in the years ahead. It will also legislate laws in tune with the injunctions of the Koran, and it will ensure propriety in the functioning of the executive. The executive council will run the day-to-day affairs of the *ummah el haraf* and execute the decisions and planning of the planning council. A council of the *sheikhs el nuqta* will ensure that none of the councils and their functionaries abuse their authority nor misappropriate public assets.

b) The councils of the *ummah el haraf* are autonomous bodies acting in roles assigned to them by the *ummahs el nuqta* and *el haraf* as enshrined in the constitution.

c) The communities of *ummah el haraf*, consisting of twenty-five thousand families, will in consultation and in consensus select from among themselves one able person of impeccable character, ability, and experience every two years for a four-year term to represent their interests at the provincial and national levels.

d) A council of

ten *sheikhs el haraf* from ten *ummahs el haraf*,

ten representatives of the *sheikh el nuqta* from the *nuqta* communities,

ten representatives of the mushir*s* of the *nuqta* communities,

twenty-five representatives of various organizations, guilds, ulema, professions, universities, and so on

will constitute a *majlis-e-ijma*. *Majlis-e-ijma* will act as the consultative body acting as the eyes, ears, and voice of an adult population of one million people of the region. This *majlis* will comprise an equal number of men and women. Each *majlis-e-ijma* will select two of its members to sit on the national and the *villayat ijma* councils to coordinate the national consensus on policy matters, which will be binding on the executive.

e) This *majlis-e-ijma* will, on an ongoing basis, consult the communities in their area in matters of mutual interest and arrive at a consensus of opinion on that matter and continually liaise with their *naibs* on the *majlis-e-watanniya, majlis-villayat,* as well as the provincial and the national executives, the ministries of these governments, and the officials and functionaries of these two levels of government.

f) The *majlis-e-ijma* will, every two years, appoint the ten elected representatives, the *naibs*, to one of the following task forces as assigned by the constitution to the *ummah el haraf:*
   1. The lower house of the national legislature, the *majlis-e-watanniya,*
   2. The provincial legislature, the *majlis-villayat,*
   3. The national executive,
   4. The provincial executive,
   5. The planning council, formulating strategies and policies concerning the nation in all spheres such as defense, foreign policy, fiscal matters, trade and commerce, population, education, health issues, Sharia and legal matters, transport, ports, cultural affairs, agriculture, mining, industry, civic planning, scientific research, and so on, delineating the course of the country in the short and long terms.
   6. The security commission, *majlis-e-naazir,* a watchdog and oversight bureau watching unobtrusively all the functions of the national and provincial governments, the government ministries and agencies, intelligence services, the armed forces, and the law enforcement agencies and the courts.

This council of *naibs,* as a body, will create and strengthen institutions based on Koranic democratic principles that the sovereignty of the *ummah* and the Dar es Salaam devolves from the individual believer to a collective repository of executive sovereignty of the whole *ummah* as a trust from Allah. The people entrusted with authority to administer the *ummah*'s affairs by contract are the *wakil* and the servants of the *ummah* and not the masters or the rulers. The legislative, executive, policy and planning, and security institutions will in clear and no uncertain terms derive their authority from individual believers, collectively from the *ummah*, as prescribed by the Koran. This authority will be passed from below upward through the *mushirs* and the *naibs*. The *majlis-e-ijma* in the middle is the eyes, ears, voice, and conscience of the *ummah*. It will—in consultation with the community and the institutions of the legislature, the executive, the policy and planning bureau, and the security council—develop a consensus of opinion and formulate the policies and agenda for the government to act on.

The Muslim society, at grass roots, has always been democratic, and it will, for the first time, universally have a democratic government with solid legislative and executive institutions. The authority will, in effect, devolve from the common man and woman believer at the grass roots, and they will, for fixed periods, assign it to their representatives and to the head of the state and his executive. The governance will function like a pyramid, with the people forming the solid foundation and, at the apex, the government resting on the secure and firm institutional structure.

Political Structure: Based on Consultation and Consensus at the Grass Roots

- When the blessed *nabi* died each believer inherited the Koran, the *din*, and the Dar es Salaam. The sovereignty of Islamic state belongs exclusively to Allah, whose will and command binds the community and state. The dignified designation in the Koran of the community as vicegerent of Allah on the earth makes the Muslim community, the *ummah*, a repository of the "executive sovereignty" of the Islamic state. The community as a whole, after consultation and consensus, charges people from among themselves with authority to manage its affairs (*ulil amri minkum*). Those charged with authority act in their capacity as the representative (*wakil*) of the people and are bound by the Koranic mandate to obey Allah and the *rasul* in the management of the affairs of the *ummah* and to consult with the community. The community, in consultation and in consensus, has the authority to depose a person charged with authority, including the head of state, in the event of gross violation of Allah's laws.

- The believers will, from time to time, choose their *wakil* to manage the affairs of the Dar es Salaam. Such affairs will be administered on the basis of the commandments of Allah in accordance with His covenant. In this scheme of affairs, each believer is connected to Allah, and the believer's relationship with Allah is exclusive. There are no intermediaries between Allah and His believers. There are no priests, no politicians, no professional kings, no hereditary rulers, nor any political parties. In summary, Allah is the Sovereign of the universe. The sovereignty of the Dar es Salaam rests with the Muslim *ummah*, which is the aggregate of individual believers, who do the bidding of Allah as His vicegerent on the earth.
- Each believer will elect or nominate six representatives or *wakil* to administer their part of the affairs designated to them in their capacity as the "repository of the executive sovereignty" that Allah has bestowed on them as His vicegerents on the earth. This tremendous responsibility of the executive sovereignty that Allah has bestowed on the believers involves the well-being of all of Allah's creatures—human, animal, and

vegetation. That includes the environmental well-being of the earth. Allah, in His mercy, has bequeathed His guidance to the believer in His covenant. Each believer is obliged to ensure that his or her *wakil* fulfills Allah's guidance in the covenant of Allah.

Every believer, man and woman, as a member of the *ummah* and as a citizen of the Dar es Salaam has the democratic responsibility to elect or appoint six public officials as their *wakil.*

a) Two *mushirs*, one man and one woman, to be appointed by a thousand adults of the *nuqta* community from among themselves for a four-year term every two years. The community will find people of faith; of impeccable character, record of accomplishment, and ability; and with *taqwa* of Allah from among themselves. It will, in consultation and consensus, choose or elect the officials from a short list of people forwarded by various citizen groups. Emphasis will be on the citizens' choice rather than self-recommendation and self-aggrandizement by individuals.
b) The *sheikh el nuqta*, man or a woman, to be selected by the *nuqta* community for a four-year term from among people of impeccable character and proven ability.
c) One *naib*, a man or a woman, to be elected alternatively every two years for a four-year term by the aggregate of ten *nuqta* communities, the *ummah el haraf*, constituting one hundred thousand adults.
d) A *raiis*, a man or a woman, will be elected by universal suffrage for a four-year term to run the administration of the vilayet as its chief executive.
e) An *emir* or a *caliph.* The whole adult population of the *ummah* from around the world will, for a six-year term, elect an emir

or a caliph, the chief executive of the Dar es Salaam, from a list of people prepared by the national council of the *majlis-e-ijma* in consultation with all major organizations and ordinary citizens. The candidate nominated for this position should be of impeccable reputation and character, administrative ability, and communication and interpersonal skills. He should be a *momin*, having submitted to the absolute will of Allah, with his actions and relationship with Him being governed by *taqwa* of Allah. The emir or the caliph should act in accordance with the three types of knowledge: *ilm al-yaqin*, *ain al-yaqin*, and *haqq al-yaqin* (knowledge of certitude, eye of certitude, and truth of certitude). He should be known to be in a state of constant submission to Allah. The caliph should be a natural leader, leading through example, piety, and humility through the guidance of his covenant with Allah. The caliph will guide and administer but will not rule. He and his family will have no privileges other than those defined by his office. The caliph will carry no titles or honors other than those pertaining to his office.

f) A council of the states composed of the *raiis* of every state or his deputy will form the upper house of the *majlis-e-wataniya* to protect the rights of each state.

g) There will be no obvious opposition party in the *majlis-e-villayats* or in the *majlis-e-wataniya* as in the Western democracies. The Islamic system has a built-in check and balance system within the framework of consultation and consensus at all levels of the government. The *majlis-e-ijma* and its national and state councils as well as the policy and planning councils are, at all times, open to the special interest and lobby groups to present their viewpoint. The security council and the *majlis-e-ijma* will unobtrusively oversee the conduct of the governments and their functionaries, putting an end to any irregularities before they take root and become entrenched.

Ummah el Villayat

The autonomous Muslim states that exist today will become the autonomous vilayets of the Dar es Salaam. All Muslim countries that function today as independent states will amalgamate into one united country, the Dar es Salaam: Afghanistan, Albania, Algeria, Bahrain, Bangladesh, Benin, Bosnia, Brunei, Burkina Faso, Cameroon, Chad, Chechnya, Comoros, Djibouti, Egypt, Ethiopia, East Turkistan, Gabon, Gambia, Guinea, Guinea-Bissau, Guyana, Indonesia, Iran, Ivory Coast, Iraq, Jordan, Kashmir, Kazakhstan, Kosovo, Kuwait, Kyrgyzstan, Lebanon, Libya, Malaysia, Maldives, Mali, Mauritania, Morocco, Mindanao, Mozambique, Niger, Nigeria, Oman, Pakistan, Palestine, Qatar, Saudi Arabia, Senegal, Sierra Leone, Somalia, Sudan, Suriname, Syria, Tajikistan, Tanzania, Togo, Tunisia, Turkey, Turkmenistan, Uganda, United Arab Emirates, Uzbekistan, and Yemen.

The population will form one united *ummah*, the *ummah wast* as proclaimed by Allah in the Koran, and their present rulers will cease to exercise every form of authority. Their authority will revert to the *ummah* as commanded by Allah. The sixty or so countries will become vilayets—states that will unite to form the Dar es Salaam, with autonomy to run their own affairs internally in the fields of health, education, agriculture, irrigation, highways, law and order, forestry, fisheries, municipalities, industry, internal trade, and commerce.

1. The states or the vilayets will be totally autonomous in the internal affairs as described above.
2. The legislative assembly, the *majlis-e-villayats*, will have authority to enact legislation in accordance to the tenets of

the covenant of the Koran. It will also act as watchdog over the executive. The *naibs* appointed by the *ummah el haraf* will constitute the *majlis*, will derive their authority from the *ummah el haraf*, and will act in consultation and in consensus with *ummah el haraf* and the *majlis-e-ijma* of their district in the best interests of the nation.

3. The head of the executive, the *raiis*, and his deputy will be elected directly by the *ummah el villayat* in consultation and in the consensus from a number of people recommended by the council of *majlis-e-ijma* of the vilayet for a four-year term.
4. The *raiis* will administer with the help of a cabinet of his selection from the *naibs* and other experts approved by the *majlis-e-villayats* for a four-year period.
5. A policy and planning bureau composing of *naibs* and experts in their fields will on an ongoing basis formulate alternate policies in every sphere of the jurisdiction of the vilayet. The policies will be discussed by the legislature and the executive in an open forum of the legislature; modified, accepted, or rejected by the *majlis* and the executive; and then implemented by the executive.
6. Task forces composing of the representative *naibs* and experts in various fields will research and collect information to advise various ministries on policy matters concerning their subject. Various interest groups will be invited for their opinions on the subject matter, and their advice and interest should be given due consideration in formulating a policy.
7. The *raiis* will derive his authority from the *ummah* and will act according to Allah's covenant and with the consent and the consensus of the *ummah* through the *majlis-e ijma*, *majlis-e-villayats*, policy and planning council, and various interest groups.

8. All citizens of any race, caste, creed, religion, gender, age, and wealth shall stand equal in the eyes of the law, same as in the eyes of Allah. There shall be no elite in the state, and no one shall use a title or a name to show superiority over other beings. All titles bestowed, inherited, or self-assumed shall extinguish.
9. The services of every person to the *ummah* and to the nation given selflessly will be recognized to be as such, and no person shall have precedence in recognition of such services in the form of land grant or with funds from the public treasury, which are not available to other citizens.
10. For the purposes of law and citizenship, any person declaring his submission to Allah and His covenant is a believer and a Muslim. For the purposes of the state, there will be no sects, and the rights of all citizens will be protected.

Ummah el Dar es Salaam: Ummah Wast

The Dar es Salaam is the composite political entity representing the home of every member of the *ummah* around the world. It is an amorphous landmass in which every home and place of worship of the believer is included. The state of Dar es Salaam will nurture every human under the commandments of Allah's covenant. In the Dar es Salaam, every human—man and woman, from the highest to the lowest, from the first to the last—shall have equal, unimpeded, and unquestionable right to liberty; right to practice his faith in accordance with his beliefs as, in Islam, there is no compulsion in matters of religion; right to life, which means intellectual, physical, and emotional well-being; right to safeguard one's property; right to intellectual endeavors, acquisition of knowledge, and education; right to earn a living; and right to free speech and action to enjoin good and forbid evil. In enjoying these freedoms, the individual will ensure that his activities do not impinge on the rights and freedom of others.

Every believer inherited the Koran, the covenant of Allah, the *din*, and the Dar es Salaam upon his or her submission to Allah. When the blessed *nabi* passed away, the Koran and the *din* were bequeathed to every believer. This custodianship of the Koran, the covenant, the *din*, and the Dar es Salaam rests with every believer individually until the last day. In the Dar es Salaam, individual believers collectively and for a defined period delegate this custodianship to a person or persons of their choice with conditions; in return, that individual is to exercise authority to manage the affairs of the Islamic state. While this authority may be bestowed, it can also be withdrawn if that individual fails to exercise his charge to the satisfaction of the majority of believers. During the period of discharge of his duties, this appointee will be called the caliph.

At the top of the pyramidal hierarchy of the *ummah*, the head of state and the successor to the temporal power of the blessed *nabi* of Allah is the caliph, appointed to office by universal suffrage by every adult believer for a period of six years. The national council of *majlis-e-ijma* and other organizations will nominate suitable candidates after consultation with citizens. Those nominated for the position of caliph will be presented to the people by the *majlis-e-ijma*. For this position, there will be no electioneering and no self-recommendation. The lessons of schism and disunity of Islam caused by Mu'awiyah's seizure of the caliphate in the sixty-sixth year of hijra will not be forgotten.

Ten *naibs* or deputies elected by the composite of fifty *haraf* communities every two years will be assigned to serve on the following bodies for a four-year term:

1. *Majlis-e-wataniya* (national parliament).
2. *Majlis-e-villayats* (provincial parliament).

3. National executive.
4. Provincial executive.
5. The planning councils formulating strategies and policies concerning the nation in all spheres such as defense, foreign policy, trade and commerce, fiscal matters, population, education, agriculture, health issues, Sharia and legal matters, transport, ports, cultural affairs, mining, civic planning, scientific research, security and intelligence, and so on. This committee will plan the possible course for the nation in the short and the long terms.
6. The security commission (*majlis-e-naazir*), a watchdog and an oversight bureau watching unobtrusively all functions of the provincial and national governments, the government ministries and agencies, the intelligence services, the armed forces, the law enforcement forces, and the courts. *Majlis-e-naazir* is autonomous and independent of the executive branch of the government.
7. One member will represent their *haraf* community on the advisory committee of the caliph and the *raiis*. These members' services will be allocated to various subcommittees as required by the needs of the day.
8. One member appointed to the *ijma council*. The function of this council will be to consult with the *ummah* and assess the consensus of public opinion on various issues in the public domain. The committee's function will also include education of the public opinion through provision of true and honest information on the state matters of concern to the citizens. The *ijma* council is autonomous and independent of the executive branch of the government.
9. The Dar es Salaam's modus operandi shall be based on truth and trust as advocated by the covenant of Allah.

These *haraf* community representatives will represent the public consensus on issues under consideration to their assigned committees, commissions, and the *majlis.* These ten members from their communities will be the best education tools to enlighten their communities on the workings of an Islamic system of governance based on Allah's covenant. Honest two-way communication from the base to the apex of the pyramid of governance and vice versa will smash any barriers of misunderstanding between the levels of administration and the people. This web of communication will unify the *ummah.* Rules, laws, and conduct of governance based on the thirty-seven commandments of the covenant of Allah will drive away Satan and humans controlled by him. These ten representatives of *haraf* communities, representing a population of five million, will meet regularly with the citizen groups to deal with their questions and problems in a formal, documented setting to find the solutions to the questions from the officialdom of the state.

The *nuqta* communities of one thousand adults, totaling a population of about twenty-five hundred, will be the basic community of the Dar es Salaam. This community holds the executive sovereignty of the Dar es Salaam. Six hundred thousand such autonomous communities form the basis of consultation and consensus of decision-making in all issues relating to the Dar es Salaam, where the democratic control over the nation begins at the grass roots and disseminates all the way to the top.

The believer's covenant with Allah reforms the individual by setting him or her to Allah's straight path. Similarly, reformed individuals in the community reinforce one another's resolve and actions in accordance with the straight path. Every believer when reciting *shahadah* in the daily prayer also pledges obedience to the covenant of Allah:

Verily those who pledge their allegiance unto you (O Muhammad), pledge it unto none but Allah; the Hand of Allah is over their hands. Thereafter whosoever breaks his Covenant does so to the harm of his own soul, and whosoever fulfils his Covenant with Allah, Allah will grant him an immense Reward. (Al-Fath 48:10, Koran)

The actions of believers reflect their faith and total submission to Allah—the only Reality; the Knower of the hidden and the manifest; the *Rahman* and the *Rahim*; the Sovereign; the Pure; the Hallowed, Serene, and Perfect; the Protector; the Almighty; the Supreme; the Creator; the Most High; the Most Great. Allah sent the blessed Muhammad and other blessed *rasuls* as witnesses to mankind, bearing glad tidings that Allah is the only reality and that everything else is dependent on Allah. Allah revealed the divine message, the Koran, to Blessed *Nabi* Muhammad as guidance and a covenant to humankind. Those who obey the covenant and Allah as guidance and hold on to Allah receive His grace, mercy, benevolence, and protection. The believers are conscious of Allah's presence with them at all times. And all their actions are with the awareness that Allah is with them; though they may not see Him, He sees them.

The believers in Allah pledge to

- fulfill their covenant with Allah;
- serve Allah and His creation with generous, beautiful, and *righteous* deeds, pledging to provide their kin, neighbors, community, and those in need with sustenance from their means and wealth;
- be just and truthful;
- shun shameful deeds, *Fahasha*;
- be united within the *ummah*;

- seek protection of Allah as the *Waliy* and reject Jews, Christians, and the infidels as their *awliya* or protectors;
- fight in Allah's cause;
- fight injustice, unbelief in Allah, *fitnah*, and tyranny until there is no more and until justice prevails altogether and everywhere;
- forbid murder and not to take life, which Allah has made sacred;
- not betray the trust of Allah and his *nabi* with theft, deception, fraud, corruption, and dishonesty;
- not devour usury nor hoard wealth;
- be good, kind, and caring to their parents;
- not kill or deprive their children because of poverty (abortion and murder);
- treat one another in kindness and on the basis of equality and justice;
- not crave those things of what Allah has bestowed His gifts more freely on some than others as men and women are assigned what they earn;
- be just and stand firmly for justice and truth as witness to Allah;
- always speak the truth and always deal justly that he shall not be dealt with unjustly;
- invite others to what is good and right and forbid what is wrong;
- avoid suspicion, which leads to sin;
- not ridicule other believers;
- avoid secret counsels, which are inspired by Satan;
- not use intoxicants, gambling, carrion, blood, flesh of swine, and any food on which a name other than that of Allah has been invoked;

- not prohibit and make unlawful the good things that Allah has made lawful;
- commit no excess as Allah does not love people given to extremism;
- respect other people's privacy and enter not their houses without first asking permission.

On ninth day of *Zul-hajj* in tenth year of hijra, Allah in His mercy proclaimed to humankind through His blessed *rasul* that *Allah had perfected the* din *of the believers,* bestowed on them His blessings, and decreed Islam as the *din* of believers.

In Sura Al-Kahf, Allah proclaims, "*We have explained in detail in this Qur'an, for the benefit of mankind every kind of similitude,* but man is in most things contentious."

In Taha, it says, "*So We have made the Qur'an e*asy in your own tongue that with it you may give glad tidings to the righteous and warnings to people given to contention."

And in Ad-Dukhan, it says, "*Ha Mim. By the Book that makes matters lucid; We revealed it during blessed night, verily We are always warning against Evil. Therein is proclaimed every wise decree, by command from Our Presence, for We are ever sending Revelations, as a Mercy from Your Lord, for He is the Hearer and the Knower.*"

In these suras, Allah proclaims that His message to mankind in the Koran "*is perfect, detailed, easy and lucid.*" Accordingly, Allah's *din* is not to be tampered by humans at any time. After that day, any additions and alterations to the *din* of the believers are a man-made innovation.

Chapter Eight

The Knowledge of Certainty: The Covenant of Allah

Knowledge[41] is defined as "the perception of agreement and disagreement between our 'ideas' and the reality of the world." The immediate object of our mind is to perceive ideas. The mind, in all its thoughts and reasoning, has no other object but to contemplate its own ideas. Therefore, our own knowledge is conversant only with our own ideas. Knowledge, it seems therefore, is nothing more than perception of and in consensus with any of our own ideas. Where this perception is, there is knowledge; and when there is no such perception, we come short of knowledge.

Faith in Islam, like in any religion, is never blind. Although belief in the unseen is important, there comes a point when a spiritual human being transcends the level of simple faith. At this point, the person's spiritual consciousness has penetrated the fog of the unseen, leading to knowledge of the true nature of things. The Koran speaks of this progression from *faith* to *knowledge* as an inward metamorphosis in which belief *(iman)* is transformed into certainty *(yaqin)*. This certainty is expressed in the Koran in terms of three types of knowledge of Allah.[42]

The most basic and fundamental knowledge is the "knowledge of certainty" (*ilm al-yaqin,* Koran 102:5.) This type of certitude refers to knowledge that results from human capacity for logical reasoning and the appraisal of what the Koran calls "clear evidences" (*bayyinat*) of Allah's presence in the world.

---

[41] *An Essay Concerning Human Understanding (1690)* (Oxford: Clarendon Press, 1964).

[42] Cornell, "Fruit."

Over time and under the influence of contemplation and spiritual practice, the knowledge of certainty may be transformed into a higher form of knowledge of Allah that the Koran calls the "eye of certainty" (*ain al-yaqin*, Koran 102:7). This term refers to the knowledge that is acquired by spiritual intelligence, which believers in the East locate metaphorically in the heart. In this context, heart and the mind are the seat of intuitive, logical, and deductive knowledge.

Once opened spiritually, the heart receives knowledge as a type of divine light or illumination (*nur*) that leads the believer toward the remembrance of Allah. Just as with the knowledge of certainty, with the eye of certainty, the believer sees Allah's existence through His presence in this world. With the eye of certainty, what lead the believer to the knowledge of Allah are not the arguments to be understood by the rational intellect but by theophanic appearances (*bayyinat*) that strip away the veil of worldly phenomenon to reveal the divine reality underneath.

The third and most advanced type of knowledge builds on transcendent nature of knowledge itself. The highest level of consciousness is called the "truth of certainty" (*haqq al-yaqin*). It is also known as *ilm ladduni* or knowledge "by presence."

The Koran seeks to establish a common foundation for belief that is based on such shared knowledge, perceptions, and experiences. Over and over again, the Koran reminds the reader to think about the truths that lie behind the familiar or mundane things of the world, such as signs of Allah in nature. The Koran, therefore, appeals to both reason and experience in determining the criterion for distinguishing between truth and falsehood.

The faith of Islam is based on certain knowledge that provides both freedom and a restriction. It is freedom in the sense that certainty of divine reality allows the human spirit to expand outward to take in the physical world, upward to realize his ultimate transcendence of the world through his link with the Absolute, and then inward to reconcile all that with his intellectual and emotional self. With this expansion outward, upward, and inward, the consciousness becomes three dimensional. Nevertheless, it is also a restriction because with the knowledge of God comes a concomitant awareness of the limits and responsibilities imposed on a person as a created being. Unlike a secular humanist, a true Muslim who submits to Allah cannot delude himself by claiming that he is the sole author of his destiny as he knows that a person's fate is routinely controlled by factors beyond his control.

Knowledge: Knowledge of the secular world is defined as the perception of agreement and disagreement between our "ideas." There are three kinds of knowledge: intuitive, demonstrative, and sensitive. The immediate object of our mind is to produce ideas. There are four ways of understanding the agreement and disagreement between our ideas.

Identity or diversity: The first act of the mind is to perceive its ideas. By the natural power of *perception* and *distinction*, it perceives what the idea is and distinguishes it from any other ideas; for instance, round is what it is, and therefore, it cannot be a square. *Identity* perceives that an idea agrees with itself, and *diversity* is the perception that that distinct ideas disagree with each other.

Relative: In any kind of ideas, the mind perceives a relationship between any two ideas, any sorts of agreements and disagreements, or any comparisons between the ideas. The agreement or disagreement is limited by our ability to discover *intermediate ideas* with which to demonstrate the agreement. It is this way of understanding agreement or disagreement (knowledge) that provides the basis of deduction. A deductive reasoning process by finding pair wise agreement in a sequence of steps that allows us to find agreement between the starting and ending points. Relation gives us, in our scheme of knowledge, basic rules of inference.

Coexistence or noncoexistence: The third type of agreement or disagreement in our ideas is that of coexistence or noncoexistence in substances. Our ideas of substances consist in collections of such *coexisting* complexes.

Real existence: The perception of agreement or disagreement to the idea is actual and that of *real existence.* Some of our ideas are "caused" by external objects, some things outside our mind. This kind of agreement or disagreement is not strictly between ideas; it is between the idea and its physical referent, the external stimulus.

Within these four parameters is contained all the knowledge we are capable of having. For all that, we know or can affirm concerning any *idea* that:

> *It is, or it is not the same with some other idea,*
>
> *it does or does not coexist with another idea in the same subject,*
>
> *it has or does not have any relation to some other ideas,*
>
> *or the idea has real existence without the mind as that God is.*

All our knowledge is based on the ideas our mind produces. Clarity of our ideas produces clearness of our knowledge, which in turn depends on the way our mind perceives and harmonizes or diverges with any of our ideas. When the mind perceives this agreement or disagreement with two ideas immediately without the intervention of any other, we call it *intuitive knowledge,* in which case the mind perceives truth as the eye sees light. It is upon this *intuition* that all the *certainty* and evidence of other knowledge depends.

The next degree of knowledge is where the mind cannot perceive agreement or disagreement in our ideas immediately and therefore has to depend on the intervention of other ideas for such a perception. This process is called *reasoning*. In this case, the mind has no intuitive knowledge and has to depend on intervening ideas to shore up agreement between any other two ideas. These intervening ideas are called *proofs*. A quickness of mind to find such proofs is called *sagacity*, and the process of finding proofs is called *demonstration*. Although *demonstrative knowledge is certain*, it lacks the clarity of intuitive knowledge. To arrive at the certainty of demonstrative knowledge, the mind will require a sequence of steps to confirm intuitive knowledge with the next intermediate idea as proof, without which there will be no new knowledge. It is evident that with every step of reasoning to acquire knowledge, the mind perceives *intuitive certainty*, and no further steps are required to confirm ideas, to achieve certainty. The *intuitive perception* and conformity of intermediate ideas in each sequence of steps in the demonstration must be carried out precisely in the mind. In long sequence of deductions, the memory cannot easily retain ideas; and therefore, this knowledge becomes imperfect and uncertain than the intuitive knowledge. Therefore, people are more likely to embrace falsehoods for demonstrations and arrive at false conclusions.

From the above discussion, it follows that

- we can have no knowledge further than we have ideas;
- we can have no knowledge further than our perception and concurrence with our ideas;
- we cannot have intuitive knowledge that shall extend itself to all our ideas; because we cannot examine and perceive the relationship, they have one to another;

- our rational knowledge cannot reach to the whole extent of our ideas; between two different ideas that the mind examines, we cannot always find proofs that connect one to the other with intuitive knowledge in the sequence of deduction and reasoning.

From all of the above, it is evident that our knowledge not only lags behind the reality of things but also is to the extent of our own ideas.

The ideas that require concurrence and connection through intermediate ideas to confirm their validity through reason form the largest field of knowledge that has expanded the most during the last fourteen hundred years. The *idea* of Supreme Being as

> Allah, Knower of the hidden and the manifest, the Rahman, the Rahim, the Sovereign, the Pure, and the Hallowed, Serene and Perfect, the Custodian of Faith, the Protector, the Irresistible, the Creator, the Sculptor, the Adorner of color and form, the Almighty and All Wise. (Al-Hashr 59:18–24, Koran)

Will, when duly considered, afford us the foundation of our obligations to Allah and His creation and *morality* among intermediate ideas in a demonstration of Allah's existence. It is evident, then, that this idea, when established and with the names annexed to it, informs us that such a proposition is true. It is evident, then, that these ideas thus established with these names annexed to them form a proposition that we know to be true. Such moral ideas are more complex and are not considered to be capable of demonstration. This difficulty is remedied by definitions, by setting down a *term* for each of the collection of simple moral ideas and then using these terms steadily and repeatedly for that precise collection.

And for the knowledge of real and actual existence of things, we have an intuitive knowledge of our own existence, a demonstrative knowledge of existence of God, and a sensitive knowledge of the objects that present themselves to our senses. The causes of our ignorance are precisely these three: (a) lack of ideas, (b) lack of a discoverable connection between the ideas we have, and (c) lack of identification of our ideas and inability to locate the *intermediate idea.*

Our knowledge follows the nature of our ideas. If our ideas are *abstract*, whose agreement or disagreement we perceive, our knowledge is universal. For what is known of such general ideas will also be true of everything in which that essence or *abstract idea* is to be found. What is once known of such ideas will remain true forever, in perpetuity. So all the general knowledge we search we find only in our own minds. And it is only by examining our own ideas that we acquire general knowledge. Truths belonging to the essence of things (abstract ideas) are eternal and are to be found out only by contemplation of those essences as the existence of such things is known only through experience.

All knowledge lies only in the perception of the agreement or disagreement of our own ideas, in the perception of sight and senses, and through reasoning. If our knowledge of our thoughts goes no further, our most serious thoughts will be of little consequence, and we have nothing else but knowledge of our ideas. It is evident that our mind knows things only by the intervention of ideas our mind has. Our knowledge is real only if there is conformity between our ideas and reality of things.

The mind does not make ideas by intention. Making of ideas must be the effect of unknown factors operating on our mind in a natural way to produce perception of things without our control. Conformity between our simple ideas and existence of things is sufficient for real knowledge.

All our complex ideas except those of substances are *archetypes* of the mind's own making and thus do not require conformity necessary for real knowledge. What is not designed to represent anything but itself can never be capable of wrong representation. Here, the ideas themselves are considered to be archetypes. Hence, moral knowledge is capable of *real certainty*. Certainty is the perception of the agreement or disagreement of our ideas and a demonstration of perception of agreement by the intervention of other ideas, our *moral ideas*, which are archetypes themselves; and hence, they are adequate and complete ideas. What is requisite to make our knowledge certain is the clarity of our ideas.

Truth means joining or separating of signs as the things signified by them agree or disagree with one another. The joining or separation of signs is called *propositions*. So truth properly belongs only to propositions. Propositions are of two sorts, *mental* and *verbal*, as there are two sorts of signs commonly made use of, *ideas* and *words*. It is not possible to treat mental propositions without verbal because when speaking of mental, we must use words, and then they become verbal. People, in their reasoning, use words instead of ideas, especially when the subject of their thoughts contains complex ideas. When we make propositions on complex ideas—such as *perseverance, oppression, fragrance,* or *fortitude*—we put a *name* to the idea because the ideas that these names stand for are confusing, imperfect, and misunderstood. The names, on the other hand, are more distinct and clearer.

We must observe two sorts of propositions that we are capable of making. *Mental propositions* are where ideas in our understanding are put together or separated by the mind while perceiving or judging their agreement or disagreement. *Verbal propositions* are words put together or separated in affirmative or negative sentences so that the proposition consists in joining or separating signs, and truth consists in putting together or separating these signs according to the things they stand for.

Truth and knowledge can be distinguished as *verbal* and *real* (*verbal truth*), wherein terms are joined according to the agreement or disagreement of ideas they stand for without regarding whether our ideas are capable of having an existence in nature. But then they contain *real truth* when these signs (ideas and words) are joined and our ideas agree—when we know that our ideas are such that they are capable of existing in nature because they have done so in the past. Truth is the marking down in words the agreement or disagreement of ideas *as it is*.

Falsehood is the marking down in words the agreement or disagreement of ideas *otherwise than it is*. So long as these ideas that are marked down conform to their archetypes, they are the real truth. The knowledge of this truth consists in knowing what ideas the words stand for and the perception of agreement of those ideas.

In the sixth century, around the world, reading and writing skills were limited. Literacy was perhaps limited to less than 5 percent of the population in the courtesan and clerical circles. Among the population in general, knowledge was transmitted through oral traditions and limited to practical matters of livelihood, trade, and religion. Books and scriptures were not accessible to the population at large. Therefore, concepts and principles were based on cultural experiences that were hard to change. This situation caused diversity among neighborly communities. Unity of ideas occurred often through compulsion from above when conquerors pushed through the ideas of their culture to the subject people.

Had the blessed *nabi* Muhammad, in the year 610 of the Common Era, opened an office across from the Kaaba and from there distributed printed and bound copies of the Koran to the pilgrims coming from all across Arabia, he would have made no impact on the psyche of that population. The people did not possess the ability to grasp the concepts and precepts of knowledge of the unity of Allah, *taqwa* of Allah, and the criterion to distinguish between good and evil (*husna* and *Fahasha*) at that time.

The precept of tawhid: The Koran laid the foundation of the idea of one universal God, and from this fount arose all that is known and all that will ever be known. It laid this foundation for the believers in the first twelve years of Blessed Muhammad's prophecy, and it took another ten years to establish the precepts of truth, justice, covenant, equality, good, and evil. The Koran laid out these principles in clarity for all times to come.

In the sixth century, Arabia—at the time of the birth of the blessed *nabi* the Arabian Peninsula—was steeped in ignorance, superstition, spirit worship, and idol worship. There was no belief or concept of one universal God. In the Mediterranean Basin, the one God was a tribal deity of the Jews, and the God of Christians was accessible to man through the creed of Trinity, in which God had incarnated into the human Jesus, and Jesus into the divine God.

The Muslims believe that Allah is the universal God and that He is the Creator and God of all that has been, all that is, and all that will be. Today we believe that the universal God is the center of the belief among followers of all the three monotheistic religions—Judaism, Christianity, and Islam. Nothing could be farther from the truth.

The Koran tells us of the guidance Allah gave to the people of old times, the children of Israel, through His blessed prophets:

> And this was the Legacy that Abraham left to his sons, and so did Jacob; "O my sons! Allah hath chosen the Faith for you; then die not except in the state of submission (to Allah). Were you witnesses when Death appeared before Jacob? Behold he said to his sons: "What will you worship after me?" They said: "We shall worship thy God and the

God of thy fathers, - of Abraham, Isma'il and Isaac, - the One (True) God: to Him we bow (in Islam)." (Al-Baqarah 2:132–34, Koran)

We gave him Isaac and Jacob: all (three) We guided: and before him, We guided Noah, and among his progeny, David, Solomon, Job, Joseph, Moses, and Aaron: thus, do We reward those who do good: And Zachariah and John, and Jesus and Elias: all in the ranks of the Righteous: And Isma'il and Elisha, and Jonah, and Lot: and to all We gave favor above the nations. (Al-An'am 6:84:86, Koran

Allah guided the prophets of old, who were among the righteous. Allah was pleased with them, and He rewarded them. When these prophets had passed away, their followers wrote the scriptures, the biblical accounts of the guidance and lives of the old-time prophets. Scholars, teachers, and writers of scriptures—the books of the Bible—left for posterity their impressions of their gods, the lives of the prophets, and the interaction between the gods and the prophets. By the eighth century BCE, when the writers of the first five books of the Bible had completed their works, it would appear from their accounts that the writers themselves and the Israelites had already reverted to paganism. Their gods were tribal, personal, and open to negotiation with the prophets.

Here are certain insights from Karen Armstrong's book on God, Judaism, Christianity, and Islam.[43] According to Karen Armstrong, the third wave of Hebrew settlements occurred in about 1200 BCE, when tribes who claimed to be descendants of Abraham arrived in Canaan from Egypt. Their story, as narrated in the Bible, states that they had been enslaved by the Egyptians but had been liberated by a deity called *Yahweh*, who was the God of their leader, Moses. After they forced their way into Canaan, they allied themselves with the

[43] Karen Armstrong, *A History of God* (New York: Alfred A. Knopf, 1993).

Hebrew tribes there and began to call themselves the people of Israel. The Bible makes it clear that the people we know as the ancient Israelites were a confederation of various ethnic groups bound together principally by their loyalty to *Yahweh*, the God of Moses. The biblical account was written years later in about eighth century BCE, though it drew on earlier narrative sources.[44]

During the nineteenth century CE, some German biblical scholars developed a critical method that discerned four different sources of the first five books of the Bible: Genesis, Exodus, Leviticus, Numbers, and Deuteronomy. These books were later collated into the final text of what we know as Pentateuch during the first century BCE. This form of criticism exposing different sources of the biblical accounts has come in for a good deal of harsh treatment, but nobody has yet come up with a more satisfactory theory that explains the way there are two quite different accounts of key biblical events as the Creation and the Flood and why the Bible often contradicts itself.

According to biblical scholars, the two earliest biblical authors—whose work is found in Genesis and Exodus—were probably writing during the eight century BCE, though some will give them an earlier date. One is known as *J* because he calls his God *Yahweh*, the other *E* since he prefers to use the more formal divine title *Elohim*. By the eighth century, the Israelites had divided Canaan into two separate kingdoms. J was writing from the southern kingdom of Judah, while E came from the northern kingdom of Israel. Later, there were two more sources of the Pentateuch—the Deuteronomist (D) and the priestly (P) accounts of the ancient history of Israel.

In chapter 12 of the Bible, the man Abram—who later came to be known as Abraham, *the father of a multitude*—is commanded by *Yahweh* to leave his family in Haran, which is now in eastern Turkey,

---

[44] Ibid.

to migrate to Canaan near the Mediterranean Sea. Yahweh tells Abraham that he has a special destiny; he will become the father of a mighty nation that will one day be more numerous than the stars in the sky, and one day his descendants will possess the land of Canaan as their own. J's account of the call of Abraham sets the tone of the future history of this God. Who is this Yahweh? Did Abraham worship the same God as Moses, or did he know him by a different name? This would be a question of prime importance to us today.

But the Bible seems curiously vague on the subject and gives conflicting answers to this question. J says that men had worshipped Yahweh ever since the time of Adam's grandson, but in the sixth century BCE, P seems to suggest that Israelites had never heard of Yahweh until he appeared to Moses in the burning bush. P makes Yahweh explain that he really was the same God as the God of Abraham as though this was rather a controversial notion: He tells Moses that Abraham had called him *El Shaddai* and did not know the divine name *Yahweh*[45]. This discrepancy did not seem to worry the biblical writers or their editors. J calls his god *Yahweh* throughout; by the time he was writing, Yahweh was the God of Israel, and that was all that mattered. Israelite religion was pragmatic and less concerned with the kind of speculative detail that would worry us. Yet we should not assume that either Abraham or Moses believed in their God as we do today.

Accordingly, we assume that the three patriarchs of Israel—Abraham, his son Isaac, and his grandson Jacob—were monotheists, that they believed in only one God. This does not seem to have been the case according to the accounts of the Israelite Bible. Indeed, it is more accurate to call these early Hebrews *pagans* who shared many of the religious beliefs of their neighbors in Canaan. They would certainly have believed in the existence of such deities as Marduk, Baal, and

45 Matthew 13:14–15.

Anat. They may not have worshipped the same deity; it is possible that the God of Abraham, the Fear or Kinsman of Isaac, and the Mighty One of Jacob were three separate gods.

It is highly likely that Abraham's God was *El,* the high god of Canaan. The deity introduces himself to Abraham as *El Shaddai* (El of the Mountain), which was one of El's traditional titles.[46] Elsewhere, he is called *El Elyon* (the Most High God) or *El of Bethel.* The name of the Canaanite high god is preserved in such Hebrew names as *Isra-El* or *Ishma-El.* They experienced him in ways that would not have been unfamiliar to the pagans of the Middle East. We shall see that, centuries later, Israelites found the *mana* or the holiness of *Yahweh* a terrifying experience. On Mount Sinai, for example, he would appear to Moses in the midst of an awe-inspiring volcanic eruption, and the Israelites had to keep their distance.

In comparison, Abraham's god, El, is a very mild deity. He appears to Abraham as a friend and sometimes even assumes human form. When the Israelites looked back to their own golden age, they saw Abraham, Isaac, and Jacob living in familiar terms with their god. El gives them friendly advice, like any sheikh or chieftain; he guides their wanderings, tells them whom to marry, and speaks to them in dreams.

In chapter 18 of Genesis, J tells us that God appeared to Abraham by the oak tree of *Mamre* near Hebron. Abraham had looked up and noticed three strangers approaching his tent during the hottest part of the day. With typical Middle Eastern courtesy, he insisted that they sit down and rest while he hurried to prepare food for them. In the course of the conversation, it transpired that, quite naturally, one of the men was none other than his god, whom J always calls *Yahweh.* The other two men turned out to be angels.

---

[46] Isaiah 6:13.

Karen Armstrong writes of Jacob's experience of God as mentioned in the Bible[47]. Before he left Bethel, Jacob decided to make the god he had encountered there his Elohim; this was a technical term signifying everything that the gods could mean for men and women. Jacob had decided that if El (or Yahweh as J calls him) could really look after him in Haran, he was particularly effective. He struck a bargain in return for El's special protection; Jacob would make him his Elohim, the only god that counted.[48] Israelite faith in God was deeply pragmatic. Abraham and Jacob both put their faith in El because he worked for them; they did not sit down to prove that he existed. El was not a philosophical abstraction. In the ancient world, *mana* was a self-evident fact of life, and a god proved his worth if he could transmit this effectively.

Years later, Jacob left Haran with his wives and family. As he reentered the land of Canaan, he experienced another strange epiphany. At the ford of Jabbok on the West Bank, he met a stranger who wrestled with him all night. At daybreak, like most spiritual beings, his opponent said that he had to leave, but Jacob held on to him; he would not let him go until he had revealed his name. In the ancient world, knowing somebody's name gave you a certain power on him, and the stranger seemed reluctant to reveal this piece of information. Jacob became aware that his opponent had been none other than El himself.

Jacob then made his request. "I beg you, and tell me your name." But he replied, "Why do you want to know my name?" And he blessed him there. Jacob named the place *Peniel* (El's face) "because I have seen El face to face," he said, "and I have survived."[49]

---

[47] Armstrong, *History*, 17.

[48] Isaiah 1:11–15.

[49] Isaiah 1:15–17.

In the final text of Exodus edited in the fifth century BCE, God is said to have made a covenant with Moses on Mount Sinai (supposed to have occurred around 1200 BCE). The idea of the covenant tells us that the Israelites were not yet monotheistic since it made sense only in polytheistic setting. The Israelites did not believe that Yahweh, the God of Sinai, was the only God but promised, in their covenant, that they would ignore all other deities and worship him alone. It is hard to find a single monotheistic statement in the whole of Pentateuch. Even the Ten Commandments delivered on Mount Sinai take the existence of other gods for granted:

There shall be no strange gods for you before my face [50].

The Bible shows that people were not true to their covenant. Although Yahweh's cult was fundamentally different in historical bias, it often expressed itself in paganism. When Solomon built a temple for *Yahweh* in Jerusalem, the city that his father, David, had captured from Jebusites, it was similar to the temples of Canaanite gods. It consisted of three square areas that culminated in a small cube-shaped room known as holy of holies, which contained the ark of the covenant, the portable altar that the Israelites had with them during their years in wilderness. Inside the temple was a huge bronze basin representing Yam, the primeval sea of Canaanite myth, and two forty-foot pillars, indicating the fertility cult of *Asherah.*

In about 622 BCE, during the reign of King Josiah of Judah, extensive repairs to the temple were carried out. At that time, people carried out worship of gods of Canaan alongside *Yahweh.* King Manasseh (687–42) had put up an effigy to Asherah in the temple, where there was a flourishing fertility cult since most Israelites were devoted to *Asherah* and some thought that she was *Yahweh's* wife. While the workmen

---

[50] Exodus 20:2.

were turning everything upside down, the high priest Hilkiah is said to have discovered an ancient manuscript that purported to be an account of Moses's last sermon to the children of Israel. When the young king heard the account in the manuscript, he was horror stricken; no wonder Yahweh had been so angry with his ancestors. They had totally failed to obey his strict instructions to Moses.[51]

It is now almost certain that the "book of law" discovered by Hilkiah was the core of the text that is now known as *Deuteronomy.* There have been various theories about its timely "discovery" by the reforming party. Some have suggested that it had been secretly written by Hilkiah with the help of the prophetess Huldah, whom Josiah immediately consulted. We shall never know for certain, but the book certainly reflected a new mood in Israel that reflected a seventh-century perspective. Eight hundred years after he died, Moses in his last sermon is made to give a new centrality to the covenant with the idea of the special *election* of Israel by *Yahweh.*

> *Yahweh had marked Israelites as His people, from all the other nations, not because of any merit of their own but because of his great love.*

The core of Deuteronomy includes the declaration that will become the Jewish profession of faith:

> Listen (*shema*), Israel! Yahweh is your Elohim, Yahweh
> alone (*ehad*)! You shall love Yahweh with all your heart,
> with all your soul, with all your strength. Let those words
> I urge upon you today be written on your hearts[52].

[51] 2 Kings 32:3–10, 2 Chronicles 34:14.

[52] Deuteronomy 6:4–6.

The stage for the appearance of Deuteronomy is set at a time when Israelites were in conflict with the seven tribes that occupied the land in which the Israelites had settled.

They must make no covenant with them or show them any pity.

They were to wipe out the Canaanite religion: "**tear down their alters, smash their standing stones, cut down their sacred poles and set fire to their idols.**"[53]

To suit the conditions of the time in the ongoing conflict between the Israelites and the Canaanites, the Bible was edited and rewritten. Moses, eight hundred after he had died addressees the Israelites to wipe out the Canaanite religion:

"tear down their alters, smash their standing stones, cut down their sacred poles and set fire to their idols"[54].

This was a land grab in the name of God. Twenty-five hundred years later the Zionist Jews used the same words inscribed in Deuteronomy to massacre and uproot the Palestinians.

The Evangelical Euro-Christians of America in the twenty-first century read the same words written by the Priest Hilkiah as an act of faith. The American support of Israel against Islam is based upon the fabrications of the High Priest Hilkiah.

When they recite Shema today, Jews give a monotheistic interpretation: Yahweh, our God, is one and unique. The Deuteronomist had not yet reached this perspective. "Yahweh *ehad*" did not mean God is one, but Yahweh was the only deity whom it was permitted to worship. Other gods were still a threat; their cults were

[53] Deuteronomy 7:3.

[54] Ibid.

attractive and could lure Israelites from Yahweh, who was a jealous God. If they obeyed Yahweh's laws, he would bless them and bring them prosperity; but if they deserted him, the consequences would be devastating.

Josiah immediately began a reform. All the images, idols, and fertility symbols were taken out of the temple and burned. Josiah also pulled down a large effigy of Asherah (regarded by some worshippers as Yahweh's wife) and destroyed the apartments of temple prostitutes.

The reformers rewrote Israelite history. The historical books of Joshua, Judges, Samuel, and Kings were revised according to the new ideology; and later, the editors of Pentateuch added passages that gave a Deuteronomist interpretation of the Exodus myth to the older narrative of J and E. Yahweh was now the author of a holy war of extermination in Canaan. The Israelites are told that the native Canaanites must not live in the country[55], a policy that Joshua is made to implement with unholy thoroughness:

> Then Joshua came and wiped out the Anakim from the highlands, from Hebron, from Debir, from Anoth, from highlands of Judah and all the inhabitants of Israel: he delivered them and their towns over to ban. No more Anakim were left in Israelite territory except at Gaza, Gath and Ashod [56].

This was genocide and a holocaust of the Canaanites.

Not all the Israelites subscribed to Deuteronomist practice in the years that led to the destruction of Jerusalem by Nebuchadnezzar in 587 BCE and the deportation of Jews to Babylon. In 604, the year of Nebuchadnezzar's accession, the *nabi* Jeremiah received the

---

[55] Exodus 23:33.

[56] Joshua 11; 21-2.

iconoclastic perspective of Isaiah that turned the triumphalist doctrine of the chosen people on its head: God was using Babylon as his instrument to punish Israel, and it was Israel's turn "to be put under a ban."[57] This time, Israelites were taken into slavery and transported to Babylon. In exile, the Israelites sat beside the rivers of Babylon; some of the exiles felt that they could not practice their religion outside the Promised Land. Pagan gods had always been territorial, and for some, it seemed impossible to sing the songs of Yahweh in a foreign country. They relished the prospect of hurling the Babylonian babies against a rock and dashing their brains out[58]. A new *nabi* preached tranquility. Nothing is known about him except that his works were added to the oracles of Isaiah, and he is called the second Isaiah.

In Babylon, the Israelites could not take part in liturgies that had been central to their religious life at home. Yahweh is all that they had.

Second Isaiah took this one step further and declared that *Yahweh* was the *only* God. In his rewriting of Israelite history, the myth of Exodus is clad in imagery that reminds us of the victory of Marduk over Tiamat, the primal goddess of the sea. If *Yahweh* had rescued Israel in the past, he could do it again; all the goyim were nothing but a drop of water in a bucket. Second Isaiah imagined the old deities of Babylon being bundled into carts trundling off into sunset[59].

For the first time, the Israelites became seriously interested in Yahweh's role in creation perhaps because of renewed contact with the cosmological myths of Babylon. If Yahweh had defeated the monsters of chaos in primordial time, it would be a simple matter for him to redeem the exiled Israelites.

---

[57] Jeremiah 25:8–9.

[58] Psalm 137.

[59] Isaiah 51:9-10 Psalms 65:7.

In 538, Cyrus issued an edict permitting the Jews to return to Judah and rebuild their own temple. Most of them elected to stay behind, and only a minority moved to Judah. In Judah, they imposed their Judaism on their bewildered brethren who had remained behind.

We can see what this entailed in the writings of the priestly tradition, which were written after the exile and inserted into the Pentateuch. This gave its own interpretation of the events described by J and E and added two more books, Numbers and Leviticus. As might be expected, P had an exalted and sophisticated view of *Yahweh.* He did not believe that anybody could actually see God the way J had suggested. He believed that there is a distinction between the human perception of God and the reality. In P's story of Moses on Sinai, Moses begs for a vision of *Yahweh,* who replies, "You cannot see my face, for no man can see and live."[60] Instead, Moses must shield himself from the divine impact in the crevice of a rock, where he could catch a glimpse of Yahweh as he departed as a kind of hindsight. P had introduced an idea that would become extremely important in history of God. Men and women can see only the afterglow of the divine presence, which he calls the "glory (*kavod*) of divine presence."

When P looked back at the old stories of Exodus, he did not imagine that Yahweh accompanied the Israelites during their wanderings; that will be unnecessary anthropomorphism. Instead, he shows the "glory of Yahweh" filling the tent where he met Moses. Similarly, it would be only the glory of Yahweh that would dwell in the temple.[61]

P's most famous contribution to the Pentateuch was, of course, the account of creation in the first chapter of Genesis, which drew on the *Enuma Elish* (the Babylonian epic of creation). P began with the waters of primordial abyss (*tibom*, a corruption of "Tiamat"), out of

60 Exodus 30:20.

61 Exodus 40:34, 35; Ezekiel 9:3.

which Yahweh fashioned the heavens and the earth. There was no battle of the gods, however, or struggle with Yam, Lotan, or Rahab. Yahweh alone was responsible for calling all things into being. There was no gradual emanation of reality; instead, Yahweh achieved order by an effortless act of will. Naturally, P did not conceive the world as divine, composed of the same stuff as Yahweh. Indeed, the notion of "separation" is crucial to P's theology: Yahweh made the cosmos an ordered place by separating night from day, water from dry land, and light from darkness. At each stage, Yahweh blessed and sanctified the creation and pronounced it "good." Unlike the Babylonian story, the making of man was the climax of the creation, not the comic afterthought.

As in *Enuma Elish*, the six days' creation was followed by the sabbatical rest on the seventh day; in the Babylonian account, this had been the day when the great assembly had met to "fix the destinies" and confer the divine title on Marduk. In P, the Sabbath stood in symbolic contrast to the primordial contrast to that had prevailed on Day One. The didactic tone and repetitions suggest that P's creation story was also designed for liturgical recital, like the *Enuma Elish*, to extol the work of Yahweh and enthrone him as Creator and Ruler of Israel[62].

Naturally, the new temple was central to P's Judaism. In the Near East, the temple had often been seen as an act of *imitatio dei,* enabling humanity to participate in the creativity of the gods themselves. During the exile, many Jews had found consolation on old stories of the ark of the covenant, the portable shrine in which God had "set up his tent" (*shakan*) with his people and shared their homelessness. When he described the building of the sanctuary, the tent meeting of the wilderness, P drew on the old mythology. Its architectural design

[62] Cf. Psalms 74 and 104.

was not original but a copy of the divine model. Moses is given very long and detailed instructions by Yahweh on Sinai:

> *Build me a sanctuary so that I may dwell among you. In making a tabernacle and the furnishings, you must follow exactly the pattern I shall show you.*[63]

The long account of construction of this sanctuary is not clearly intended to be taken literally; nobody imagined that the ancient Israelites had really built such an elaborate shrine of

> *gold, silver and bronze, purple stuffs, of violet shade, and red crimson stuffs, fine linen, goat's hair, rams' skin, acacia wood [and so forth].*[64]

This lengthy interpolation is heavily reminiscent of P's creation story, written eight hundred years after Moses's encounter on Mount Sinai. At each stage of construction, Moses "saw all the work" blessed the people, like Yahweh on the six days of creation. The sanctuary was built on the first day of the first month of the year. Bezalel, the architect of the shrine, was inspired by the spirit of God (*ruach Elohim*), which also brooded over the creation of the world. And both accounts also emphasize the importance of the Sabbath rest.[65]

The work of priestly tradition was included in the Pentateuch alongside the narratives of J and E and the Deuteronomist. Some Jews would always feel more drawn to the Deuteronomist God, who had chosen Israel to be aggressively separate from the goyim; some extended this into the Messianic myths that looked forward to the Day of Yahweh at the end of time, when he would exalt Israel and humiliate other nations. These mythological accounts tended to see

---

[63] Exodus 25:8–9.

[64] Exodus 25:3–5.

[65] Exodus 39:32, 43; 40:33; 40:2, 17; 31:3, 13.

God as a very distant being. It had tacitly agreed that, after the exile, the era of prophecy had ceased. There was to be no more direct contact with God; this was achieved in symbolic visions attributed to the great figures of the remote past, such as Enoch and Daniel.

Jesus: Again, borrowing quotes from the authoritative work of Karen Armstrong, we follow the trail of the deification of Jesus. About five centuries after the Jews returned from the captivity, a new charismatic faith healer and teacher began his own career in the north of Palestine. Very little is known about Jesus. The first full account of his life was Saint Mark's Gospel written around some forty years after his death. By that time, historical facts had been intertwined with mythical elements that expressed the meaning Jesus had acquired for his followers. During his lifetime, many Jews in Palestine had believed that he was the Messiah; the first Christians saw him as the new Moses, a new Joshua, and a founder of new Israel.

By the time of Jesus's death, the Jews had become passionate monotheists, so nobody expected the Messiah to be a divine figure. Mark's Gospel, the earliest chronicle of Jesus's life, presents Jesus as a perfectly normal man with a family that included brothers and sisters. No angels announced his birth or sang over his crib. He had not been marked out in infancy or adolescence in any remarkable way.

During the first century, Christians continued to think about God and pray to him like the Jews, and the churches were similar to synagogues. There were some acrimonious disputes in the '80s of the first century with the Jews, when Christians refused to observe the Torah, and the Christians were ejected from the synagogues.

In the Roman Empire, Persia, and India, people worshipped their gods to ask for help in times of turmoil and crisis, to seek a divine blessing for their situation, and to experience a therapeutic sense of continuity with their past. Religion was a matter of cult and rituals rather than philosophy and logic; it was based on emotion and not on dogma and ideology. Many people in today's world find solace in religious services and rituals of their religion that give them a sense of security and a link with their tradition. Pagans of antiquity worshipped their ancestral gods generation after generation; their rituals gave them a sense of identity. Celebration of traditions and old rituals gave them assurance of continuity with their known past. New ideas and changes in liturgy posed a threat of the unknown and uncertainty of the future. In a similar manner, the Israelites felt threatened by the break with their gods of the old. It took them over seven hundred years to accept the idea of Moses's one God. Even then, it required several edits of the Pentateuch by biblical writers to paint the new face of Yahweh with which Israelites felt comfortable. What finally put an end to the continual reversion of the Israelites to paganism was their own tribal God, Yahweh[66].

The election of God had set Israel apart from the goyim and a promised land that placed them in their eyes above all other inhabitants.

> *They must make no covenant with them or show them any pity.*

They were to wipe out the Canaanite religion:

> *Tear down their altars, smash their standing stones, cut down their sacred poles and set fire to their idols*[67].

Even then, Yahweh was the God and the King of Israel who would reside in the temple built by the Israelites. He would accompany them in their wanderings in the ark of the covenant, the portable shrine in

---

[66] Armstrong, *History*.

[67] Deuteronomy 7:3.

which God had *"set up his tent" (shakan)* to be with his people to share their homelessness.

Both Plato and Socrates had been "religious" about their philosophy; their scientific and metaphysical studies had inspired them with a glory of the universe. Platonism was one of the most popular philosophies of the late antiquity. In the first and second centuries, people were attracted to Plato, not as the ethical and the political thinker but as the mystic. His teachings helped one understand one's inner self by liberating the soul from the earthly body and ascend to the divine world. His thinking used cosmology as an image of continuity and harmony.

> The One Reality existed in serene contemplation of itself beyond the ravages of time and change at the pinnacle of the great chain of existence. All existence derived from the One as a necessary consequence of its pure being the eternal forms had emanated from the One, and had in turn animated the sun, stars, and moon each in their respective sphere. Finally, the gods, who were now seen as the angelic ministers of the One, transmitted the divine influence of the sub stellar world of men. The Platonist needed no barbaric tales of a deity who suddenly decided to create the world or who ignored the established hierarchy to communicate directly with a small group of humans. He needed no grotesque salvation by means of a crucified Messiah. Since he was akin to the God, who had given life to all things, a philosopher could ascend to the divine by means of his own efforts, in a rational ordered way.

By the second century, Christianity had moved into the world where Greek philosophy and Platonic ideas predominated. The Christian thinkers tried to explain their own religious experience; they naturally turned to the new Platonic vision of Plotinus and his pagan disciples. Plotinus (205–270) found Christianity a thoroughly objectionable creed, yet he influenced generations of future monotheists in all three of the God religions—Judaism, Christianity, and Islam. Plotinus synthesized the main currents of a millennia of Greek thought and transmitted them in a form that has continued to influence scholarship in our time. Plotinus evolved a system that helped achieve understanding of *self.* He was not looking for a scientific explanation of the universe or attempting to explain the physical origins of life. Instead of looking to the outside for objective explanations, he withdrew into himself to explore the depths of the psyche. Plotinus came to the conclusion:

Human beings become aware that something is wrong with their inner Self; they feel in conflict with themselves, out of touch with their inner nature and they feel perplexed. This conflict and complexity characterize human existence. The human's intrinsic impulse constantly seeks to remedy this inner conflict. It seeks to unify the multiplicity of experiences causing conflict, and disconnection, and reduce them to an integral whole. The drive for unity of the whole is the fundamental way in which the human mind works to reflect the essence of things in nature. To find the underlying truth of Reality, the soul must refashion, undergo a period of purification, and engage in contemplation. To do so one has to look beyond the cosmos, beyond the sensible world and even beyond the intellect to see deep into the core of Reality. And this reality is not beyond us but lies in the deepest recesses of our mind.

This ultimate reality is a primal unity, which Plotinus called the One. All things owe their existence to this potent reality. The One is simplicity itself. It just was. Consequently, the One was nameless. If we are to think positively of the One, there was more truth in silence[68]. We cannot say that it exists, since as Being itself, "it is not a thing distinct

[68] *Enneads* 5.6.

> from all things"[69]. Indeed, Plotinus explained, "It is Everything and Nothing; it can be none of the existing things, and yet it is all"[70].

In fact, the Koran calls the same underlying truth of the reality as the *ain al-yaqin* (Koran 102). Over time and under the influence of contemplation and inner search, the knowledge of certainty may be transformed into a higher form of knowledge of Allah that the Koran calls the eye of certainty (*ain al-yaqin*, Koran 102:7). This knowledge is acquired through spiritual intelligence that metaphorically lies in the heart of the believer. Before attaining this type of knowledge, the heart of the believer must first be "opened to Islam."

> Is one whose heart Allah has opened to Islam, so that he has received enlightenment from Allah. Woe to those whose hearts are hardened against celebrating the praises of Allah! They are manifestly wandering (in error)! (Az-Zumar 39:22. Koran)

Once opened, the heart receives knowledge through the divine light, the *nur* of Allah, which leads the believer toward the remembrance of Allah. Just as with the knowledge of certainty, with the eye of certainty, the believer sees Allah's existence through His presence in this world. With the eye of certainty, what lead the believer to the knowledge of Allah are not the arguments to be understood by the rational intellect but through divine inspiration that strips away the veils of worldly phenomenon to reveal the divine reality underneath.

From the spiritual perspective, the one who perceives the reality through the knowledge of Allah is the true sage. Unlike a scholar who develops his skills through years of formal study, the spiritual intellectual does not need book learning to apprehend the divine light,

---

[69] Ibid. 5.3.11.

[70] Ibid. 7.3.2.

the *nur* of Allah. A spiritual intellectual can be anyone, scholarly or otherwise, whose knowledge extends both outward to take in the physical world and upward to realize his ultimate transcendence of the world through his link with the Absolute. Without such a vertical dimension of spirit, the scholars' knowledge, whatever its extent may be in academic terms, is of little worth.

The third and most advanced type of knowledge builds on the transcendent nature of knowledge itself. The highest level of consciousness is called the "truth of certainty" (*haqq al-yaqin).* It is also known as *ilm ladduni*, knowledge "by presence." This form of knowledge partakes directly of the divine reality and leaps off directly across the synapses of human mind to transcend both cognitive reasoning and intellectual vision at the same time. The truth of certainty refers to a state of consciousness in which a person knows the Real through direct participation and communion with the reality. This type of knowledge characterizes Allah's prophets and *rasuls*, whose consciousness of truth is both immediate and participatory because it comes through direct inspiration.

Christian thinkers tried to explain their religious experience on the basis of Plotinus's vision. The notion of enlightenment was impersonal, beyond human categories, and natural to humans. After bypassing the superficial differences, there were profound similarities between the monotheistic religions and the Hindu and Buddhist ideal in India. When human beings contemplate the Absolute, they have very similar ideas and experiences. The sense of presence, ecstasy, and dread in the presence of a reality—called nirvana, the One, Allah, Brahman, or God—seems to be a state of mind and a perception that are natural and endlessly sought by human beings.

The religious impulse behind the startling divination of Jesus may be connected to religious developments in India and Persia at the same time. In both Hinduism and Buddhism, there had been a surge of devotion to exalted beings such as Buddha himself or Hindu gods, which had appeared in human form. This kind of personal devotion is known as bhakti. These kinds of devotions expressed perennial human longing for personal humanized gods, whom they could approach, converse with, and seek comfort from hardships and calamities. It was a new departure in Buddhism and Hinduism, and it was integrated into religion without compromising essential principles.

Nagarjuna, the Buddhist philosopher who founded the void school in the first century, suggested that the ultimate truth could only be grasped intuitively through the mental disciplines of meditation. Buddhists, who adopted this philosophy, developed a belief that everything that we experience is an illusion. The Absolute, which is the inner essence of all things, is a *void*, a nothing, that has no existence in a normal sense. It was therefore natural to identify the void with nirvana. Since Buddha had achieved nirvana, it followed that in some indefinable way, he had become nirvana and identical with the Absolute. Thus, everybody who sought nirvana was also seeking to identify with the Buddhas. It is easy to see that this bhakti or devotion to Buddha was similar to the Christian devotion to Jesus. There had been similar welling up of bhakti in Hinduism at the same time. It centered on the figures of Shiva and Vishnu, two of the most important Vedic deities. The Hindus developed a trinity of Brahman, Shiva, and Vishnu. The three were symbols or aspects of single indefinable reality.

Origen, a priest in Alexandria, developed a theology that stressed the continuity of God with this world. God was the spirituality of light, optimism, and joy. Origen adapted his Platonist philosophy to the Semitic scriptures. Thus, the virgin birth of Jesus was not to be taken as a literal event but as birth of the divine wisdom in the soul. Step by step, a Christian could ascend the chain of being until he reached God, his natural element, and home. Belief on the divinity of Jesus the man was a phase that would help the Christian to transcend and see God face-to-face.

By 235, Christianity became one of the most important religions of the Roman Empire. It was beginning to appeal to the highly intelligent men who were able to develop the faith along the lines that the Greco-Roman world could understand. The new church attracted women; its scriptures taught that in Christ there was neither male or female and insisted that their men cherished their wives as Christ cherished his church. Christianity had the advantages that had made Judaism once an attractive faith without the disadvantages of circumcision and the burden of 613 mitzvoth (commandments). Pagans were particularly impressed by the welfare system that the churches had established and their compassionate behavior toward one another. The church had become multiracial, catholic, international, and ecumenical. It was administered by efficient bureaucrats.

In about 320 CE, a severe theological debate seized the churches of Egypt, Syria, and Asia Minor. Christianity within itself had failed to resolve the true ideology of God.

It had taken Judaism eight hundred years to resolve the issues about who Yahweh, the God of Moses, was. In the end, with additions and changes to the Pentateuch by the fifth century BCE, a resolution of sorts was achieved. In the final text of Exodus edited in the fifth century BCE, God is said to have made a covenant with Moses on Mount Sinai (supposed to have occurred around 1200 BCE). The idea of the covenant tells us that the Israelites were not yet monotheistic since it made sense only in a polytheistic setting. The Israelites did not believe that Yahweh, the God of Sinai, was the only God but promised, in their covenant, that they would ignore all other deities and worship him alone. It is hard to find a single monotheistic statement in the whole of Pentateuch. Even the Ten Commandments delivered on Mount Sinai take the existence of other gods for granted:

> There shall be no strange gods for you before my face[71].

The debate in the churches of the Near East arose first from unresolved issues left over from the separation of Christianity from Judaism and second from the issues brought over by the influence of the Greek thought to the new Christianity. The controversy had been kindled by Arius, a charismatic presbyter of Alexandria: How could Jesus Christ have been God in the same way as God the Father? Arius was not denying the divinity of Jesus; he called Jesus "strong God" and "full God," but he argued that it was blasphemous to think that he was divine by nature.[72] Jesus had specifically said that the Father was greater than he was. The controversy became so heated that the emperor Constantine himself intervened and summoned a synod to Nicaea, in modern Turkey, to settle the issue.

There has been much speculation about the nature of Jesus's teachings and mission. Very few of his words seem to have been recorded in the Gospels, and much of the material of the Gospels has been influenced by later developments in the church founded by Saint Paul. There are clues that point to the essentially Jewish nature of Jesus's career. After Jesus's death, his followers decided that he had been divine.

The doctrine that Jesus was God in human form was not finalized until the fourth century. The development of Christian belief in the incarnation was a gradual, complex process. Jesus himself certainly never claimed to be God. He never claimed that he had divine powers or *dynameis* confined to him alone. He had promised his disciples that if they

---

[71] Exodus 20:2.

[72] In a letter to Eusebius, his ally, and in the Thalia. Quoted in Robert C. Gregg and Dennis E. Groh, *Early Arianism: A View of Salvation* (London, 1961), 66.

had "faith," they could have these powers too. By faith, he did not mean adopting the correct theology but cultivating an inner attitude of surrender and openness to God. Centuries later, Muhammad taught the same surrender and openness to God.

After Jesus's death, his followers could not abandon their faith that Jesus somehow presented an image of God. From a very early date, they had begun to pray to him. Saint Mark's Gospel, written forty years after Jesus's death, presents Jesus as a perfectly normal man with a family that included brothers and sisters. No angels or magi announced his birth or sang over his crib. During his lifetime, a very few of his words seem to have been recorded, leading to speculation about the exact nature of his mission. Jesus never claimed to be God, yet after his passing, his followers decided that Jesus had been divine.

The Gospels tell us that God had given Jesus divine powers (*dynameis*) that enabled him to perform godlike tasks to heal the sick and to forgive their sins. Jesus never claimed that that these divine "powers" were confined to him alone. Jesus did not believe that the Spirit was for the privileged and the Jews only but believed that even goyim could receive the Spirit. Paul called Jesus "Son of God" in the Jewish sense and certainly did not believe that Jesus had been the incarnation of God himself. When Paul explained the faith that was handed down to him, he said that Jesus had suffered and died *"for our sins."* There were no detailed theories about the crucifixion as an atonement of the "original sin" of Adam. This theology did not emerge till the fourth century and was only important in the Roman world.

Euro-Christianity: After Jesus's death, his followers among the poor continued to live in their native communities. They continued to worship as their Jewish ancestors did. Moreover, they did follow the law and the covenant of the prophets. As it usually happens, the prosperous, the educated, and those familiar with the Greek and the

Roman ways moved to the center of power of the Roman Empire. The reign of Emperor Constantine is often taken to mark the beginning of a new period in the history of the Roman Empire. Constantine transferred his capital from Rome to Constantinople, on the site of the Greek city of Byzantium, in the year 324. He maintained the Roman legal and political structure and the economy, and the military remained unchanged. The elite spoke Latin, and the common people maintained their Greek language and culture. In 313 CE, in the Edict of Milan, Constantine legalized Christianity. With the Greek and Roman influences, Christianity in the Roman Empire acquired significant aspects of pagan Greco-Roman culture as the Christians came to play a more important and more public role in the life of the empire.

An icon (in Greek *eikon* or "image") was a panel painted with a sacred subject intended for veneration and worship among the Greeks of Asia Minor. The icon's imitation of a holy figure enabled the image to take on the essence and sanctity of a god or of the saintly figure portrayed. By venerating the image, the worshipper honored the saintly figure through the pathway of the icon. The Greco-Roman tradition of painted panels of the gods placed in homes with candles lit around them inspired the development of icons among the early Christians. It started with the images of Jesus, Virgin Mary, and other people regarded as saints. People of the empire continued the veneration and the worship of Jupiter, Apollo, Adonis, Venus, Athena, and Aphrodite, and some of them added a new god, Jesus, to their worship. Icons with Christian subjects, at first, were worshipped in private; but gradually, they entered the church. Because of their pagan roots and because they violated the second of the Ten Commandments, that forbade the making of idols; segments of society rejected icons. This rejection eventually led to the iconoclastic controversy and to the separation of Christianity from Judaism in the Byzantine Empire.

First Ecumenical Council of Nicaea—AD 325: The Byzantine emperor Constantine invited an ecumenical council of 318 church leaders on June 19, 325, to sort out many internal disputes on the nature of Jesus and his message among the Roman Christians. This was the first ever meeting of the leaders of Christianity. The odd thing about this convention was that the council of the Christian church was called by an emperor who was neither pious nor a Christian. Internal disputes within the Christian community had prevented it from presenting an intelligent and coherent view of Jesus's mission to others in the Roman Empire, which caused conflict. After much argument and debate, a unanimous statement on the Christian profession of faith was not achieved. Persuasion and, according to some, coercion by the emperor finally achieved a documented compilation of the Christian profession of faith that, with some changes, is still in effect today. This council also called for the compilation of a scripture for this new faith.

Jesus was an observant Jew, and Christianity originally developed as a part of Judaism. The historical Jesus is thought to have lived from about 3 BC to AD 33. He lived and taught in Palestine, primarily among fellow Jews. Christianity separated from the main body of Judaism for two major reasons:

1. Christianity came to regard Jesus as God's presence in human form. This was unacceptable to most Jews.
2. Judaism is defined by a covenant made between God and the Israelites. Part of this covenant is the law, a set of religious and ethical rules and principles. Most Christians came to regard both this covenant and law as *superseded* by Jesus's teaching and the community that he established.

After Jesus's time, his word spread to Persia, Egypt, and the Greek world. Over the next three hundred years, the epicenter of Christianity shifted from the Semitic Jerusalem to the Greek world of the Byzantine Empire. Jesus's message based on the God of Abraham and Moses, the Jewish law, and the covenant came to be understood differently by his followers in Persia, Egypt, and parts of the Roman Europe. Various gods and goddesses of the ancient world—Jupiter, Apollo, Adonis, Venus, Athena, and Aphrodite—heavily influenced the culture of Asia Minor and Mesopotamia. In Asia Minor, there were temples dedicated to these gods and goddesses. There were the temple of the goddess of victory, Nike, in the city of Nicaea; Zeus's temple in Bursa; temples of Athena in Truva and in Assos; temples of Trajan and Athena and altar of Zeus; temple of Heracles; temple of Hera; temple of Dionysus; temple of Serapis in Pergamum; and the sixth century BCE temple of mother goddess in Ayvalik.

Other cultures in the Near East had other names for the same gods. In the fourth century CE, when Christianity had not yet gained a popular following in the Middle East, al-'Uzza of the Arabs was Venus and Aphrodite among the Greeks and the Romans and Isis of the Egyptians. Al-Lat of Arabs was the Athena of the Greeks. Manat of the Arabs represented the goddess of fate for the Persians and the Romans. Hubal was the Semitic Baal, Adonis of the Syrian and Greek Pantheon, and Tammuz, the consort of Ishtar of the Babylonians; and a six-day "funeral" for this god used to be observed even at the very door of the Israelite temple in Jerusalem, to the horror of the reformer Ezekiel. Temples for the worship of Baal, Adonis, Tammuz, Venus, Athena, al-'Uzza, Aphrodite, and Isis were commonplace in the Byzantine and Roman Empires. These gods formed the collective pantheon for the whole known world. The temples of the gods were open to every person who was able to make offerings to the gods. Every temple had a hierarchy of priests who served the gods.

The Byzantines converted the temple of Serapis in Pergamum to a church. During the Byzantine rule, the first of the first seven churches was built in Pergamum. The temple of the goddess of victory, Nike, in the city of Nicaea was converted into the Christian church of Ayatriponos. The First Ecumenical Council, Constantine's council, was held in Nicaea in 325 CE and the Seventh Ecumenical Council in 723 CE.

In Ephesus, in the early period of Christianity, due to the efforts of Paul and John, the Virgin Mary came to be recognized as Artemis, the successor of the goddess Cybele, and Jesus came to be recognized as Apollo, the successor to Artemis's son Attis. A Virgin Mary church was built in Ephesus. Byzantine church council meetings were held in Ephesus. Other temples in Ephesus were dedicated to Emperor Augustus and the goddess Rhea and Serapis. The Byzantines converted the temple of Serapis into a church. On the Seljuk Hill lie the remains of a basilica and a church built to honor Saint John during the Byzantine period. On the western slope of this hill lie the remains of the Temple of Artemis, considered as one of the Seven Wonders of World. This temple belonged to the Etruscan mother goddess, Cybele. Cybele was later identified as Artemis, and the temple was rebuilt for her. In Miletus on the temple of Serapis, the Byzantines built a basilica. In Priene, a city of sanctuaries of Egyptian gods Isis, Serapis, Anubis, and Harpocrates, a Byzantine church was built in the grounds of the theater and the temples.

Churches and other places of worship sprang up in Mesopotamia and Asia Minor in the second century, where the new Christians continued to worship in the manner of the Jews. The archeological sites in present-day Turkey show that original churches were near or adjacent to the temples, and in the fourth century, churches moved right into the temple buildings. In the process, there was a gradual assimilation of pagan traditions into the teachings of Jesus. The priesthood of the church assumed a hierarchy similar to that of the temples of gods. The priests of the temples were free to make creed and dogma for their gods. The Greeks were originally pagans and attached to their personal gods. For over five thousand years before the arrival of Christianity, the inhabitants of the land had built temples for the worship of their gods; and later on, the same site churches came to stand in every city of Asia Minor and Mesopotamia. The church fathers took up the Greek tradition of establishing the rules and dogma of their church. Eventually, many different competing traditions raised controversies and arguments among the church fathers in Egypt, Syria, and Asia Minor.

Emperor Constantine called the First Council of Nicaea. Pagan Constantine invited 318 church leaders from all over the empire. The major churches were represented, and the small and poor parishes were not aware of what was going on. The emperor hosted the gathering and sat amid the discussions while they lasted. These events ended in the *merger* of the church of Christianity and the pagan world of the Greeks and Romans, whereby a new religion sprang up. This gathering made a total split from Jesus's Judaic traditions. The new religion has, by today, evolved into Euro-Christianity and the Western civilization. The Council of Nicaea in 325 CE met in the city named after the temple of the goddess of victory, Nike, and put a stamp of approval on the merger of Christian teachings and the pagan world of Asia Minor. In this merger, the Semitic part of Christianity maintained the Judaic view of God:

> We believe in one God the Father all powerful, maker of all things both seen and unseen.

And the pagans also maintained their personal human god:

> And in one Lord Jesus Christ, the Son of God, the only begotten, begotten from the Father, that is from the substance *(Gr. ousia, Lat. Substantia)* of the Father, God from God, light from

> light, true God from true God, begotten *(Gr. gennethenta, Lat. Natum)* not made *(Gr. poethenta, Lat. Factum), Consubstantial Gr. homoousion, Lat. unius substantiae (quod Graeci dicunt homousion)* with the Father[73].

It was this First Ecumenical Council, Constantine's council, of Nicaea in 325 CE that requested a Christian scripture, the New Testament, from what historians know to be an editing of thousands of Christian manuscripts and letters, to be formed for the emperor Constantine's subjects in the *Holy Roman Empire.* The manuscripts and Gospels that did not agree with this council's views were carefully gathered and put to a bonfire throughout the empire on the orders of the patriarch and the emperor.

All the first- and the second-century primary source documents, letters, and manuscripts that the First (325 CE) and Second (381 CE) Ecumenical Councils abridged, changed, and declared as heresy have been lost to posterity because they were destroyed by the church. There are no Gospels or epistles in Aramaic or Greek; those are of the period of Jesus Christ. Theologians point to one or two so-called second-century CE fragments that contain less than two paragraphs as primary sources, but these fragments are miniscule and on mediums that are impossible to date. There are no early Christian documents like the Dead Sea Scrolls known despite the fact that all the great apostolic works were gathered under the Holy Roman Empire in a time of great triumph for Christianity. The earliest New Testament Gospels we have, by any factual standard, are the Codex Vaticanus and Codex Sinaiticus of the mid-fourth-century CE. They are both in ancient Greek and cannot easily be translated into English due to the complexity and age of the lexicon.

---

[73] The Christian profession of faith.

Second Ecumenical Council: It was not until the Second Ecumenical Council held in Constantinople in 381 CE, sixty-six years after the First Council of Nicaea,

> *that the third person in the Trinity was recognized, and a full three hundred and fifty years after the crucifixion of Jesus Christ.*

The infallible papal edict of 381 CE that

> *God is the Holy Spirit, and the Holy Spirit is God*

revealed the great mystery of Christianity, three persons in one God. It was the Nicene Creed of 325 CE that introduced the word *homoiousious* or *consubstantial*, meaning "of one substance," explaining how only one God can exist in two different distinct forms, God the Father and God the Son. The third part of the Trinity was eventually revealed by the infallible papal edict of 381 CE that *God is the Holy Spirit, and the Holy Spirit is God,* finalizing the Christian profession of faith and revealing the great mystery of Christianity, three persons in one God.

> *We believe in one God the Father all-powerful, maker of heaven and of earth, and of all things both seen and unseen. And in one Lord Jesus Christ, the only-begotten Son of God, begotten from the Father before all the ages, light from light, true God from true God, begotten not made, consubstantial with the Father, through whom all things came to be; for us humans and for our salvation he came down from the heavens and became incarnate from the holy Spirit and the virgin Mary, became human and was crucified on our behalf under Pontius Pilate; he suffered and was buried and rose up on the third day in accordance with the scriptures; and he went up into the heavens and is seated at the Father's right hand; he is coming again with glory to judge the living*

and the dead; his kingdom will have no end. And in the Spirit, the holy, the lordly and life-giving one, proceeding forth from the Father, co-worshipped and co-glorified with Father and Son, the one who spoke through the prophets; in one, holy, catholic, and apostolic church. We confess one baptism for the forgiving of sins. We look forward to a resurrection of the dead and life in the age to come. Amen.

Third Ecumenical Council: The Third Ecumenical Council was held in Ephesus in 431 CE. In the Council of Ephesus, four hundred years after the crucifixion of Jesus, 200 bishops gathered and defined the true personal unity of Christ

and declared Mary, the mother of Jesus as the Mother of God (theotokos).

These foundational tenets of Christianity are not the Gospels according to Matthew, Mark, Luke, and John. They are the Gospels according to the Councils of Nicaea (325 CE), Constantinople (381 CE), and Ephesus (431 CE), in which mortal humans met and made declarations about the nature of God, Jesus, and his mother, Mary.

- A council of *318* mortal men who met in Nicaea in June 325 CE created Jesus, the only begotten son of God, as God the Creator.
- *One hundred and fifty* mortal men met in Constantinople in the year 381 CE and passed a resolution creating a Holy Spirit or the Holy Ghost.
- In the year 431 CE, *200* men met in Ephesus to make Virgin Mary the Mother of God.
- This leap of faith suggested that these men were divinely inspired when they abridged at least fifty Gospels into four and made Jesus God and his mother, Mary, Mother of God. These men, the hierarchical priests, came from the same flock of men as today's clergymen, some pious, while

others, albeit a small minority, tarnished the church around the world for raping little boys and girls in residential schools and churches. The council of priests of the fourth-century Nicaea, Constantinople, and Ephesus could have been no more divinely inspired than the council of priests of the twentieth-century Europe and America.

- The point of this argument is that humans are fallible and subject to God's will and not the other way around. God makes humans. Humans do not make God. Pagan priests of the old times, however, did invent their gods—Jupiter, Apollo, Adonis, Venus, Athena, and Aphrodite—and established rules for their service. This, however, does not occur in revealed monotheism.

It is impossible to learn what the apostles' firsthand account of Jesus really was as the original texts are missing. We do know, however, that a lot about the history of Christianity from the Council of Nicaea in 325 CE to the present. At the Council of Nicaea, the bishops and theologians were bitterly split, with some maintaining Jesus was a prophet, while others claimed Jesus was the Son of God but a separate "divine entity" (Arius), while the Constantine majority held fast to their belief that Jesus is God and God is Jesus (homoiousious). Unfortunately, there are no primary source manuscripts, letters, and carvings in wood or stone to allow anyone to study the ancient and apostolic texts to draw scholarly conclusions. All New Testament scholars must rely on faith that the Codex Vaticanus and Codex Sinaiticus (about 425–450 CE) are true to the accounts of the apostles, Mary, Paul, and Mary Magdalene. No primary proofs exist from the time of Jesus Christ that can give evidence that the New Testament is accurate to Jesus's message to humanity.

By making Jesus an incarnation of God on the earth, a redeemer, and the only notion of religious truth in the world, the Christians surpassed the Israelites and the Jews as the exclusive holders of truth and the knowledge of God. The Israelites continued to phase in and out of paganism for over eight hundred years. Faith in matters of cult and rituals based on emotion rather than philosophy and logic provides most people solace and comfort. Personalized and humanized gods are simpler to talk to and to ask for help in mundane matters.

The debate over the Nicene Creed was still simmering in the non-Hellenized world when a new vision of monotheism appeared in the seventh-century Arabia. With a sigh of relief from the Greek Trinitarianism, people in Africa, Mesopotamia, Persia, Syria, and Asia Minor flocked to the new faith of one universal God. These people had been perplexed by the mystery of God expressed in an idiom that was alien to them. Three hundred years after the bishops met in Nicaea at the behest of Constantine, at the time still a pagan, majority of Christians and Jews in the southern and eastern basins of the Mediterranean embraced the faith of one universal God, Islam.

The majority of Israelites, Jews, and Christians of Asia Minor, Mesopotamia, Egypt, and Africa embraced the *din* of one universal God, Islam. It was the faith of the God of Abraham. This was the legacy that Abraham left to his sons, and so did Jacob:

> Behold, Jacob said to his sons: "What will you worship after me?" They said: "We shall worship thy God and the God of thy fathers, - of Abraham, Isma'il and Isaac, - the One True God: to Him we bow." (Al-Baqarah 2:132–34, Koran)

> We guided Noah, and among his progeny, David, Solomon, Job, Joseph, Moses, and Aaron: thus, do We reward those who do good: And Zachariah and John, and Jesus and Elias: all in the ranks of the

Righteous: And Isma'il and Elisha, and Jonah, and Lot: and to all We gave favor above the nations: (Al-An'am 6:84:86, Koran)

Knowledge of God: Humans have always looked at God at two levels. *Emotionally*, it is a personal and humanized god that is tribal. This god has favorite children whom he protects and rewards over and above others. He is readily accessible in a temple, shrine, mausoleum, or mosque and has priests in attendance as intermediaries. The priest class formulates dogma, creed, and rituals to appease the god. This god is unpredictable—loving or demanding, subject to anger and joy in accord with the deeds and sacrifices of his devotees.

He has a specially trained class of helpers who act as cheerleaders and who perform crowd control for him. These hierarchies of helpers are the popes, bishops, priests, ayatollahs, rabbis, imams, ulema, pundits, and various classes of religious police. Proximity to their god provides this hierarchy power over other men and women. This source of power naturally leads to competition and often wars between the devotees. Wars fought in the name of this god leads to injustice and usurpation of rights of others.

The priest class, scholars, and writers introduced and interjected ideas that made their god dependent on creed and dogma invented by them. Writers of the Old and the New Testaments fashioned Yahweh and Jesus according to their own caprice. Muslim scholars produced Hadith and interpreted Sharia that made Allah and Muhammad subject to their own fancy and caprice. Such collective manipulations, at first, divided humans and then splintered communities into factions. Marriages of Henry XIII fragmented the Christian Europe, and nonsuccession of Ali split the Muslim world. These mechanizations of men interrupted the message of the God of Abraham that Moses, Jesus, and Muhammad had come to teach. In the fundamental emotional nature of humans, there is an essence of paganism under the surface that wells over in times of stress, grief, and failing belief. The signs of disbelief, mistrust, and *shirk* lies in the faith in astrology, horoscope, saint worship, amulets, and worship of gods of wealth, power, and politics.

Intellectually, humans wholeheartedly accept the concept of God as the Creator of everything that is. He wills, and it is. He is beyond human comprehension, and His divine systems do not conform to human concepts, creed, and dogma. Allah, God the Creator, created the galaxies, worlds, stars, sun, moon, little atoms, protons, neutrons, and tiny particles that show the complexity of His genius. Allah, the Lord of creation, sends water from the heavens for the sustenance of life on the earth. Allah directs sunshine to the earth to provide warmth and light to sustain, human, plant, and animal life. Allah formed the sun, moon, and stars to create equilibrium in the universe, every object in its intended place, revolving in its fixed orbit in perfect harmony and balance. Allah created the secrets and the mysteries of the heavens and the earth, the so-called sciences, and the knowledge of particles, elements, cells, mitochondria, chromosomes, gravity, and black holes, only a minute portion of which he revealed to man. Allah clearly provided humans a mind to wonder at His infinitesimal wisdom. Yet man is conceited and arrogant to believe that God is driven by man-created creed, testament, dogma, Sunna, and Sharia.

Allah does not require a shrine, a temple, a tent, or a talisman to live in. His presence is everywhere. He is present in the smallest particle (*nuqta*) and in the greatest expanse. He is accessible to each and every object He has created. Every object obeys Allah's will except for man. Man has been given free will. The covenant of the Koran presents us with the scope of the freedom of choice that humans have in doing what is wholesome and beautiful or what is corrupt and ugly and in the human role among the creation that distinguishes right activity, right thought, and right intention from their opposites. It reminds us of how the scales of Allah's justice—the two hands of Allah, His mercy and His wrath—are reflected in the human domain, where people have been appointed Allah's vicegerents. Deeds of goodness and wholesomeness are associated with mercy, paradise, and the beautiful. Evil and corruption is rewarded with wrath, hell, and the ugly.

Allah the Divine is open to the most miniscule of beings. From this little particle, the *nuqta*, the connection to Allah, the Cherisher and the Nourisher of the universe, extends into the vastest of expanse. Within this communion of the Divine with the creation passes the Spirit of Allah into His creatures. Man lays his heart and mind open to Allah in submission to receive His Spirit and guidance.

In the space and emptiness of the universe, there flow currents and whispers of wind and energy. These winds of silence, light, and sound carry the divine whisper, and in this sound is Allah's message. This message descends into the believer's receptive heart in peace, silence, and tranquility. When the angels and the Spirit descend with Allah's guidance, the eyes perceive the most beautiful divine light, the ears hear the softest tinkle of the bell, the nose smells the fragrance of a thousand gardens, and the skin feels the most tranquil of the gentle breeze. When this happens, the soul has seen nirvana. The believer is in communion with Allah. This is the knowledge of Allah.

Allah sent thousands of prophets to mankind to teach man precepts and principles to His straight path of unity, truth, and goodness. Over thousands of years, these precepts and principles spread around the world through civilizations till mankind, as a whole, began to comprehend the message of one universal God, the Creator of every particle and every being in the whole universe. Man listened and occasionally regressed into his inherent paganism, greed, selfishness, and egotism. Allah bestowed on man a vicegerency on the earth, a mind, a free will, and a covenant. Allah then announced that there would be no more prophets. The era of prophecy had ended. Man, in stages, had received the knowledge required to live in submission to Allah's will in peace and harmony on the earth in accordance with the divine laws, which were sent down as a guidance to every human community to a life of truth justice, goodness, and peace. Such knowledge consisted of the following:

Unity: There is one absolute Being from which all stems; the universe of galaxies and all the living things in it are all connected to one another and cannot be separated from that absolute Being. Everything alive—humans, animals, plants, and microorganisms—is created by the absolute Being, all nurtured with the same organic matter, all breathing the same air; and in turn, their physical self disintegrates to the same elements that then return to the earth and the universe. In this cycle of creation and disintegration, the only permanence is of the Real, the Absolute. All else is an illusion and a mirage. One moment you are here, and in the next, you are gone. Nothing is left behind—no riches, no honor, no ego, and no pride. What is left, however, is an account of your deeds, on which one day you will be judged.

Mind: Man is bestowed with a mind and free will. The mind has the ability to perceive ideas and knowledge from the Divine and from the signs of Allah. The whisper of the Divine, the rustle of the wind, the light of God, the fragrance of God's creation, and the sensation of the Divine touch all inspire the human mind with an endless stream of ideas and knowledge. Man has been granted the ability to process his thoughts and the knowledge with free will.

The verse of the light encompasses the totality of the message and guidance that God sent to man through His prophets. The pagan in man confused God's message and instead began to worship the *rasul*. With the end of the era of the prophets, man has to open his heart to the light of Allah and learn to recognize the goodness of God within himself, in his own heart.

Allah is the Light of the heavens and the earth. The parable of His Light is as if there were a Niche and within it a Lamp: the Lamp enclosed in Glass; the glass as it were a brilliant star: lit from a blessed Tree, an Olive, neither of the East nor of the West, whose Oil is well-nigh luminous, though fire scarce touched it: Light upon Light! Allah doth guide whom He will to His Light: Allah doth set forth Parables for men: and Allah doth know all things. (Lit is such a light) in houses, which Allah hath permitted to be raised to honor; for the celebration, in them, of His name: in them is He glorified in the mornings and in the evenings, (again and again). (An-Nur 24:35-36, Koran)

The parable of divine light is the fundamental belief in one universal God for the whole humankind.

Allah is the Light of Heavens and Earth. His light illuminates' hearts and minds of those who love Him, place their Trust in Him and open their heart and soul in submission to Him. Once hearts and minds are open to Allah in submission, they form the niche in which Divine light, Spirit and Wisdom of Allah glows in the human. The glow and the luminescence of the Spirit and Wisdom shines with the brightness of a star that is lit from the light of Divine Wisdom, the Tree of Knowledge, the knowledge of Allah's Signs. For those who Believe, Allah is within. The Believer is aglow with Allah's radiance, Light upon Light! The dwellings, where praised and glorified is Allah's name in the mornings and evenings, are aglow with Allah's light.

Allah has granted knowledge and the wisdom of *furqan* and *taqwa* to the believers who have opened their hearts and minds to Him. Man has been granted the freedom of choice in doing what is wholesome and beautiful or what is corrupt and ugly. It is only man among the creation that has been given the knowledge to distinguish right activity, right thought, and right intention from their opposites. This knowledge reminds man of the scales of Allah's justice; the two hands of Allah, His mercy and His wrath, are reflected in the human domain, where people have been appointed Allah's vicegerents. Deeds of goodness and wholesomeness are associated with mercy, paradise, and what is beautiful. Evil and corruption is rewarded with wrath, hell, and what is ugly.

The fundamental knowledge is the "knowledge of certainty" (*ilm al-yaqin*, Koran 102:5). This type of certitude refers to knowledge that results from the human capacity for logic and reasoning and the appraisal of what the Koran calls "clear evidences" (*bayyinat*) of Allah's presence in the world. This knowledge also comes through the study of Koran, the teachings of the prophets, and the signs of Allah. The signs of Allah encompass the whole knowledge of the creation; man's scientific and philosophical disciplines include only a miniscule fragment of this knowledge. The knowledge of certainty is rational and discursive, a point that the Koran acknowledges when it admonishes human beings to:

> Say: "Travel through the earth and see how Allah did originate creation; so, will Allah produce a later creation: for Allah has power over all things. (Al-'Ankabut: 29:20, Koran)

> It is He Who gives life and death, and to Him (is due) the alternation of Night and Day: will you not then understand? (Al-Mu'minun 23:80, Koran)

Over time and under the influence of contemplation and spiritual practice, the knowledge of certitude may be transformed into a higher form of knowledge of Allah, which the Koran calls the "eye of certitude" (*ain al-yaqin*, Koran 102:7). This term refers to the knowledge that is acquired by spiritual intelligence that believers in the East locate metaphorically in the heart. Before attaining this type of knowledge, the heart of the believer must first be "opened to Islam."

> Is one whose heart Allah has opened to Islam, so that he has received enlightenment from Allah. Woe to those whose hearts are hardened against celebrating the praises of Allah! They are manifestly wandering (in error)! (Az-Zumar 39:22, Koran)

Once opened, the heart receives knowledge as a type of divine light or illumination (*nur*) that leads the believer toward the remembrance of Allah. Just as with the knowledge of certainty, with the eye of certainty, the believer sees Allah's existence through His presence in this world. With the eye of certainty, what lead the believer to the knowledge of Allah are not the arguments to be understood by the rational intellect but by theophanic appearances (*bayyinat*) that strip away the veil of worldly phenomenon to reveal the divine reality underneath.

From the spiritual perspective, the one who perceives reality through the knowledge of Allah is a true "intellectual." Unlike the scholar, who develops his or her skills through years of formal study, the spiritual intellectual does not need book learning to understand the divine light. A spiritual intellectual can be anyone, scholarly or otherwise, whose knowledge extends both outward to take in the physical world and upward to realize his or her ultimate transcendence of the world through his or her link with the absolute. Without such a vertical dimension of spirit, the scholar's knowledge, whatever its extent may be in academic terms, is of little worth.

The third and most advanced type of knowledge builds on transcendent nature of knowledge itself. The highest level of consciousness is called the "truth of certitude" (*haqq al-yaqin).*

> But truly (Revelation) is a cause of sorrow for the Unbelievers.
> But verily it is Truth of assured certainty. So, glorify the
> name of thy Lord Most High. (Al-Haqqah 69:50–52)

It is also known as *ilm ladduni* (knowledge "by presence"). This form of knowledge partakes directly of the divine reality and leaps off directly across the synapses of human mind to transcend both cognitive reasoning and intellectual vision at the same time. The "truth of certainty" refers to a state of consciousness in which a person knows the Real through direct participation in it without resorting to logical proofs. This type of knowledge characterizes God's prophets and *rasuls*, whose consciousness of the truth is both immediate and participatory as what it is based on comes from direct inspiration.

Many Islamic scholars believe that divine inspiration could remain accessible to believers even after *Nabi* Muhammad's death. This possibility is symbolized in Islamic tradition by the figure of Khidr. Khidr first appeared in the Koran as an unnamed servant of Allah and as a companion of *Nabi* Musa (Moses). Khidr was endowed with knowledge of the unseen, which *Nabi* Musa lacked. The Koran describes this sage, who is not a *nabi* yet partakes of divine inspiration:

> So they found one of Our servants, on whom We had
> bestowed mercy from Ourselves and whom We had taught
> knowledge from Our own Presence. (Al-Kahf 18:65, Koran)

According to both the word of Allah as expressed in the Koran and the tradition of the *nabi* Muhammad, faith in Islam has as much to do with theoretical and empirical knowledge as it does with simple belief. This multidimensional conception of knowledge comprehends a reality that lies hidden within the unique world yet can be revealed by the human mind and the vision of the spiritual intellect through the signs of Allah that are present in the world itself. In the Koran, Allah calls humanity:

So, I do call to witness what you see

And what you see not,

(This is) a Message sent down from the Lord of the Worlds.

But verily it is Truth of assured certainty. (Al-Haqqah 69:38–39, 43, 51, Koran)

The Koranic notion of religious belief (*iman*) as dependent on knowledge is actualized in practice in the term *islam*. The term *islam* signifies the idea of surrender or submission. Islam is a religion of self-surrender; it is the conscious and rational submission of a dependent and limited human will to the absolute and omnipotent will of one universal God of all creation, Allah. The type of surrender Islam requires is a deliberate, conscious, and rational act made by a person who knows with both intellectual certainty and spiritual vision that Allah, who is the subject of Koranic discourse, is the Real. The knower of God is a Muslim (fem. *Muslimah*), "one who submits" to the divine truth and whose relationship with God is governed by *taqwa*, the consciousness of humankind's responsibility toward its Creator.

Consciousness of God alone is not sufficient to make a person a Muslim. Neither is it enough to be merely born a Muslim or to be raised in an Islamic cultural context. The concept of *taqwa* implies that the believer has the added responsibility of acting in a way that is in accordance with three types of knowledge: *ilm al-yaqin*, *ain al-yaqin*, and *haqq al yaqin* (knowledge of certainty, eye of certainty, and truth of certainty). The believer must endeavor at all times to maintain himself or herself in a constant state of submission to Allah. By doing so, the believer attains the honored title of "slave of Allah" (*abd Allah*, fem. *amat Allah*), for he recognizes that all power and all agency belongs to God alone:

> Allah has willed it. There is no power but Allah's. (Al-Kahf 18:39, Koran)

Trusting in the divine mercy of his divine Master yet fearing God's wrath, the slave of God walks the road of life with careful steps, making his actions deliberate so that he will not stray from the path that God has laid out for him:

> Thee do we worship, and Thine aid we seek, Show us the straight way, The way of those on whom Thou hast bestowed Thy Grace, those whose (portion) is not wrath, and who go not astray. (Al-Fatihah 1:5–7)

It is an all-encompassing and highly personal type of commitment that has little in common with academic understanding of Islam as a civilization or a cultural system. The universality of religious experience is an important premise of the Koran's argument against profane or secular life. Along with commitment to the belief and submission to the Divine comes the obligation to obey the covenant of Allah. It is the same covenant that God offered to the followers of the old-time prophets of the Israelites, and the people failed in their commitment to the covenant. The covenant is still open to obedience of the whole mankind.

After submission (*islam*) and faith (*iman*), *ihsan* forms the third dimension of the *din*. The word *ihsan* is derived from the word *husn* that designates the quality of being good, beautiful, virtuous, pleasing, harmonious, or wholesome. The Koran employs the word *hasana*, from the same root as *husn*, to mean a good or a beautiful deed, for example:

> Whatever beautiful touches you, it is from Allah, and whatever ugly thing touches you, it is from yourself. And We have sent thee as a Rasool to (instruct) humanity. And enough is Allah for a witness. (An-Nisa 4:79, Koran)

> If any does beautiful deeds, the reward to him is better than his deed; but if anyone does evil, the doers of evil are only punished (to the extent) of their deeds. (Al-Qasas 28:84, Koran)

Such verses reveal that Allah loves humans who do what is beautiful, who have *taqwa* of Allah and are God-wary, who repent, who ask for forgiveness and cleanse themselves, those who have trust in Allah, and who are just and fair. Twenty-three verses in the Koran mention traits in humans that Allah does not love: *Munafiqeen* (truth concealers), *kafirun* (the wrongdoers), *zalimun* (workers of corruption), *mufsidun* (the transgressors), and *ta'adda* (the immoderate, the proud, and the boastful).

In the Koran, Allah's love is always directed at humans, and such a love designates the special relationship between Allah and human beings, the special trust in the form of vicegerency only given to mankind. However, Allah does not love human beings whose love is not directed at Him. How can humans love Allah, about whom they know nothing? Once people come to know Him, the first spark of love of Allah lights up in the human. This spark is the *nur* of Allah. According to the Koran, the person must follow the *nabi* by moving toward Allah through *islam* (submission to Allah), *iman* (the right faith), and *ihsan* (doing what is beautiful). Through Allah's love, they will reach salvation. Allah commands the *nabi* to utter these words:

> Say, if you love Allah, follow me and Allah will love you and forgive your sins. Allah is Forgiving, Compassionate. Say, "Obey Allah and the Rasool". But if they turn their backs, Allah loves not those who reject faith. (Ali 'Imran 3:31–32, Koran)

Allah wants people to love Him, and their love for Him follows His love for them. Human love precedes divine love. It is Allah who, in His mercy and bounty, kindles the spark of love for Him in the human heart. How is it possible for anyone to love Allah unless it has been instigated by Him? How could anyone love God without the intervention of His mercy?

> O you who believe! If any from among you turn back from his Faith, soon will Allah produce a people whom He will love as they will love Him, lowly with the Believers, mighty against the Rejecters, fighting in the Way of Allah, and never afraid of the reproaches of such as find fault. That is the Grace of Allah, which He will bestow on whom He pleases. And Allah encompasses all, and He knows all things. (Al-Ma'idah 5:54, Koran)

The End

O my Allah! I have labored in your path of
Truth, Justice, Unity and Peace.

May this work please Thee. O my Allah shower
thy Blessings on this work and on

those who read it and follow Thine Path of Mercy. Aameen.

Munawar Sabir

Appendix

adalah: One capable of adjudication.

'adl: Justice.

ad-deen: Commitment, obligation, responsibility, pledge, promise, oath, contract, compact, covenant, pact, and treaty agreement.

ahd: Commitment, obligation, responsibility, pledge, promise, oath, contract, compact, covenant, pact, and treaty agreement.

***ahkam*:** Legal verdict, judgment, permissible.

ain al-yaqin: Eye of certainty.

ardh: The earth, man's domain.

amanah: Trust.

amilu: Deeds.

aql: Intellect, human reasoning.

awliya: Friends and protectors.

ayah: Verses of the Koran.

***ayan*:** Local notables.

babas: Sufi holy men.

batil: Falsehood, untruth, opposite of *haqq*.

beys: Local notables.

bhakti: Sanskrit: love and attachment to God.

burka: Head-to-foot garment worn by some women in the Middle East and South Asia.

covenant: Commitment, obligation, responsibility, pledge, promise, oath, contract, compact, pact, and treaty agreement.

Dar es Salaam: The abode of peace; the land of Islam.

darar: Hardship.

din: Total belief system based on the practice of total submission to God's will, accompanied by acts of beautiful deeds that endeavor to set things right and restore harmony, peace and balance. A synthesis of *islam*, *iman*, and *ihsan*.

***devsirme* class:** Ottoman custom of taking young slaves from among the Slavic peoples for use in bureaucracy and as loyal officers in the army.

dhikr: Remembrance of Allah.

dynameis: Greek: divine "powers."

ehad: Hebrew: one. Equivalent of Arabic *ahad*.

Enuma Elish: The Babylonian epic of creation.

Fahasha: Shameful, indecent; sexual misconduct.

faqih: Jurist.

fasiq: Impostor.

fasiqun: Rebellious transgressors.

fatwa: A religious edict; decree in matters of religious law.

fay: Income from the captured territories.

fiqh: Science of jurisprudence.

fuqara: Those who ask or beg.

furqan: Criterion to judge between right and wrong.

ghazzu: Tribal raids of pre-Islamic times, practiced by the likes of Ibn Sa'ud.

goyim: Hebrew, Yiddish: a pejorative term for non-Jews, used in Talmud, Jewish literature, and speech Hadith; a story; saying and deeds of the prophet.

Hadith: A story; saying and deeds of the prophet.

hajj: Pilgrimage to Mecca.

halal: That which is permitted.

Haleem: Magnanimous.

Hanafi: Followers of the school of jurisprudence of Abu Hanifah.

Hanbali: Followers of the school of jurisprudence of Imam Hanbal.

haqq: Absolute truth.

haqq al-yaqin: Truth of Certainty.

haraj: Harm.

haram: Unlawful; illegal.

harramma: Unlawful.

hasana: Beautiful, wholesome, good.

***hubb*:** Love.

hukm: Command; edict.

husn: Good, beautiful, wholesome.

husna: Beautiful, good.

ihram: Precincts of Kaaba; in the state of piety and dress for the *hajj.*

ihsan: Doing good and wholesome deeds.

ijma: Mutual consultation.

ijtihad: Capacity to find answers to the dilemmas of the community.

Ikhwan: Brothers.

ilm al akhlaq: Knowledge of conduct of the faith.

ilm al kalam: Knowledge of dogmatic theology; knowledge of reason or rational investigation.

ilm al-yaqin: Knowledge of certainty.

***ilm ladduni*:** Knowledge from Allah.

iman: Faith of Islam; second dimension of Islam.

imam: A person who leads the congregation prayers. In Shiite Islam, a descendant of the prophet who is looked on as the leader of the community.

imitatio dei: Latin: imitation of God.

insan: Mankind, humankind, humans.

iqtas: Land grants in lieu of services.

Islah: Establishing wholesomeness, reform.

islam: A voluntary submission to the will of Allah.

Isr: A firm covenant, compact, or contract that if one does not fulfill becomes liable for punishment.

Jannat: Paradise. Garden of eternity.

***Jannat adn*:** Gardens of eternity.

Jammaa: Community of Muslims.

jihad: Struggle to the utmost; striving to purify oneself; struggle against oppression and tyranny.

jum'ah: Friday (prayers).

kafir: The nonbelievers; infidel, pagan, ungrateful.

kafirun: The plural of *kafir.*

kafireen: The plural of *kafir.*

kavod: Hebrew: glory of divine presence.

khankahs: Sufi hospices.

Kharijites: Seceders, those who disaffiliate.

kufr: The act of disbelief in Allah; ingratitude.

ma'ashiyyat: Economics.

madrassas: Religious schools.

madhab: Fraternity or school of jurisprudence.

madhahib: Plural of *madhab.*

ma'eeshat: Life of hardship; economic hardship.

masha'ikhs: Leaders of fraternities of jurisprudence.

mawla: Protector and helper.

millet: Autonomous religious communities in the Ottoman Empire.

mihnah: Inquisition.

mithaq: Tie of relationship between two parties.

mitzvoth: Hebrew: commandments.

mufsidun: Worker of corruption.

muhsin: Performer of wholesome deeds.

mufti: A jurist and scholar of Islamic law.

malaika: Angels.

Munafiqeen: Hypocrites, truth concealers.

***Munkar*:** Wrong.

mushrikun: Unbelievers.

mushirs: Advisers, representatives.

Mutaffifeen: Purveyors of fraud.

muttaqeen: One with *taqwa*; a true believer.

***nabi*:** The one who is given the divine revelation. It does not mean "prophet." *Prophet* is a Jewish and Christian terminology that means "clairvoyant or a forecaster of events."

nirvana: Sanskrit: the sense of ecstasy or dread in the presence of a reality.

nur: Allah's blessed light.

padishah: An Iranian and Indian title of a king.

pasha: High-ranking official in the Ottoman Empire.

Qarmatian: a Sufi sect organized around khankahs and religious communities.

qutb: An imaginary divine axis representing justice.

Rabb: Lord.

Rahamat: Divine mercy.

Rahim: Most merciful.

Rahman: Most gracious.

rashidun: Righteous.

***rasul, rasool*:** The one who receives a revelation and then communicates it to others. "Messenger" is a mistranslation of *rasul*. The *rasul* knows and understands the revelation and, on the basis of this knowledge, communicates this word of Allah.

reava: Flocks; Turkish subjects.

şabr: Patience, fortitude.

şābir: Patient one.

şabbār: Patience.

şābara: Plural for the ones who are patient.

Sahaba: Companions of the Prophet.

salat: Contact prayers; prayers that require standing, bowing, and kneeling to Allah in submission.

salihat: Wholesome.

sama: The heavens; the sky.

shakan: Hebrew: to set up a tent.

Shakoor: Appreciative

Sura: Chapter.

tabi'un: Governors.

***Taslim*:** Last part of the salat prayer asking for blessings on the people on the left and the right.

***tapulu*:** Lands given to the military in lieu of services.

***taqwa* of Allah:** Awareness of Allah's presence.

timars: Endowment of estates in lieu of military service.

Tawhid: Unity of Allah.

ulema: Scholars of Islam; those knowledgeable in Islamic law.

***ulil amri minkum*:** A person appointed to administer affairs of a community.

ummah: Islamic community; the nation of the Muslims.

ummah el nuqta: *Nuqta* is a dot. Thus, the *ummah el nuqta* forms the lowest level or the basic community in a democracy.

ummah wast: The middle nation; the nation given to moderation.

wakil: Representative.

waqf: Endowment

yashmak: Veil; a head-to-toe garment worn by some Muslim women.

zakat: Mandatory charity; cleansing of oneself.

zalimun: Evildoers.

About the Author

Dr. Munawar Sabir was born in Kenya, then a British colony. He received his education in Kenya, Pakistan, England, and Canada. As a product of Muslim and secular heritages of Africa, Asia, Europe, and North America, he has gone back to delve deep into his original heritage of the *din* and the Koran.

Dr. Munawar Sabir has written six books on contemporary Islam, the covenant of the Koran, and the historical events that have shaped the current state of Islamic societies. These books are the culmination of over thirty years of observation, study, and research on Islam and the sociopolitical development of Islamic societies in relation to their fulfillment of the covenant of Allah.

Munawar Sabir is a fellow of the Royal College of Physicians and Surgeons of Canada. He has practiced medicine in Britain and Canada for over fifty-eight years and has published scientific papers on neurological disorders of the musculoskeletal system.

In this book, Dr. Munawar Sabir argues that the Koran is a living, vibrant communion between Allah and His creatures. The lines of thought and the step-by-step guidance laid out by Allah for the individual believer fourteen hundred years ago continue to vitalize the community of believers as it did in the course of early Islam's belief, thought, and history. The sense of the word read, recited, and explained by the scholars of Islam has remained anchored to the meaning given to it by the *masha'ikhs* of the schools of jurisprudence at the time of the Umayyad and the Abbasid caliphates of the Middle Ages. The religion that passes as Islam today—that is, the Islam of the masses, the scholars, and the ruling classes both of the Shia and the Sunni—is the fossilized version of the Islam of the Middle Ages. The present-day Muslims adhere to the rituals without observance of the guidelines of the covenant of Allah.

It is not the Islam of the Koran, nor it is the Islam of the blessed *nabi.* It is in the Koran that the Muslims will find the answers to their resurrection, and the remedy to the ills of modern-day Islamic world lies in the pages of the holy book in the step-by-step guidance of Allah.

The covenant of the Koran is a total belief system of an individual based upon total submersion of one's personality with Allah with total awareness and *taqwa* of Him at all times through observance of all the thirty-seven commandments of Allah's covenant. This communion is not only with Allah but also, through Him, with other humans and Allah's creation, both alive and inanimate. The phrase *amilu al saalihaat* (to do good, to perform wholesome deeds) refers to those who persist in striving to set things right, who restore harmony, peace, and balance. Other acts of good works recognized in the covenant of the Koran are to show compassion, to be merciful and forgive others, to be just, to protect the weak, to defend the oppressed, to be generous and charitable, to be truthful and to seek knowledge and wisdom, to be kind, to be peaceful, to love others, and to perform beautiful deeds.

Through the fulfillment of the covenant of Allah, the *ummah* is now ready to roll over artificial borders and barriers dividing the Dar es Salaam, to assume its *executive sovereignty* over the land of Islam, and to establish the governance of the *ummah* in accord with the covenant of Allah through justice, consultation, and consensus of the community. The greatest miracle of Islam is the revelation and preservation of the divine word, the Koran. The next greatest miracle is survival and continuing expansion of the *ummah* through centuries of tyrannical and turbulent sultanic and colonial rule. In spite of the alien systems of governments of sultans and dictators founded on self-aggrandizement and personal power, the common people and the community of Islam have continued to receive nurturing and spiritual enlightenment through love of Allah and His blessed *nabi.* Holy men, sages, Sufis, and other humble religious teachers have continued to nurture the love of Allah in the heart of the people. They have sought to teach unity, *taqwa*, and knowledge of Allah in humility and sincerity.

Insignificant raindrops fall on parched land singly and disappear forever; however, the same raindrops coalesce in strength to form little streams and then little rivulets and then join together to become mighty rivers flowing further, dropping into powerful and majestic waterfalls, yet again joining together with other rivers, lakes, and more hill torrents, to end up in mighty oceans ever increasing in size, in length, in depth, and in power yet at all times obedient to the will of Allah. An insignificant human without faith is like a drop of water on parched land. Yet the same human, a believer strengthened by his covenant with Allah, joins others with the covenant to form a little community that, in communion with Allah and in unity, becomes the *ummah* of believers around the world, a powerful united people witnessing over other nations, with Allah and His *nabi* witnessing over them. At the turn of the twenty-first century, there are more believers than ever in the history of mankind. These believers of Allah are in Islam and in other religions. It is the obligation of every Muslim to commune with every believer of Allah in the brotherhood of the people of *haqq*.

The house of Islam, the Dar es Salaam, is spread over territories of the *ummah* whose boundaries were demarcated by the un-Koranic conquering sultans and the colonial West in their sweep of plunder of the Muslim world. In the land of the believers, these artificial borders do not exist. They are the figment of the imagination of the un-Koranic rulers, their armies, and their intelligence services.

The *ummah* is one community in one land, the abode of peace, the Dar es Salaam, ordained by Allah. For the believer, there are no borders between Muslim communities. Our land is one land.

During the last two hundred years, Muslims have lost in the battlefield in every conflict against the West; and in doing so, they have been subjected to humiliation and colonization lasting more than a century. Why did that happen? Muslim communities are beset with traitors and *Munafiqeen.* They look like Muslims, dress like Muslims, and pray like Muslims. They frequently go for *umrah* and hajj, yet for a price, they disobey every article of the covenants of the Blessed *Nabi* Muhammad and of the Koran, for the price of a kingdom and a fiefdom, they betray their *din* and the *ummah.*

During the last three centuries, the Muslim states had had many external enemies whose motives were varied. All of them used disgruntled Muslim princes, noblemen, and tribes with the temptation of wealth and territory in fostering their aim. Once the conquering armies managed to gain a stranglehold on the Muslim territory, the traitors were discarded like rags once their usefulness was over. Yet in Muslim history, there had never been shortage of such traitors. In recent history, those who invited and aided the infidels in the occupation of the lands of Islam are the generals of the Pakistan Army, Northern Alliance of Afghanistan, Kurds of Iraq, the Shias of Iraq, the Saudi royal family, the Jordanian royals, and the sheikhs of Qatar, Kuwait, Bahrain, United Arab Emirates, and Oman. The result is the occupation of Afghanistan and Iraq, with the resulting loss of life of over one million believers in Afghanistan, Syria, Libya, Yemen, and Iraq in the years 2002–2021. The loss of life of more than one million Iraqis caused by the United Nations sanctions was aided and abetted by the rulers of the Arabian Peninsula, Turkey, Jordan, and Iran. In fact, all the Islamic states combined are in no better position now to solve their problems of defense, disunity, infighting, poverty, illiteracy, and poor world image than they had in 1909, when Caliph Abdulhamid was deposed by their ilk. When the Koran says the following, it might as well have been addressed to the present rulers of Islam:

> They have made their oaths a screen for their misdeeds, thus they obstruct men from the Path of Allah: truly evil are their deeds. That is because they believed, then they rejected Faith: so, a seal was set on their hearts: therefore, they understand not. When you look at them, their exteriors please thee; and when they speak, you listen to their words. They are as worthless as rotten pieces of timber propped up, unable to stand on their own. They think that every cry is against them. They are the enemies; so, beware of them. The curse of Allah be on them! How are they deluded away from the Truth! (Al-Munafiqun 63:4)

It is not only the Koran that makes the believers aware of the tricks of such people. Jesus spoke of them in these terms:

> Beware of false prophets, which come to you in sheep's clothing, but inwardly they are ravenous. You shall know them by their fruits. Do men gather grapes of thorns, or figs of thistles? Even so every good tree brings forth good fruit, but a corrupt tree brings forth evil fruit. "A good tree cannot bring forth evil fruit; neither can a corrupt tree bring forth good fruit." Every tree that brings forth bad fruit is hewn down and cast into the fire. Therefore, by their fruits shall you know them.

Dr. Munawar Sabir